PIRARO 8/12
UNFINISHED SELF-PORTRAIT
©DAN PIRARO·1995/ DIST. BY UNIVERSAL PRESS SYND.

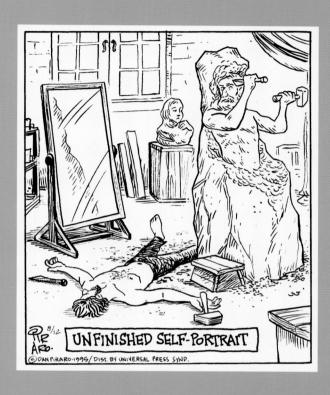

Bizarro

AND OTHER

For Edna & Larry —

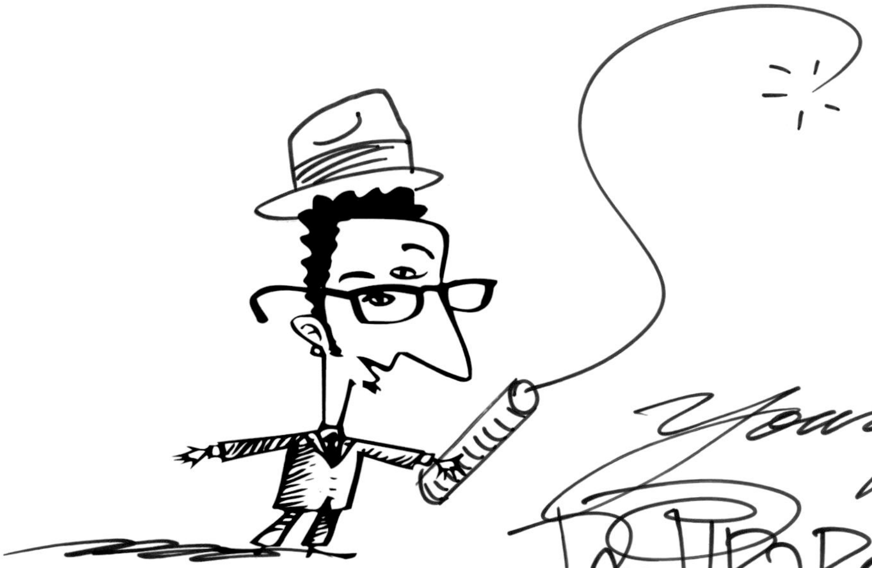

Your pal,
Dan Piraro.
SCHULZ MUSEUM 2010

STRANGE MANIFESTATIONS OF THE ART OF

Dan Piraro

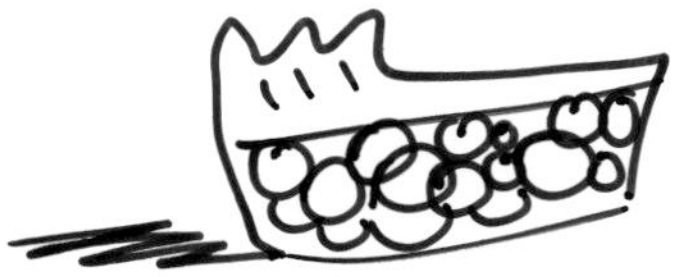

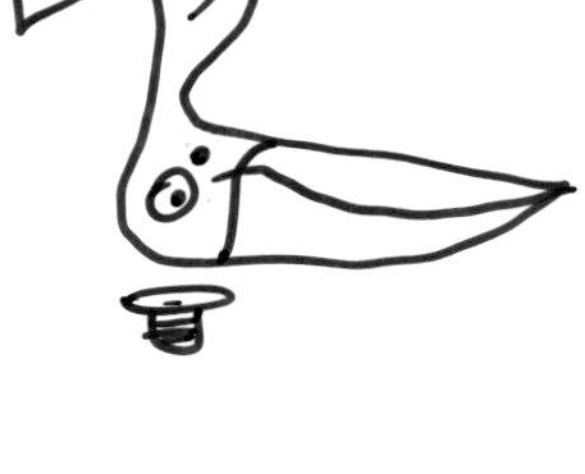

Abrams, New York

Editor: Sharon AvRutick
Designer: Brady McNamara
Production Manager: Maria Pia Gramaglia

Library of Congress Cataloging-in-Publication Data

Piraro, Dan.
    Bizarro and other strange manifestations of the art of Dan Piraro / Dan Piraro.
    p. cm.
  ISBN 0-8109-9221-3 (pbk.)
1. Piraro, Dan. 2. Cartoonists—United States—Biography. 3. United States—Social life
and customs—Caricatures and cartoons. 4. American wit and humor, Pictorial. I. Title.
  NC1429.P58A2 2005
  741.5'973–dc22
                                                            2005021773

Printed and bound in China

10 9 8 7 6 5 4 3 2 1

Page 155, above and center: Reproduced by special permission of *Playboy* magazine.
Copyright © 2003, 2004 by *Playboy*

HNA ▉▉▉▉▉
harry n. abrams, inc.
a subsidiary of La Martinière Groupe
115 West 18th Street
New York, NY 10011
www.hnabooks.com

For my wife, Ashley, who has changed my life for the better in more ways than I imagined existed. Corny and disgustingly sweet, but true. Read this book and find out how.

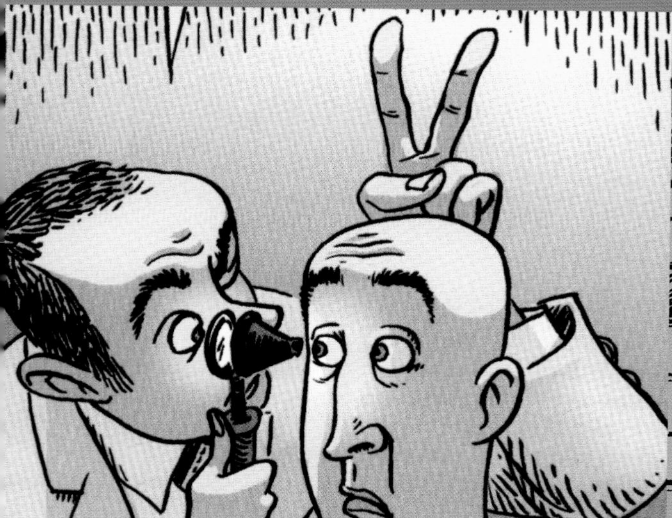
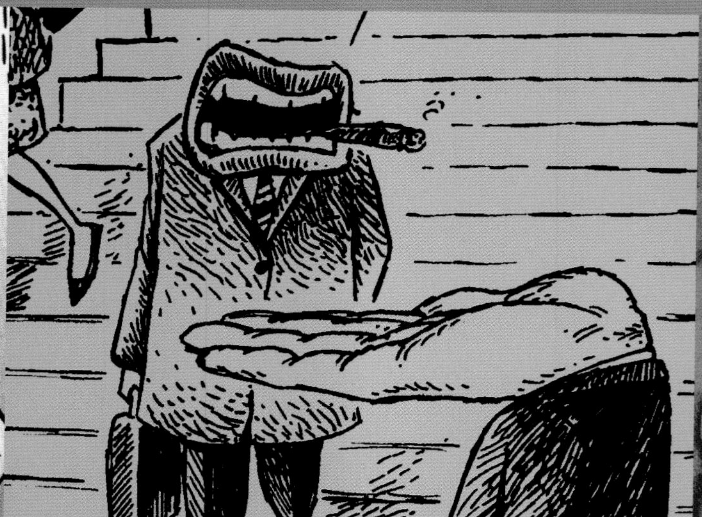
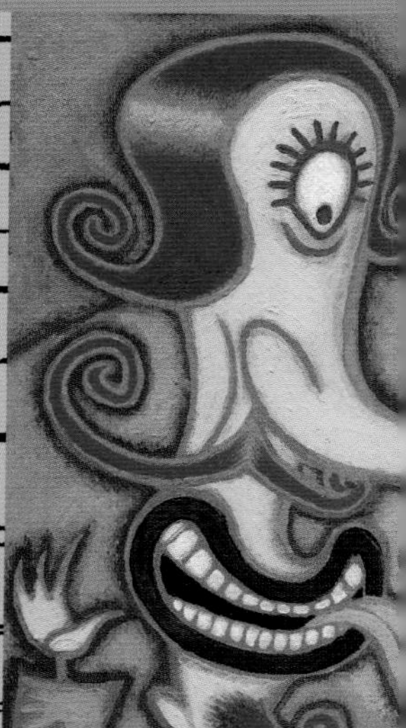

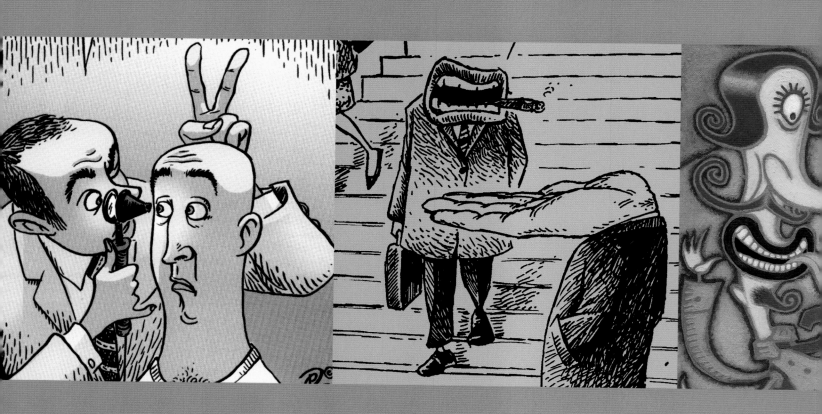

Contents

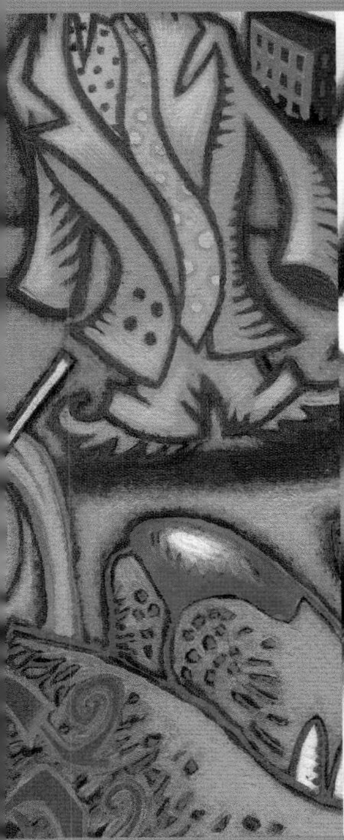

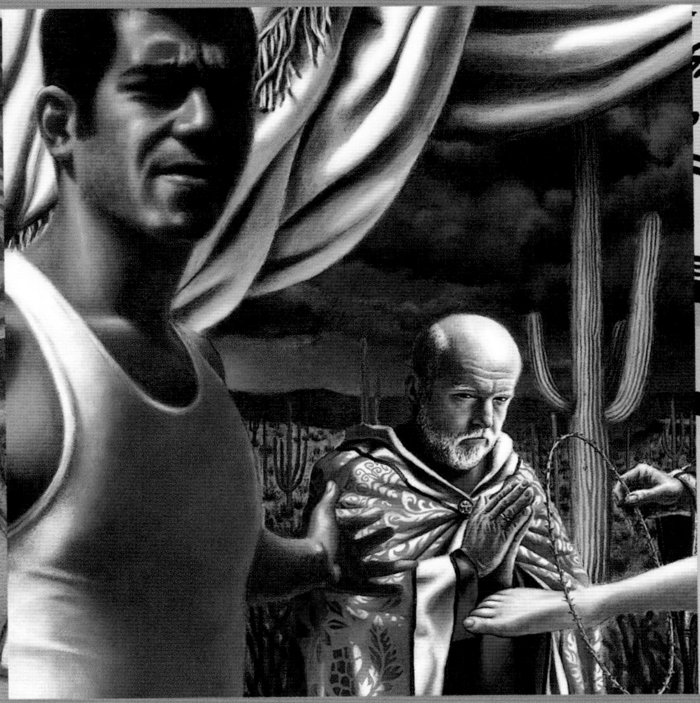

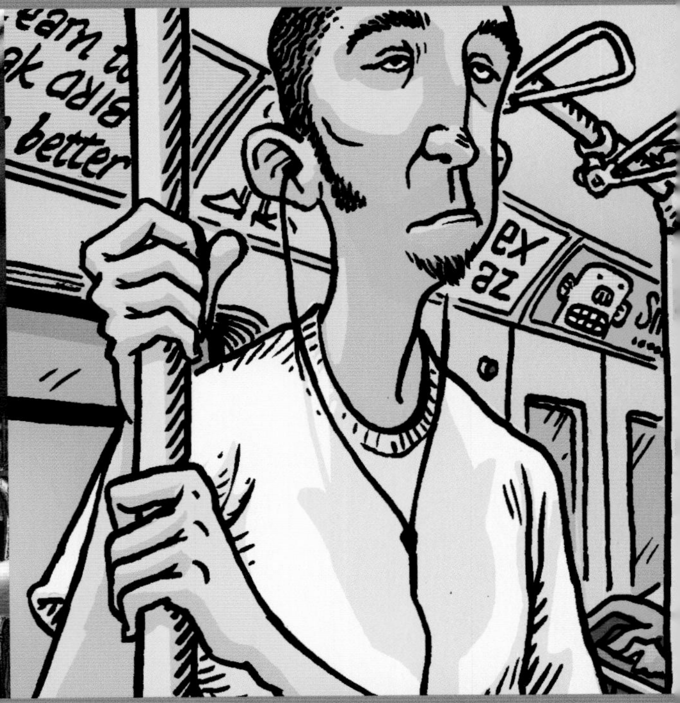

Chapter one

Bible Belt
baby

On the morning of October 7, 1958, the sun rose slowly over the hideous specter of another day in the Bible Belt. In a small apartment in Kansas City, a city once called "Cow Town" because of some relationship it probably had with cows, a young woman sat up in bed and said, "Fred, I think it's time."

My mother was that woman, and Fred was her husband, as well as the man she believed to be my father. She cried out to him as she was feeling the first of many pains I would give her over the next several decades. What she didn't know was that I was about to be born. Well, she knew *someone* was about to be born, of course, but she didn't know that it was me, specifically. For instance, a year and a half earlier, on April 9, the same thing had happened, and it turned out to be my older sister. But this time, it was my turn.

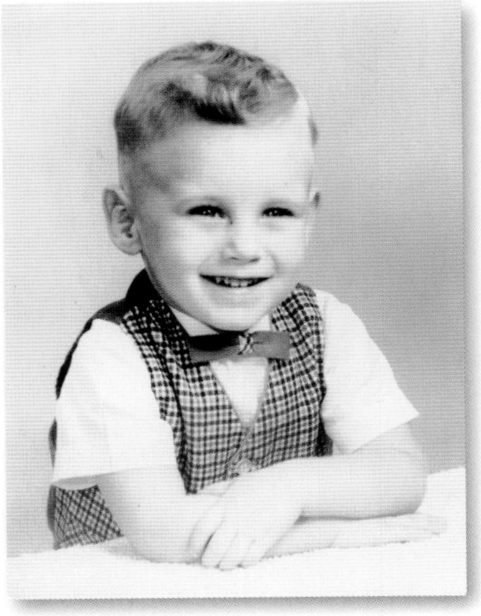

My birth was a great embarrassment to everyone involved. It was the first (and I wish I could say the only) time I appeared in a room full of strangers, soaking wet and buck naked. It took my mother nearly three days in bed to recover from the shame, and even then she had to be taken out of the hospital in a wheelchair.

Being born in the middle of the country was a mixed blessing for me. When I was four my family moved from Kansas City to Ponca City, and then to Tulsa, Oklahoma, where I would spend the vast majority of my time until I was old enough to leave home. I used to find this fact both disappointing and embarrassing. Most of the creative people I know—artists, writers, actors, musicians, comedians—were raised by artistic types or academics in culturally interesting cities and traveled extensively. Some were even the offspring of felons on the lam. How cool is that?

But I, much to my chagrin, was mired in the pudding of mediocrity and mainstream values every day of my life until I went to Europe at the age of twenty. I say "mixed blessing" because while on the one hand there were no positive artistic or cultural influences in my life whatsoever (all I knew of art or aesthetics was what I could glean from picture books and television), on the other hand my ability to draw big-butted ladies with gigantic, poufy hairdos is almost unparalleled.

PREVIOUS PAGE: For the entire year of 1960, my parents dressed me like Jack Parr.

A glimpse of what I looked like in a bathing suit in 1961, and will look like again in my sixties.

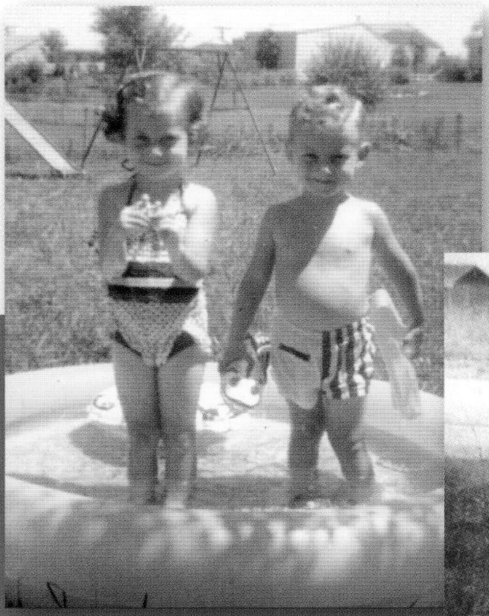

Me and my first dog. I was five. She was a terrier-type mutt and I wanted to name her Spike or Fang or something appropriately "butch." But my older sister won out and we named her Penny. Penny and I were very close when I was young but as I got into my teens I almost never played with her. My parents didn't want her in the house, so she spent her last few years very lonely in the backyard. It still breaks my heart.

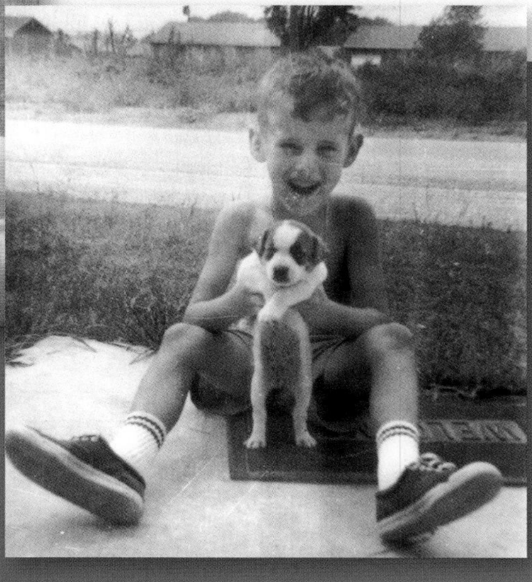

This is either my sister, Karen, and me the day of our first holy communion, or my parents married me off when I was very young and I've blocked the memory. (Ponca City, Oklahoma, 1965)

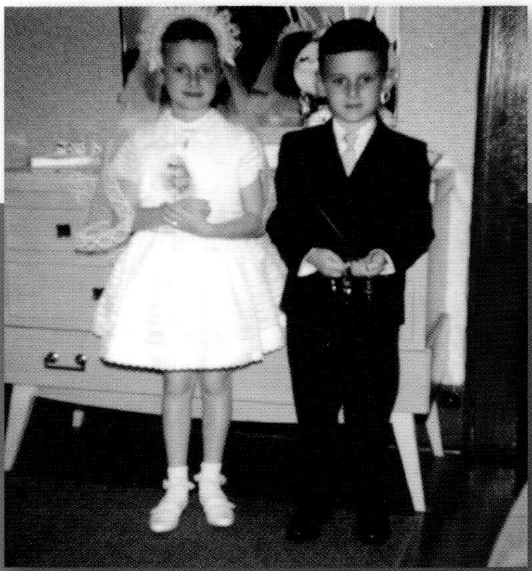

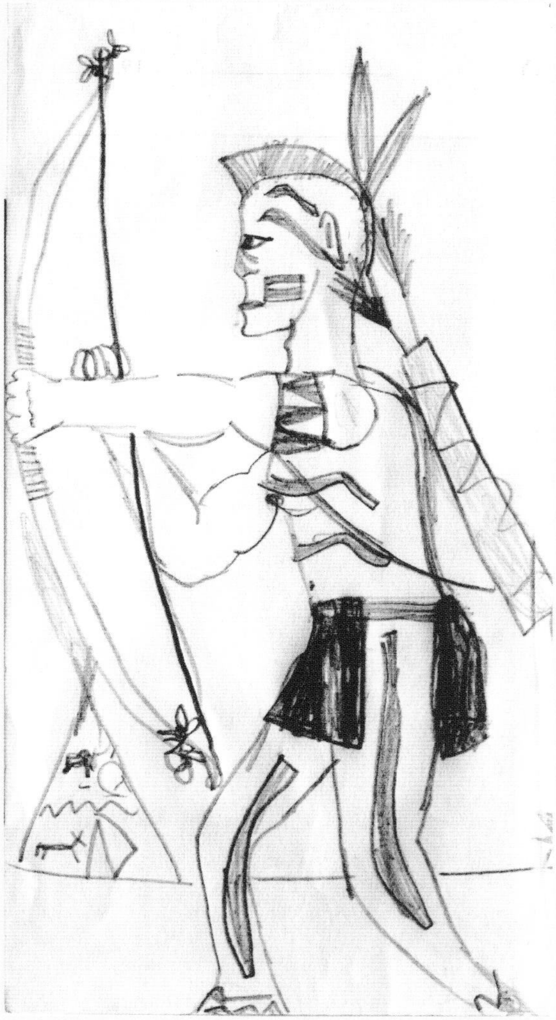

Drawn at age five from one of the many TV shows about the Old West that were popular during the early sixties. I begged my parents to let me have a Mohawk haircut, but of course, they denied me. Little did any of us know, the style would become popular fifteen years later among punk rockers. (1964)

BELOW: I drew this after attending the circus at age five. I now regularly picket animal circuses. They are notoriously abusive to their animals, and the Cirque de Soleil–style circuses are far more entertaining anyway. (1964)

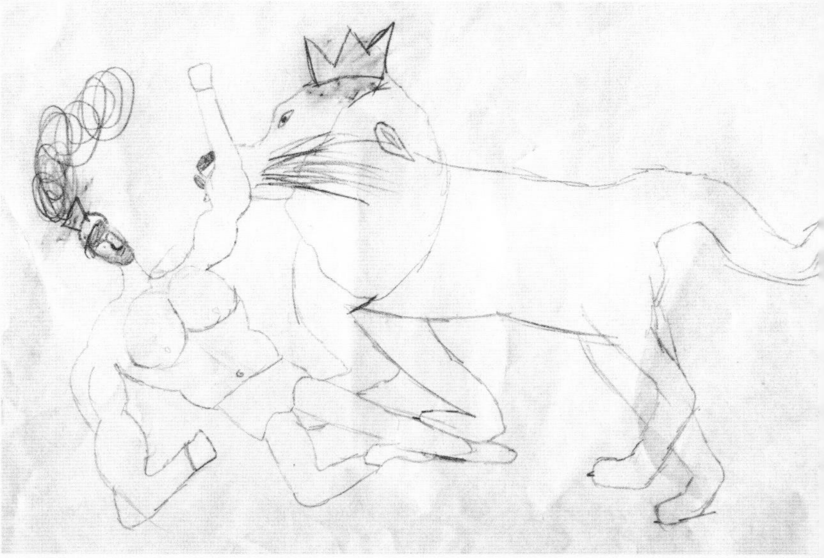

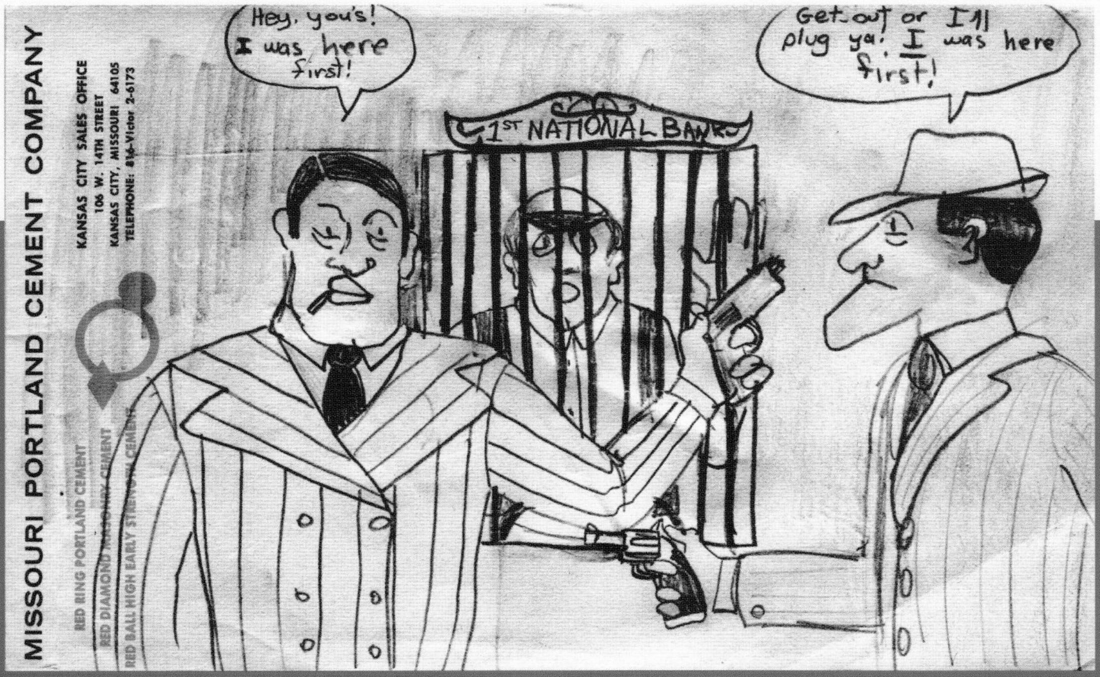
MISSOURI PORTLAND CEMENT COMPANY
KANSAS CITY SALES OFFICE
106 W. 14TH STREET
KANSAS CITY, MISSOURI 64105
TELEPHONE: 816-Victor 2-6173
Hey, you's! I was here first!
Get out or I'll plug ya! I was here first!
1ST NATIONAL BANK

A very early attempt at something like a cartoon. (1966)

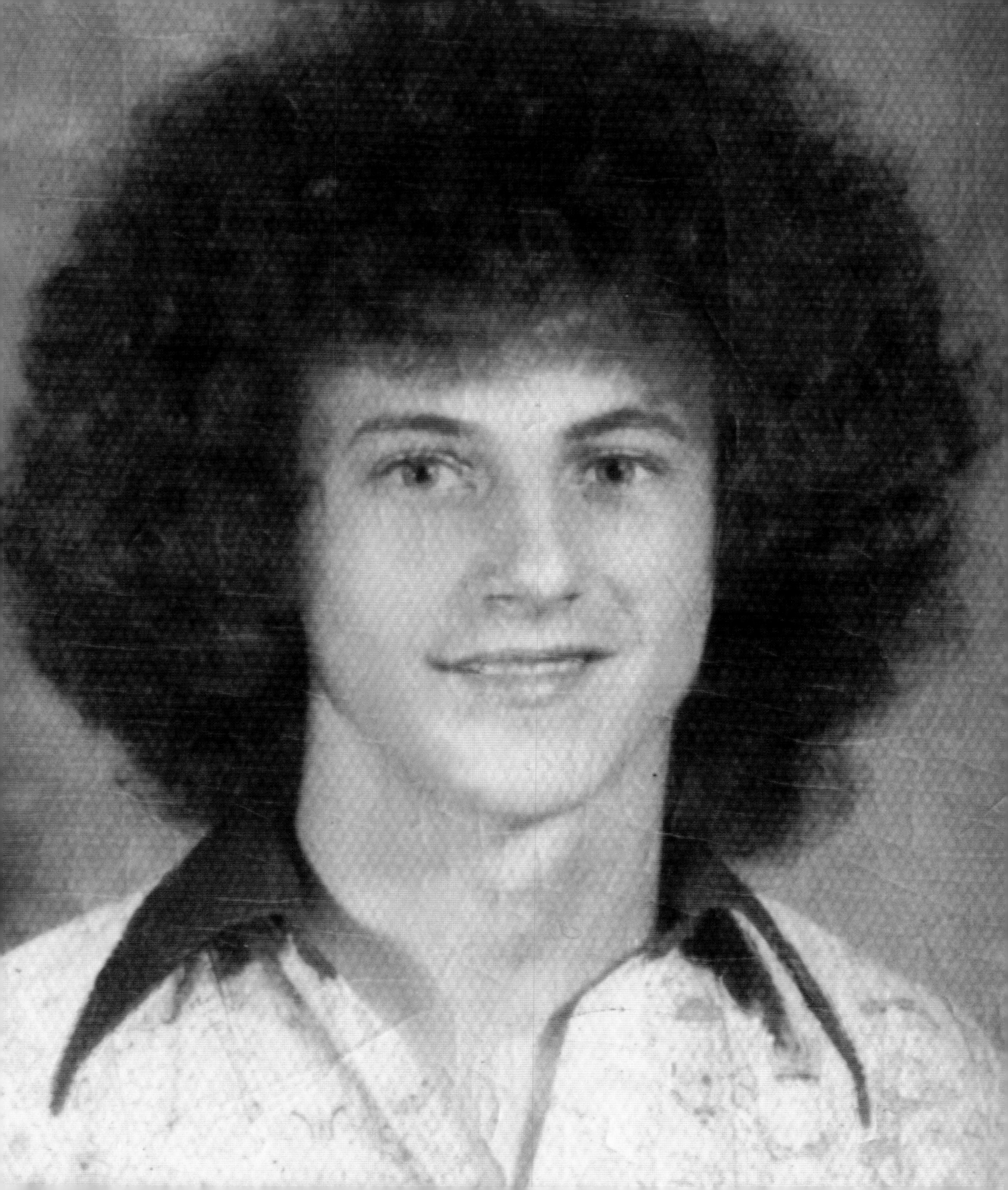

Based entirely on television and film evidence, I had dreamed of living in New York or Paris or London (or anywhere not like Oklahoma) since childhood. As far back as I can remember, drawing was my favorite pastime, and in high school I began to enjoy writing, music, and acting as well. As a senior, heavily influenced by The Who's *Tommy,* I wrote my own rock opera and convinced the theater teacher, music teacher, and choir director to mount the production. We worked on it for weeks but ran out of time, and my epic never actually saw the stage. But the rehearsals were immense fun and gave me a taste for the myriad possibilities of life as a creative person. I remember well one evening in the mid-1970s when my mother came into my room while I was painting. We talked about all my various projects: the painting I was working on, the play I was acting in, the musical we were trying to produce, and God knows what else. She asked, "Why do you have to go in a million different directions at once? Why can't you concentrate on doing the one thing you do best—your artwork?"

I don't remember my exact response, but being a typically invincible smart-ass teenager with more ambition than brains, it was probably something like, "When I've won an Oscar, a Grammy, a Tony, and a Pulitzer, and have paintings in every major museum by the age of twenty-one, you'll call me from the mansion I bought you for Christmas and thank me for not listening to you."

Still fighting the curly hair, combing it down, wishing it looked like Paul McCartney's. (Tulsa, 1970)

With my dad, my sparkly T-shirt, and the Spanish-style candelabra on the fireplace. The look on Dad's face says to me: I'm determined to be proud of this kid in spite of the fact that he's well on his way to looking like a transvestite. (Tulsa, 1975)

OPPOSITE: Groovy Dude Dan, one of the top ten coolest juniors at Booker T. Washington High School, Tulsa, 1975. Put this head on bell-bottom jeans and platform shoes and you've got a party.

When I graduated high school, however, my mother's recommendation changed. Suddenly she joined my father in his quaint notion that I should get a college degree in something at which I might actually be able to make a living. "Be an artist if you want, but have a medical degree to fall back on," they would chant in unison. They didn't understand that I was going to be rich and famous just for being me. They had never been ambitious young geniuses bursting with talent, so what could they know about it?

Finally a compromise was reached, and I agreed to go to Washington University in St. Louis on a fine-arts scholarship. My mother had found out about it, gathered my work into a portfolio, and applied for it on my behalf. When I think back on that I am embarrassed by what a lazy, foolish jackass I was. If I had a son like me I'd sell him to gypsies and give the money to a foundation searching for a cure for teenage hubris.

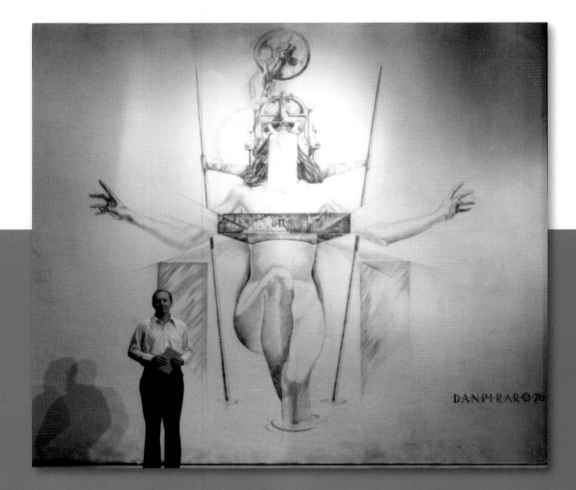

My high school theater director, Darrell Goode, standing in front of a backdrop I drew with litho crayon. No reason, just wanted to. I originally drew the breasts, but the school administrators made me cover them up. Boobies are dirty and God wants us to be ashamed of them. (1976)

I'M not touching that! It's GROSS!
Well, I'M sure not! I'm wearing brand-new scrubs.
Don't look at ME! I HATE slimy stuff!
Ooooh! I think I just saw it wiggle!
©DAN PIRARO. 7·24·01

Too squeamish and irreverent to achieve the medical degree my mother had hoped for me, I draw upon those shortcomings to create doctor cartoons.

You'd charge a lot, too, if you had to look at people like you naked all day.
BIZARRO.COM
Dist. by King Features
©DAN PIRARO 4·15·03

I'm writing you a prescription for some clothes—wear them whenever you leave the house.
©DAN PIRARO. 10·6·00

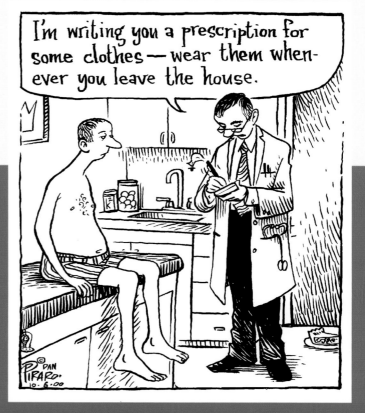

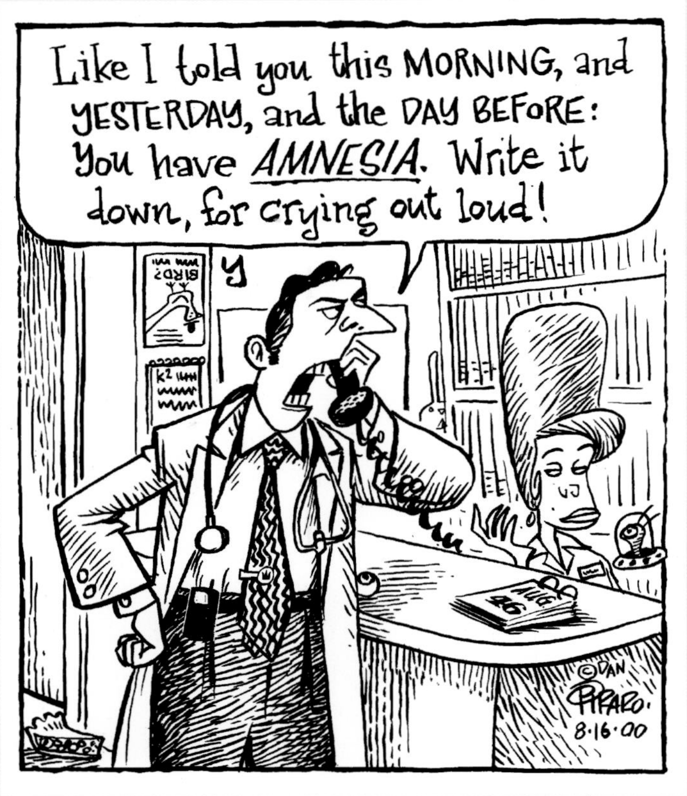
Like I told you this MORNING, and YESTERDAY, and the DAY BEFORE: You have AMNESIA. Write it down, for crying out loud!
©DAN PIRARO. 8·16·00

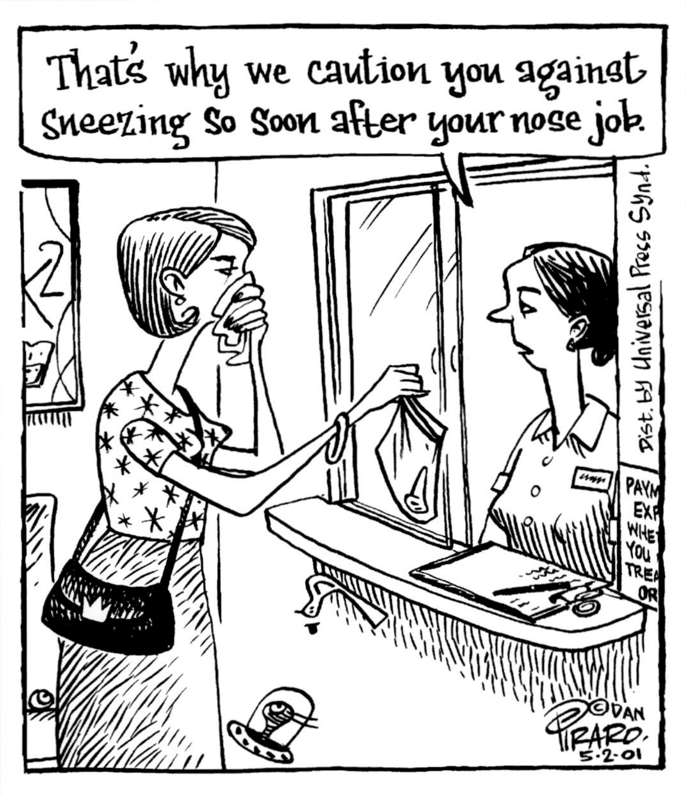
That's why we caution you against sneezing so soon after your nose job.
Dist. by Universal Press Synd.
©DAN PIRARO. 5·2·01

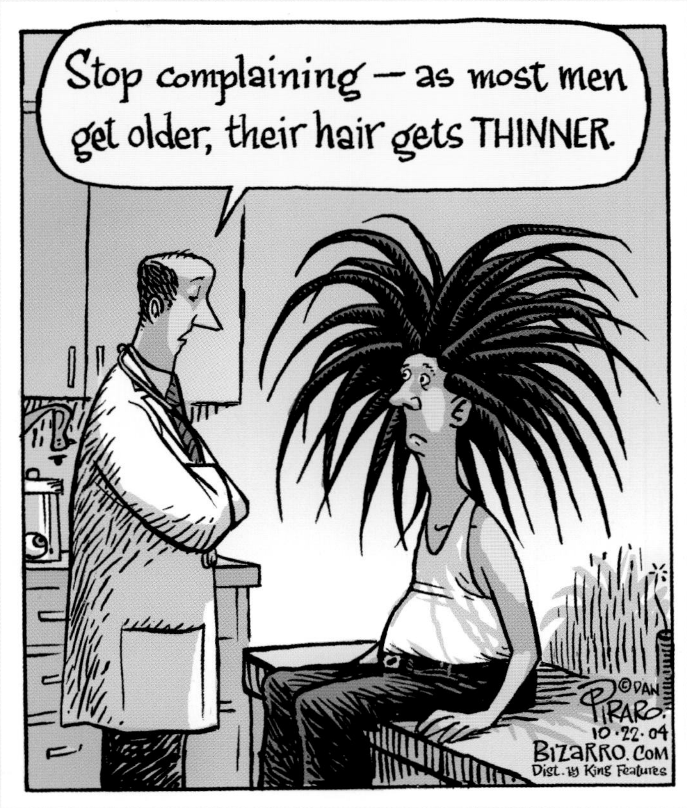
Stop complaining — as most men get older, their hair gets THINNER.
©DAN PIRARO. 10·22·04
BIZARRO.COM
Dist. by King Features

As my hair continues to thin, I continue to do hair-loss cartoons. By the time I accept it and move on, I'll be doing incontinence cartoons.

Although leaving for college in St. Louis wasn't much of a step toward international fame and fortune, I was almost excited. At least it wasn't Oklahoma. Still, I wasn't sure it was going to work. More institutionalization and routine in the middle of the country was the last thing I wanted. But I'd promised my parents I would give it a go, so off I went.

After what I deemed to be an adequate amount of "go" (one semester), I dropped out and returned to Tulsa with delusions of grandeur and a plan: I would live with my parents for a few months, save money, and then move somewhere cool to be "discovered." Somehow.

It didn't work as well as I'd hoped. I worked at a series of crap jobs until I had enough money to get an apartment of my own across town. After I moved out, I promptly slipped into depression over the idiotic trap I'd dug for myself.

Luckily, a business associate of my father's was living and working in Italy and fancied himself a patron of the arts. He invited me to use his spare bedroom in Milan as a jumping-off point if I wanted to explore Europe and see the great museums. Knowing that Tulsa had little to offer me and that the armed forces would never accept me, my parents encouraged me to take him up on the offer. So after a year or so of saving money from debasing, minimum-wage jobs I would wish only on the privileged children of wealthy Republicans, in the summer of 1979 I set off for Europe with a backpack and a Eurail Pass to wander the world and discover my destiny.

This trip turned out to be seminal in my development both as an artist and as a human being. I hitchhiked, slept in strange places, met and went home with unusual people (I consider anyone who would invite me home unusual), smoked hash, viewed art, experienced foreign cultures, got drunk, got laid, got robbed, sketched, philosophized in bars and coffee houses, and spent countless hours alone walking and observing. In the end I learned that what I'd seen on TV and in films was true: the world is a fascinating place. I regularly recommend this sort of activity to the estimated 90 percent of Americans who have never left the country. The average "expert" foreign policy you hear from every bozo on the sidewalks of Mainstreet U.S.A. might change drastically if that happened.

A photo I took on a whim in the attic of a castle in Germany. A friend and I were on a tour, and ducked under a rope and went exploring on the upper floors. This was a spontaneous attempt to be "classical." (1979)

Another important thing I discovered while in Europe was the fact that there are a lot of very talented people in the world, and it was going to take more than a desire to be rich and famous to build a life I would be happy to get out of bed for. I was also probably going to have to put off the purchase of a mansion for my parents for a while longer. After four months away, I was still determined to live the life of an artist back at home, but I was thinking more in terms of climbing the ladder one rung at a time.

Instead, I made the colossal mistake of moving to Dallas, Texas. There was a small but growing nightclub scene in Dallas at the time, in which new wave/punk bands played original music, causing purple-haired young people with safety pins through their cheeks to thrash about in front of the stage. It reminded me of clubs I had frequented in London and seemed like a viable place to launch a career in music. The year before going to Europe I had formed a band, but now found the Lynyrd Skynyrd–cover-band atmosphere of Oklahoma inhospitable. As a Tulsa teen, my main influences were early The Who and Peter Gabriel. But after my European epiphany, I was gaga over the likes of Elvis Costello and The Clash. I was the lead singer and co-songwriter for The Doo (we meant it like "doo-wop" or "dooby dooby doo," but in that era of punk rock, most people took it to refer to "dog doo") and Costello was the perfect role model for me. Twenty-five years later I can say that, unfortunately, I share his hairline but none of his musical brilliance.

Three of the four members of my band joined me in Texas, and an older friend who was the PR guy for some record stores agreed to manage us to fame, fortune, and groupies. Our plan was to play the club scene in Dallas and in Austin for a year or so until we felt we had an album's worth of brilliance to unleash on the world, and then we'd move to New York or Los Angeles. The rest would be history. I would simultaneously paint and become known as an artist. Somehow. I had become a little more realistic, but I was still only twenty-one and, apparently, a very slow learner.

Three-fourths of The Doo. From left: Mark Veale, me, Colin Marsh. Plainly evident is my ongoing battle with obesity. Of the many regrets I have about this photo, perhaps the greatest is that sideburns were not in style. (Hot Klub, Dallas, 1980)

hot line:
526-9432
PRESENT
BAG OF WIRE
THE NUMBERS
quad
pi
OPEN 3:30 PM
BEER
Fleshtones
SPECIAL GUESTS
telefones

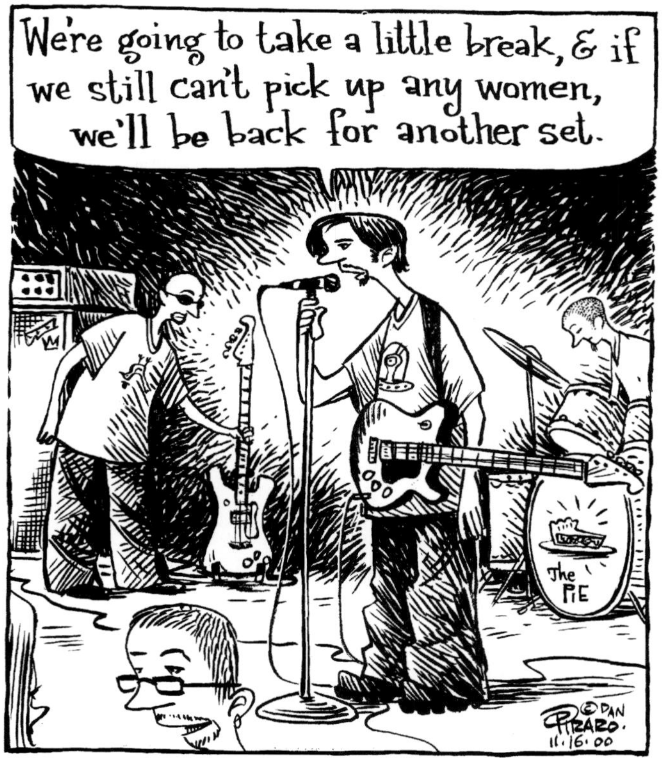
We're going to take a little break, & if we still can't pick up any women, we'll be back for another set.
The PiE
©DAN PIRARO. 11.16.00

Drawn from my days in The Doo. (2000)

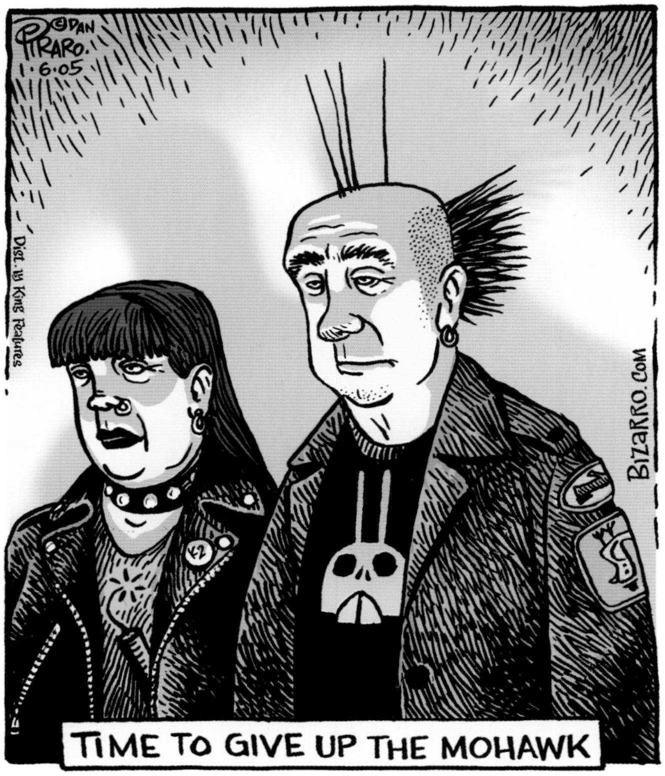
©DAN PIRARO. 1.6.05
Dist. by King Features
BIZARRO.COM
TIME TO GIVE UP THE MOHAWK

In New York, as in many big cities, you see a lot of aging hipsters who won't let go of the "look." One such groovy granddad on the subway made me think of this sight gag. (2005)

Pleasant Meadows
A GATED COMMUNITY OF FEARFUL, WHITE CONFORMISTS
BIZARRO.COM
Dist. by King Features
©DAN PIRARO 6·16·04

Can we still have cake & ice cream if we're NOT happy he was born?
HAPPY BIRT
SOY
BIZARRO.COM
Dist. by King Features
©DAN PIRARO 9·30·04

I was raised in middle-class suburban Tulsa and apparently was the only one of my family with the "get the hell out of suburbia as soon as possible!" gene. I left for the big city as soon as I was old enough. My sisters and parents are still there.

You seem unusually tense today.
BIZARRO.COM
Dist. by King Features
©DAN PIRARO 9·3·04

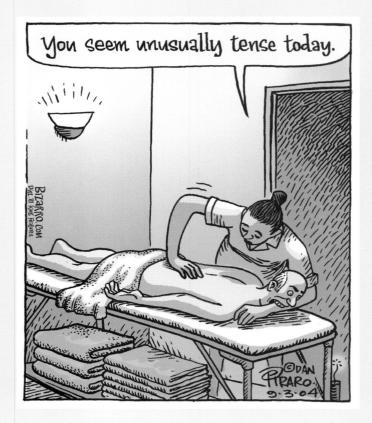

There was no money in weekend club dates (or sitting at home painting), so I got more crappy, minimum-wage jobs. I hated this kind of work so I eventually decided it was time to find better, career-style employment. Because I had no education and couldn't do anything as well as I could draw, I got into commercial illustration. I soon found out that if you're willing to sell your soul and draw tortilla chips and soda pop, you can make a lot more than minimum wage. A *lot* more.

But when you make more money you get more comfortable, and with that comfort comes a growing impatience with the drug addicts, alcoholics, pathological liars, and general ne'er-do-wells of the nightclub and garage-band world. Before you know what hit you, you're married, have two kids, two dogs, two cars, a big house in Dallas, and it's been ten years since you played in a band. At least, that's how it worked for me.

Although I liked the money and I loved my kids, I was desperately unhappy with the 9-to-5 grind of the advertising world and the same old Middle American attitudes about culture, religion, and politics that I had sworn off as a young man. I was also too tired from working all day and playing with the kids at night to get any painting done. I often felt I was drowning.

I tried in earnest to move the family to San Francisco or New York a few times, but we couldn't afford it, so I plodded on. In 1996, after sixteen years, my marriage ended unexpectedly and painfully. While I had some good times and good friends in Dallas and would never wish my children away, I deeply regret that I forsook my dream—of being an artist living in a world-class city—for money and middle-class comfort.

Kids, just say no.

Two pumpkins I carved in the early nineties for the Treetop Apple Cider National Pumpkin Carving Contests. The one at left won the national grand prize, a first-class trip for four to Disney World for a week. The Cowardly Lion one won a camera the next year. At this point in my life, so little of interest was happening that this passed as a major event. I was so proud that I carried the photos around in my wallet for years. Hence their condition.

Summertime in Dallas. The kids and I used to lie around in a kiddy blow-up pool in the front yard. Here we're drying out. (1993)

Commercial art

The vast majority of commercial illustration I did early on was tedious, ugly, and utilitarian. Instead of wasting space on it, I offer instead these illustrations, most of which were done later, in the mid-nineties, when I was a freelancer.

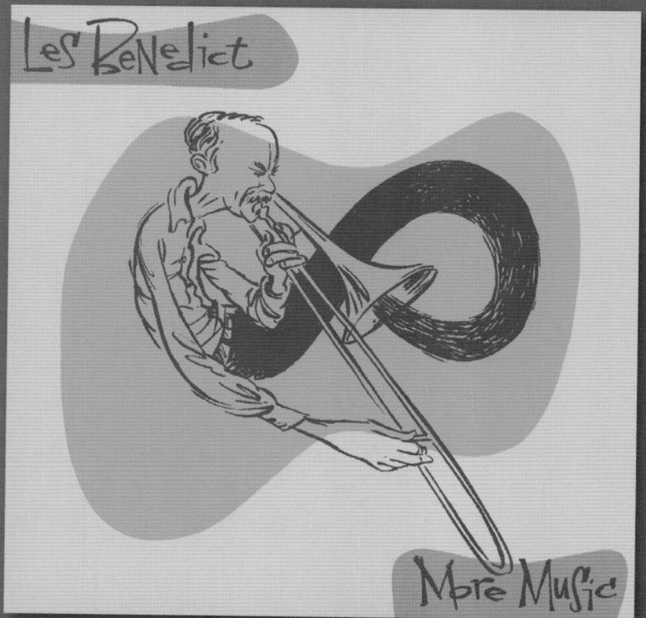
Les Benedict
More Music

A CD cover for a trombonist in California. One of his students, a fan of *Bizarro,* paid me to do the art.

RIGHT: I designed and illustrated this ad for the photostat shop affiliated with our illustration studio. I designed the jumping-cat logo for them around 1983.

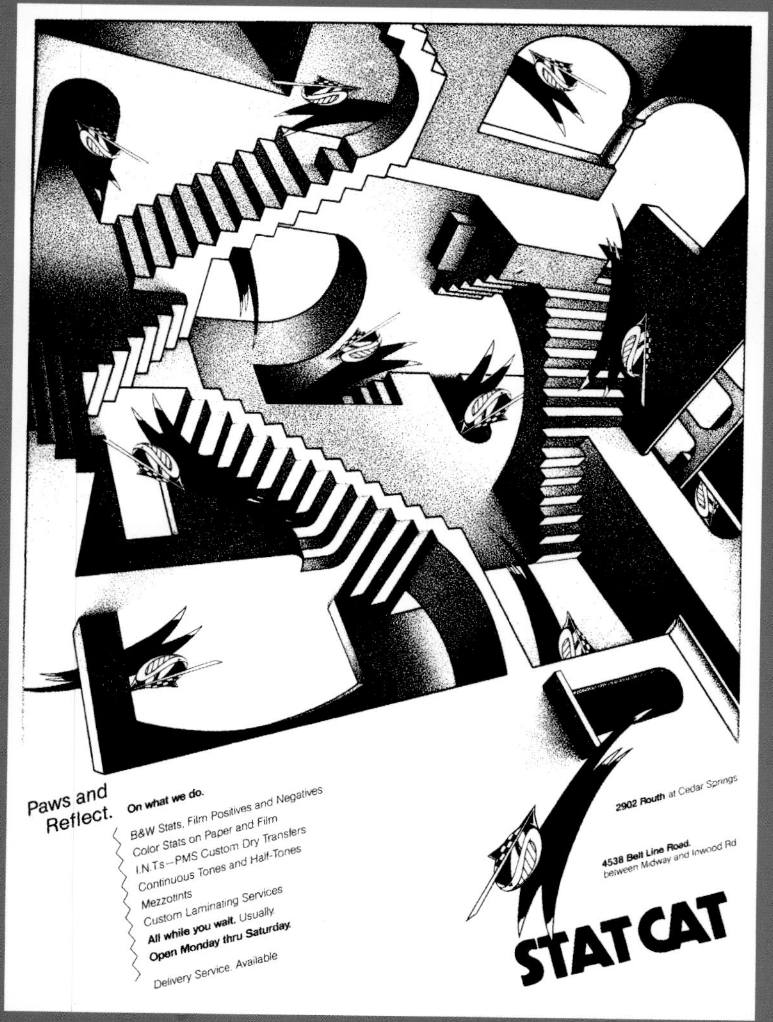
Paws and Reflect.
On what we do.
B&W Stats, Film Positives and Negatives
Color Stats on Paper and Film
I.N.T.s—PMS Custom Dry Transfers
Continuous Tones and Half-Tones
Mezzotints
Custom Laminating Services
All while you wait. Usually.
Open Monday thru Saturday.
Delivery Service. Available
2902 Routh at Cedar Springs
4538 Belt Line Road.
between Midway and Inwood Rd
STAT CAT

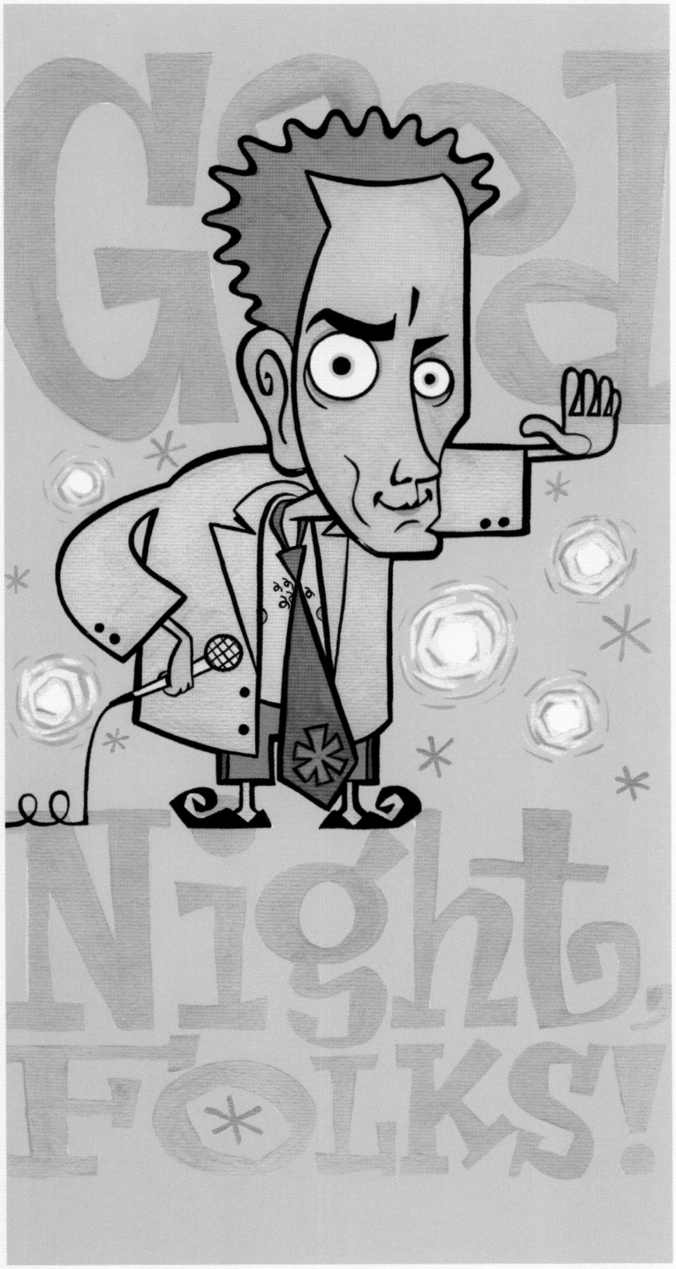
Night,
FOLKS!

A color sketch for an animation sequence to be used with the end credits of a show on VH1. Never used, never paid for. A common story in the world of freelance illustration.

RIGHT: Self-promo piece, done around 1992.

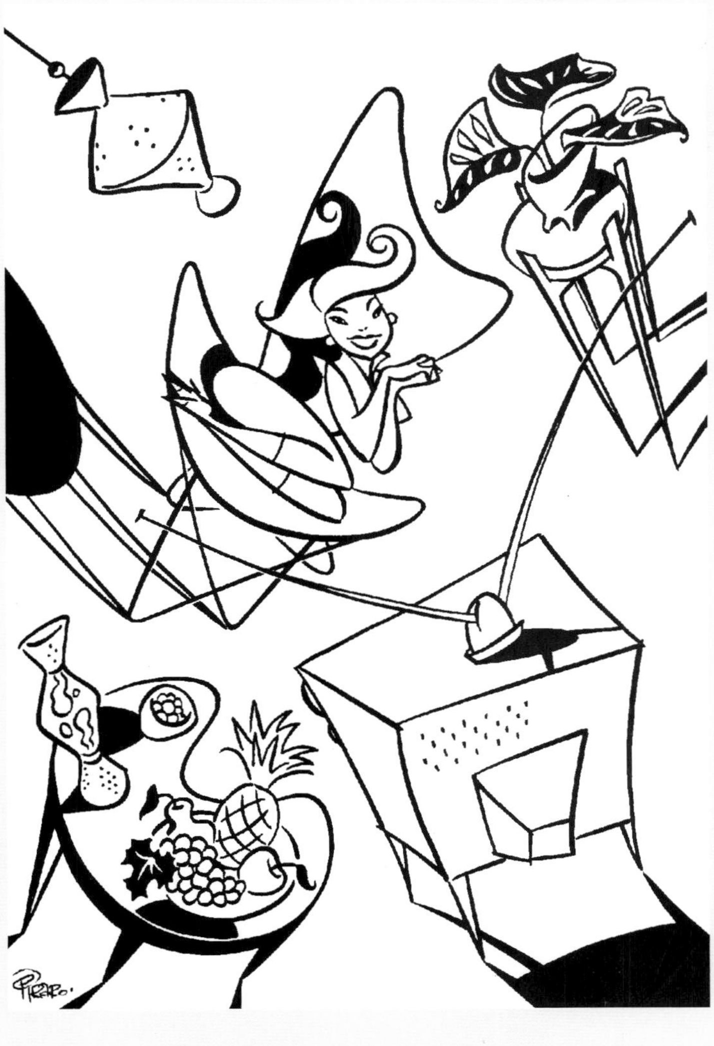

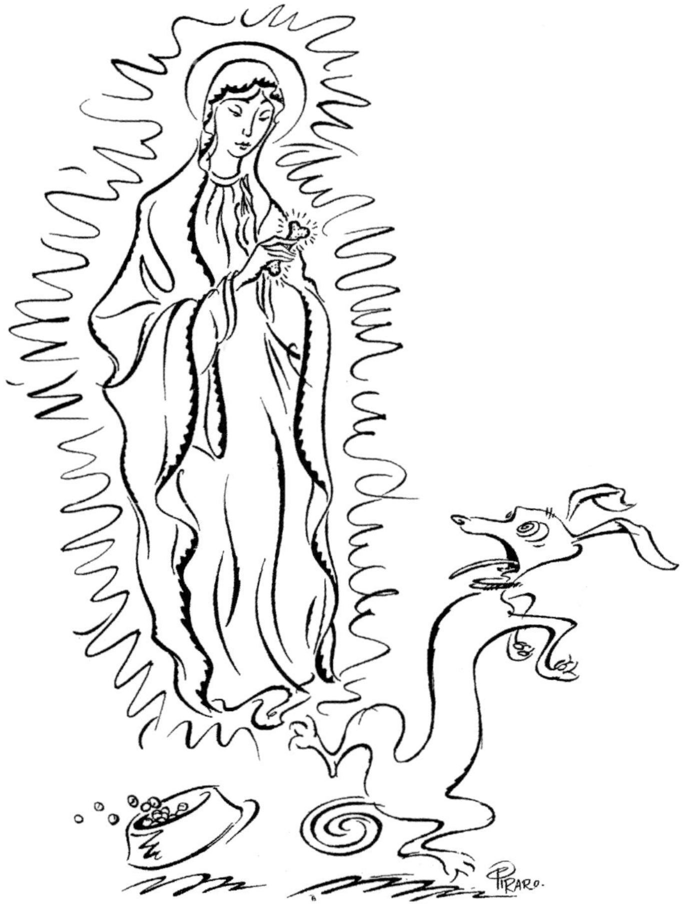
PIRARO.

An image I called "Our Lady of the Kibbles." I intended to do a line of irreverent religious T-shirts and cards, but couldn't find a company interested in marketing them. (1995)

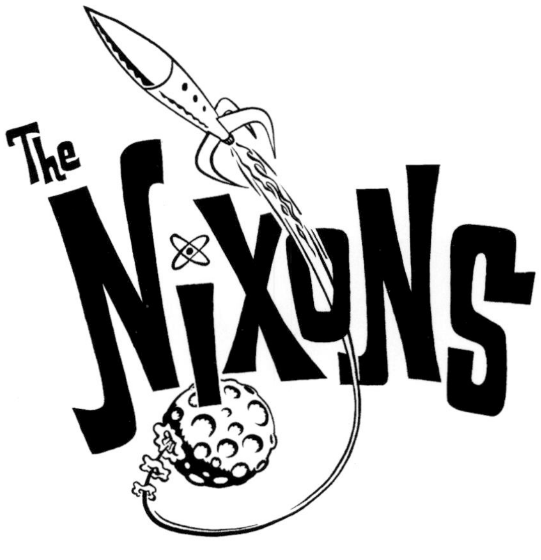
The
NIXONS

A T-shirt image I designed that was used to promote a Nixons album in the late nineties.

RIGHT: When I worked for an illustration studio, from the mid-eighties to the mid-nineties, I specialized in stipple drawings, mostly of food items. This is a promotional piece I did for the studio, which was called Catpak. It was a lot more interesting than what I was doing day to day.

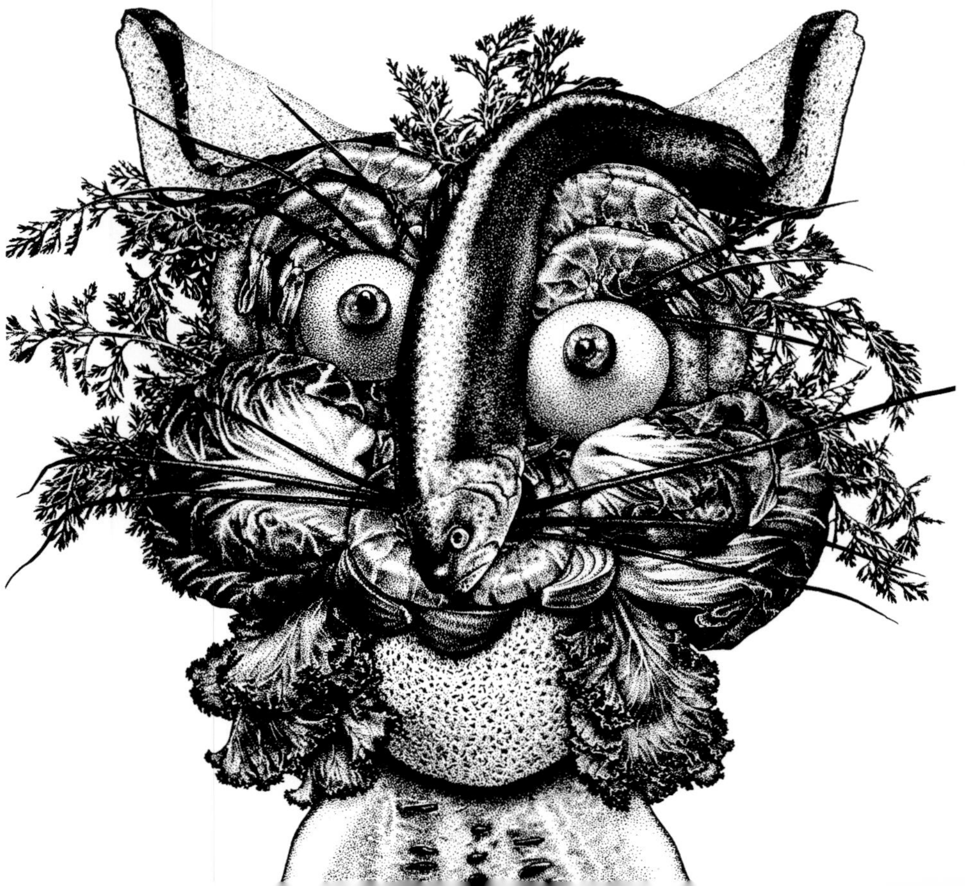

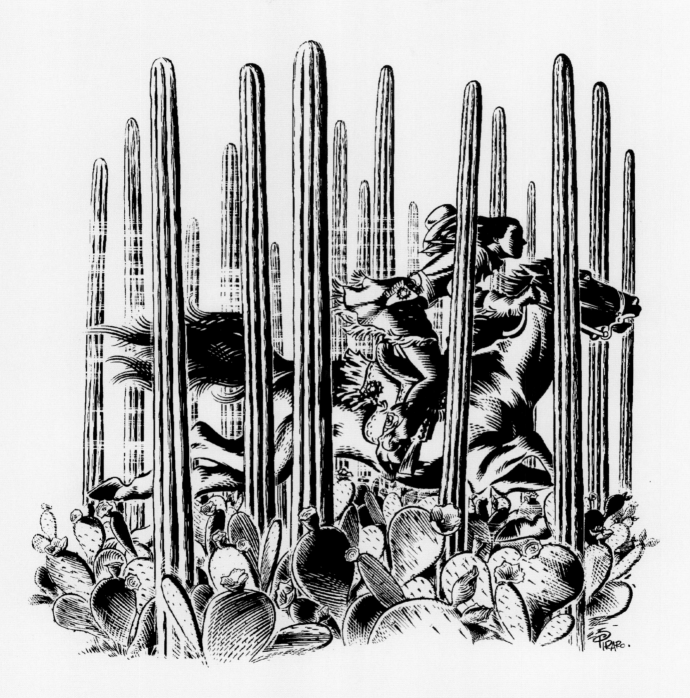

Self-promo piece from around 1994.

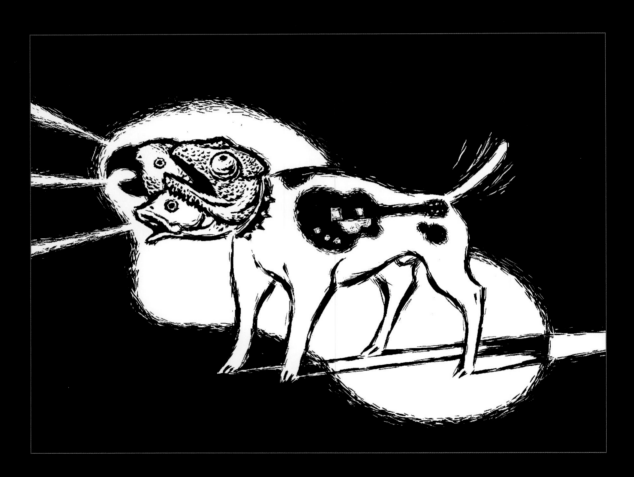

Fun image, not terribly commercial.

OPPOSITE: Self-promo piece, done around 1993.

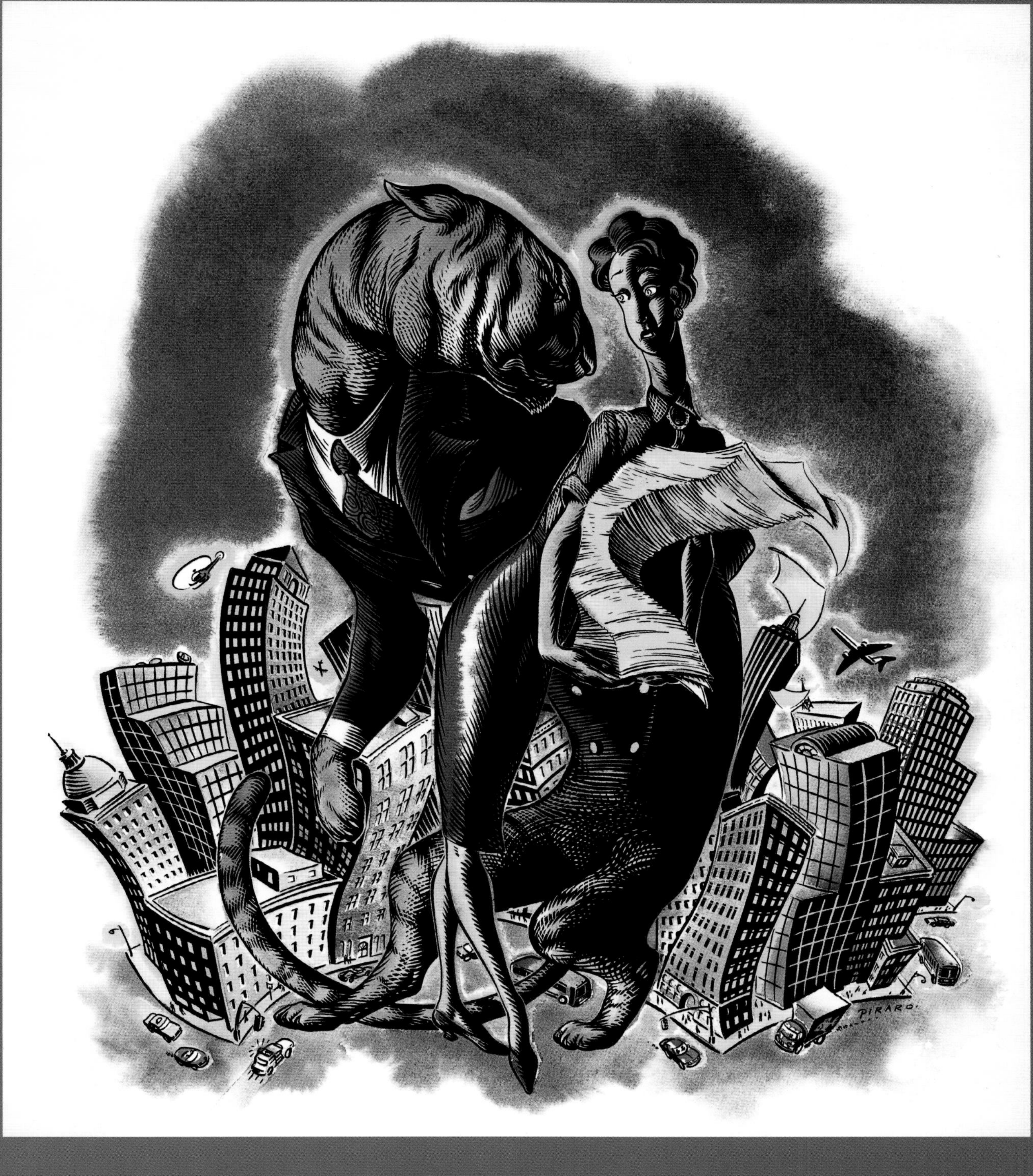
PIRARO

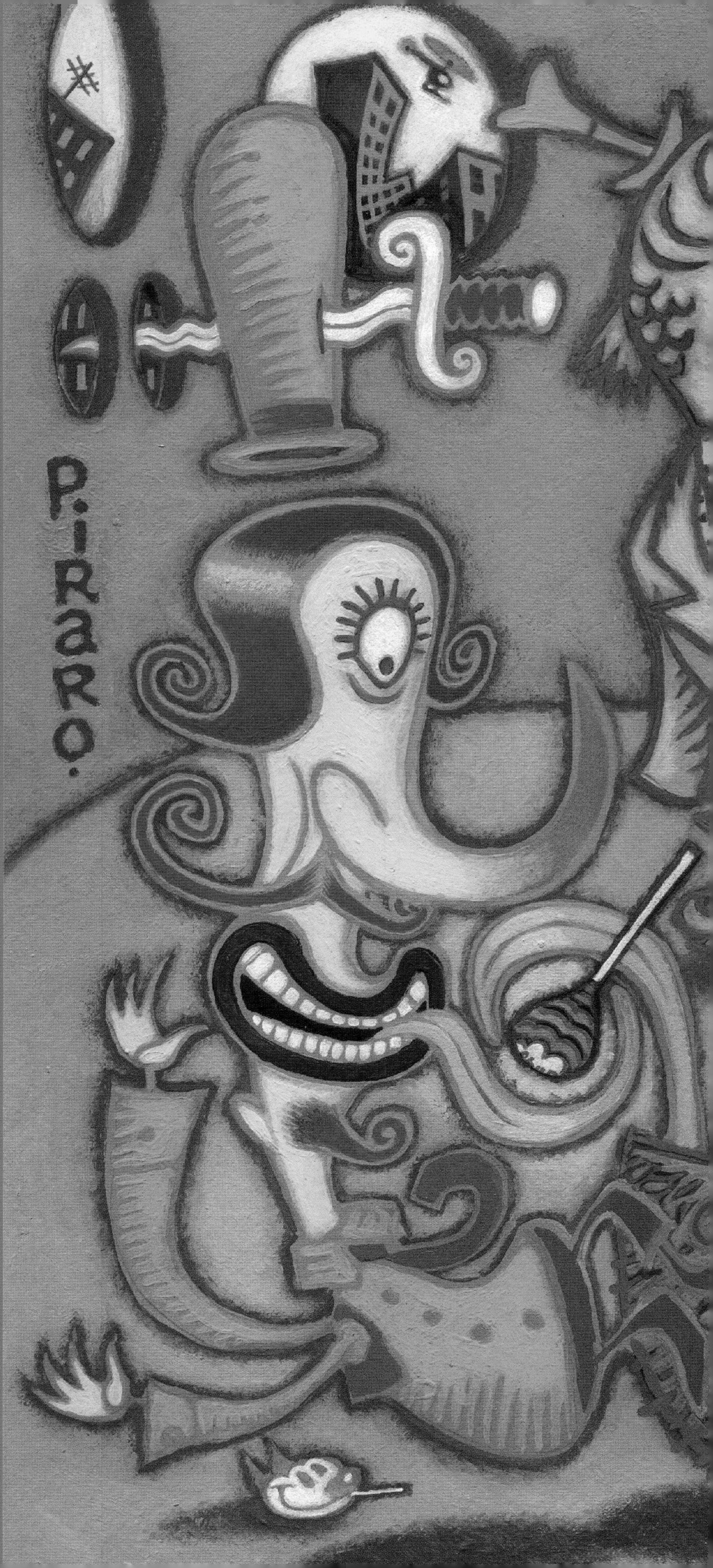
P. IRARO.

Used on the Chupa Chups website in the late nineties. Most of these characters are out of my sketchbook. I thought I'd never have any commercial use for them.

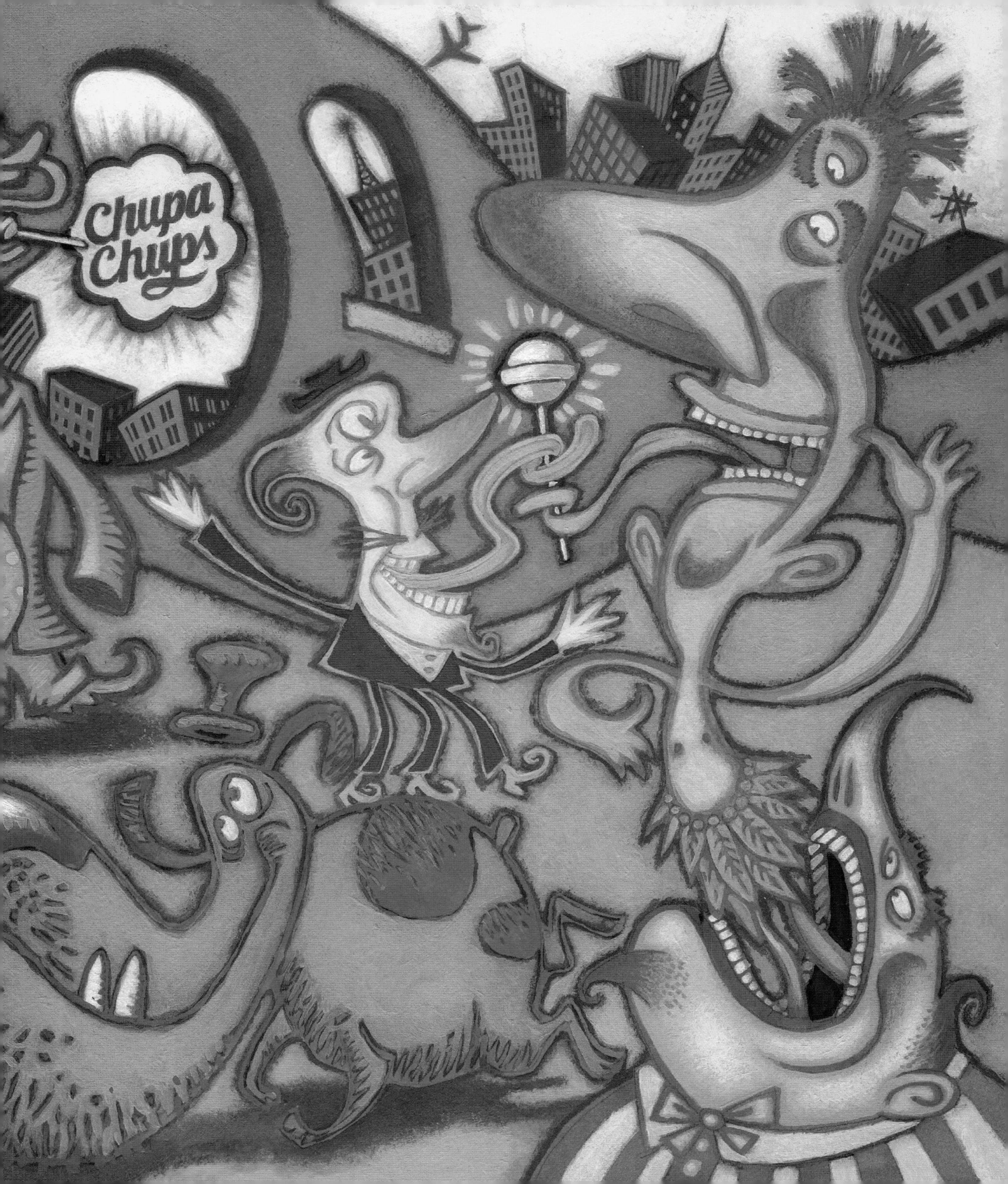
Chupa
Chups

Games and puzzles

As a kid I loved games and puzzles and occasionally enjoy creating my own versions of them for my Sunday comics.

Magical Eyeball Cartoon
©DAN PIRARO·1997
TO GET THE PICTURE & THE GAG...
Hold the image close to your nose. Move paper slowly away from you & back again like a slide trombone, for several minutes or until you become cross-eyed & dizzy. Now look around at all the people staring & laughing at you! — GET THE PICTURE? YOU'RE THE GAG!
7-6 PIRARO.
Dist. by Universal Press Synd.

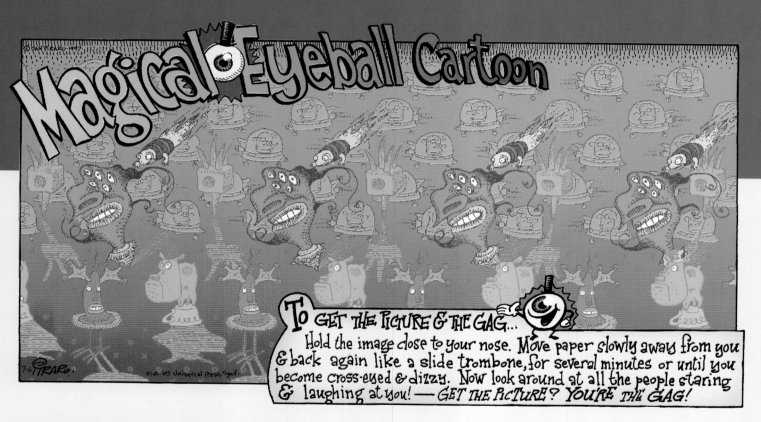

If you cross your eyes and line up a couple of like images, you actually get a sense of depth from this picture. I was proud of myself for being able to figure out how to create it from scratch. The ones they had in the newspaper feature called "Magic Eye" and that you see in books are done with a computer. Mine was just ink, paper, and good old-fashioned guesswork. (1997)

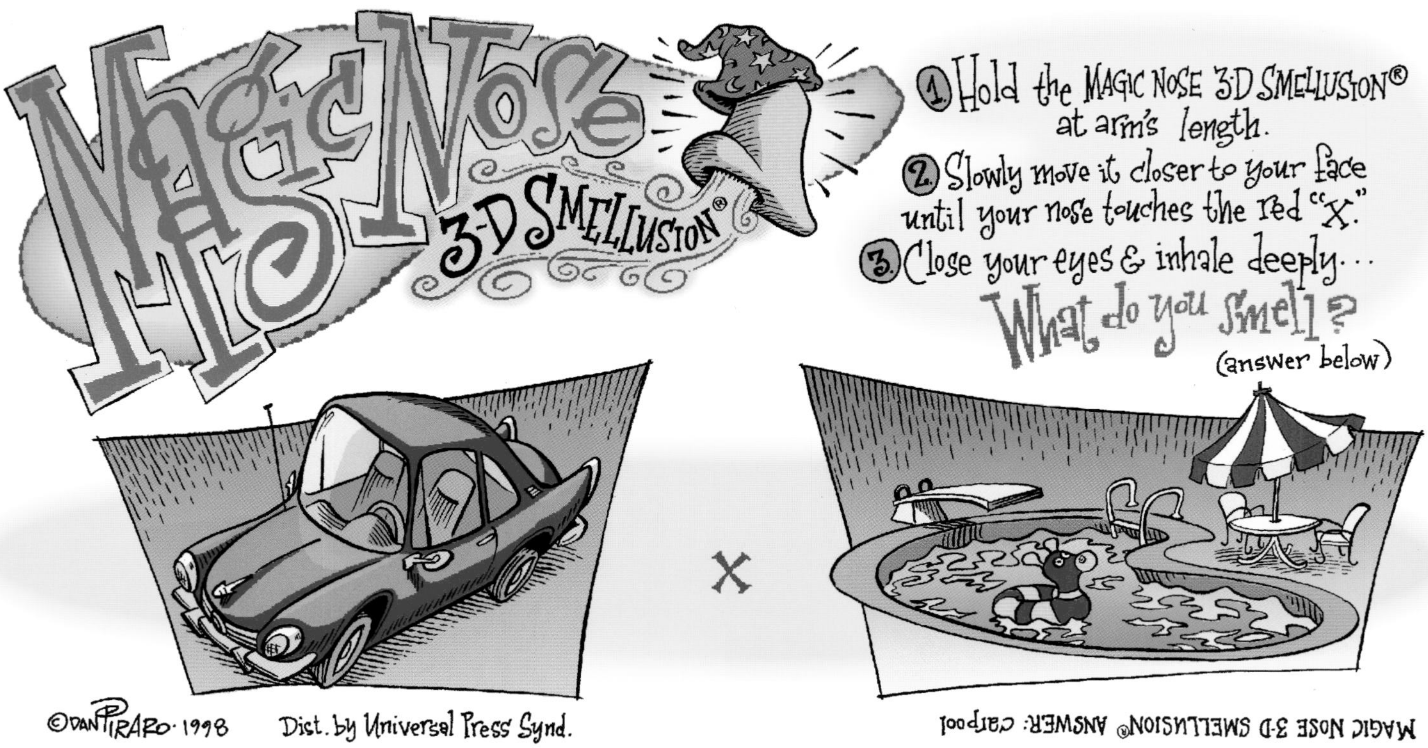
Magic Nose 3-D SMELLUSION®
1 Hold the MAGIC NOSE 3-D SMELLUSION® at arm's length.
2 Slowly move it closer to your face until your nose touches the red "X."
3 Close your eyes & inhale deeply...
What do you smell?
(answer below)
X
©DAN PIRARO 1998 Dist. by Universal Press Synd.
MAGIC NOSE 3-D SMELLUSION® ANSWER: carpool

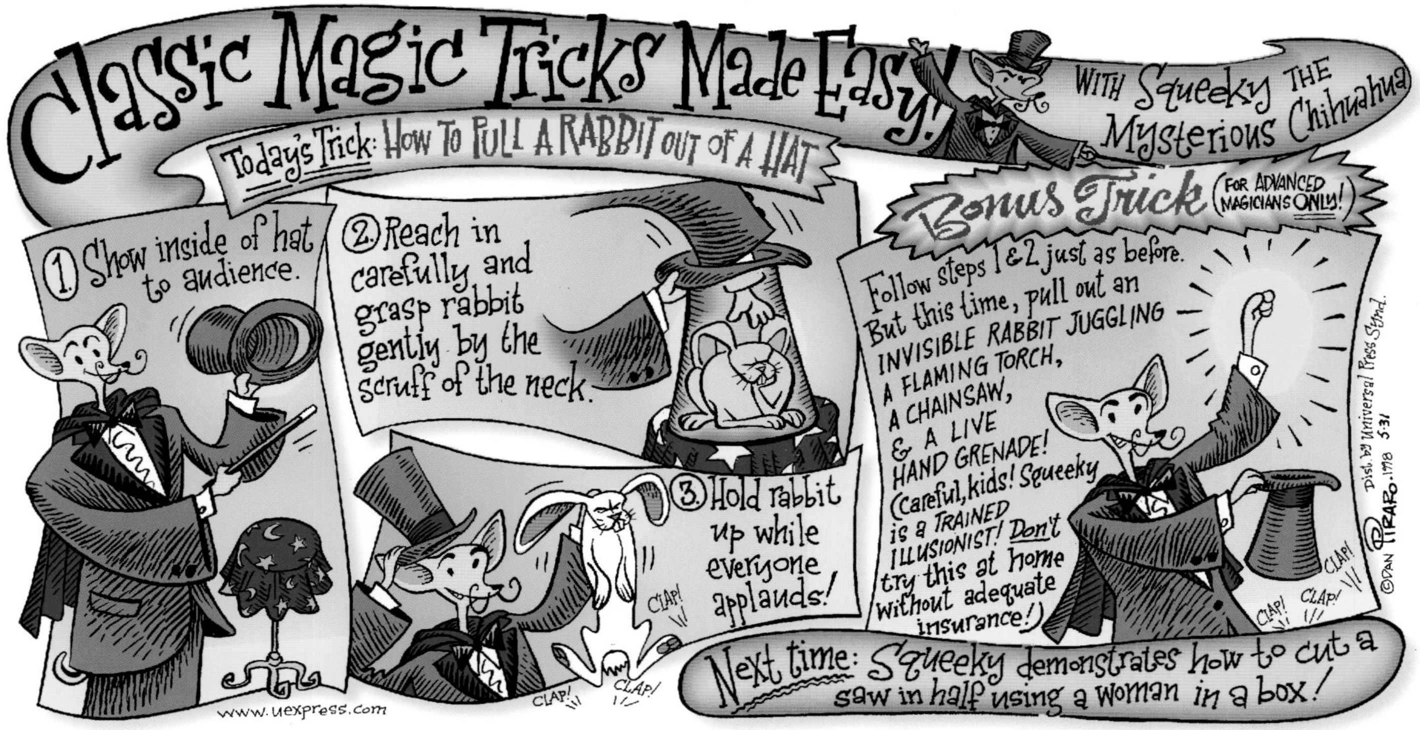
Classic Magic Tricks Made Easy!
WITH Squeeky THE Mysterious Chihuahua
Today's Trick: HOW TO PULL A RABBIT OUT OF A HAT
1. Show inside of hat to audience.
2. Reach in carefully and grasp rabbit gently by the scruff of the neck.
3. Hold rabbit up while everyone applauds!
CLAP! CLAP! CLAP!
Bonus Trick (FOR ADVANCED MAGICIANS ONLY!)
Follow steps 1 & 2 just as before. But this time, pull out an INVISIBLE RABBIT JUGGLING A FLAMING TORCH, A CHAINSAW, & A LIVE HAND GRENADE! (Careful, kids! Squeeky is a TRAINED ILLUSIONIST! Don't try this at home without adequate insurance!)
CLAP! CLAP! CLAP!
©DAN PIRARO 1998 5-31 Dist. by Universal Press Synd.
Next time: Squeeky demonstrates how to cut a saw in half using a woman in a box!
www.uexpress.com

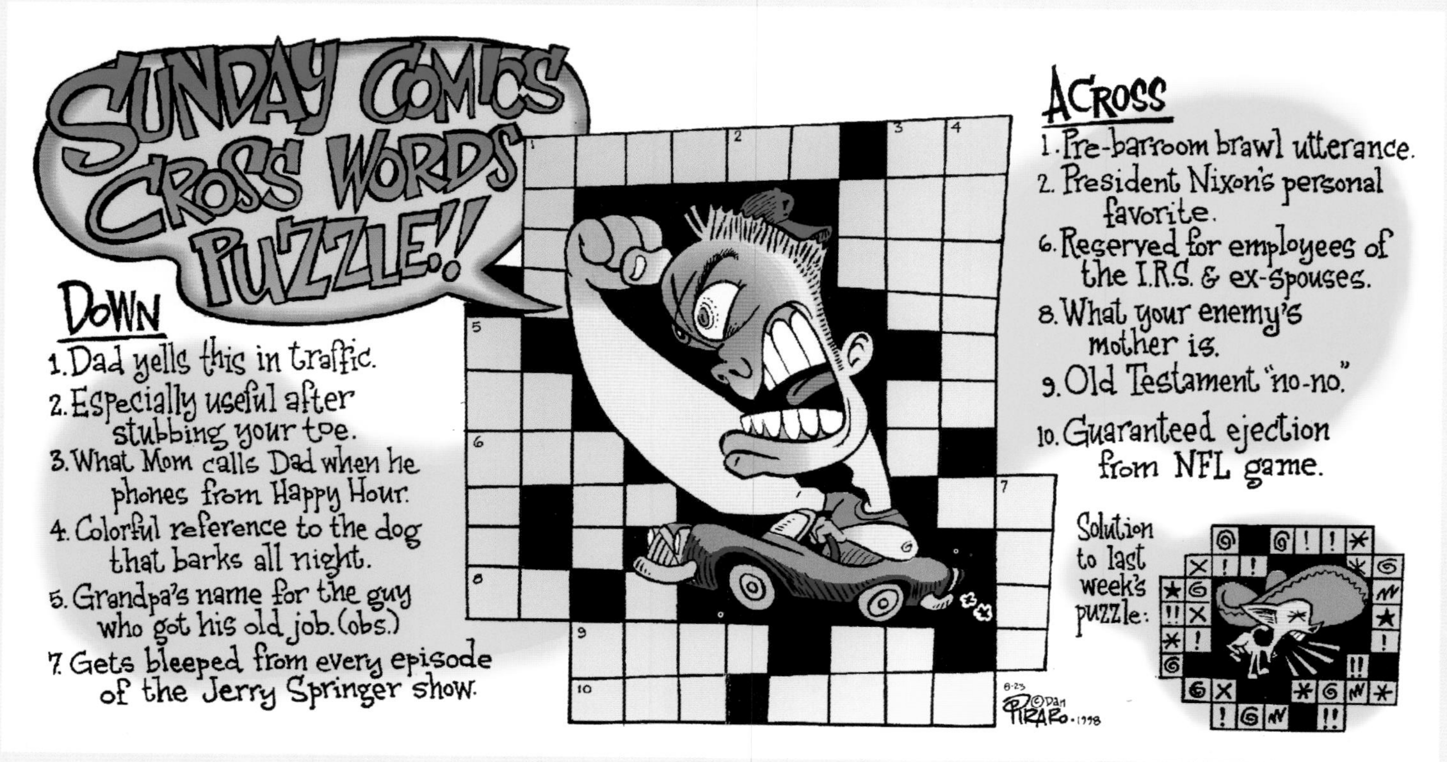
SUNDAY COMICS' CROSS WORDS PUZZLE!!
DOWN
1. Dad yells this in traffic.
2. Especially useful after stubbing your toe.
3. What Mom calls Dad when he phones from Happy Hour.
4. Colorful reference to the dog that barks all night.
5. Grandpa's name for the guy who got his old job. (obs.)
7. Gets bleeped from every episode of the Jerry Springer show.
ACROSS
1. Pre-barroom brawl utterance.
2. President Nixon's personal favorite.
6. Reserved for employees of the I.R.S. & ex-spouses.
8. What your enemy's mother is.
9. Old Testament "no-no."
10. Guaranteed ejection from NFL game.
Solution to last week's puzzle:
6-25 ©Dan Piraro 1998

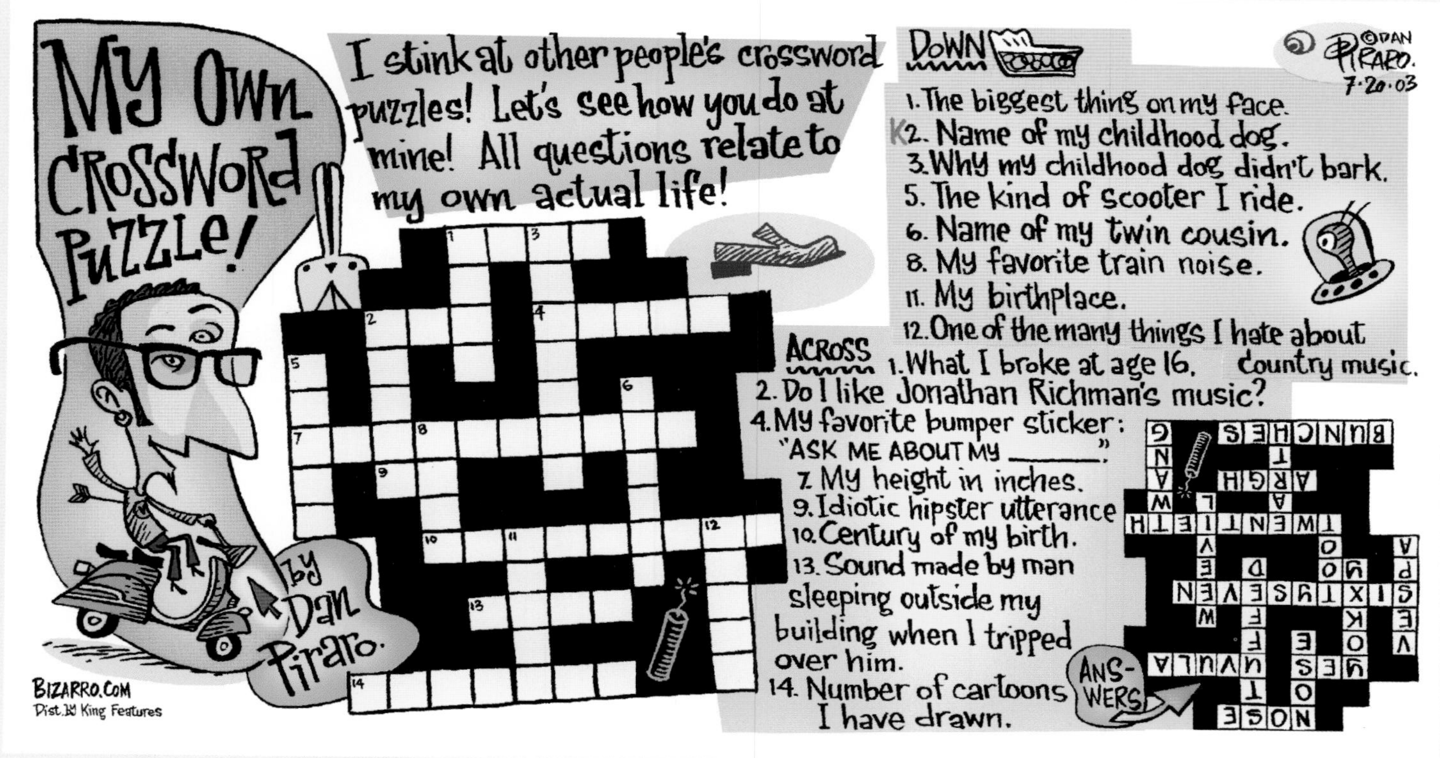
My Own Crossword Puzzle!
by Dan Piraro.
I stink at other people's crossword puzzles! Let's see how you do at mine! All questions relate to my own actual life!
DOWN
1. The biggest thing on my face.
2. Name of my childhood dog.
3. Why my childhood dog didn't bark.
5. The kind of scooter I ride.
6. Name of my twin cousin.
8. My favorite train noise.
11. My birthplace.
12. One of the many things I hate about country music.
ACROSS
1. What I broke at age 16.
2. Do I like Jonathan Richman's music?
4. My favorite bumper sticker: "ASK ME ABOUT MY ______."
7. My height in inches.
9. Idiotic hipster utterance
10. Century of my birth.
13. Sound made by man sleeping outside my building when I tripped over him.
14. Number of cartoons I have drawn.
ANSWERS
©Dan Piraro. 7-20-03
BIZARRO.COM
Dist. by King Features

Help Mr. Mouse Find His Way...
A.
B.
C.
D.
E.
Which road will lead Mr. Mouse to something CHEESY?
CHEEZ ITz
The JERRY SPRINGER SHOW
WEEKLY WORLD
DRAMATIC NEW EVIDENCE
SINATRA KIDNAPPED BY BIGFOOT & UFO
The STARR REPORT
WALMART
WALMART
©DAN PIRARO · 1998

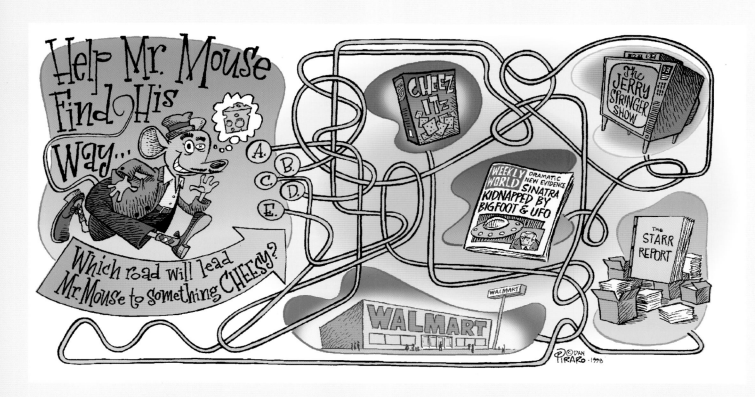

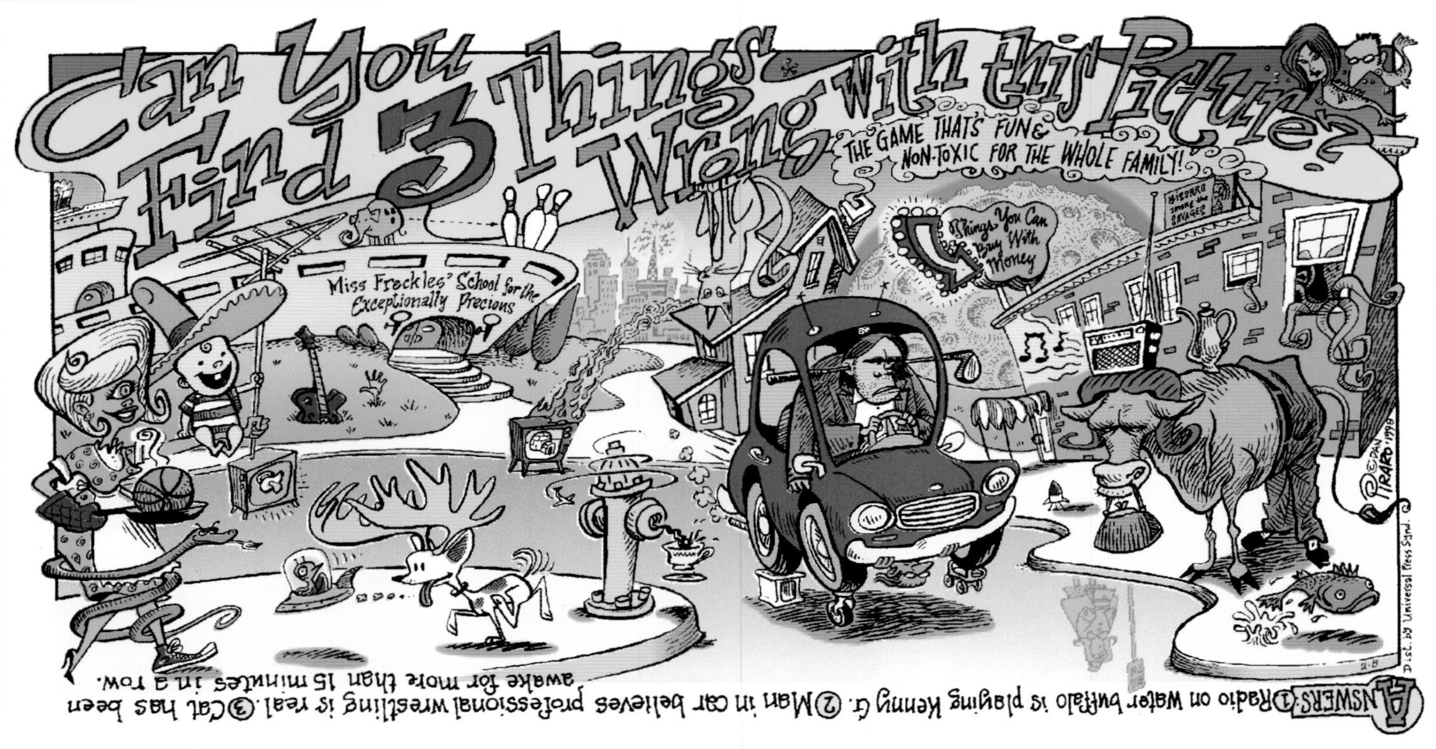
Can You Find 3 Things Wrong with this Picture?
THE GAME THAT'S FUN & NON-TOXIC FOR THE WHOLE FAMILY!
Miss Freckles' School for the Exceptionally Precious
Things You Can Buy With Money
©DAN PIRARO 1998
Dist. by Universal Press Synd.
ANSWERS: ① Radio on water buffalo is playing Kenny G. ② Man in car believes professional wrestling is real. ③ Cat has been awake for more than 15 minutes in a row.

The first of a series of "Can You Find *x* Things Wrong with this Picture?" A satire of my favorite game in *Highlights* magazine. (1998)

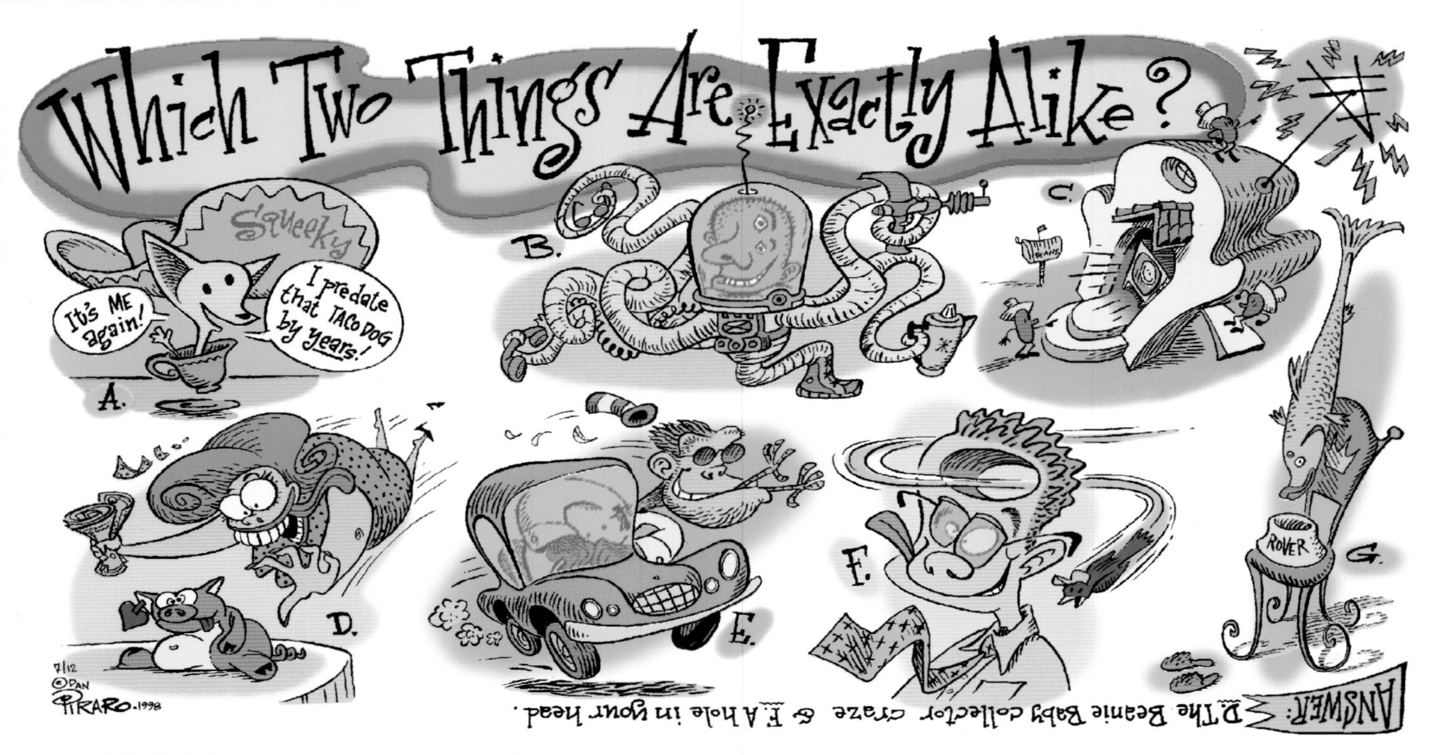
Which Two Things Are Exactly Alike?
Squeeky
It's ME again!
I predate that TACO DOG by years!
A.
B.
C.
D.
E.
F.
ROVER
G.
7/12 ©DAN PIRARO.1998
ANSWER: D. The Beanie Baby collector craze & F. A hole in your head.

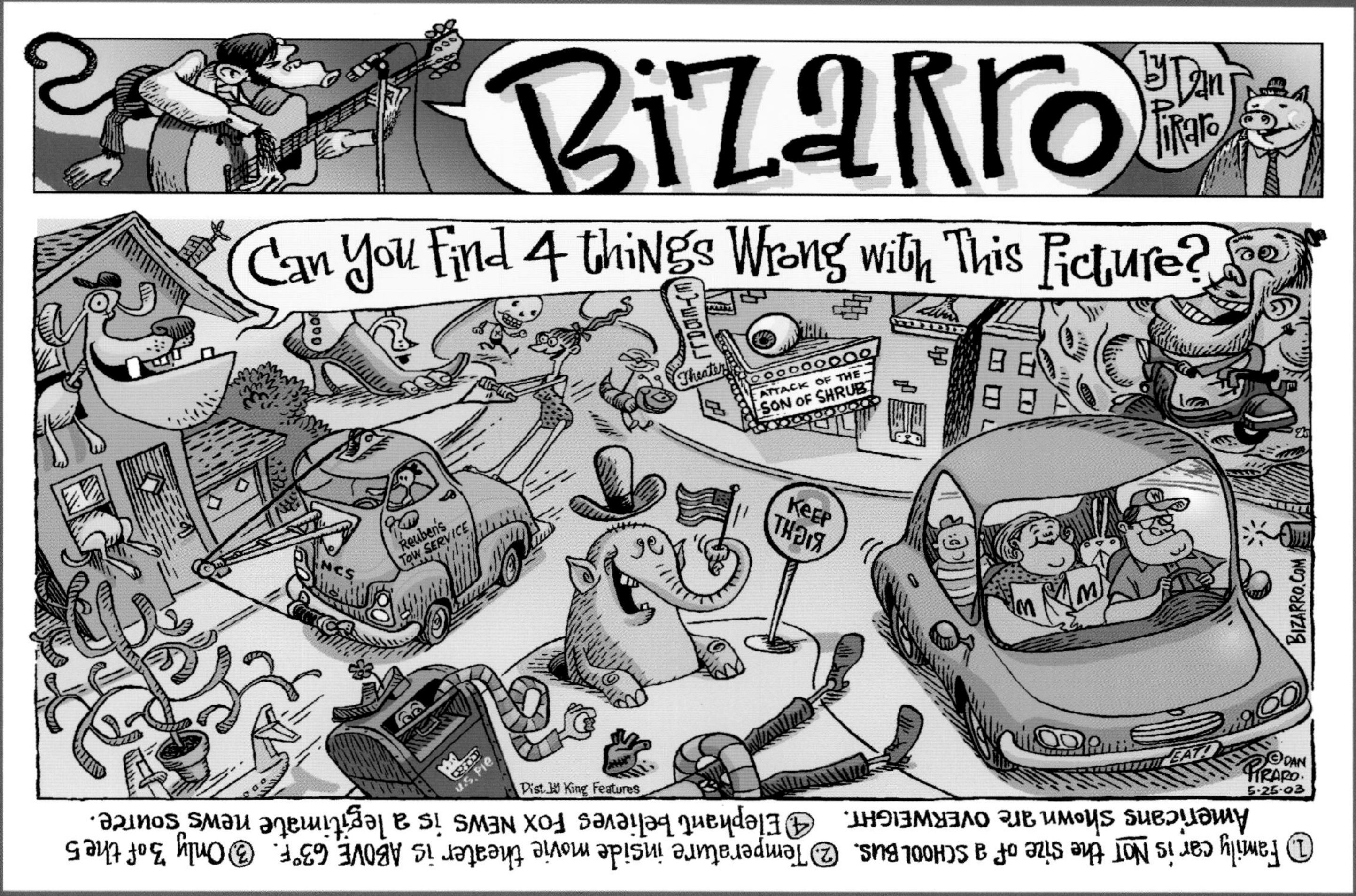
Bizarro
by Dan Piraro
Can You Find 4 things Wrong with This Picture?
EYEBALL Theater
ATTACK OF THE SON OF SHRUB
Reuben's Tow SERVICE
NCS
KEEP RIGHT
BIZARRO.COM
EAT!
U.S. Pie
Dist. by King Features
©DAN PIRARO 5-25-03
1. Family car is NOT the size of a SCHOOL BUS. 2. Temperature inside movie theater is ABOVE 63°F. 3. Only 3 of the 5 Americans shown are OVERWEIGHT. 4. Elephant believes FOX NEWS is a legitimate news source.

This represents my first blatant shot at Fox News. (2003)

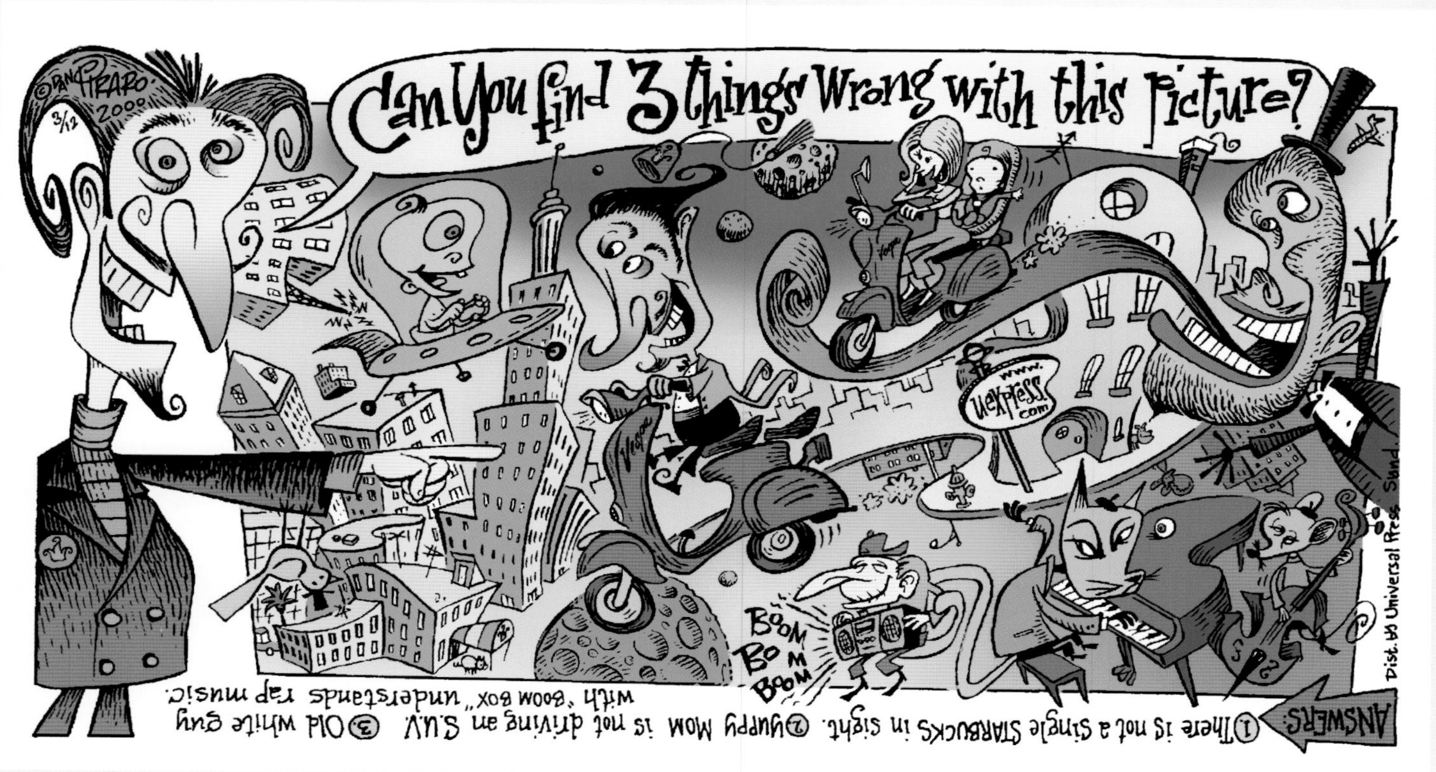
©DAN PIRARO 2000 3/12
Can You find 3 things Wrong with this Picture?
UEXPRESS.com
BOOM BOOM BOOM
Dist. by Universal Press Synd.
ANSWERS: 1 There is not a single STARBUCKS in sight. 2 Yuppy Mom is not driving an S.U.V. 3 Old white guy with "Boom Box" understands rap music.

This repeating theme offers a great chance to go ape with the art. (2000)

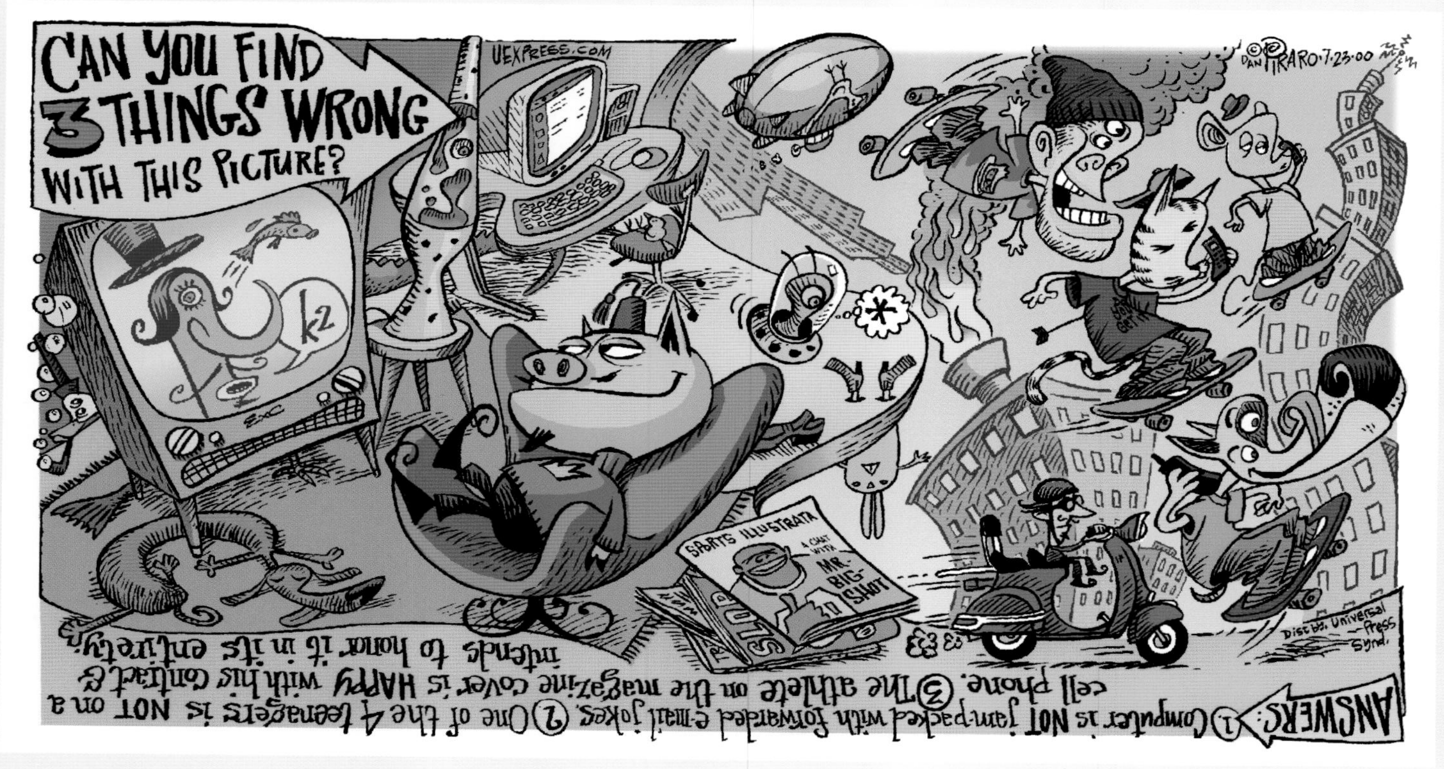
CAN YOU FIND 3 THINGS WRONG WITH THIS PICTURE?
UEXPRESS.COM
©DAN PIRARO·7·23·00
SPORTS ILLUSTRATA
A CHAT WITH MR. BIG-SHOT
Dist. by Universal Press Synd.
ANSWERS: 1 Computer is NOT jam-packed with forwarded e-mail jokes. 2 One of the 4 teenagers is NOT on a cell phone. 3 The athlete on the magazine cover is HAPPY with his contract & intends to honor it in its entirety.

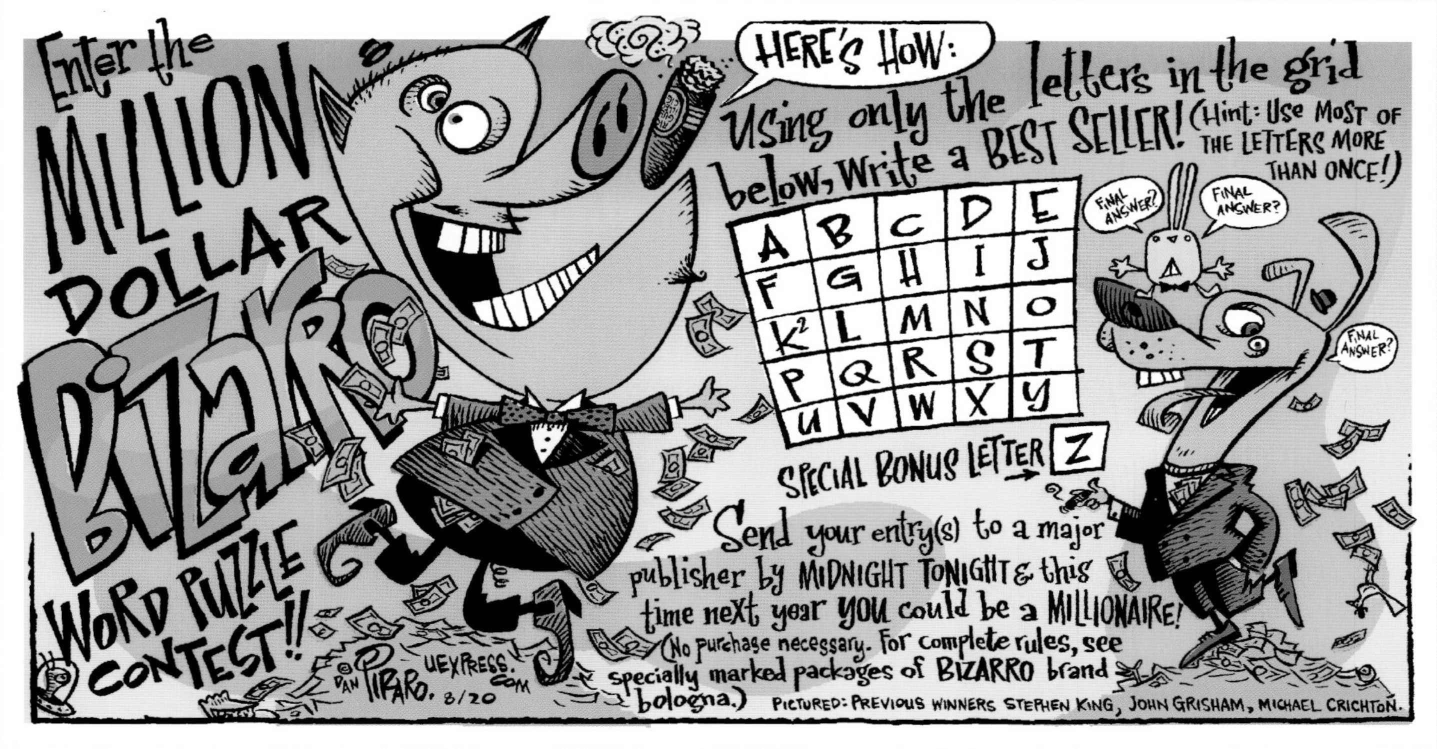

Enter the MILLION DOLLAR BIZARRO WORD PUZZLE CONTEST!!
HERE'S HOW:
Using only the letters in the grid below, Write a BEST SELLER! (Hint: Use MOST OF THE LETTERS MORE THAN ONCE!)
A B C D E
F G H I J
K² L M N O
P Q R S T
U V W X Y
SPECIAL BONUS LETTER Z
FINAL ANSWER?
FINAL ANSWER?
FINAL ANSWER?
Send your entry(s) to a major publisher by MIDNIGHT TONIGHT & this time next year YOU could be a MILLIONAIRE!
(No purchase necessary. For complete rules, see specially marked packages of BIZARRO brand bologna.)
PICTURED: PREVIOUS WINNERS STEPHEN KING, JOHN GRISHAM, MICHAEL CRICHTON.
© DAN PIRARO. 8/20
UEXPRESS.COM

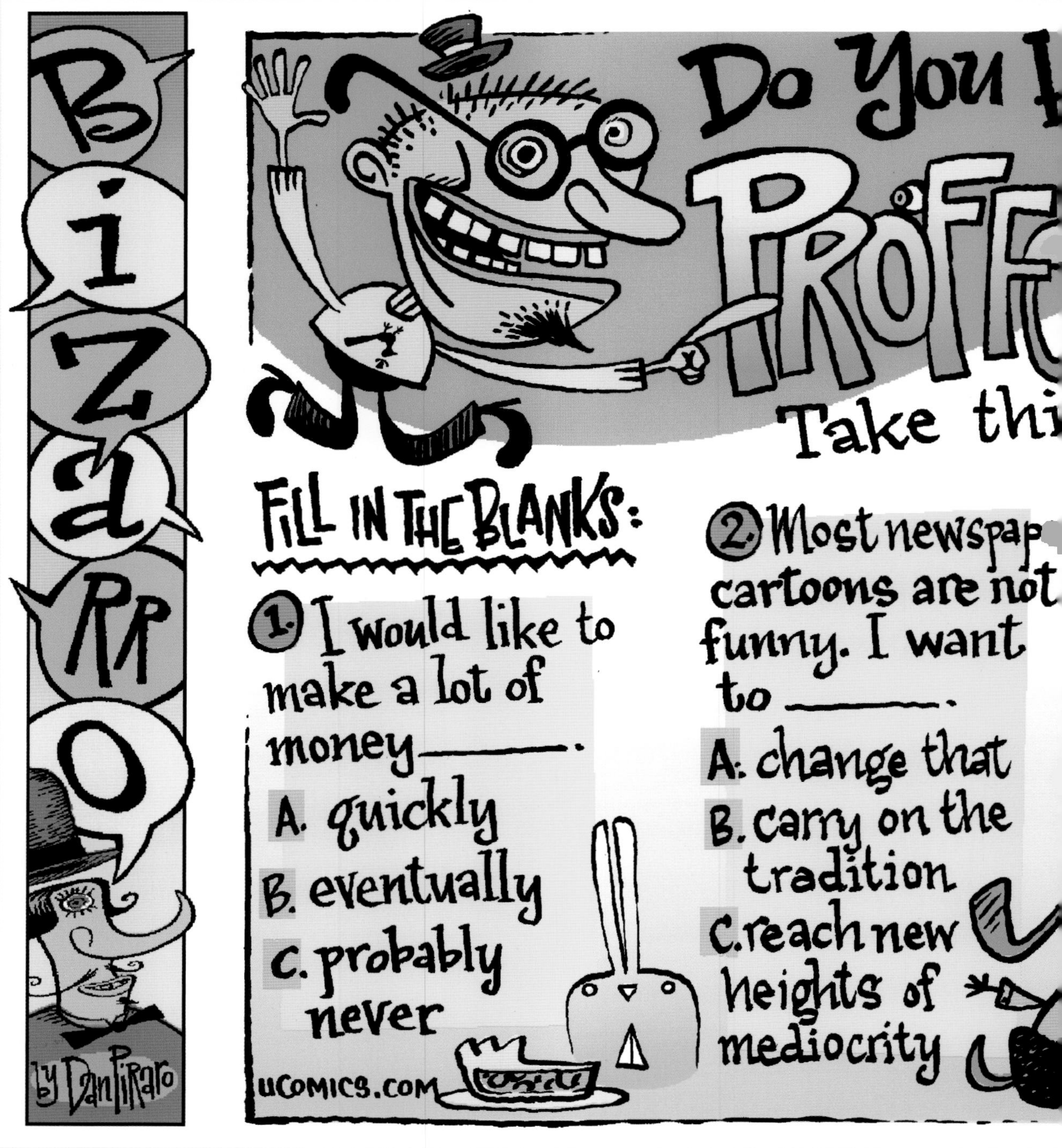
Bizarro
by Dan Piraro
Do You I
PROFF
Take thi
FILL IN THE BLANKS:
1. I would like to make a lot of money ______.
A. quickly
B. eventually
C. probably never
2. Most newspap
cartoons are not
funny. I want
to ______.
A. change that
B. carry on the tradition
C. reach new heights of mediocrity
UCOMICS.COM

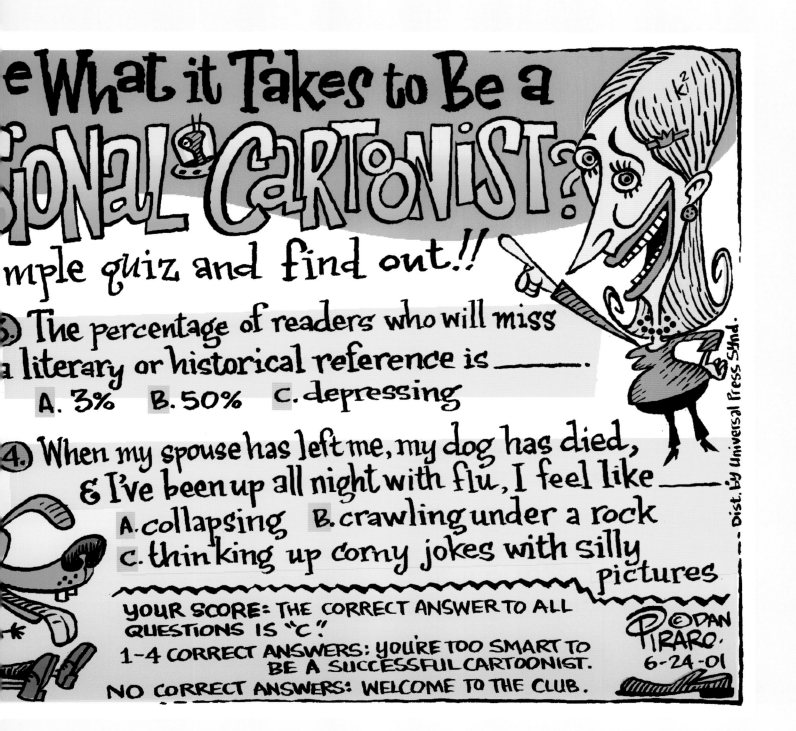

e What it Takes to Be a

iONAL CARTOONIST?

mple quiz and find out.!!

3.) The percentage of readers who will miss
a literary or historical reference is _____.
A. 3%   B. 50%   C. depressing

4.) When my spouse has left me, my dog has died,
& I've been up all night with flu, I feel like _____
A. collapsing   B. crawling under a rock
C. thinking up corny jokes with silly
pictures

YOUR SCORE: THE CORRECT ANSWER TO ALL
QUESTIONS IS "C."
1-4 CORRECT ANSWERS: YOU'RE TOO SMART TO
BE A SUCCESSFUL CARTOONIST.
NO CORRECT ANSWERS: WELCOME TO THE CLUB.

© DAN PIRARO. 6-24-01

Dist. by Universal Press Synd.

I showed this cartoon during a talk I gave to the National Cartoonists Society.
It didn't get much of a laugh. Perhaps it was too close to home. To be fair,
though, these guys are the toughest audience in the world. They don't laugh
at jokes; they process them. (2001)

Children's poems

Here is a group of Sunday cartoons that came from some children's poems I wrote. I've long intended to illustrate them properly and try to get them published, but haven't gotten around to it yet. Most are much too long for a Sunday cartoon.

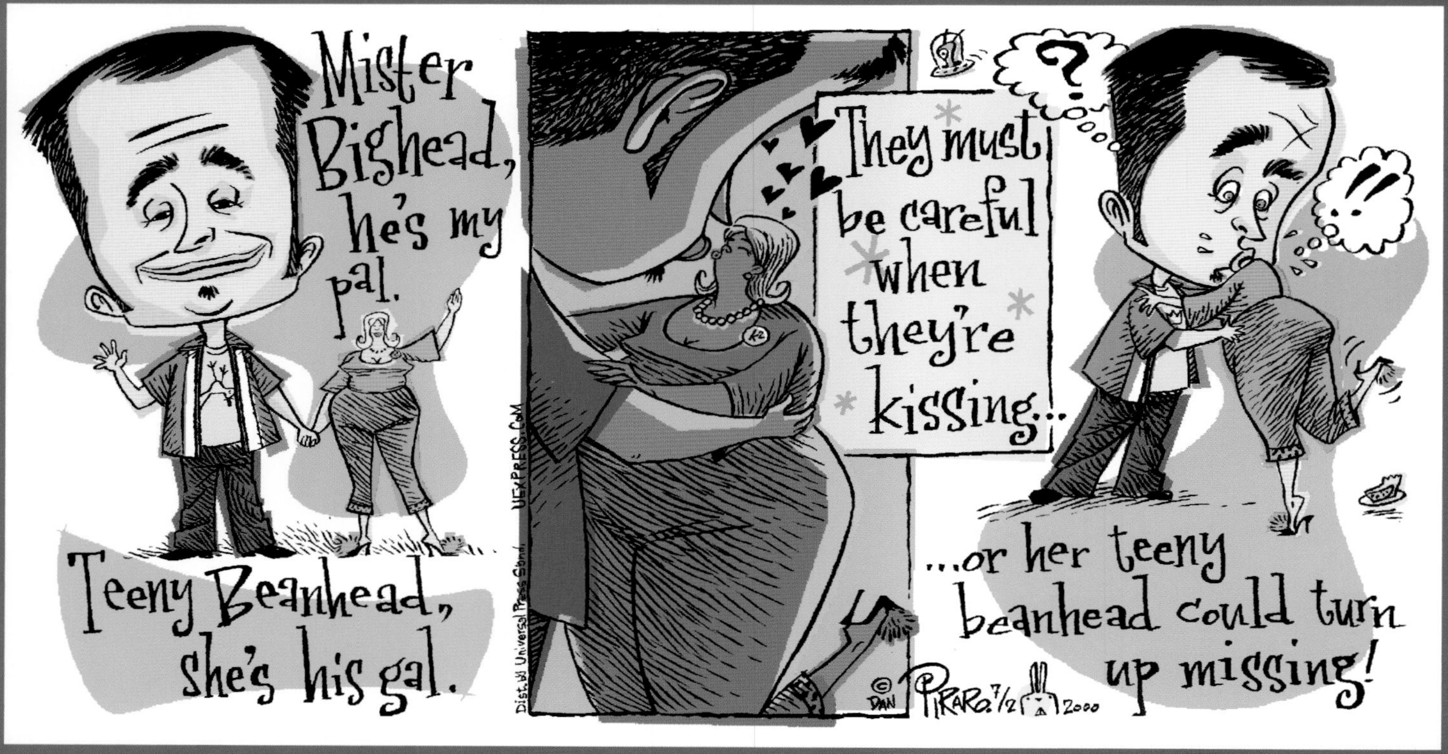
Mister Bighead, he's my pal.
Teeny Beanhead, she's his gal.
They must be careful when they're kissing...
...or her teeny beanhead could turn up missing!
Dist. by Universal Press Synd.
UEXPRESS.COM
© DAN PIRARO 7/2 2000

This is maybe my favorite of all the poems I've written. It's simple, weird, and has lots of comic illustration potential. As I look at it now, I wish the final image had been of the two separated after the kiss, a surprised look on the man's face and the woman with no head at all. (2000)

OPPOSITE, TOP: I adore Dr. Seuss and firmly believe that he alone kept me from committing suicide out of boredom from reading those damned "Dick and Jane" books they were still using when I started school in 1964. (2000)

OPPOSITE, BOTTOM: This is one of my favorite concepts but like much of what I do, it is so complicated that I fear the average reader would give up. If you stick with it, the payoff is worth it, I think. That's a fairly accurate depiction of my dad and me in the last column. (2000)

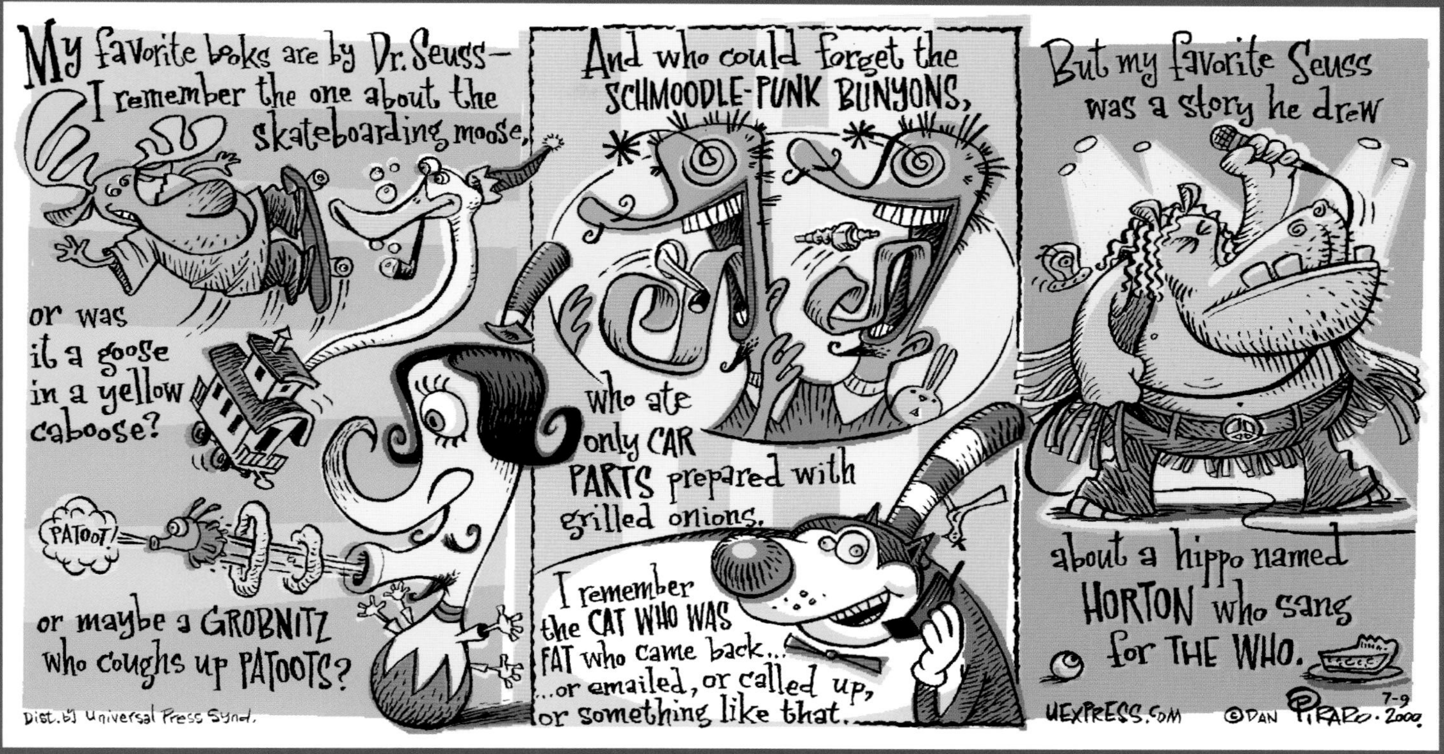
My favorite books are by Dr. Seuss—
I remember the one about the skateboarding moose,
or was it a goose in a yellow caboose?
PATOOT!
or maybe a GROBNITZ who coughs up PATOOTS?
Dist. by Universal Press Synd.
And who could forget the SCHMOODLE-PUNK BUNYONS,
who ate only CAR PARTS prepared with grilled onions.
I remember the CAT WHO WAS FAT who came back... ...or emailed, or called up, or something like that.
But my favorite Seuss was a story he drew
about a hippo named HORTON who sang for THE WHO.
UEXPRESS.COM
©DAN PIRARO 7-9 2000

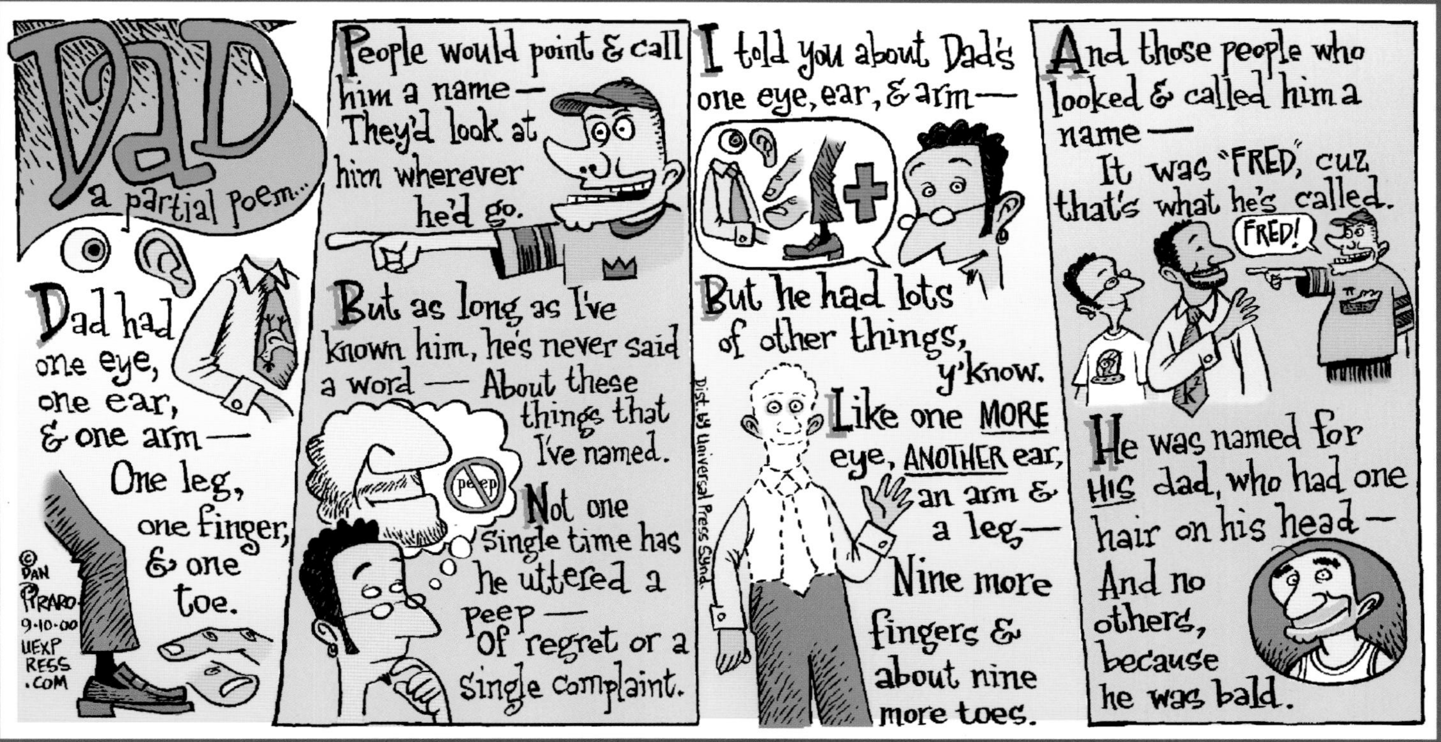
DAD
a partial poem...
Dad had one eye, one ear, & one arm—
One leg, one finger, & one toe.
© DAN PIRARO 9-10-00 UEXPRESS.COM
People would point & call him a name—
They'd look at him wherever he'd go.
But as long as I've known him, he's never said a word— About these things that I've named.
peep
Not one single time has he uttered a peep— Of regret or a single complaint.
Dist. by Universal Press Synd.
I told you about Dad's one eye, ear, & arm—
But he had lots of other things, y'know.
Like one MORE eye, ANOTHER ear, an arm & a leg—
Nine more fingers & about nine more toes.
And those people who looked & called him a name—
It was "FRED," cuz that's what he's called.
FRED!
He was named for HIS dad, who had one hair on his head—
And no others, because he was bald.

Aliens!

Presenting an outsider's view of earth is always a great way to make a statement about the current culture.

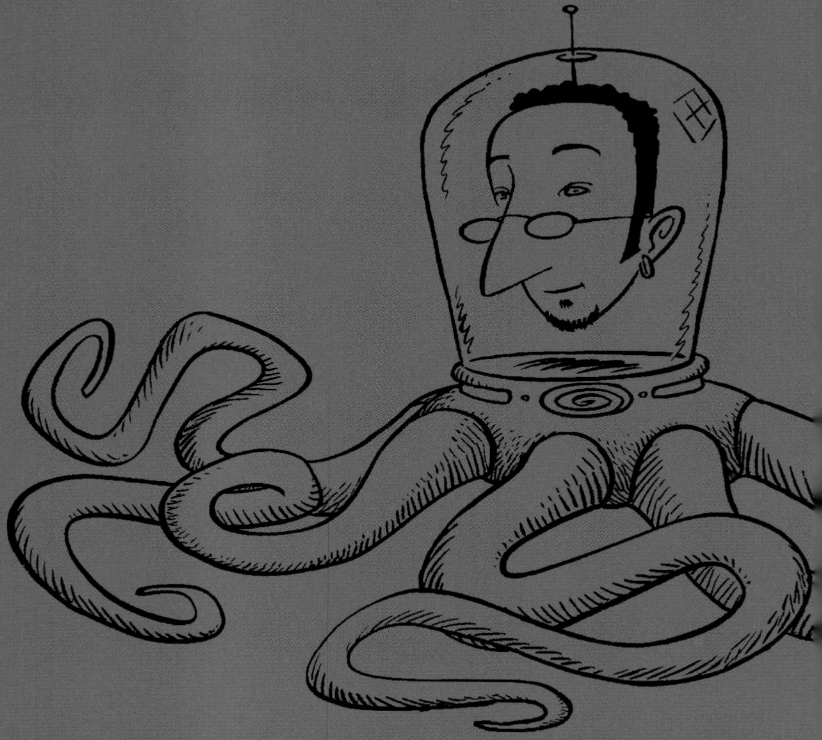

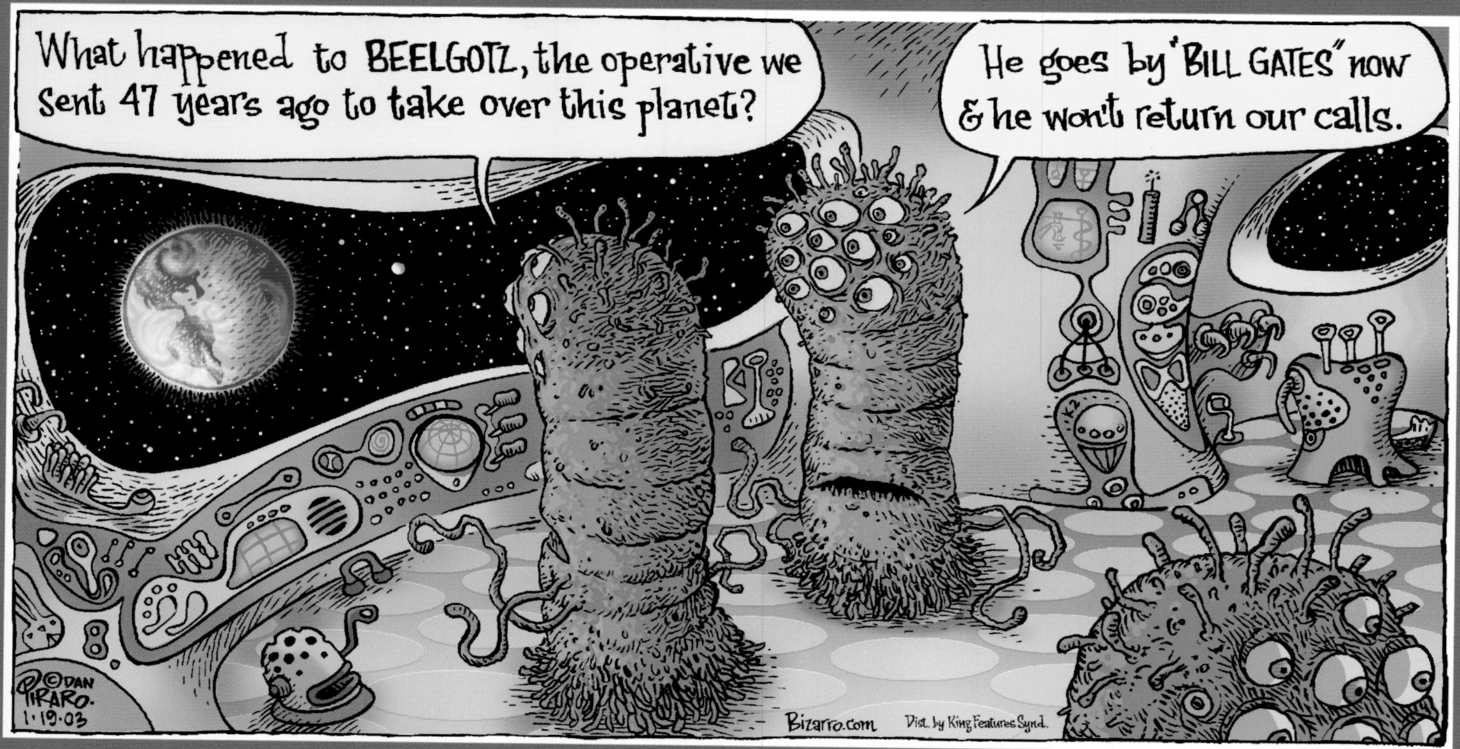
What happened to BEELGOTZ, the operative we sent 47 years ago to take over this planet?
He goes by "BILL GATES" now & he won't return our calls.
©DAN PIRARO. 1·19·03
Bizarro.com
Dist. by King Features Synd.

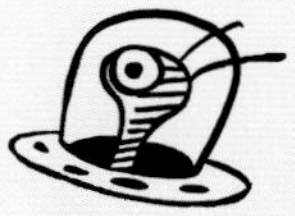

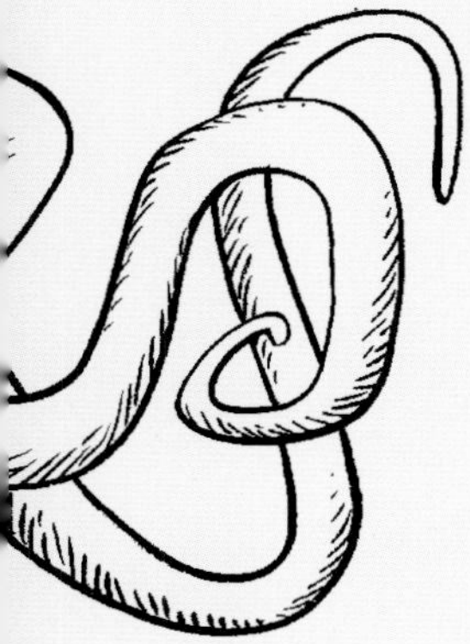

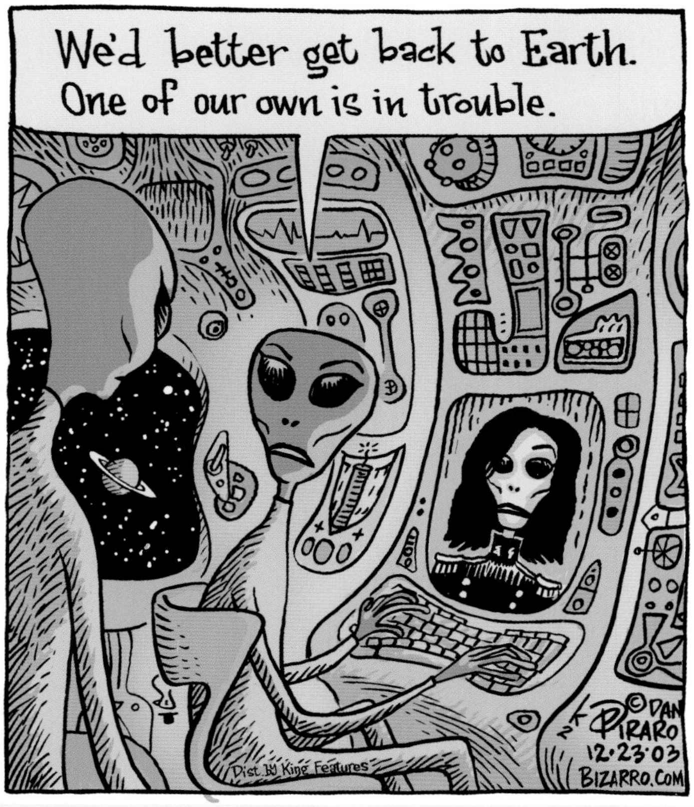
We'd better get back to Earth. One of our own is in trouble.
©DAN PIRARO 12·23·03
BIZARRO.COM
Dist. by King Features

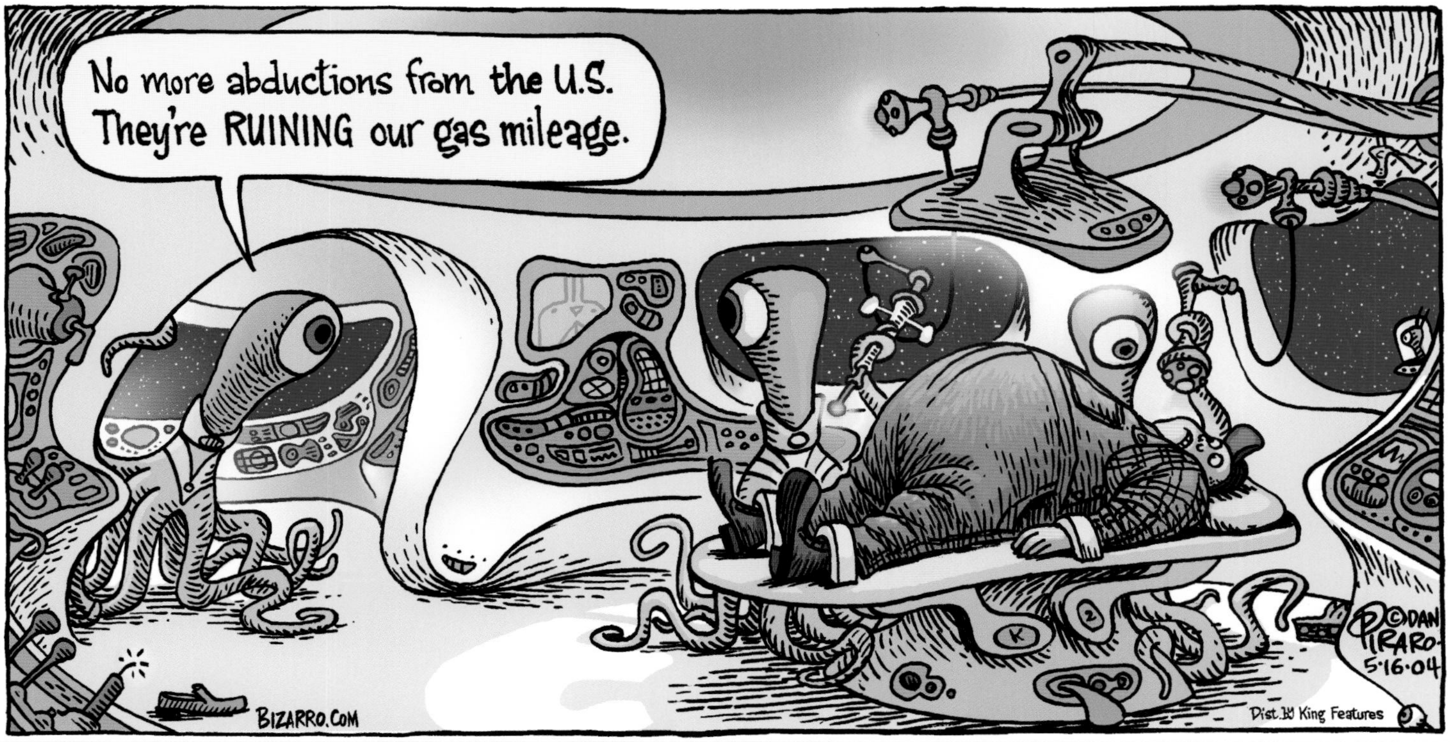
No more abductions from the U.S. They're RUINING our gas mileage.
©DAN PIRARO 5·16·04
BIZARRO.COM
Dist. by King Features

Chapter two

Cartooning
as escape

Each of us is a product of the total of our experiences, be they conscious decisions or not, wise actions or colossal mistakes, amazing good fortune or hideous bad luck. In the end, the "what if" fantasies are little more than a party game. I am extremely happy with who and where I am now, and I believe my life today is a direct result of the lessons I've learned from the mistakes I've made. Had I not buried myself under a heap of bourgeois responsibilities early on, I almost certainly would not have become a cartoonist. Although it had never been my ultimate goal, it has been a great blessing.

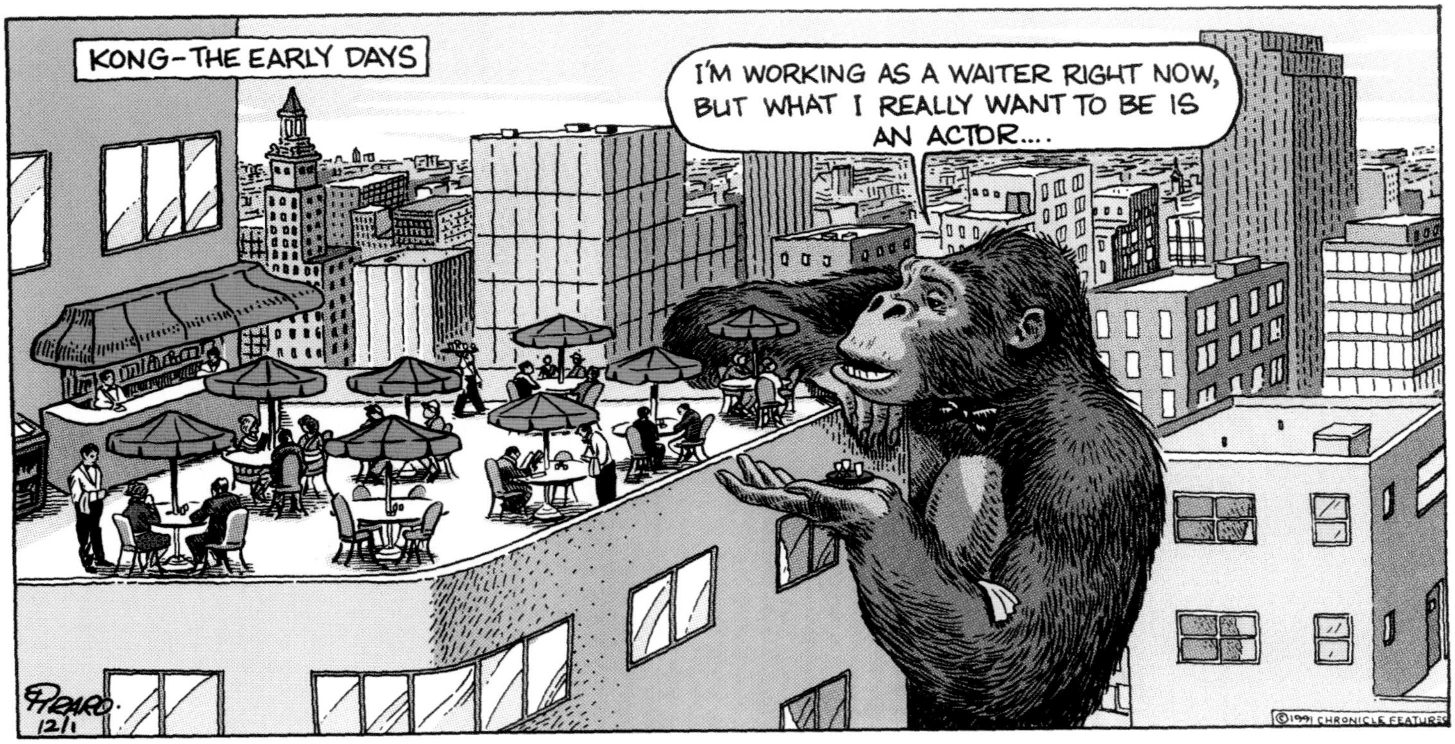
KONG–THE EARLY DAYS
I'M WORKING AS A WAITER RIGHT NOW, BUT WHAT I REALLY WANT TO BE IS AN ACTOR....
PIRARO. 12/1
©1991 CHRONICLE FEATURES

I enjoyed newspaper comics as a kid, but didn't revere them as an art form. I often thought that being a cartoonist would be fun, but I only considered pursuing it professionally out of desperation.

Several years into the daily grind of meeting deadlines at the illustration studio and with a demanding toddler and stressed-out wife at home, I was near the end of my rope. I was at serious risk of taking some of my advertising clients hostage. I considered this briefly, even drew up plans and laid out my wardrobe, but in the end a more reasonable approach seemed to be to look for a better way to make money as an artist. I had drawn odd cartoons for years to entertain myself, so it seemed logical to attempt to get paid for it. I mistakenly thought that being signed to a syndication contract and having cartoons in the paper every day would be a quick road to wealth and creative freedom. This proved no more rational than my one-year plan to move my band out to the Coast and win a Grammy.

In 1981 Chronicle Features in San Francisco had launched *The Far Side*, giving Gary Larson a five-year contract. When it expired, he unexpectedly jumped to another syndicate, leaving Chronicle with an opening in their stable for a surreal, one-panel feature such as mine. Chronicle had liked my early submissions—I'd been showing them and the other syndicates different sorts of comic ideas for more than a year—and they called and offered me a contract.

I was thrilled, of course, and thought my ship had come in. I envisioned quitting my illustration job and never looking back. In reality, the ship was more like a bamboo raft lashed together with string. As it turns out, a syndication contract basically says that you will give them an original cartoon every day for *x* years, they will do everything they can to sell it to newspapers, and you'll split whatever money comes in.

This is the first published *Bizarro* cartoon, January 22, 1985. Ugly drawing, horsey signature, goofy joke. When I look at my earliest work, I often wonder what prompted Chronicle to give me a contract.

It was another frantic day of trading at The New York Sock Exchange.

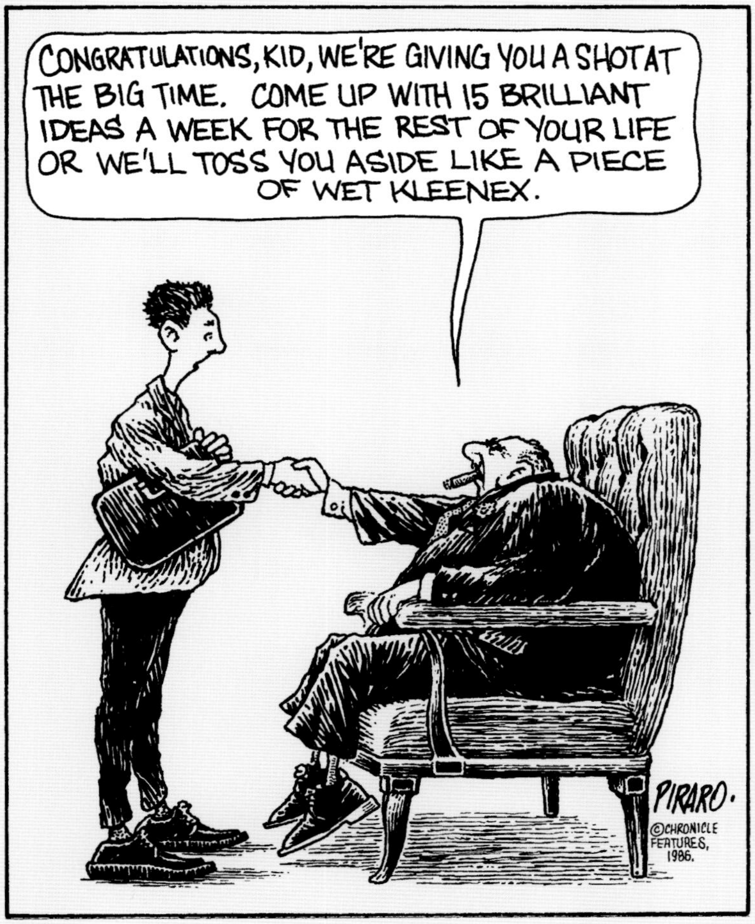
CONGRATULATIONS, KID, WE'RE GIVING YOU A SHOT AT THE BIG TIME. COME UP WITH 15 BRILLIANT IDEAS A WEEK FOR THE REST OF YOUR LIFE OR WE'LL TOSS YOU ASIDE LIKE A PIECE OF WET KLEENEX.
PIRARO.
©CHRONICLE FEATURES, 1986.

By 1986 I had begun to develop a more attractive inking style. After being disappointed by several typos in the typeset captions, such as "Sherriff" (below left), I started putting caption balloons in my drawings. The cartoon at left represented the pressures of being sentenced to having to create a joke a day for life.

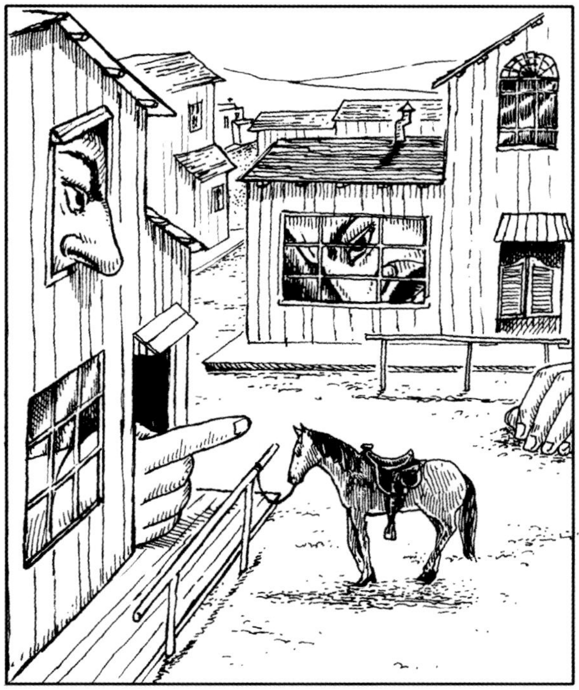

"This town ain't big enough for the both of us, Sherriff!"

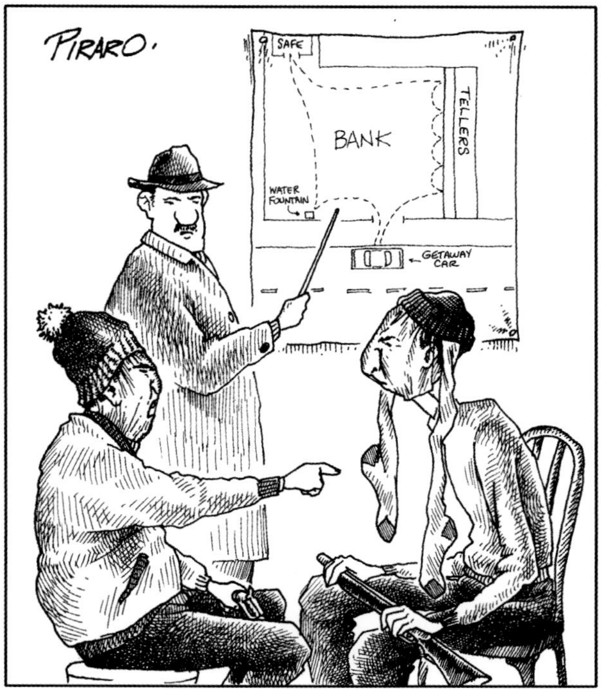
PIRARO.
SAFE
BANK
TELLERS
WATER FOUNTAIN
GETAWAY CAR

"I'm not going in that bank till he tucks the feet in!"

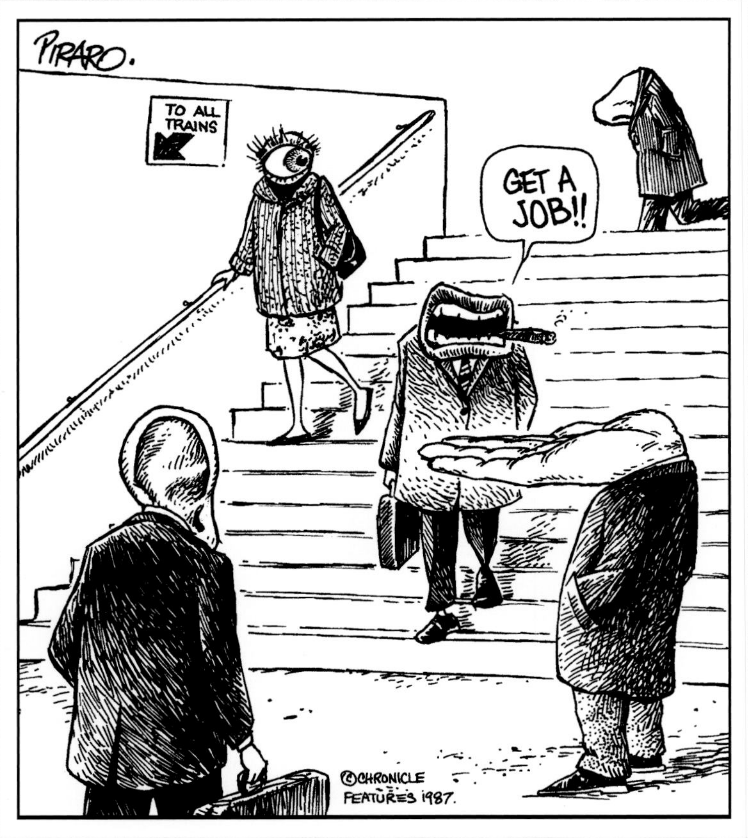
PIRARO.
TO ALL TRAINS
GET A JOB!!
©CHRONICLE FEATURES 1987.

My early love of the art of Salvador Dalí has led to a lot of surreal situations in my cartoons.

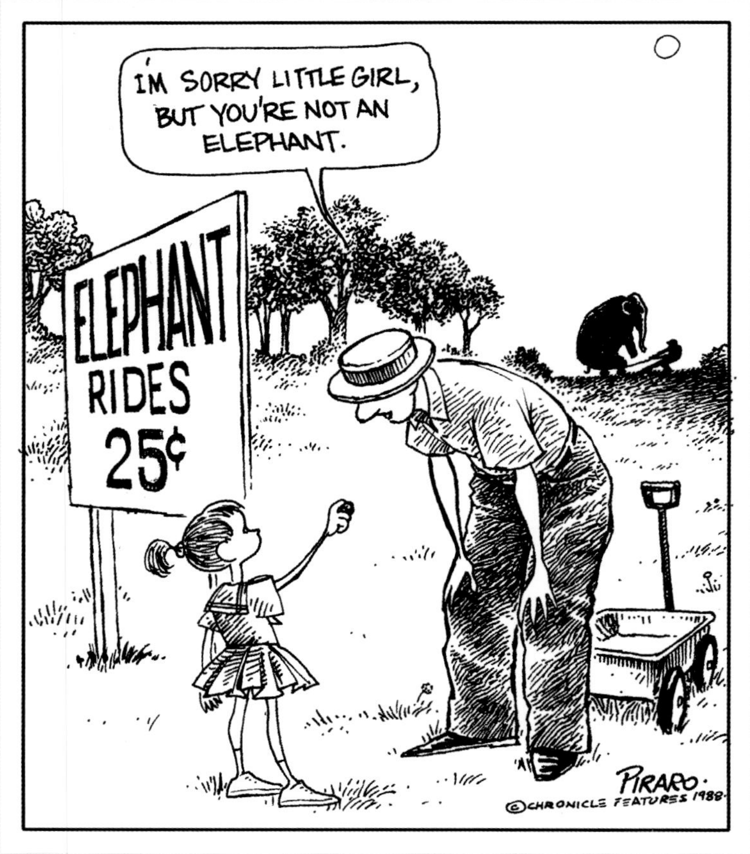
I'M SORRY LITTLE GIRL, BUT YOU'RE NOT AN ELEPHANT.
ELEPHANT RIDES 25¢
PIRARO.
©CHRONICLE FEATURES 1988.

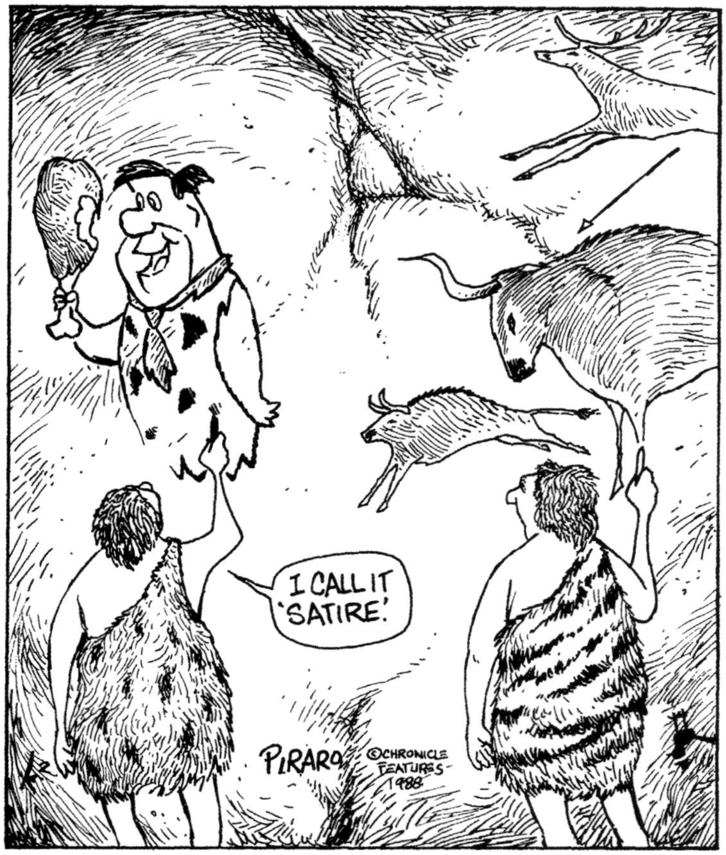
I CALL IT 'SATIRE.'
PIRARO
©CHRONICLE FEATURES 1988

How cool would it be if you could sneak into the caves at Lascaux, France, and paint Fred Flintstone amid the prehistoric cave painting there? Not very cool, perhaps, but funny. (1988)

BELOW: Typical of much of my early work. Way overdrawn and not very funny. (1993)

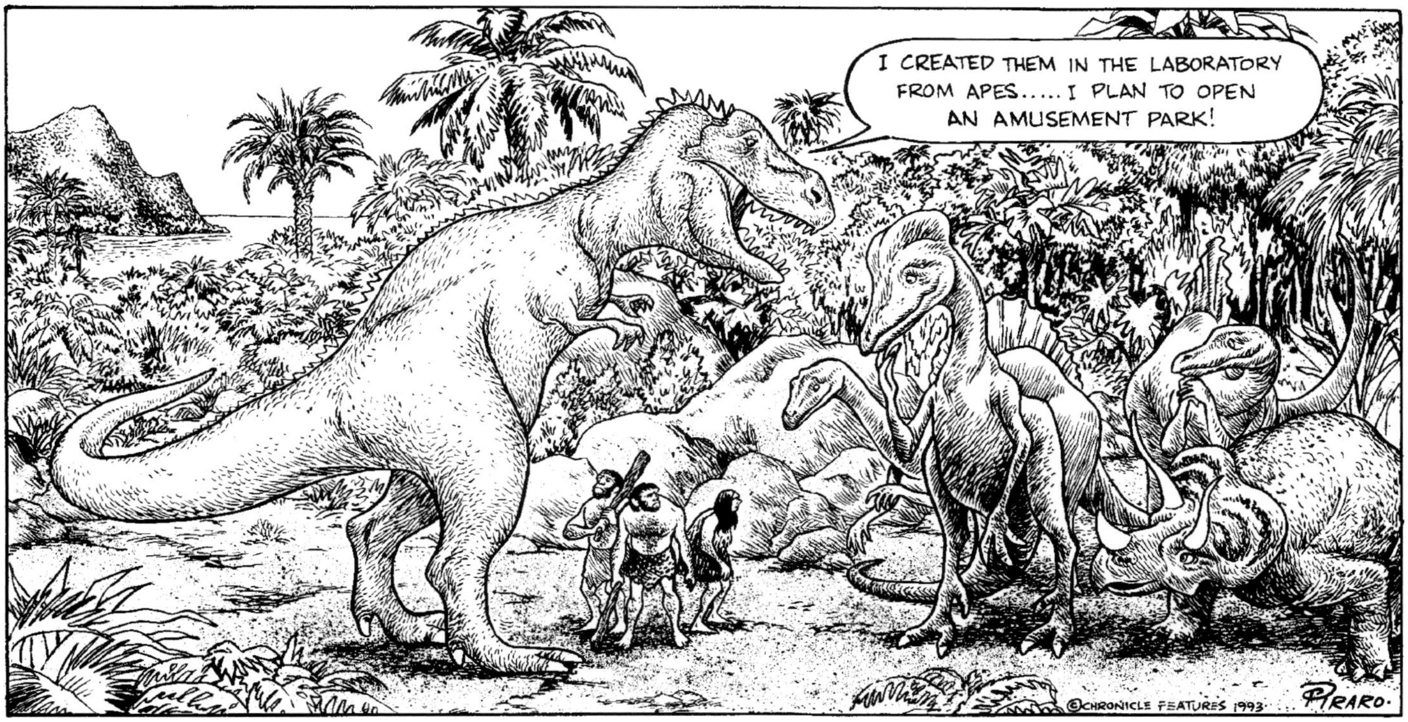
I CREATED THEM IN THE LABORATORY FROM APES..... I PLAN TO OPEN AN AMUSEMENT PARK!
©CHRONICLE FEATURES 1993
PIRARO

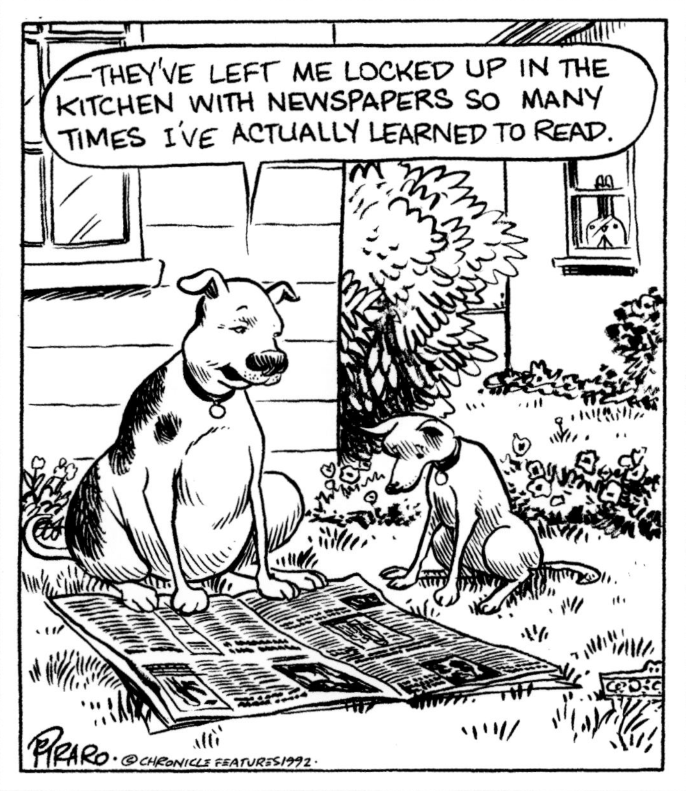
—THEY'VE LEFT ME LOCKED UP IN THE KITCHEN WITH NEWSPAPERS SO MANY TIMES I'VE ACTUALLY LEARNED TO READ.
PIRARO · © CHRONICLE FEATURES 1992 ·

Dogs are my favorite animals in the world. Some of my very closest friends have been dogs. (1992)

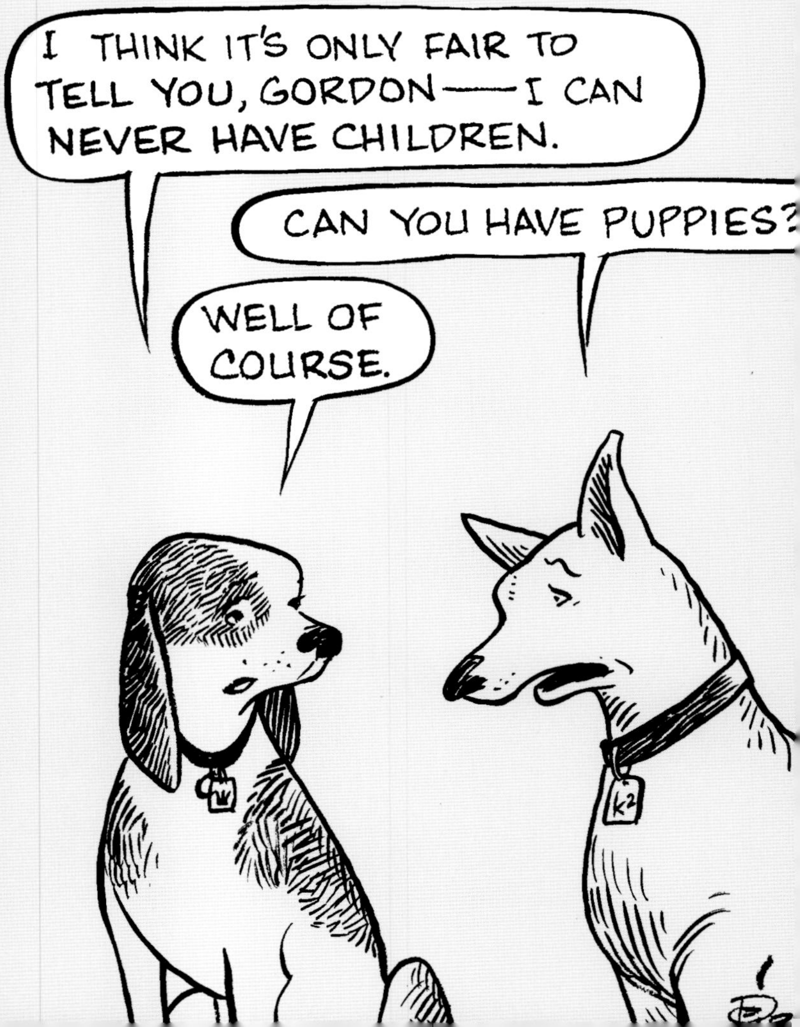
I THINK IT'S ONLY FAIR TO TELL YOU, GORDON—I CAN NEVER HAVE CHILDREN.
CAN YOU HAVE PUPPIES?
WELL OF COURSE.

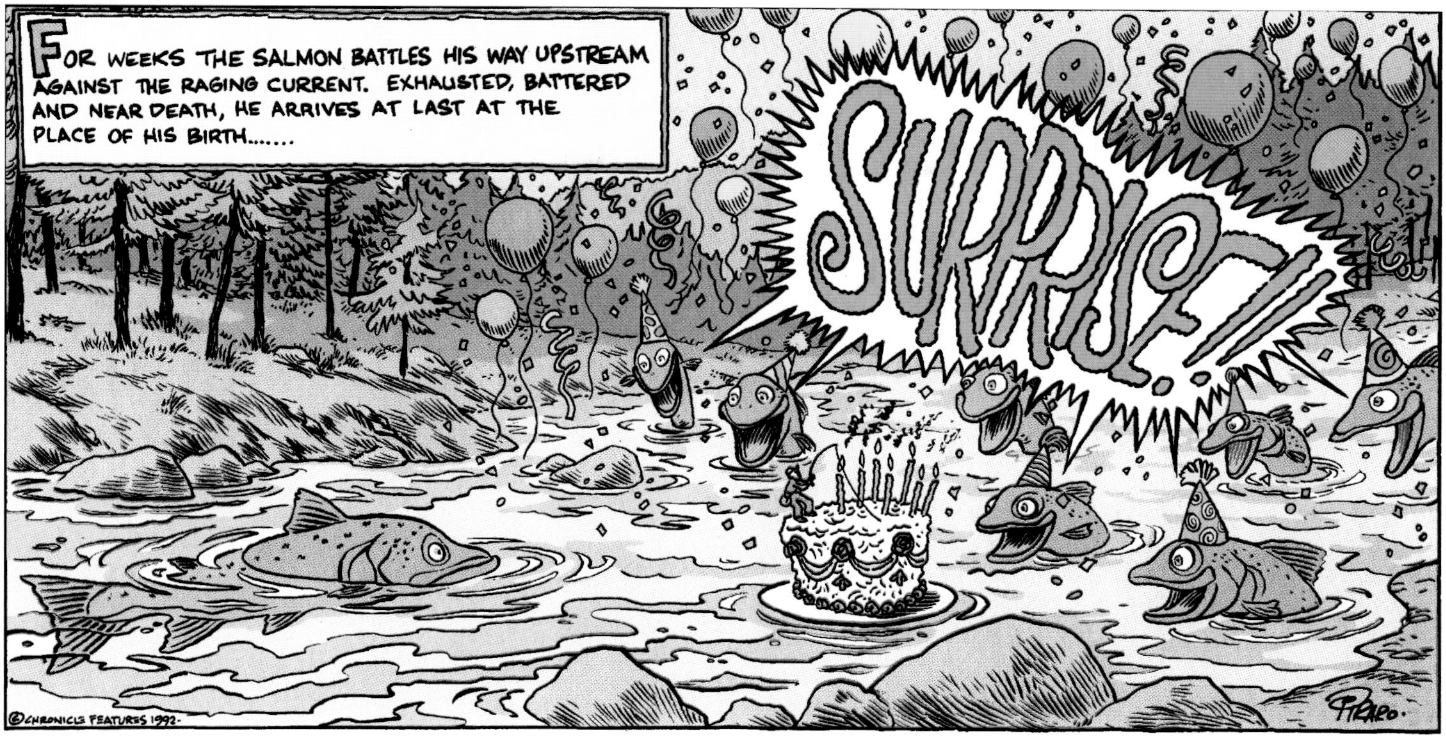
FOR WEEKS THE SALMON BATTLES HIS WAY UPSTREAM AGAINST THE RAGING CURRENT. EXHAUSTED, BATTERED AND NEAR DEATH, HE ARRIVES AT LAST AT THE PLACE OF HIS BIRTH.......
SURPRISE!!
©CHRONICLE FEATURES 1992.
PIRARO.

Bizarro sold very slowly, especially at first, and in the first year there was barely enough money in it to cover my paper, ink, envelopes, and stamps. In the late eighties, *The Far Side* had only just begun to catch on and most newspaper editors felt it was an anomaly whose popularity would pass. Few thought their comics page needed more than one such feature, and many were reluctant to have even that many. So, instead of landing a way to get out of my day job, I had added to it a nearly full-time, nonpaying night job. I was even more overworked and stressed than before. And as any newly syndicated cartoonist will attest, having to write a joke a day without fail is terrifying. I spent two years coming up with my first batch of sixty cartoons and had only sixty days to come up with the next. And so on, again and again, until I decide to retire.

I was only twenty-six, and most of my friends were still playing in bands, partying in bars, and sleeping around. I often envied them. But at least now I had a creative project that kept me from permanently slipping into a homicidal rage.

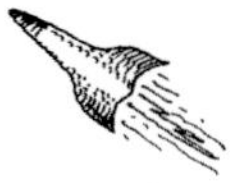

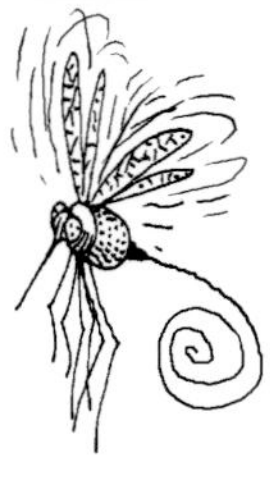

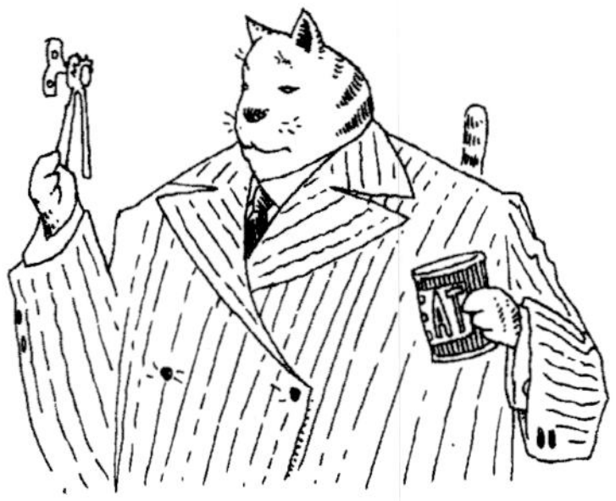

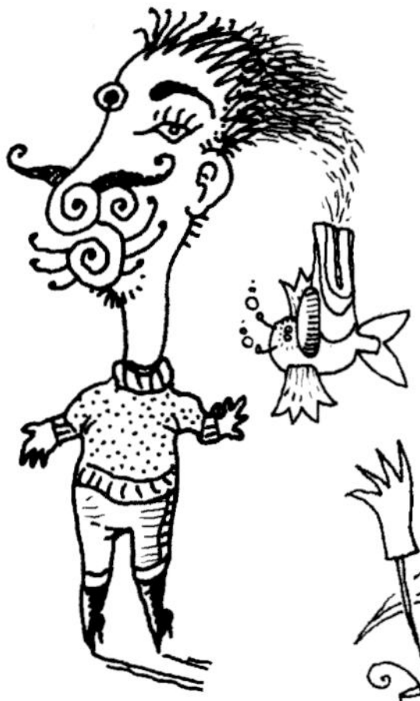

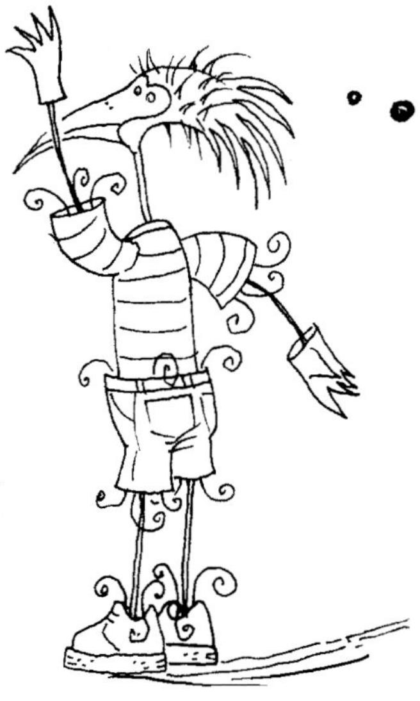

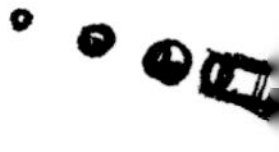

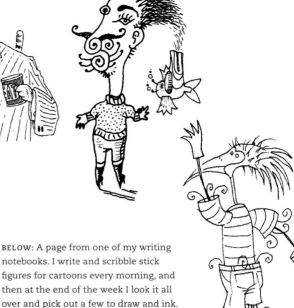

All cartoonists are asked about their process and materials.

This is so common that it has become a sort of inside joke. When we find ourselves in the audience when a colleague is giving a talk, we make a point to raise our hands and ask one or both of the questions we all hear ad infinitum: "Where do you get your ideas?" and "What kind of ink, paper, and pen do you use?"

The answers are inevitably much less interesting than people hope. I use white, acid-free paper, india ink, and a small brush. Most cartoonists use a thicker paper called bristol board, but since I have to store so many cartoons, I don't like using such thick paper. Many prefer specific brands and sizes of pens or brushes, but I don't. I just buy a small, synthetic brush (I don't buy anything made from animals) that looks and feels about right. I'm not a purist. I don't even have a drawing table. I just sit in an armchair with a piece of cardboard in my lap. After I've drawn the cartoon, I scan it into my computer and do the repairs (which used to be done with Whiteout) and the fixes and coloring there. When I've finished a week's worth, I upload them directly to King Features. Gone are the days when I would race across town to catch the last FedEx pickup the night before a deadline.

As for where my ideas come from, the answer is as simple as it is uninteresting: thin air. There's no trick, no process—either you can do it or you can't. Drawing a picture a day is easy; writing one at that rate is what differentiates a syndicated cartoonist from any other derelict. I just stare at a blank piece of paper and let my mind wander. From what I've heard, that's how most cartoonists do it. Except for Jim Davis, the creator of *Garfield.* He has a staff of writers and artists to stare at blank paper for him.

BELOW: A page from one of my writing notebooks. I write and scribble stick figures for cartoons every morning, and then at the end of the week I look it all over and pick out a few to draw and ink. The circles are my notes about ones I've deemed worthy of being drawn. After I do the final art, I cross them out. I go straight from this sketch to the final piece, with nothing in between. (2003)

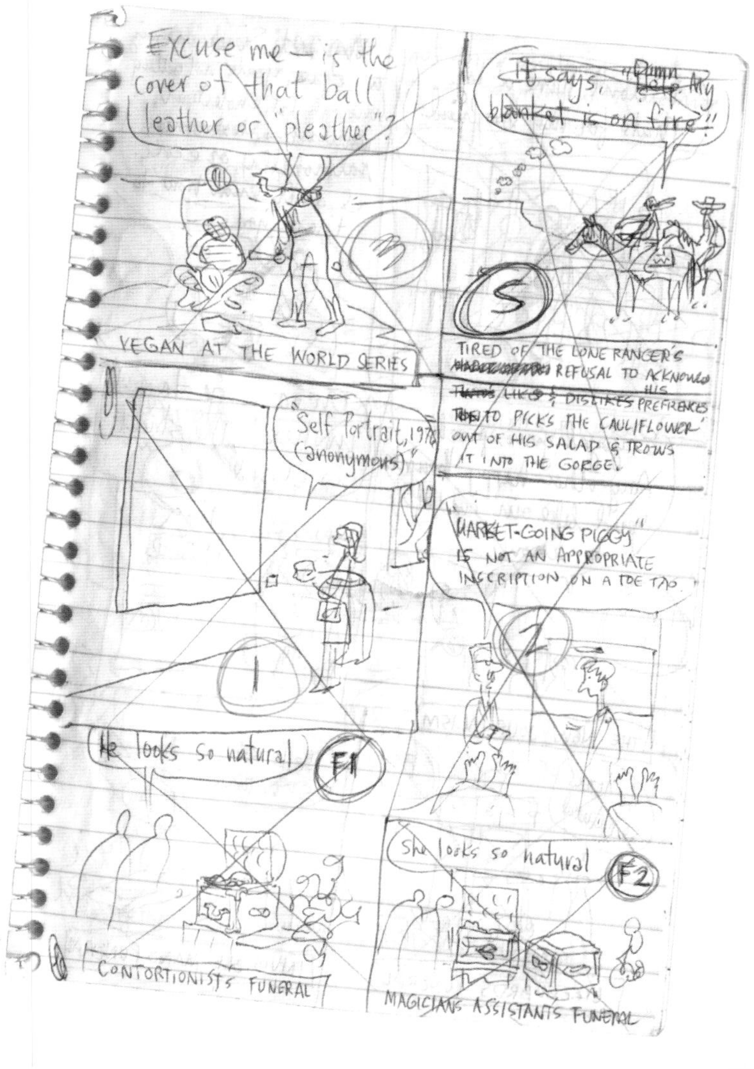
Excuse me—is the cover of that ball leather or "pleather"?
VEGAN AT THE WORLD SERIES
Self Portrait, 1970 (anonymous)
He looks so natural
F1
CONTORTIONIST'S FUNERAL
It says, "Help. My blanket is on fire!"
S
TIRED OF THE LONE RANGER'S REFUSAL TO ACKNOWLEDGE HIS PREFRENCES TONTO PICKS THE CAULIFLOWER OUT OF HIS SALAD & TROWS IT INTO THE GORGE.
"MARKET-GOING PIGGY" IS NOT AN APPROPRIATE INSCRIPTION ON A TOE TAG
She looks so natural
F2
MAGICIAN'S ASSISTANT'S FUNERAL

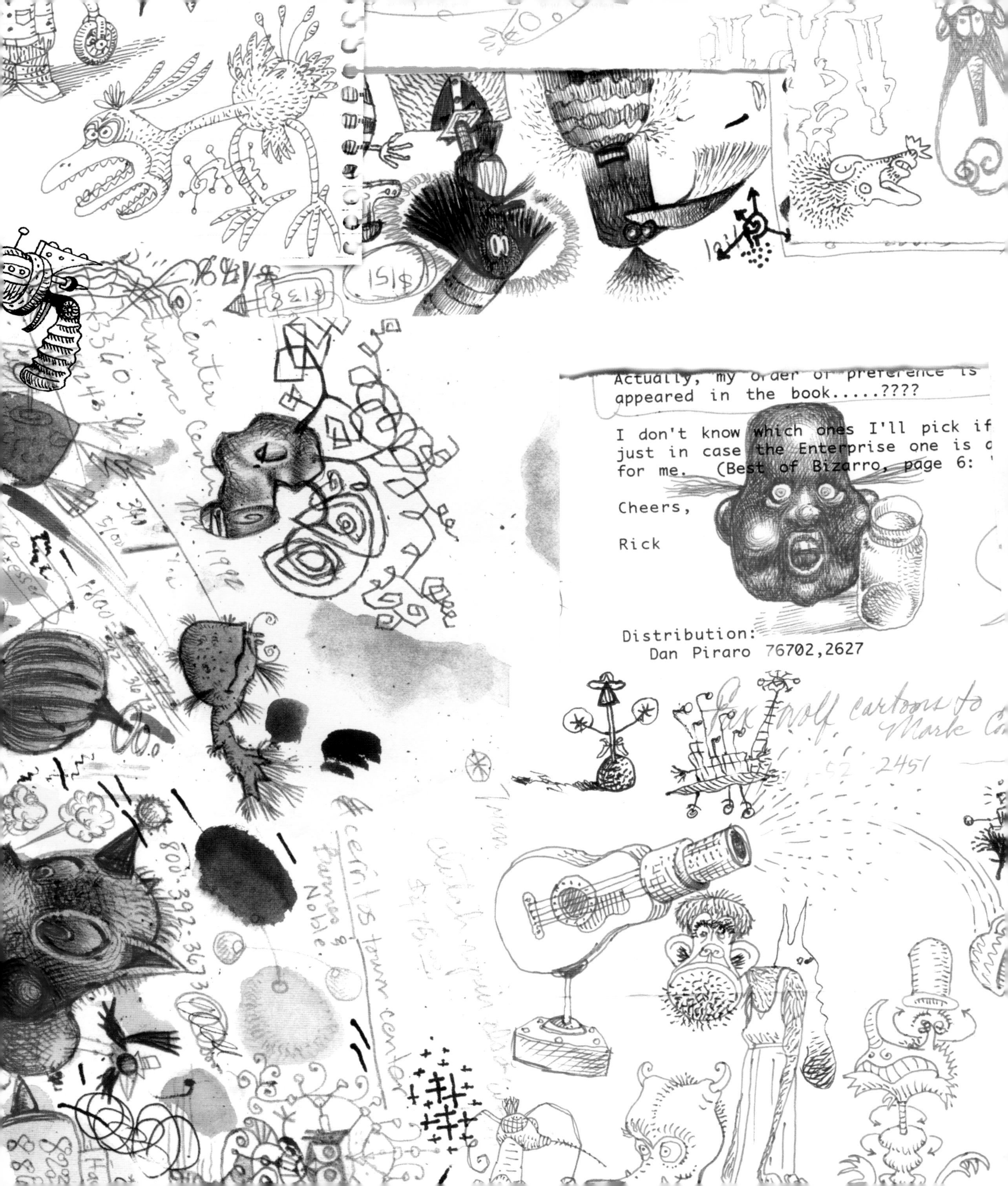

Actually, my order of preference is
appeared in the book.....????
I don't know which ones I'll pick if
just in case the Enterprise one is
for me. (Best of Bizarro, page 6:
Cheers,
Rick
Distribution:
Dan Piraro 76702,2627
fax wolf cartoons to Mark
2451
800-392-3673
Cerritos town center
Barnes & Noble
$151
$138

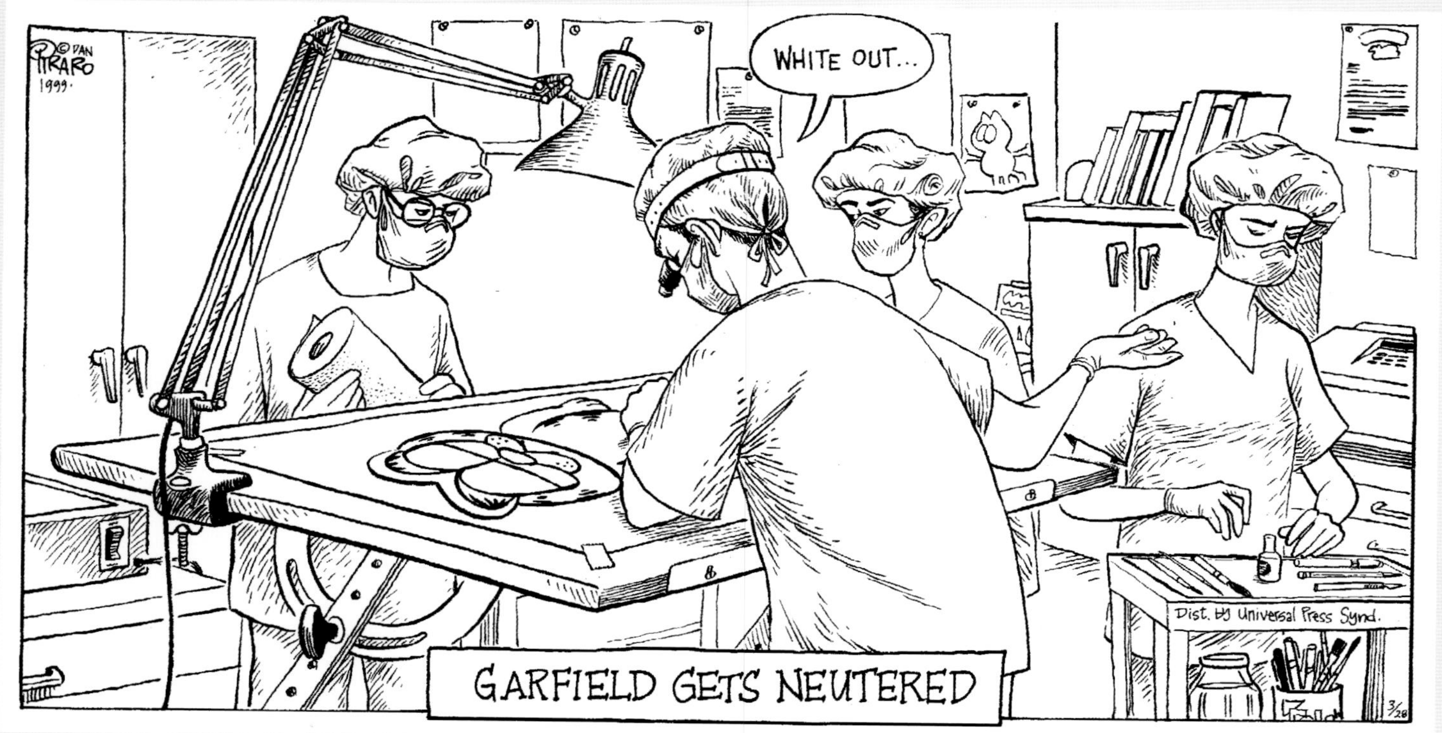
© DAN PIRARO 1999.
WHITE OUT...
Dist. by Universal Press Synd.
GARFIELD GETS NEUTERED

Will I ever get tired of slamming *Garfield*? I doubt it. (1999)

RIGHT: Drawn from the experience of my first marriage. (1991)

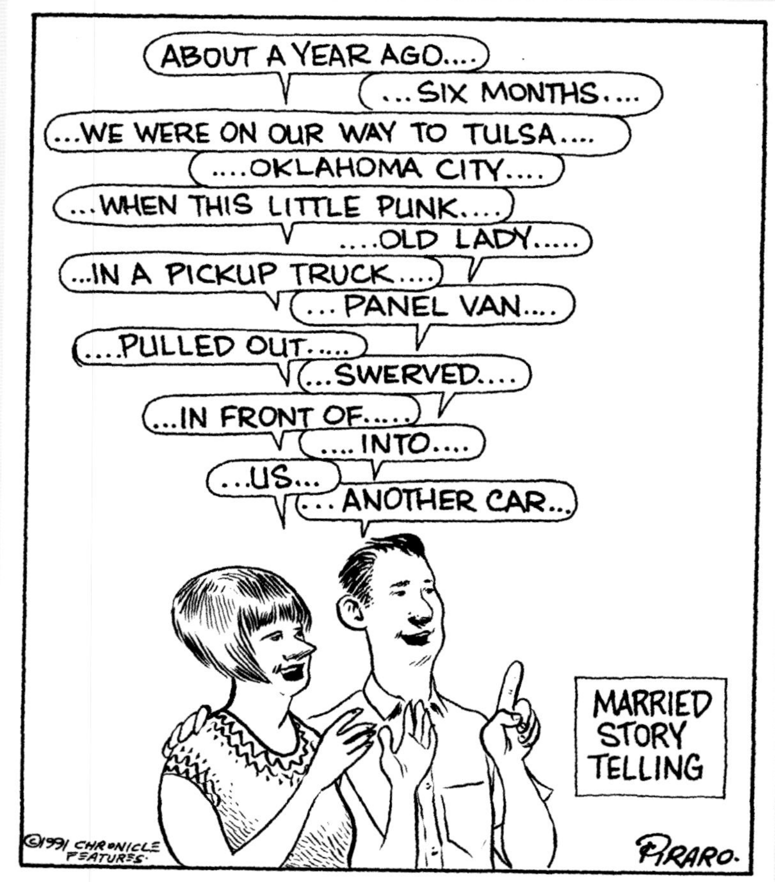
ABOUT A YEAR AGO....
...SIX MONTHS....
...WE WERE ON OUR WAY TO TULSA....
....OKLAHOMA CITY....
...WHEN THIS LITTLE PUNK....
....OLD LADY.....
...IN A PICKUP TRUCK....
...PANEL VAN....
....PULLED OUT.....
...SWERVED....
...IN FRONT OF.....
....INTO....
...US...
...ANOTHER CAR...
MARRIED STORY TELLING
©1991 CHRONICLE FEATURES.
PIRARO.

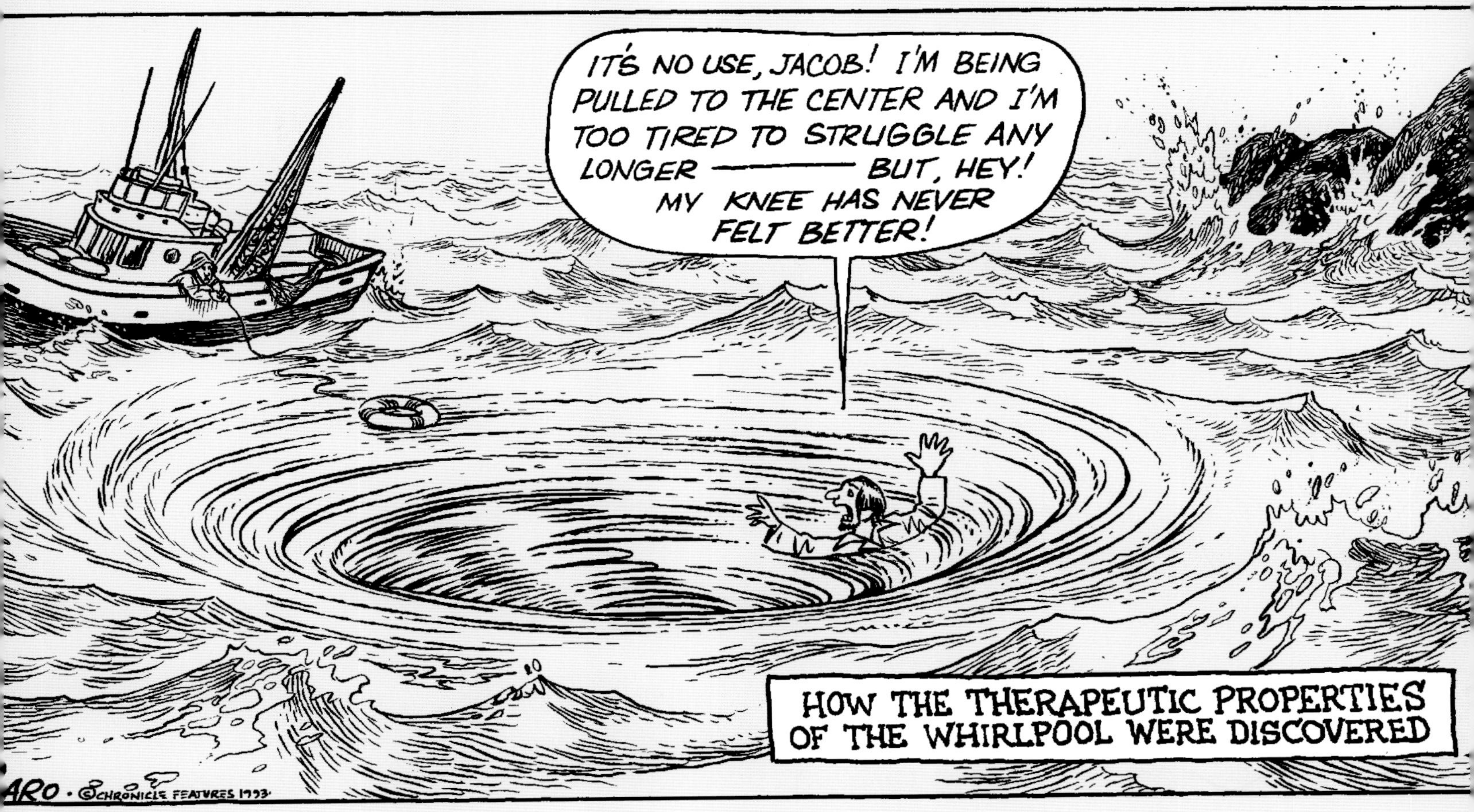
IT'S NO USE, JACOB! I'M BEING PULLED TO THE CENTER AND I'M TOO TIRED TO STRUGGLE ANY LONGER ——— BUT, HEY! MY KNEE HAS NEVER FELT BETTER!
HOW THE THERAPEUTIC PROPERTIES OF THE WHIRLPOOL WERE DISCOVERED
ARO · ©CHRONICLE FEATURES 1993

Even all these years later, I still think this is a funny idea. I can't always say that about my early work. (1993)

Although *Bizarro*'s growth was plodding, it was steady, and within a few years, as my income from cartooning rose, I began to do proportionately less illustration. By the mid-nineties, I had quit doing illustration completely and begun to turn my spare time and energy to other pursuits.

In 1992 I began to paint again and experienced a kind of rebirth. Because I had dropped out of art school and had never used oil paints in my commercial work, I knew almost nothing about the medium. But it was oil that I had always wanted to conquer, so I began to study the techniques of the great masters of the Renaissance. I made a concerted effort to learn the fundamentals so that I could one day achieve with my hands what I could see in my head. Progress was rapid. Just a few canvases and about eight months into my self-tutorial, I painted *The Virgin and Her Daughters* (opposite). I was thrilled with the result and showed it to a well-respected art collector and dealer I knew, who encouraged me to enter it in a yearly juried show at a Dallas gallery. Out of some eight hundred entries, sixty were chosen for the show, and mine was one of them. The judge, the curator of contemporary art at the Dallas Museum of Art, awarded my painting one of five "Best in Show" awards. I was ecstatic.

Even this brief and relatively insignificant brush with fine-art success reminded me that what I had really always yearned to be was a painter, not a cartoonist. But cartoons were paying the bills, so I could hardly afford to quit. The only reasonable option was to do both. Once again, I was filling nearly every waking moment with some project or other, making time to hang out with the wife and kids here and there and in between. And on top of the cartoons I did for a living and the paintings I was trying to do on the side, there was an unending stream of ancillary projects for *Bizarro*—calendars, books, T-shirts, cards—all of which needed new art or design work or revisions. (It is important to note that the fact that these products were being created doesn't mean they were selling enough to make anyone rich. The artist typically gets a very small percentage of sales of these kinds of products, so unless they catch on nationally like *The Far Side* or *The Simpsons*, you usually don't see much money from them beyond the relatively small advance.) One such ancillary project that took on an unexpected life of its own was one of the many *Bizarro* compilation books.

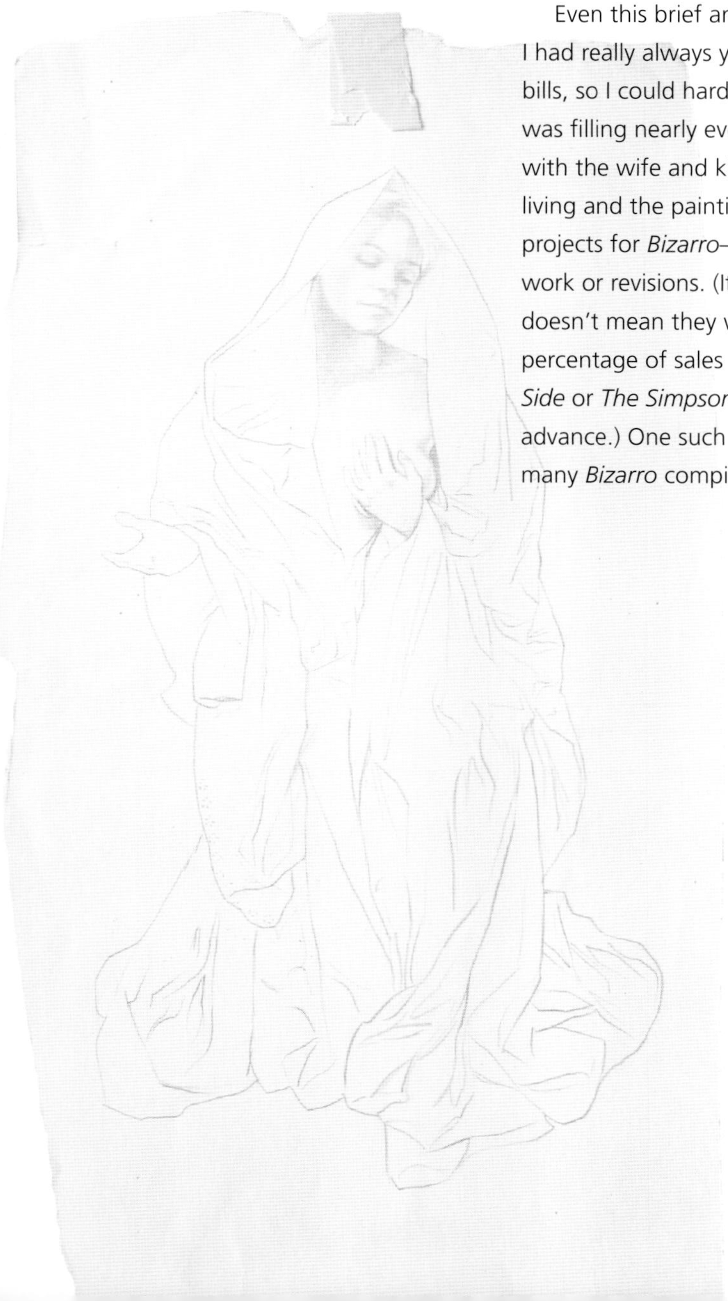

OPPOSITE: *The Virgin and Her Daughters* (1993, oil on canvas, 40" x 40"). The guy on his knee is a Dallas friend of mine who is the nephew of sixties pop singer Trini Lopez. The two girls are my daughters.

LEFT: A sketch for *The Virgin* (1993).

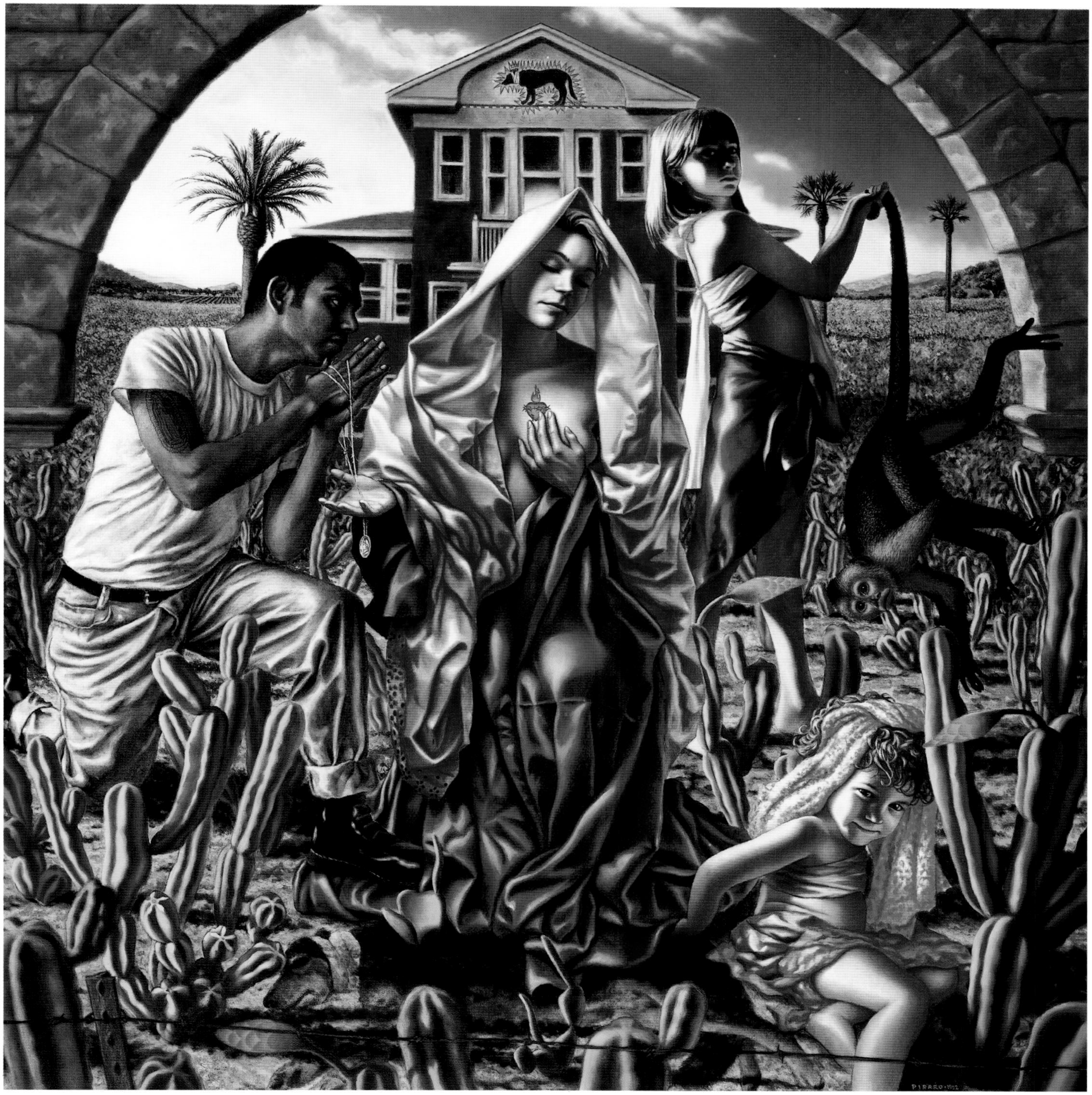

In 1995, the ninth book of *Bizarro* cartoons was about to be published, cleverly titled *Bizarro Number 9*, and I was looking for ways to promote it. There is never any money for publicity or book tours with small, paperback cartoon books, so it occurred to me one night while answering email that it might be fun to ask my readers if they'd pitch in. I'd been publishing my personal email address in my daily cartoons and routinely received thirty to fifty emails each day. I had accumulated a couple of years' worth of email addresses. I immediately composed and sent the following letter out to several thousand people:

From: piraro@earthlink.net
To: devotedfan@lol.com
Subject: 1995 Bizarro Lap of Luxury Book Tour

Dear Person Who Wrote To Me About *Bizarro*
At One Time Or Another In The Past Two Years,

Please excuse the impersonal nature of this form letter, but the following important message requires me to send the same epistle to all my email pals at once.

My new book, *Bizarro Number 9*, will be appearing in stores in the near future. I would very much like to take this opportunity to visit as many *Bizarro* cities as possible, sign books, kiss hands, shake babies, make speeches, and meet as many of my readers as I can tolerate. That is why I am proud to announce the nationwide 1995 Bizarro Lap of Luxury Book Tour. But I need your help.

I am looking for a few dozen good-hearted, fun-loving *Bizarro* fans around the country to volunteer their homes and/or services during the coming months to make this book tour a reality. Here's how you can help:

If you would like to donate a plane ticket, pick me up at the airport, drive me to a book signing, act as personal bodyguard during said signing, put me up for a night at your home, feed me dinner, drag me to parties, or any combination of the above, let me know A.S.A.P. and I will send you details on how to apply.

At this moment you may be saying, "It sounds like fun, Dan, but what if you turn out to be a chain-smoking egomaniac who teases my dog and scares the children? How do I know I really want to get involved in this revolutionary public relations gimmick and maybe end up with my picture in *People* magazine with my arm around your shoulder?" Well, that's a fair question and one I might very well ask of you, too. But let me assure you that while I am visually unusual and an avid nonconformist, I am an exceptionally polite house guest who has excellent hygiene, does not drink to excess, smoke, or use illegal drugs, and is invariably loved by animals, children, and the elderly alike.

If you or anyone you know would be interested in providing one or more of the aforementioned services, contact me at this email address and I will instruct you on how to apply. Thanks in advance for your attention!

Your talking mammal friend,
Dan Piraro

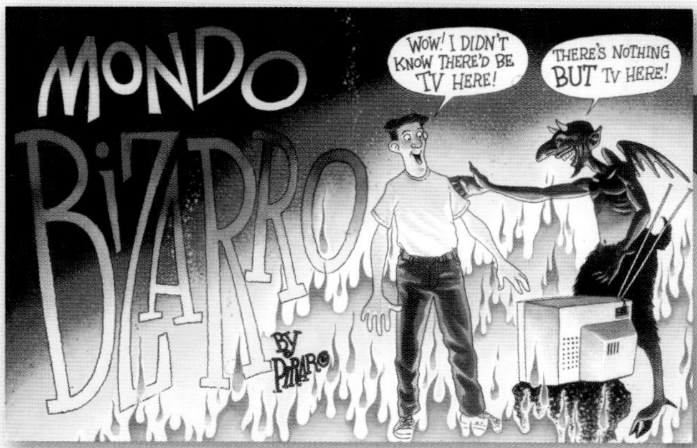
MONDO BIZARRO
BY PIRARO
WOW! I DIDN'T KNOW THERE'D BE TV HERE!
THERE'S NOTHING BUT TV HERE!

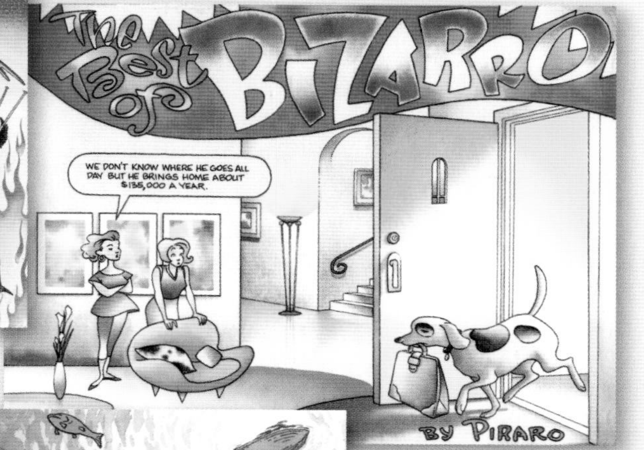
The Best of BIZARRO
WE DON'T KNOW WHERE HE GOES ALL DAY BUT HE BRINGS HOME ABOUT $135,000 A YEAR.
BY PIRARO

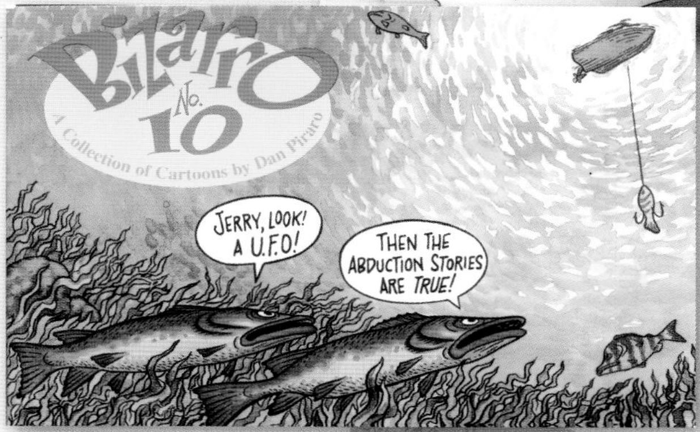
Bizarro No. 10
A Collection of Cartoons by Dan Piraro
JERRY, LOOK! A U.F.O.!
THEN THE ABDUCTION STORIES ARE TRUE!

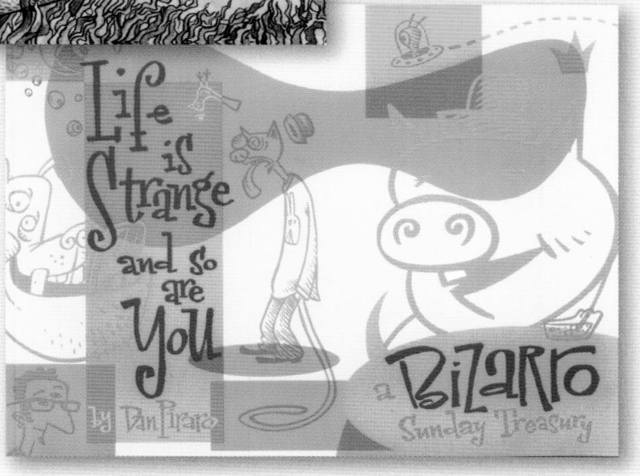
Life is Strange and so are You
by Dan Piraro
a BIZARRO Sunday Treasury

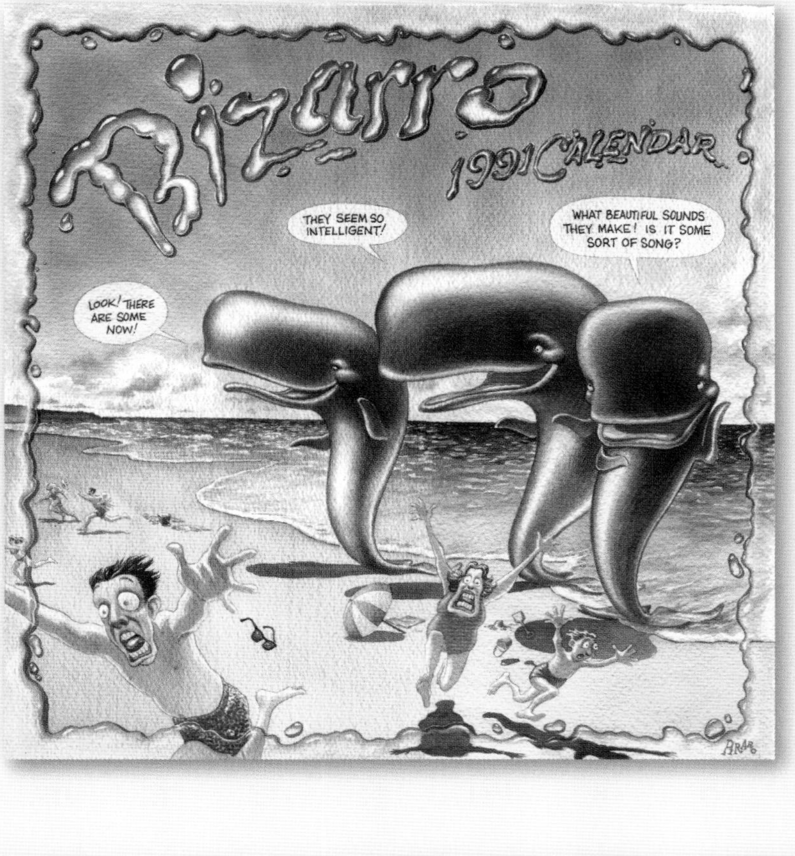
Bizarro
1991 CALENDAR
THEY SEEM SO INTELLIGENT!
WHAT BEAUTIFUL SOUNDS THEY MAKE! IS IT SOME SORT OF SONG?
LOOK! THERE ARE SOME NOW!

ABOVE: Shots from the book covers. (1989–2001)
LEFT: Fun with whales and watercolor. (1991)

What started as a whim quickly became the book tour that ate my life. Literally within minutes I had more offers than I could accept.

Over the next few weeks, I spent countless hours on the Internet and telephone arranging the details of a ten-city tour from Miami to Los Angeles. The traveling itself happened in five-to-ten-day stints with a week or two at home between each foray. While at home I was frantically working to nail down the details of the next trip and catch up on my relentless cartoon deadlines. It was an idea that sounded clever and fun on paper but was a big and unwieldy beast in practice. I chronicled the entire brain-searing experience and its surprise, catastrophic, marriage-destroying ending in a book called *Bizarro among the Savages,* published in 1997.

My divorce marked the rejuvenation of the self-discovery process that I had begun as a young man in Europe. While I didn't leave Dallas permanently for five more years—I stayed there to be a part of my children's lives—I began to travel quite a lot, something I hadn't had the time or money to do when married (because of some choices my ex-wife made, I came out of the divorce far more financially healthy than American men usually do) and I applied my energies in more creatively satisfying directions. Few things will advance a person's artistic capabilities more than experiencing personal tragedy. This began to show in both my serious artwork and my cartoons.

BIZARRO
among the
SAVAGES
A Relatively Famous Guy's Experiences on the Road with and in the Homes of Strangers
Dan Piraro

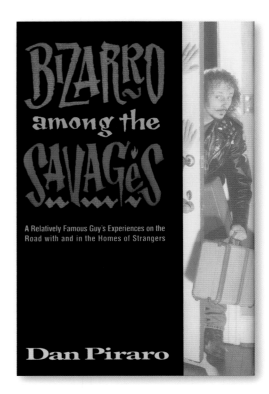

The cover photo was taken in the early stages of my Salvador Dalí mustache. (By the time I shaved it off a year later, it had gotten so long that the points were up near my eyes.) Prophetically, the hands in this photo were my wife's. Prophetic, because it was during my tour that she began her dalliances that resulted in our divorce. (1995)

That's one of our most popular features by far.
See Your EX-SPOUSE in HELL
See Your EX-SPOUSE in HELL
Dist. by Universal Press Synd.
© DAN PIRARO 9-28 12 99

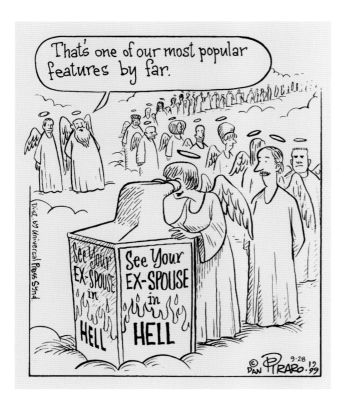

By far my favorite joke from the divorce years. This one goes over really well at my stage shows, too. (1999)

In the months immediately following the breakup, I was emotionally devastated. Every moment of every day was filled with dark thoughts and despair and among the long list of things I wished I could do (kill myself, kill my ex, kill her boyfriend), drawing funny pictures with silly punch lines was nowhere to be found. Had it not been for my children's need for my continued financial and emotional support, I might well have quit cartooning and disappeared. I fantasized about selling everything I had other than my art supplies, a chair, lamp, and mattress, and moving into a hovel far away to paint and drink as long as the money and my liver lasted. As romantic as that sounds, I'm glad I opted for a more rational path. While it might have made a good storyline for an opera, it would have been a miserable existence and I likely would have died of tuberculosis in the snow.

Since I chose to continue *Bizarro*, I had to come up with a joke a day without fail. Accordingly, many of those jokes were about relationships and divorce. One pleasant and unexpected by-product of these cartoons was the feedback I received from readers all over the country who had gone through similar situations and who appreciated my humorous and honest take. I never write cartoons thinking I'm going to help people through their day, but I'm always delighted to hear that I have.

I relied heavily on a support group to help me through the process of getting divorced. I've done many support group cartoons since. (2003)

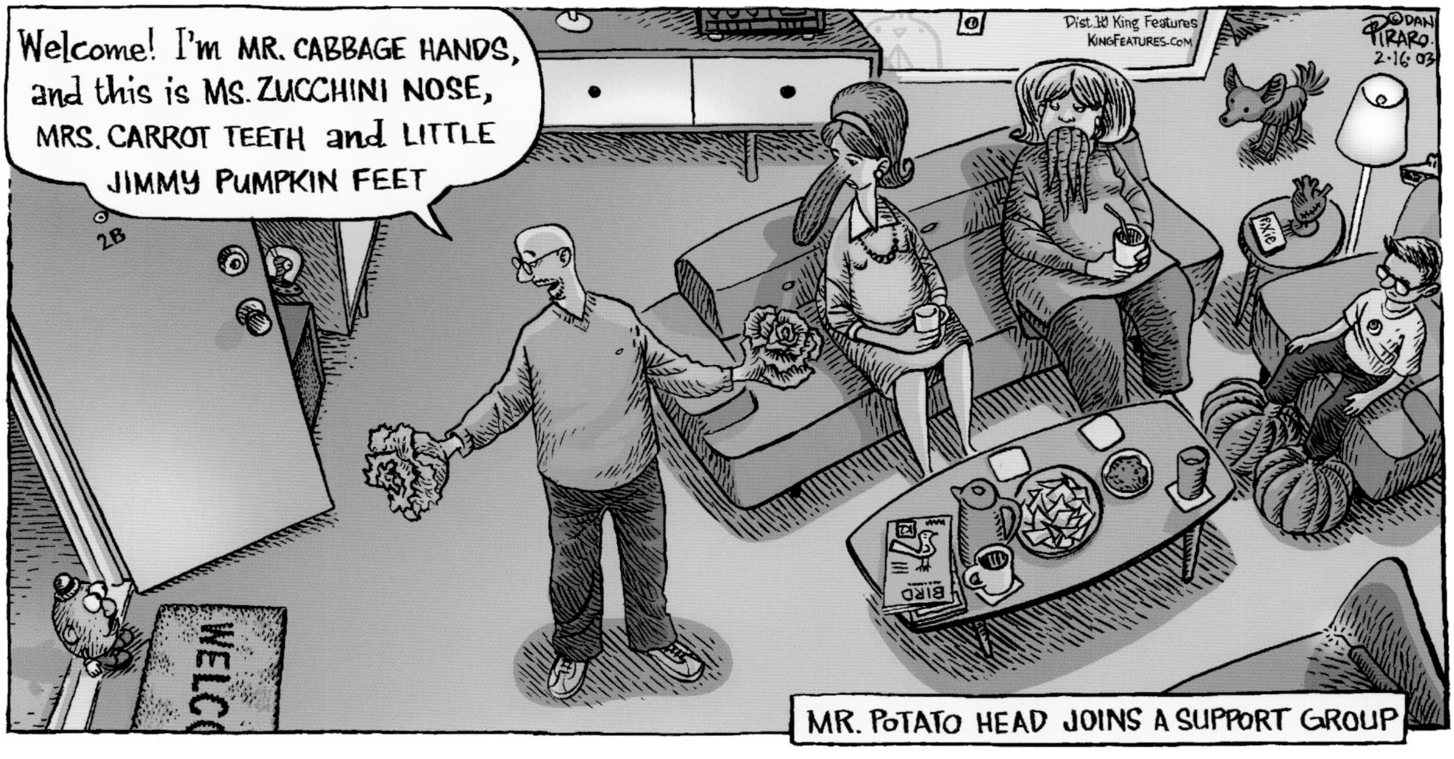
Welcome! I'm MR. CABBAGE HANDS, and this is MS. ZUCCHINI NOSE, MRS. CARROT TEETH and LITTLE JIMMY PUMPKIN FEET
Dist. by King Features
KINGFEATURES.COM
©DAN PIRARO. 2·16·03
2B
BIRD
WELC
MR. POTATO HEAD JOINS A SUPPORT GROUP

Juggling octopus

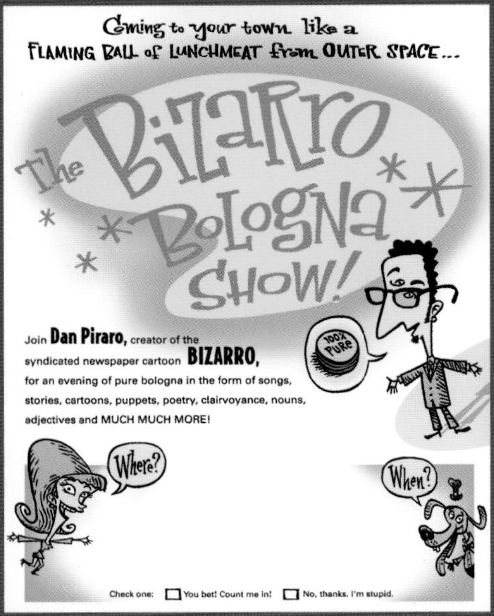

Coming to your town like a
FLAMING BALL of LUNCHMEAT from OUTER SPACE...
The Bizarro Bologna Show!
Join Dan Piraro, creator of the syndicated newspaper cartoon BIZARRO, for an evening of pure bologna in the form of songs, stories, cartoons, puppets, poetry, clairvoyance, nouns, adjectives and MUCH MUCH MORE!
100% PURE
Where?
When?
Check one: You bet! Count me in! No, thanks. I'm stupid.

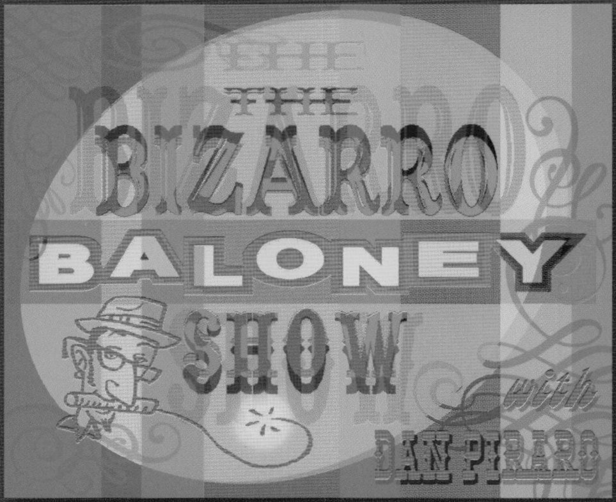

THE BIZARRO BALONEY SHOW
with
DAN PIRARO

My first one-man comedy show, in 2001, was called the Bizarro Bologna Show, using the classic spelling. Over the years I was alarmed at how many Americans would pronounce "bologna" phonetically, as if they'd never seen the word. For the new version of the show, created in 2005, I used the tag line, "New Show! New Spelling!"

I've always found there are far more things I want to do than I can manage while still eating and sleeping regularly. Today, for instance, I've got to write this essay, come up with a foreword for a colleague's book, color one batch of cartoons for *Bizarro*, sketch another, and confer with a comedian friend about some ideas for a comedy show I'm putting on for a charity next month. And this isn't a particularly busy day.

Sticking to one art form has never been enough for me. I love them all. For years I've been saying I'm going to learn to say no. "After *x* project is over, I'm going to take a break and stop working so hard," has become a mantra. But cartooning, fine art, writing, music, and performing are all too much fun to give up. Each scratches a different itch. And as I get older and better known, more people contact me with cool projects that I don't want to pass up, so it only gets worse.

It isn't that I'm a classic workaholic, the sort who is constantly chasing money and avoiding personal relationships. God knows it's not about the money—the vast majority of my projects are for fun or charity. I'm not avoiding personal relationships, either. Some of my favorite activities are hanging out with friends or bumming around with my wife. Fortunately, we both work at home or we'd never see each other.

My primary motivation is and has always been to exercise my creativity. I've been churning inside since I was a little kid. I've always enjoyed nothing more than *making* something. When I was younger, I found it profoundly frustrating that I couldn't create the things I could imagine. Either I didn't know how, didn't have the tools, equipment, or money, or I simply did not yet have the skills. At this point in my life, however, all of those problems are solvable and the possibilities actually make me high. I'm saving a fortune on recreational drugs.

Of all my interests, the strangest is the performance bug. I was a terribly shy child and found it difficult to talk to strangers even when spoken to. I'm only slightly better as an adult. Yet when I'm in front of a group and the microphone is mine, all my inhibitions melt away. I can't explain where this sudden boldness comes from.

It started when I tried out for a musical in high school. I'm not sure where I found the courage to

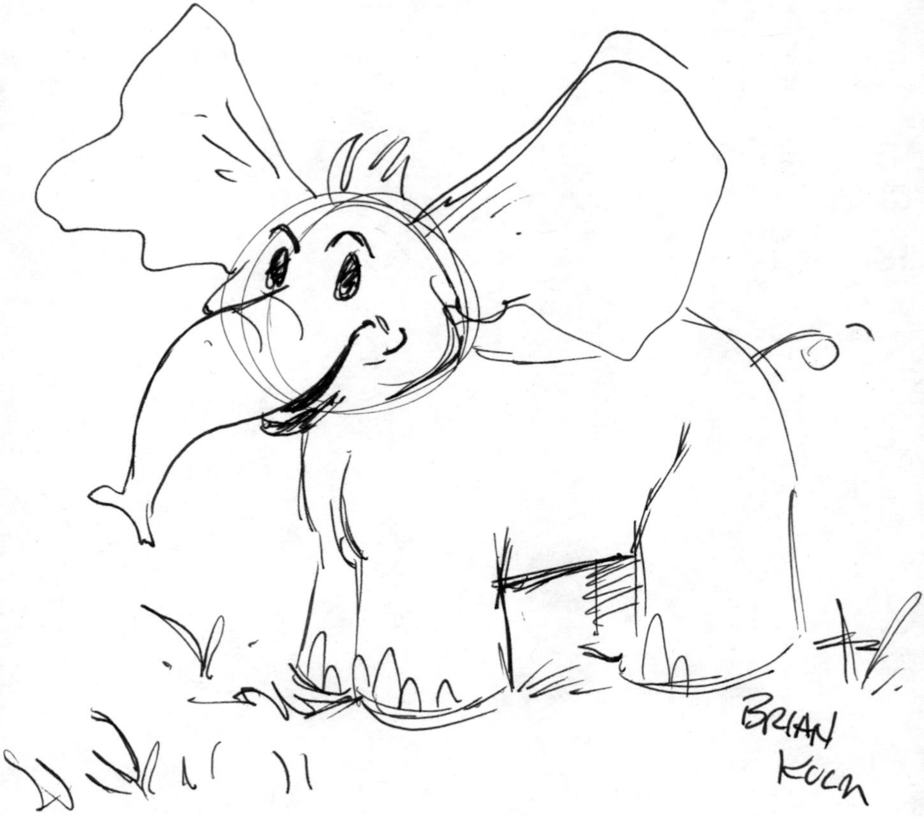
BRIAN
KOCH

RE ELEPHANT GOD ORIG ART

STAFF@ATOMICBEARPRESS.COM

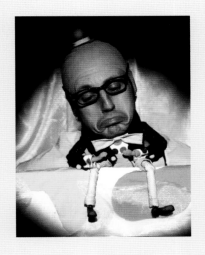

That's me as Humpty Dumpty from the Bizarro Bologna Show in 2002. In my version, Humpty is gay and sings a song about his one true love, an egg named Benedict, whom he devours on an English muffin in a fit of passion. (Photo: Jenny Warburg)

audition, but I did and found that I loved being on stage. I was in several plays in school and performed in a community theater production as well. At about the same time my best friend and I started a band, which lasted a few years. I didn't perform again until I was forty-three, when I created the one-man, multimedia show I called the Bizarro Bologna Show.

With no model or preconceived notions, I just began coming up with things I thought would be funny or interesting on stage. I fashioned a couple of dog puppets out of fake fur. I built a little puppet theater stage sort of thing out of cardboard and bright orange and yellow fabric. I constructed a small body that strapped onto my neck with arms and legs on wires. When I combined it with a bald cap, I could sling the legs over the edge of the puppet stage and make it look like Humpty Dumpty sitting on a wall. I made a cardboard guitar and wrote some songs. I created a big fortune-telling fish out of fabric and fake jewels. I bought an old slide projector and converted some of my favorite cartoons and drawings into slides.

I've performed the show a couple of dozen times around the country, changing it as I go along, adding new material, and cutting older stuff as I tired of it. With the exception of a completely disastrous preview in front of about forty friends (whom I've had to murder one by one to avoid future blackmail attempts) the show went over very well right from the start. Now, with some experience under my belt, it's gangbusters. It is quite simply the most fun I've ever had with my clothes on. It's also the strangest and most unpredictable thing in the world, with or without clothes.

Performance comedy is like voodoo. Nobody fully understands why humans laugh or what makes them do it, so there is no formula. It is all done by instinct— that's why we call it a *sense* of humor. You either have it or you don't. You can hone it, practice it, and perfect it, but you can't create it in someone who doesn't have it. No amount of training, information, drugs, or hypnotism could ever make Dick Cheney funny. (Or make Dubya as funny as he *thinks* he is.) What works one night might fail miserably the next: same venue, same time, same material. Kills one night, dies the next. No one knows why.

And that's what makes it so exciting.

Stand-up comedy is the scariest thing in the world. It takes tremendous courage to get up and do it, yet it is somehow rooted in profound insecurity. To stand in a spotlight in front of a room full of strangers and try to get them to love you is a little perverse. When it doesn't work, you feel like you've been beaten to death. They call it "dying" because that's exactly what it feels like. And you can't get good at it without dying a lot. But when you succeed, it's an exhilaration like none other. You feel as though you've conquered the world.

I've never really made any money doing the show. I usually just break even. And I spend countless hours and expend a tremendous amount of energy to pull it off. Many times I've been up half the night before, hot-gluing cardboard and fabric together, packing it all into a box the size of a bathtub, and then dragging it through subways and airports to get to a show. When I go on the road, I've got to bring art supplies and my laptop so I can keep up with my cartoon deadlines. It's a huge hassle.

But I could never give it up. I hope one day to be able to afford to build some more durable props and costumes (though I still want them to have that homemade-at-midnight-with-a-glue-gun look), have state-of-the-art projection and sound (with that used-slide-projector look) and some roadies and stagehands to help pull it all off, and play permanently a few nights a week in some off-off-Broadway theater here in New York.

But for now, I'm happy to drag my boxes, art supplies, luggage, and computer around the country like a juggling octopus with a perverse need to be loved by strangers.

63

Self-portraits

Cartoonists usually pose for a "candid" shot at their art table, as though they looked up and smiled casually just as a person with a camera entered the room. I always thought cartoon readers would like more from their cartoonists.

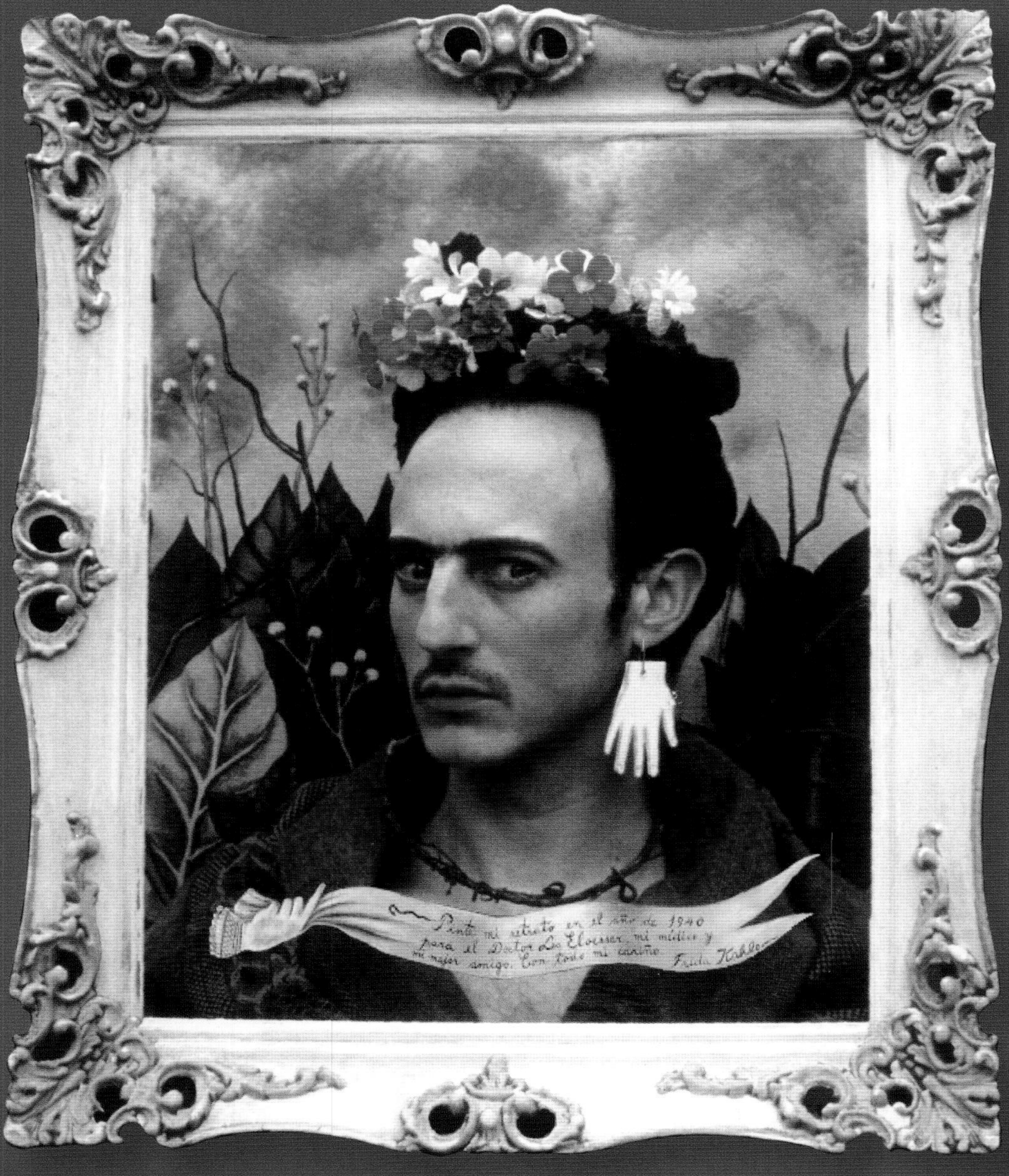
Pinté mi retrato en el año de 1940
para el Doctor Leo Eloesser mi médico y
mi mejor amigo. Con todo mi cariño.
Frida Kahlo

My favorite publicity photo ever, as Frida Kahlo, in 1994. In 2005 I wore this costume on stage as I sang a song about her in the Bizarro Baloney Show. (Photo: Hector Acevedo)

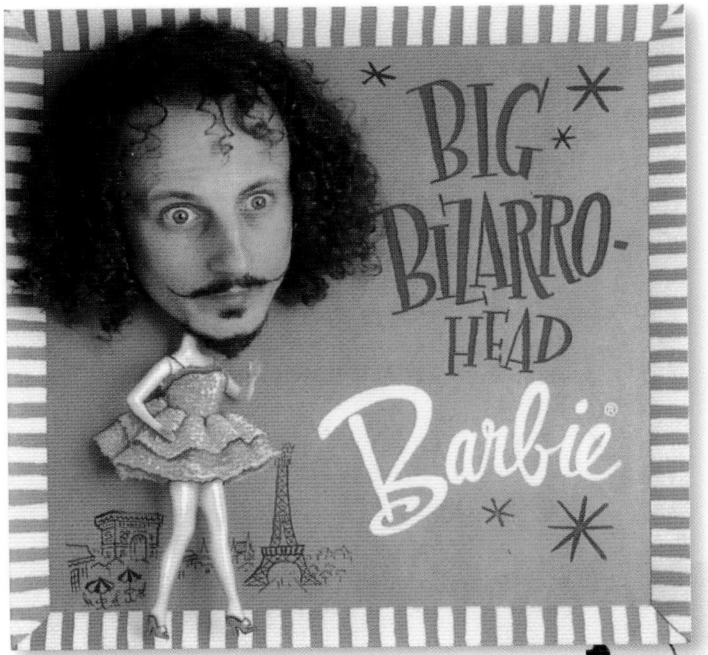
BIG
BIZARRO-
HEAD
Barbie

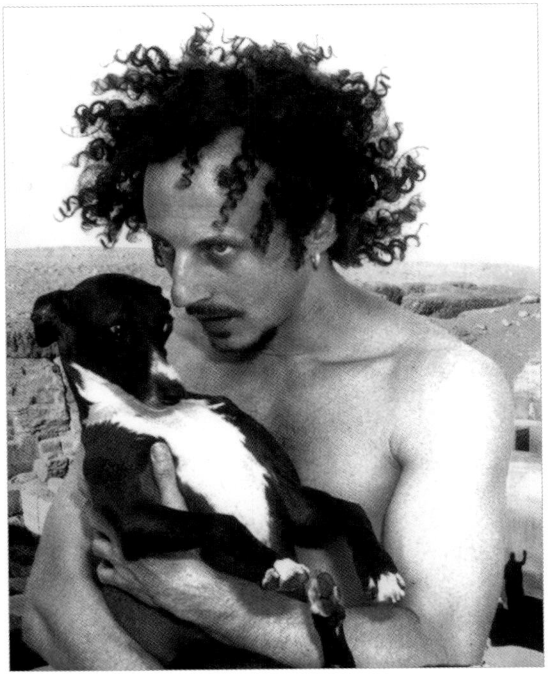

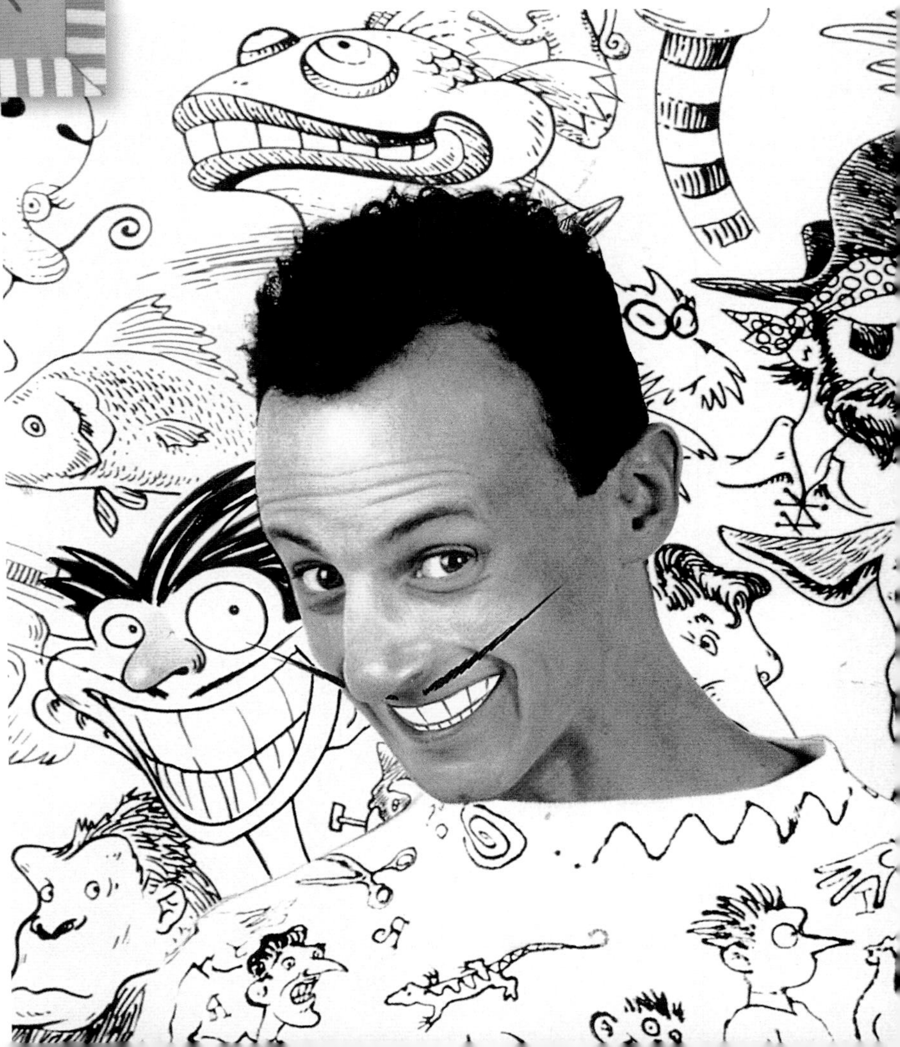

Author photo from the back of *Bizarro No. 10,* 1996. Even I have trouble believing the hair, mustache, and beard were real. (Photo: J. D. Talasek)

ABOVE, RIGHT: Author photo from the back cover of *Bizarro Number 9*, 1995, featuring me and my dog, Bruno. (Photo: Robert Greeson)

RIGHT: One of my earliest publicity photos, from 1987.

Cameos

When I was quite young, Dad pointed out to me that Alfred Hitchcock would often appear briefly in his films as a sort of trademark. I thought it was cool as hell and loved trying to spot him. I now put myself (and my wife) in many of my cartoons. Since the only people who recognize me are those of you who know me, have come to my stage shows or book signings, or are reading this book, it isn't a bid for fame. It's just fun.

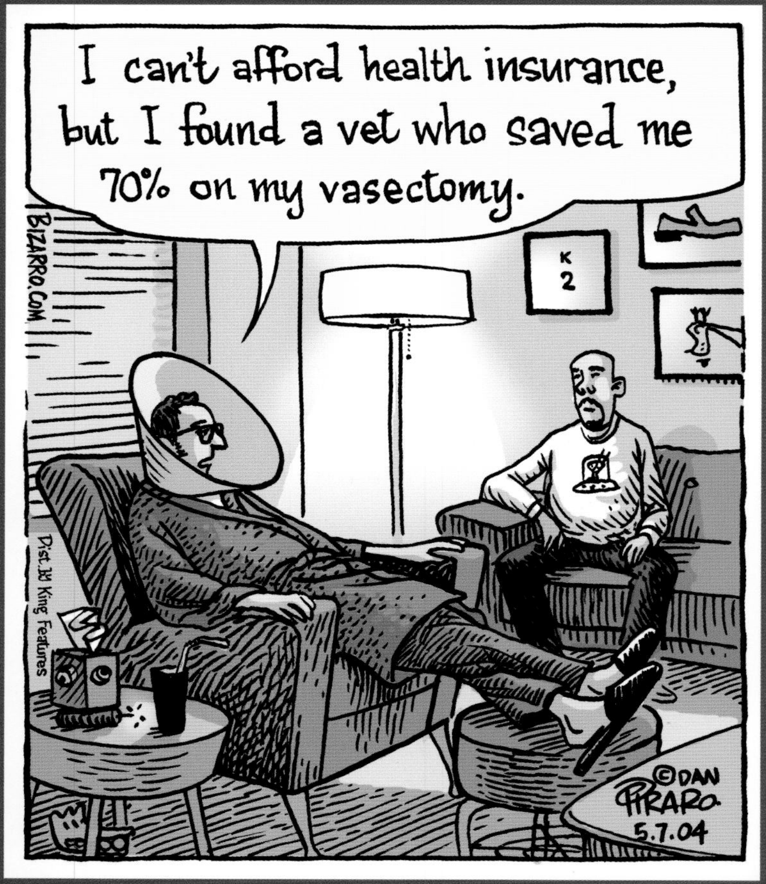
I can't afford health insurance, but I found a vet who saved me 70% on my vasectomy.
BIZARRO.COM
K 2
Dist. by King Features
©DAN PIRARO 5.7.04

I had a vasectomy in 2004 and have enjoyed talking about it ever since. (2004)

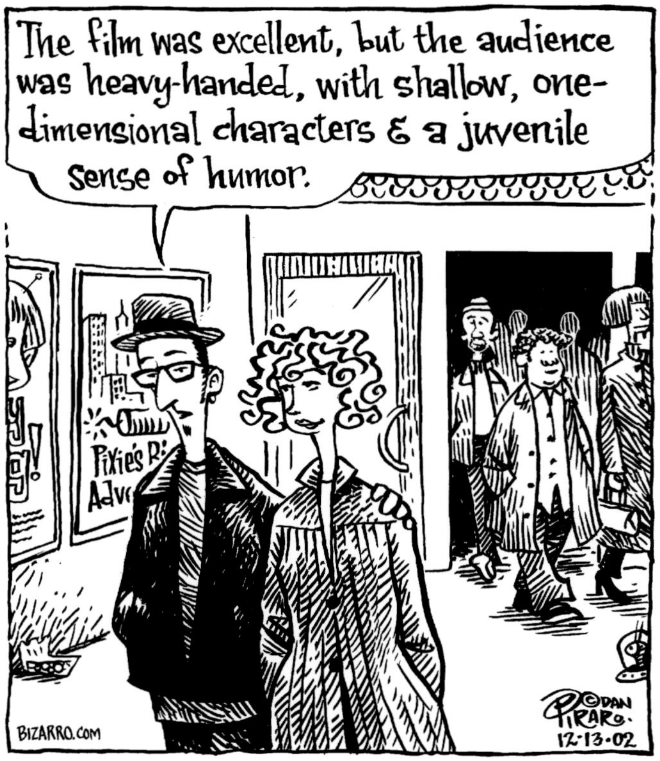
The film was excellent, but the audience was heavy-handed, with shallow, one-dimensional characters & a juvenile sense of humor.
©DAN PIRARO 12-13-02
BIZARRO.COM

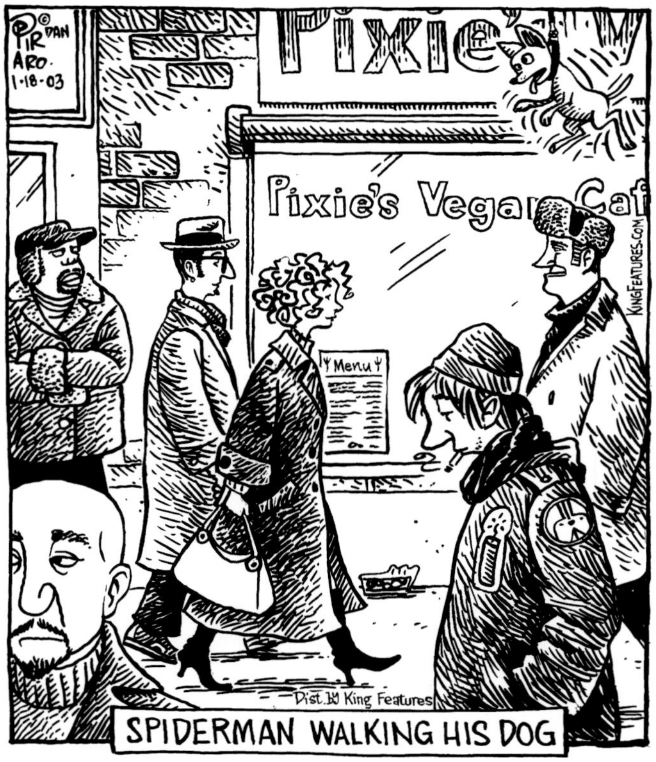
Pixie's
Pixie's Vegan Caf
Menu
©DAN PIRARO 1-18-03
KINGFEATURES.COM
Dist. by King Features
SPIDERMAN WALKING HIS DOG

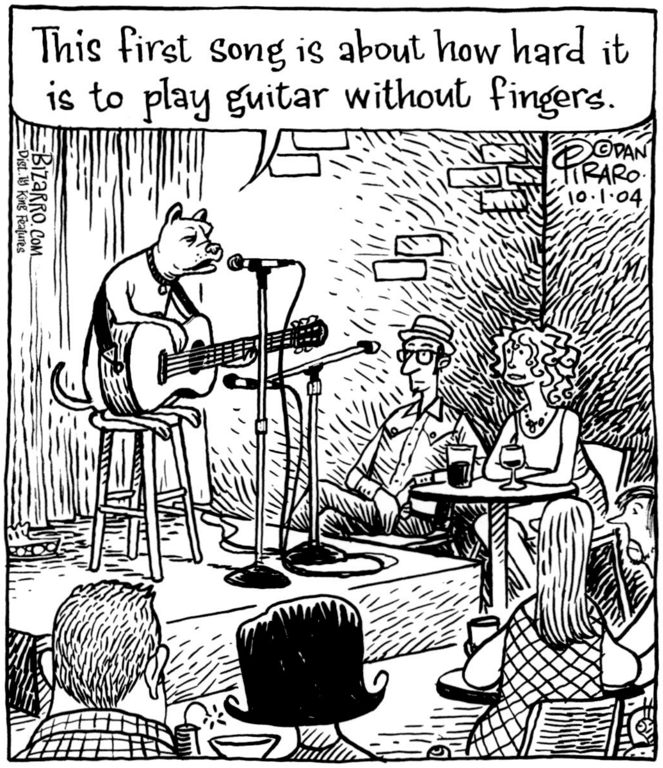
This first song is about how hard it is to play guitar without fingers.
©DAN PIRARO 10-1-04
BIZARRO.COM
Dist. by King Features

ABOVE, LEFT: A nice portrait of the wife and me. To be fair, she looks better than this, and I look worse. (2002)

ABOVE: Ashley and me in front of her imaginary vegan café. (2003)

LEFT: Ashley and I see a lot of up-and-coming music and comedy acts in small venues in New York. We have occasionally seen performers who later go on to win Grammys, Oscars, Nobel Peace Prizes, you name it. That's us on the side of the stage. (2004)

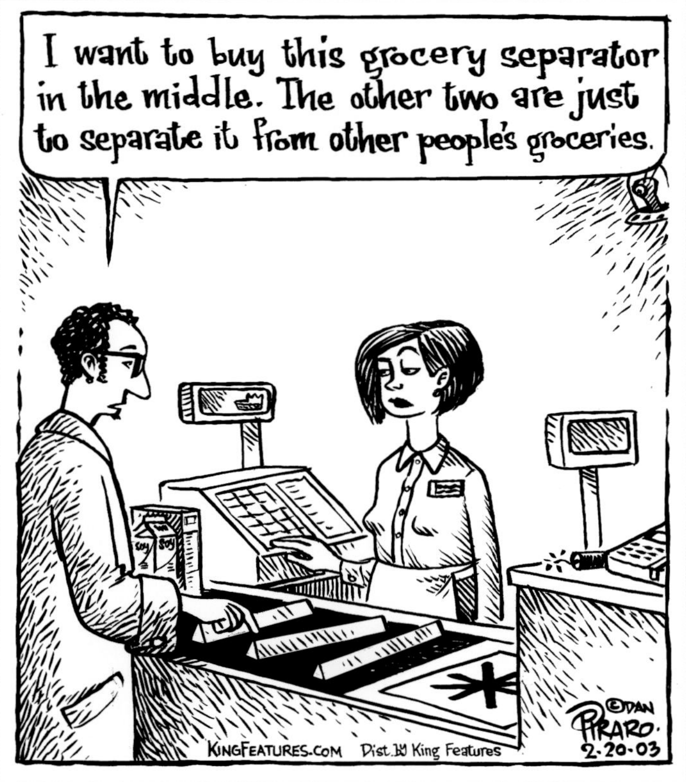
I want to buy this grocery separator in the middle. The other two are just to separate it from other people's groceries.
©DAN PIRARO. 2-20-03
KINGFEATURES.COM Dist. BY King Features

Nitpicking common phrases and their various possible meanings is something I learned from listening to George Carlin comedy albums as a kid.

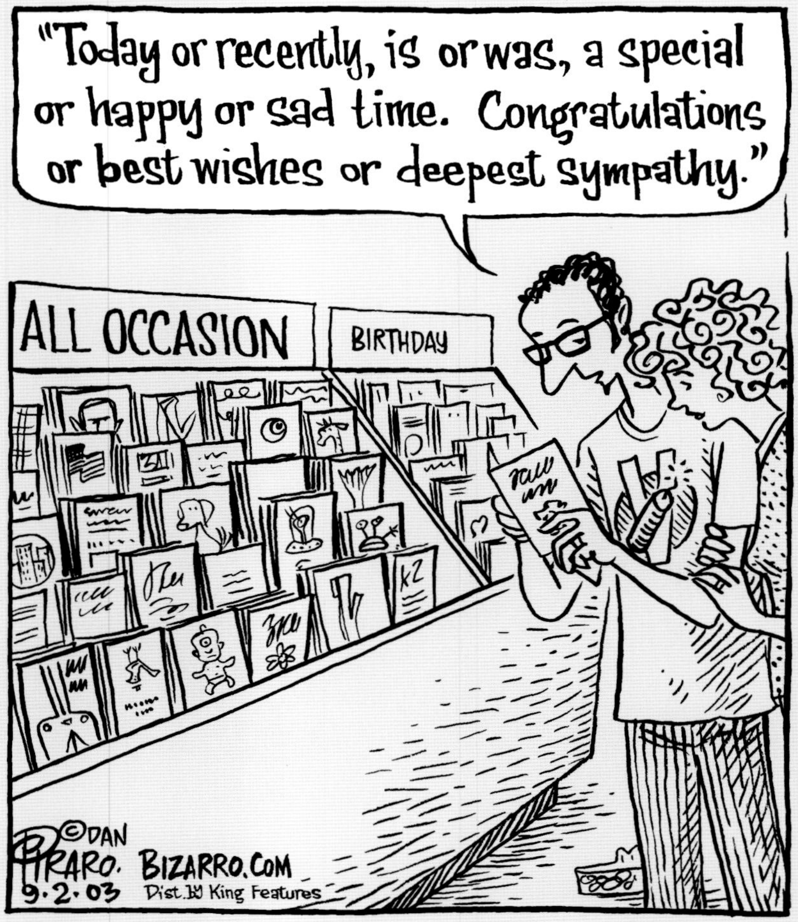
"Today or recently, is or was, a special or happy or sad time. Congratulations or best wishes or deepest sympathy."
ALL OCCASION
BIRTHDAY
©DAN PIRARO. 9-2-03
BIZARRO.COM
Dist. BY King Features

Strips

In 2000 I began offering *Bizarro* for sale as either a panel or a strip. I don't do it this way now, but at the time I drew a large, odd shaped cartoon that could then be cropped to accommodate either format. The extra drawing proved too much after a couple of years, and I found a simpler way to do it. Here are a few examples of the early ones with tons of extra art most people never even saw because so few papers ran it as a strip. Even now, most papers run it as a panel.

Say "WHEN!"
NO! NEVER!
WAITERS OF THE INQUISITION
© DAN PIRARO. 6/9 2000
UEXPRESS.COM
Say WHEN!
NO! NEVER!
© DAN PIRARO. 1·7·04
BIZARRO.COM
Dist. by King Features
WAITERS OF THE INQUISITION

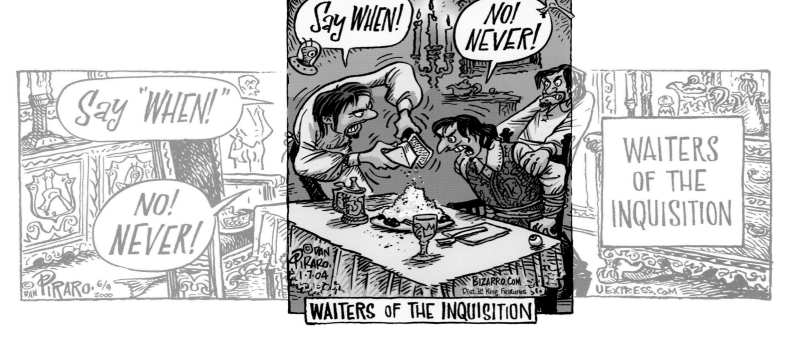

This was inspired in part by Monty Python's "Nobody Expects the Spanish Inquisition" routine. (2000)

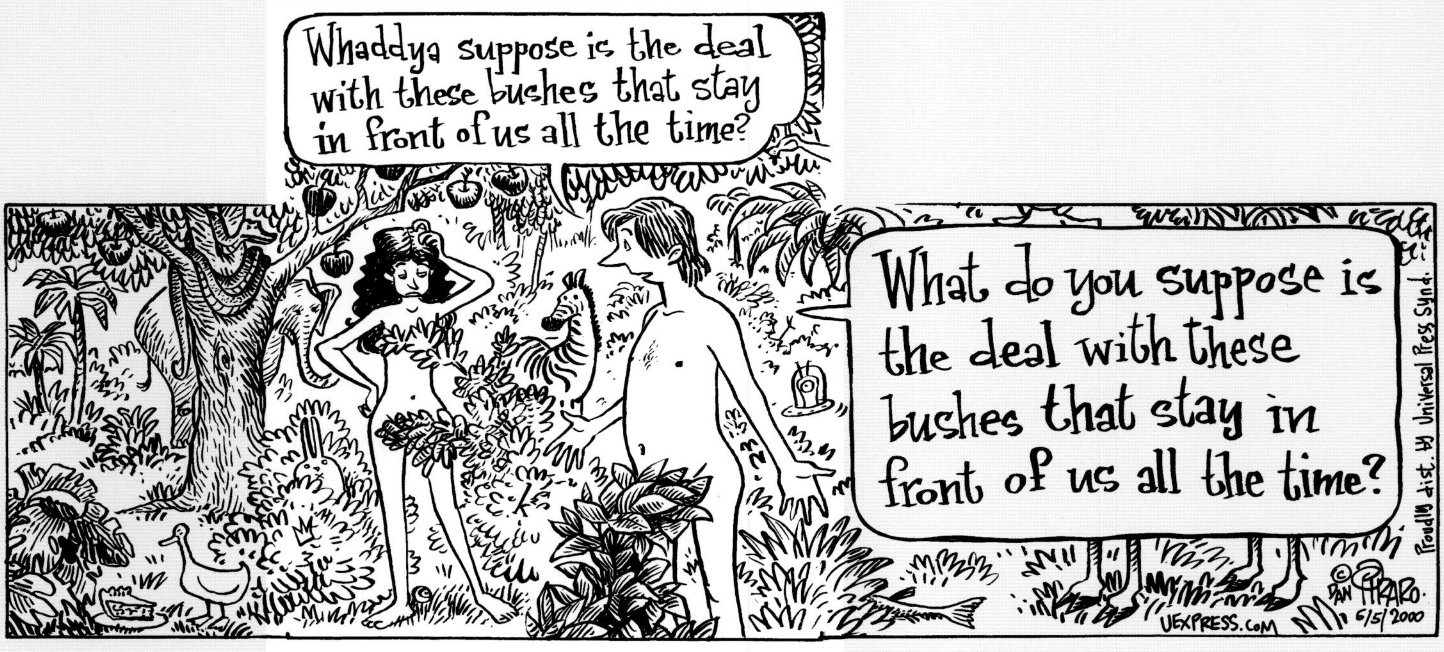
Whaddya suppose is the deal with these bushes that stay in front of us all the time?
What do you suppose is the deal with these bushes that stay in front of us all the time?
Proudly dist. by Universal Press Synd.
© Dan Piraro. 6/5/2000
UEXPRESS.COM

I asked this question of myself all the time as a small kid when looking at the illustrated depictions of Adam and Eve in my Catholic school catechism books. (2000)

I love the wordplay in this cartoon almost as much as my self-portrait as a chimp in the right corner. (2000)

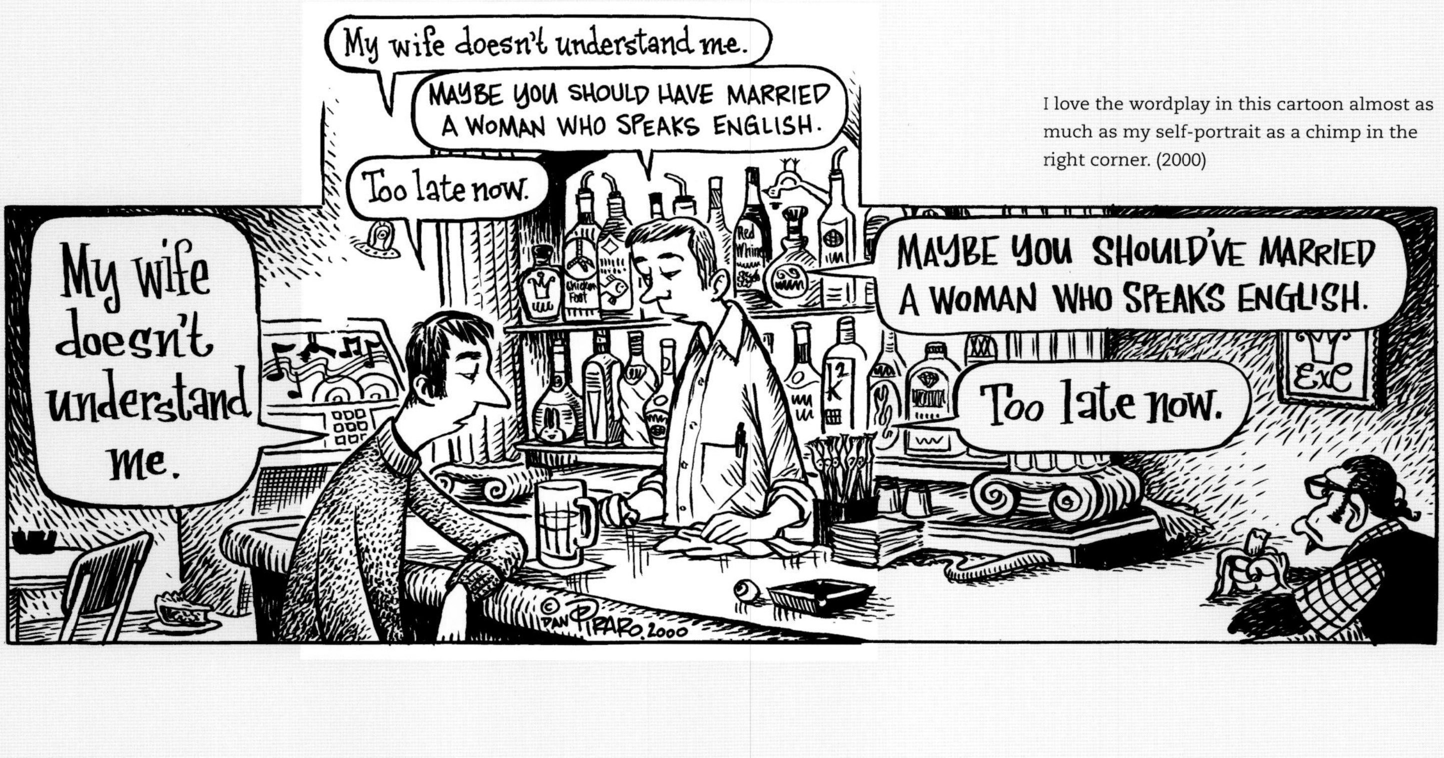
My wife doesn't understand me.
MAYBE YOU SHOULD HAVE MARRIED A WOMAN WHO SPEAKS ENGLISH.
Too late now.
My wife doesn't understand me.
MAYBE YOU SHOULD'VE MARRIED A WOMAN WHO SPEAKS ENGLISH.
Too late now.
© Dan Piraro 2000

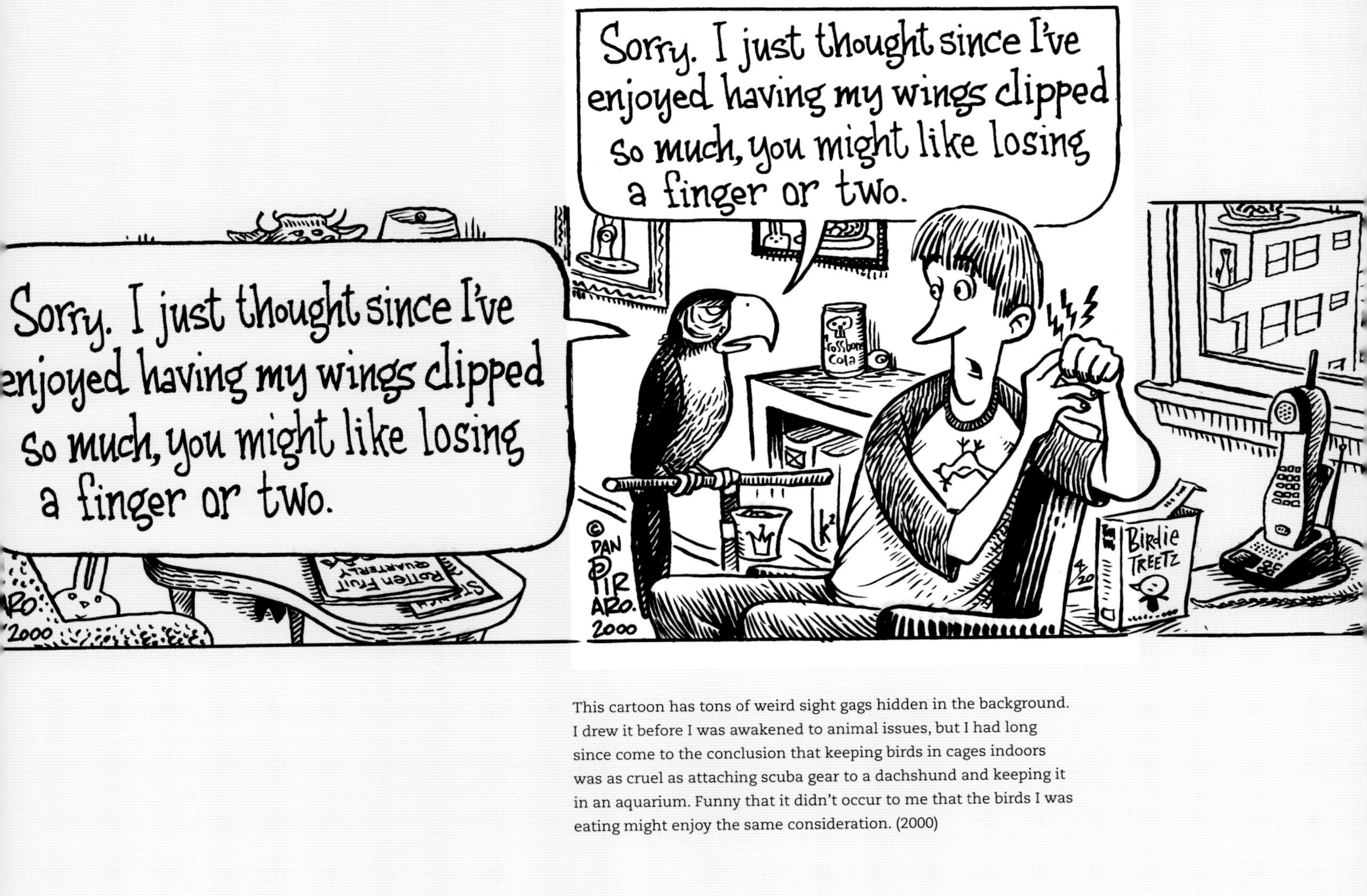
Sorry. I just thought since I've enjoyed having my wings clipped so much, you might like losing a finger or two.
Crossbones Cola
Birdie Treetz
© Dan Piraro 2000

This cartoon has tons of weird sight gags hidden in the background. I drew it before I was awakened to animal issues, but I had long since come to the conclusion that keeping birds in cages indoors was as cruel as attaching scuba gear to a dachshund and keeping it in an aquarium. Funny that it didn't occur to me that the birds I was eating might enjoy the same consideration. (2000)

Chapter three

A chance meeting with myself

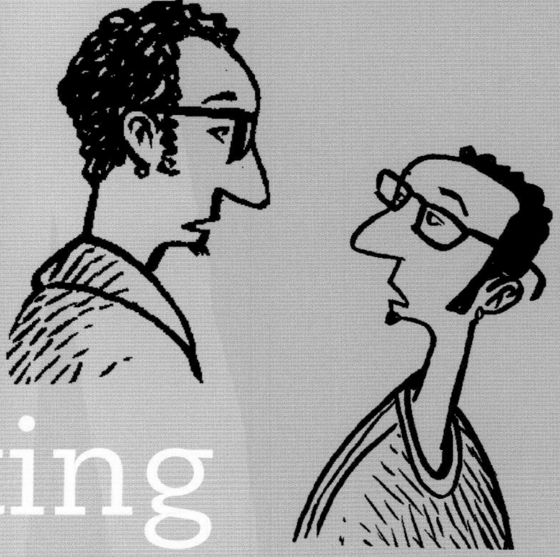

As the years after my divorce slipped by and my children got older, I began to think again about moving to New York or San Francisco. But the difference in the cost of living was still daunting. For what I was paying for a 3,000-square-foot house in a beautiful, old, hilly, tree-lined neighborhood in Dallas, I could get a damp, cardboard box near a bridge in New York City. For a box *under* the bridge, it would cost a little more. I put the idea off for a while longer, hoping something would happen that would make it seem financially feasible. Something like winning the lottery or optioning *Bizarro* for a two-picture deal with Steven Spielberg.

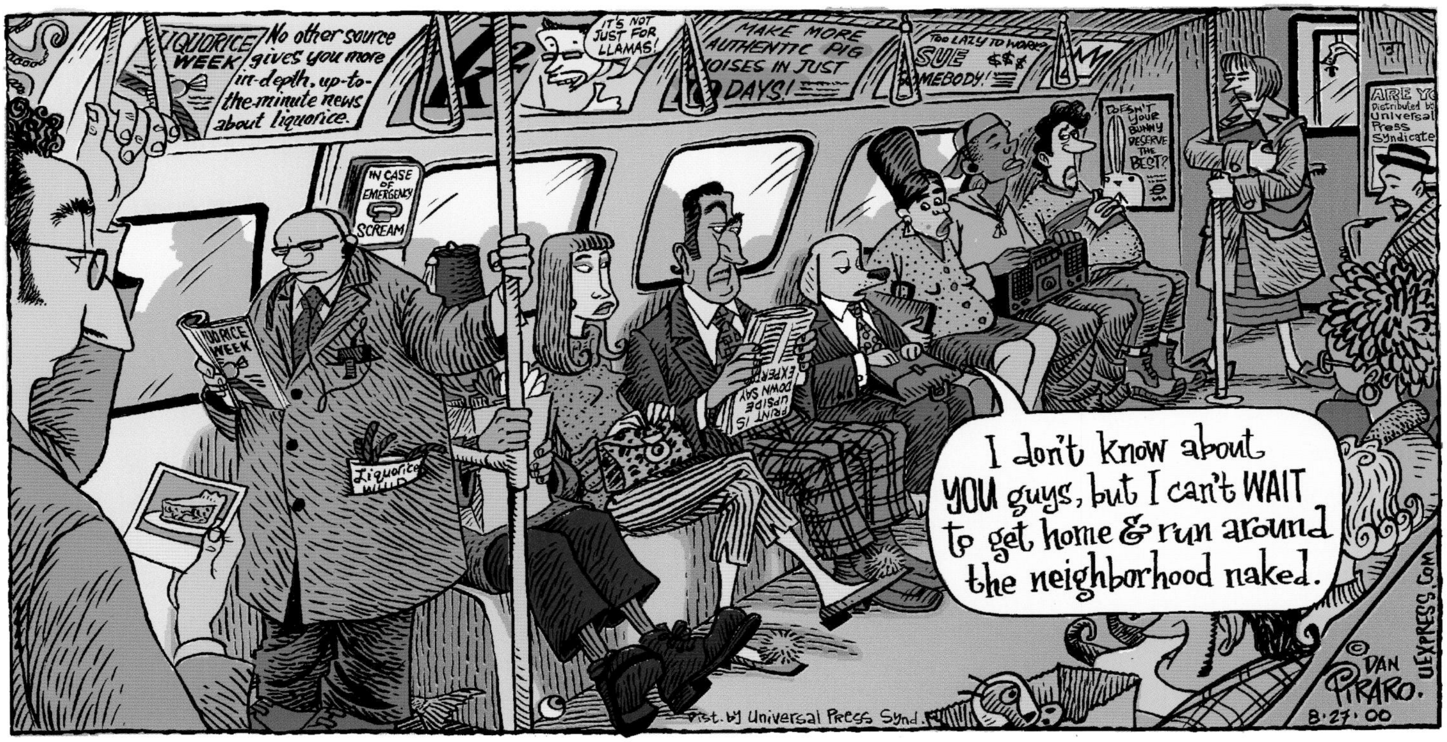
LIQUORICE WEEK
No other source gives you more in-depth, up-to-the-minute news about liquorice.
IT'S NOT JUST FOR LLAMAS!
MAKE MORE AUTHENTIC PIG NOISES IN JUST DAYS!
TOO LAZY TO WORK? SUE SOMEBODY! $$$
IN CASE OF EMERGENCY SCREAM
DOESN'T YOUR BUNNY DESERVE THE BEST?
ARE YO
Distributed by Universal Press Syndicate
PRINT IS UPSIDE DOWN SAY EXPERT
I don't know about YOU guys, but I can't WAIT to get home & run around the neighborhood naked.
© DAN PIRARO. 8·27·00
UEXPRESS.COM
Dist. by Universal Press Synd.

While I continued to move toward the artist's life, more side projects began to emerge. One grew from my public-speaking engagements. Over the years I had often been asked to speak to everyone from elementary school classes to PTA groups and at universities and literary festivals. I've always enjoyed performing and virtually never turned down a reasonable offer to speak somewhere. (A reasonable offer would be "Come to speak at our university. We'll pay your travel expenses and lodging." An unreasonable one would be "Sorry I can't afford to pay for your travel, but I loved the cartoon you did about that woman having a baby and I wonder if you'd come speak to my Lamaze class in Anchorage. We have a futon in the basement you can sleep on.") I was becoming increasingly adept at keeping audiences interested and making them laugh. In 2000 I decided to turn my "talks" into a one-man show with the intention of playing small theaters in cities where *Bizarro* runs.

I wrote a couple of hours' worth of material that was partly about being a cartoonist, but mostly just fun performance art and stand-up comedy. With no model or preconceived notions, I just began coming up with things I thought would be funny or interesting on stage. I hired a director, Lee Ritchey, to help me shape the material into a show and a small, local PR firm to help me get it publicized and booked. A few months later, I had a ninety-minute-long one-man show that consisted of songs, anecdotes, slides of cartoons, stand-up comedy, puppets (of my dogs, Steve and Bruno), and audience interaction (a clairvoyance routine with a large prop called

BELOW, LEFT: I loved the monkey and organ grinder in this picture so I used versions of them again on the copyright page of a *Bizarro* collection. (1996)

BELOW: Here I'm treading on thin ice. A cartoon I did a decade earlier about a city pool receiving a mandate to make the high diving board wheelchair accessible was nixed by a few editors who feared it would insult disabled readers. It's been my experience that able-bodied people are much more likely to complain about such things than the disabled. (2002)

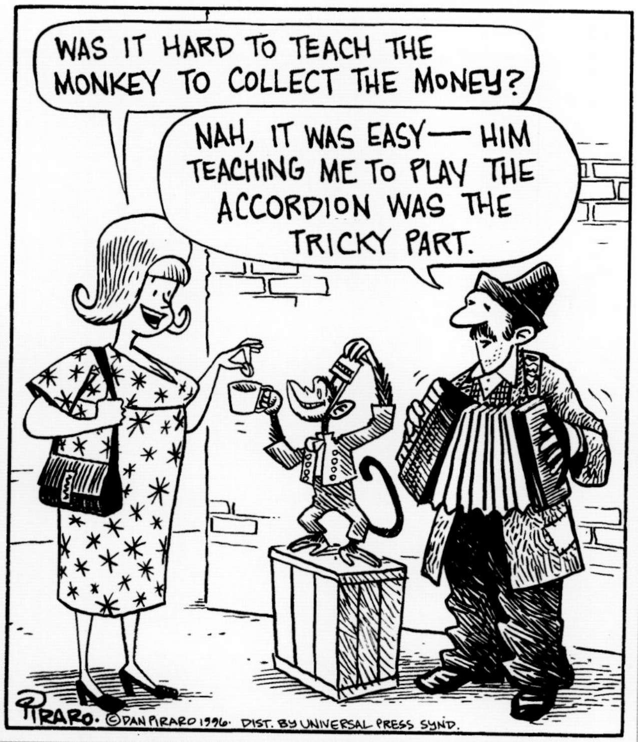
WAS IT HARD TO TEACH THE MONKEY TO COLLECT THE MONEY?
NAH, IT WAS EASY— HIM TEACHING ME TO PLAY THE ACCORDION WAS THE TRICKY PART.
PIRARO. ©DAN PIRARO 1996. DIST. BY UNIVERSAL PRESS SYND.

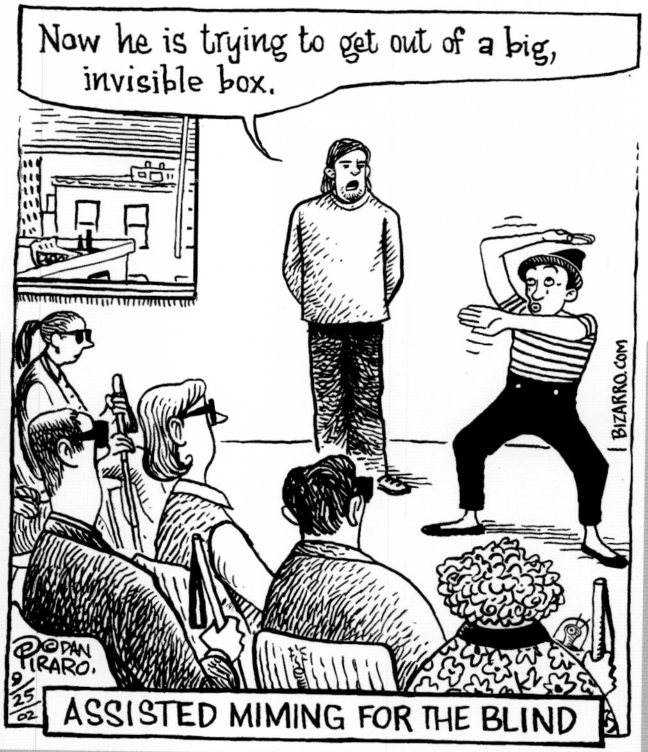
Now he is trying to get out of a big, invisible box.
BIZARRO.COM
©DAN PIRARO.
9/25/02
ASSISTED MIMING FOR THE BLIND

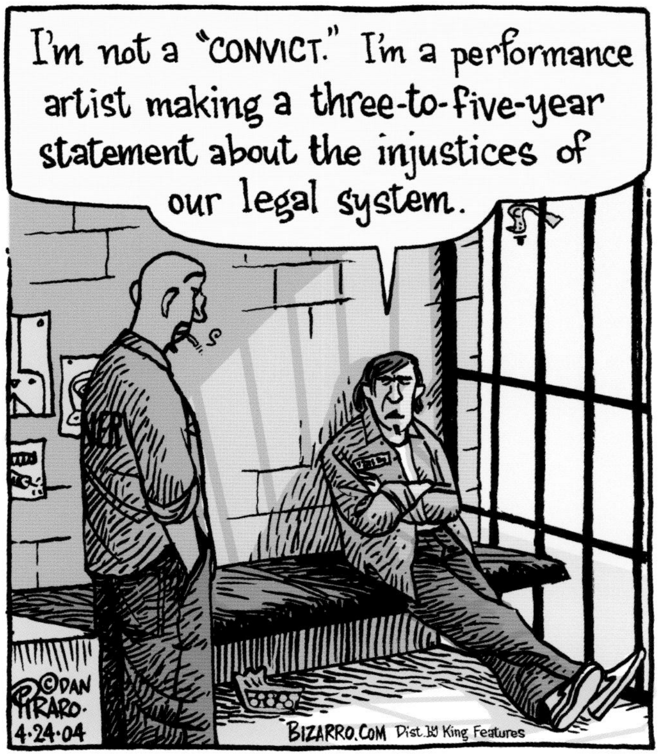
I'm not a "CONVICT." I'm a performance artist making a three-to-five-year statement about the injustices of our legal system.
©DAN PIRARO. 4·24·04
BIZARRO.COM Dist. by King Features

The Psychic Salmon), all loosely held together with a framework of handmade props, costumes, and set. I called it the Bizarro Bologna Show and performed it in Tulsa, Dallas, Houston, Raleigh, and San Francisco in late 2001. With no small amount of trepidation, I then entered it in the New York International Fringe Festival for 2002. To my delight and surprise it was accepted, was very well received, got a favorable review in *The New York Times,* and even won the festival's Best Solo Show award.

At the same time, my personal life was about to change in ways the rapidity and enormity of which I could not have imagined.

LEFT: And his effort may well be documented in a museum someday. (2004)

BELOW: Here I display some of my meager song-writing ability. Dressing up like Picasso, painting myself blue, and singing a song like this is just the sort of thing I do in my one-man show. (2003)

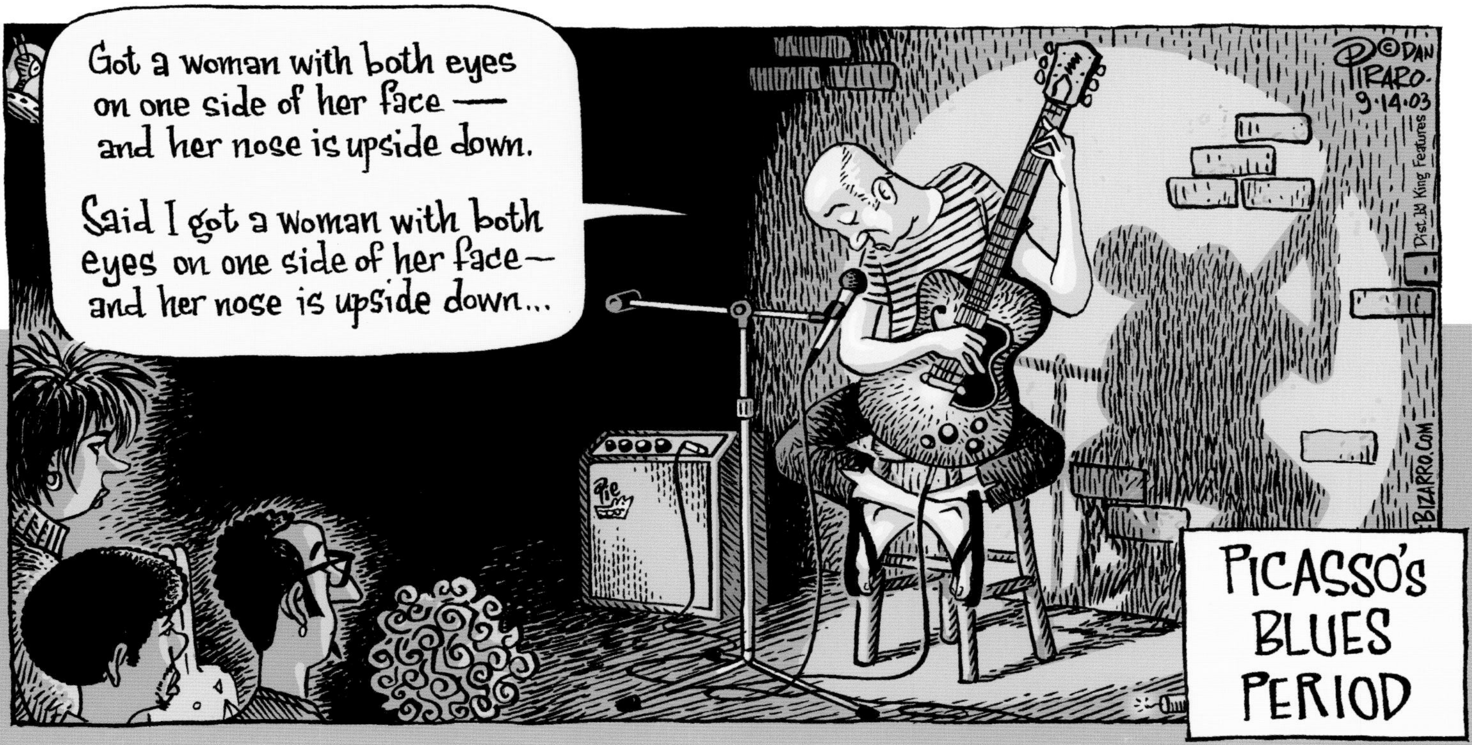
Got a woman with both eyes on one side of her face — and her nose is upside down.
Said I got a woman with both eyes on one side of her face — and her nose is upside down...
©DAN PIRARO. 9·14·03
Dist. by King Features
BIZARRO.COM
PICASSO'S BLUES PERIOD

At a National Cartoonists Society event I happened to run into Ashley Smith, a woman I had seen once a year for nearly a decade at annual conventions, but had never really spoken to. She had been attending such functions since she was a child, as both her father, Ralph Smith, and her stepfather, Chris Browne, are cartoonists by profession. Ralph has a syndicated strip called *Through Thick and Thin* and is an editorial cartoonist in Sarasota, Florida, and Chris works on his late father's creation, *Hagar the Horrible,* as well as having had his own strip, *Raising Duncan*, and publishing dozens of one-panel gags in magazines such as *Playboy* and *National Lampoon*.

This chance meeting led to a simple, yet earth-moving conversation. Ashley and I were both swept away almost instantly. We wondered how we'd eluded each other all those years. Neither of us were the sort to believe in soul mates or to act impetuously regarding matters of the heart—or so we had believed—but we found ourselves incapable of rational thought as our whirlwind romance culminated a mere two months later at a wedding chapel in Las Vegas with an Elvis impersonator. And here's the kicker: She lived in New York City.

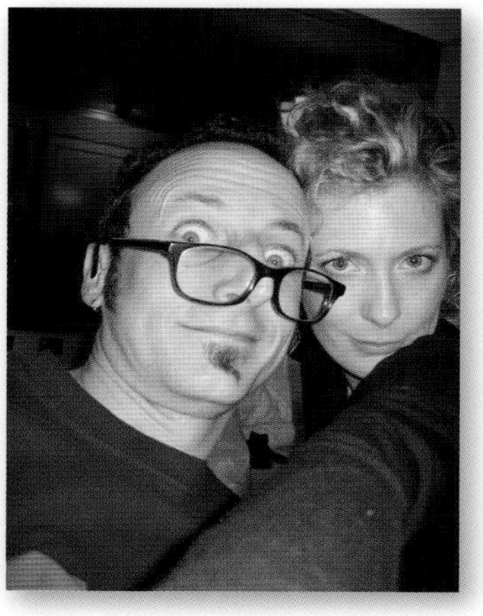

The love of a good woman was what I needed to take the plunge and move to New York, and I did so happily in the spring of 2002. My sudden marriage and move have turned out to be the most influential and beneficial choices I've made since my decision not to start a male cheerleading squad in high school. Ashley's and my relationship has continued to grow beyond even our expectations, and living in New York has been every bit as artistically rewarding as I had ever imagined. Even though I was raised in Oklahoma and lived in Texas until I was past forty, I never felt as at home there as I have in New York City since the day I arrived.

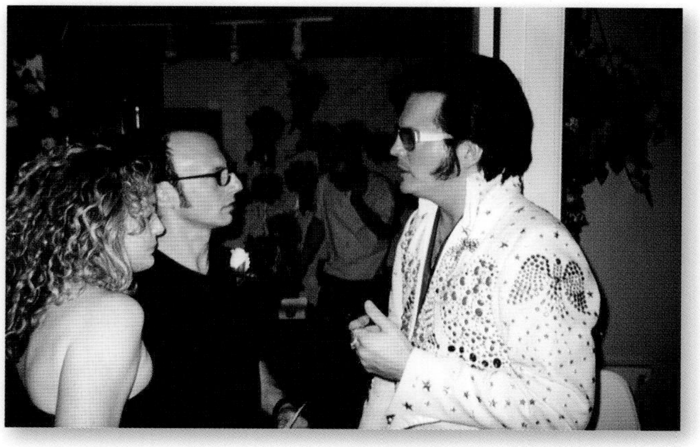

A couple of months after we began dating, I joined Ashley and six members of her immediate family on a road trip from L.A. to Las Vegas to the Grand Canyon. While in Vegas, only one day after I'd met them, I got them all into a limousine outside our hotel under the pretense of taking them to a "surprise." In the limo, I proposed to Ashley. Lucky for me she said yes and we proceeded to a wedding chapel where we were married by an Elvis impersonator. Four weeks previously, I had arranged for this cartoon (right) to run on that day. (Our middle names are Louise and Charles.) Her family has since forgiven me. (2002)

OPPOSITE: For one year, in 2002, I did a back-page cartoon for *D* magazine, a glossy, well-designed monthly in Dallas. This was my final cartoon for them. Much had changed during that year, including my getting married and moving to New York City. It was very hard to do the feature long distance as it was supposed to be about local issues and my head was not in Dallas anymore. (2003)

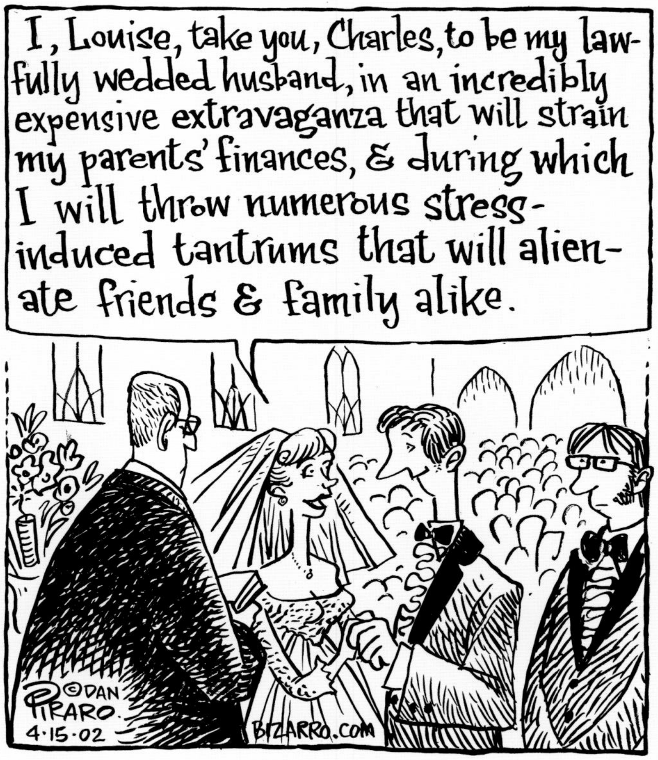
I, Louise, take you, Charles, to be my lawfully wedded husband, in an incredibly expensive extravaganza that will strain my parents' finances, & during which I will throw numerous stress-induced tantrums that will alienate friends & family alike.
©DAN PIRARO. 4·15·02
BIZARRO.COM

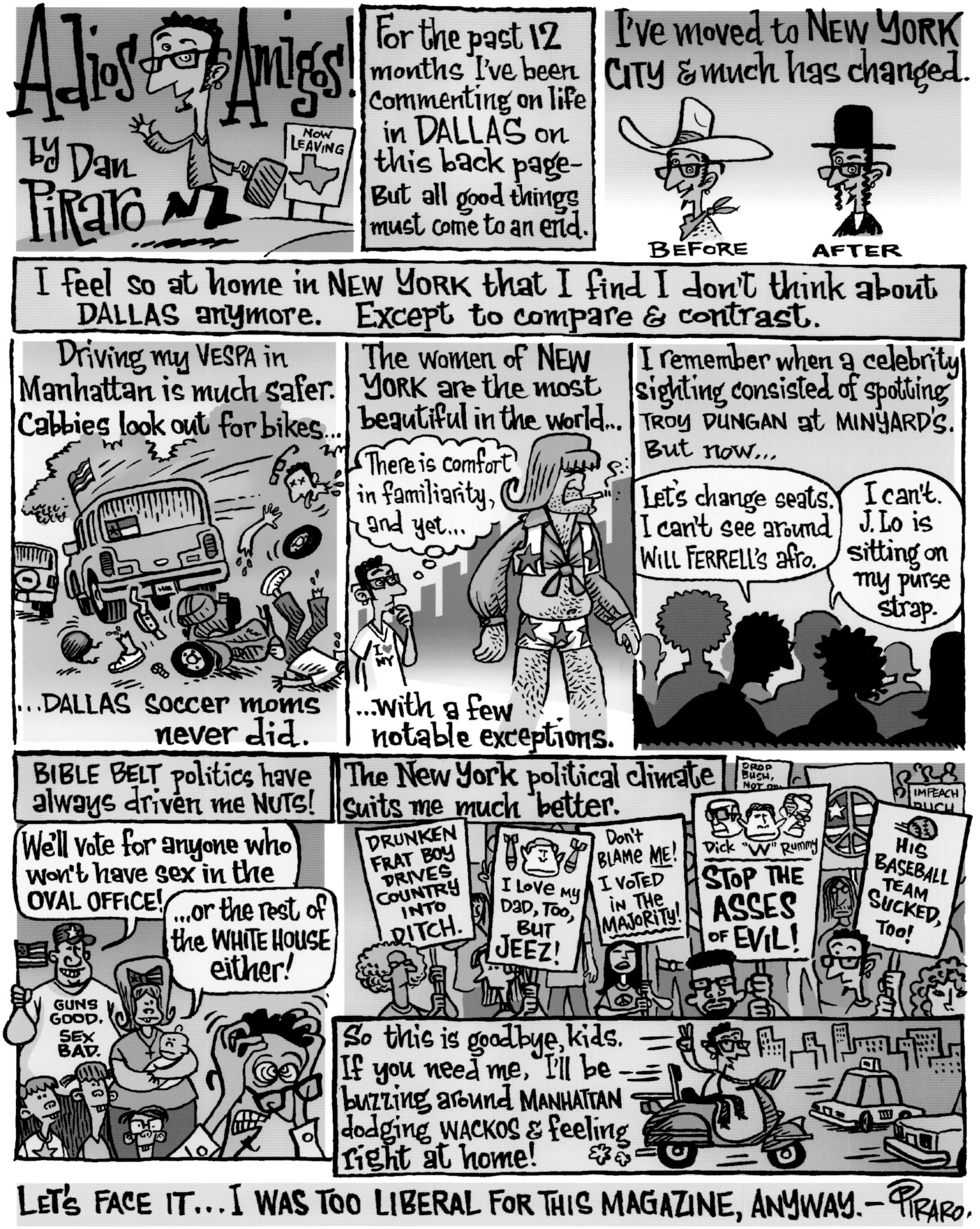
Adios Amigos!
by Dan Piraro
NOW LEAVING
For the past 12 months I've been commenting on life in DALLAS on this back page- But all good things must come to an end.
I've moved to NEW YORK CITY & much has changed.
BEFORE
AFTER
I feel so at home in NEW YORK that I find I don't think about DALLAS anymore. Except to compare & contrast.
Driving my VESPA in Manhattan is much safer. Cabbies look out for bikes...
...DALLAS soccer moms never did.
The women of NEW YORK are the most beautiful in the world...
There is comfort in familiarity, and yet...
I ♥ NY
...with a few notable exceptions.
I remember when a celebrity sighting consisted of spotting TROY DUNGAN at MINYARD'S. But now...
Let's change seats. I can't see around WILL FERRELL's afro.
I can't. J. Lo is sitting on my purse strap.
BIBLE BELT politics have always driven me NUTS!
We'll vote for anyone who won't have sex in the OVAL OFFICE!
...or the rest of the WHITE HOUSE either!
GUNS GOOD. SEX BAD.
The New York political climate suits me much better.
DRUNKEN FRAT BOY DRIVES COUNTRY INTO DITCH.
I Love MY DAD, Too, BUT JEEZ!
Don't BLAME ME! I VOTED IN THE MAJORITY!
Dick "W" Rummy
STOP THE ASSES OF EVIL!
HIS BASEBALL TEAM SUCKED, Too!
So this is goodbye, kids. If you need me, I'll be buzzing around MANHATTAN dodging WACKOS & feeling right at home!
LET'S FACE IT... I WAS TOO LIBERAL FOR THIS MAGAZINE, ANYWAY. — PIRARO.

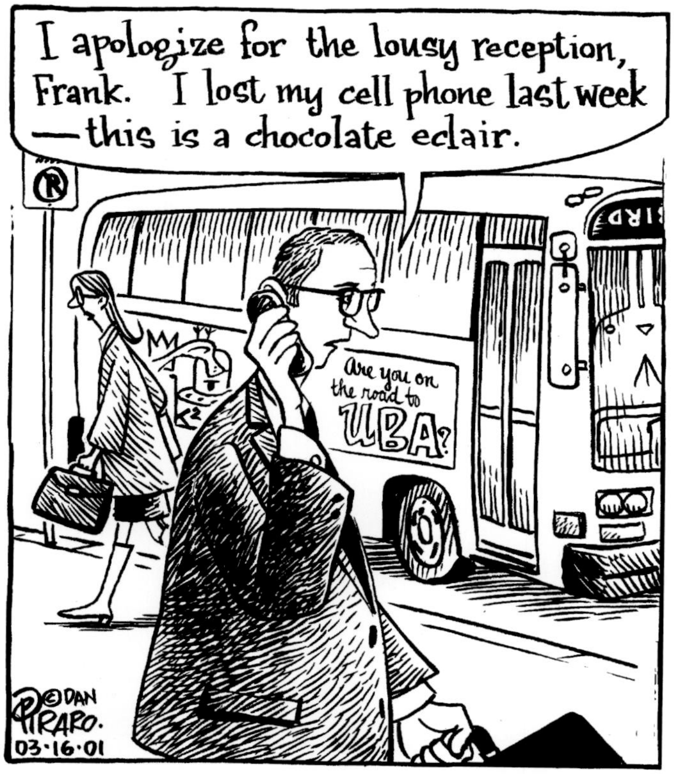
I apologize for the lousy reception, Frank. I lost my cell phone last week —this is a chocolate eclair.
Are you on the road to UBA?
©DAN PIRARO. 03·16·01

These two gags are similar, but I liked the idea enough to use the premise twice. The signs in the background below and in the window opposite below are subtle advertisements for the website promoting my Comics Against Evil political comedy tour. (2004)

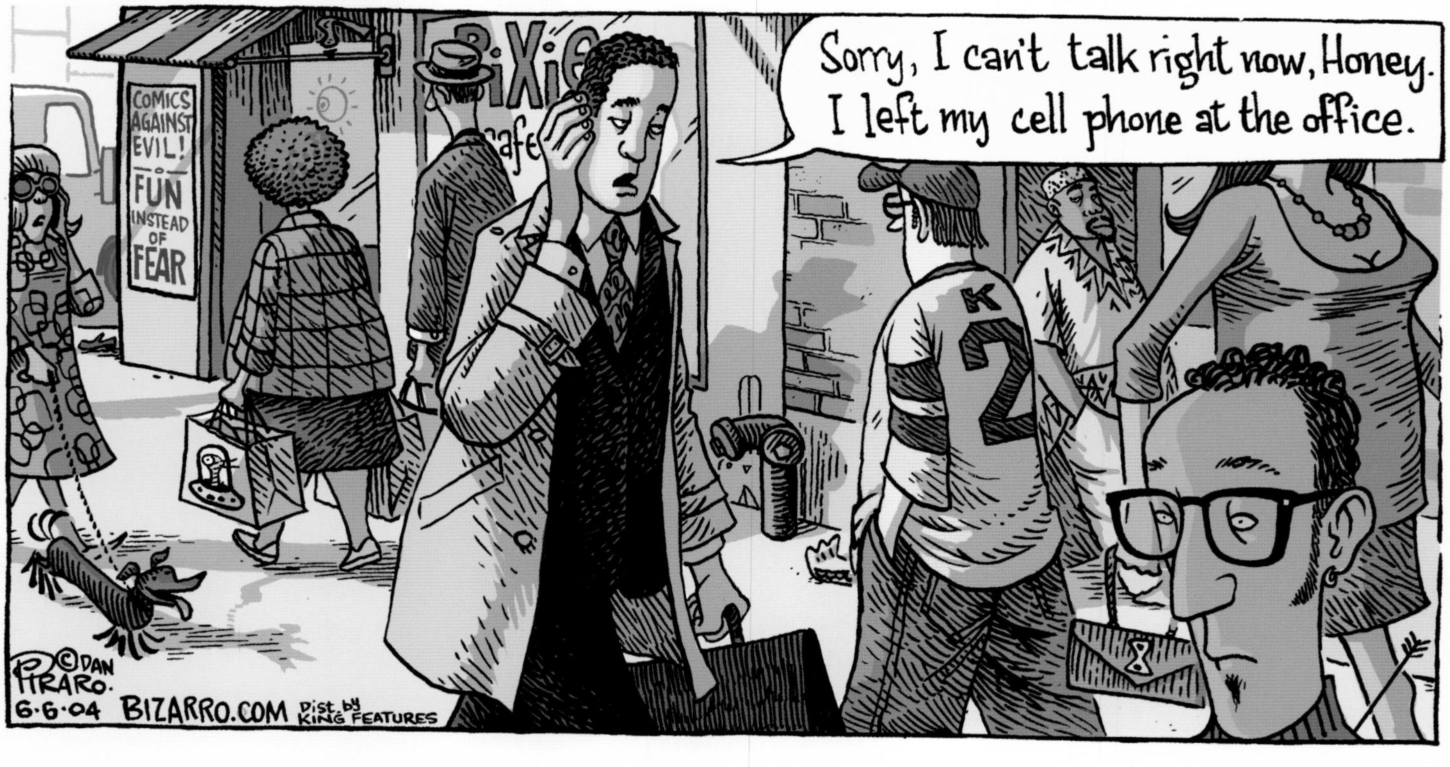
Sorry, I can't talk right now, Honey. I left my cell phone at the office.
COMICS AGAINST EVIL! FUN INSTEAD OF FEAR
©DAN PIRARO. 6·6·04 BIZARRO.COM Dist. by KING FEATURES

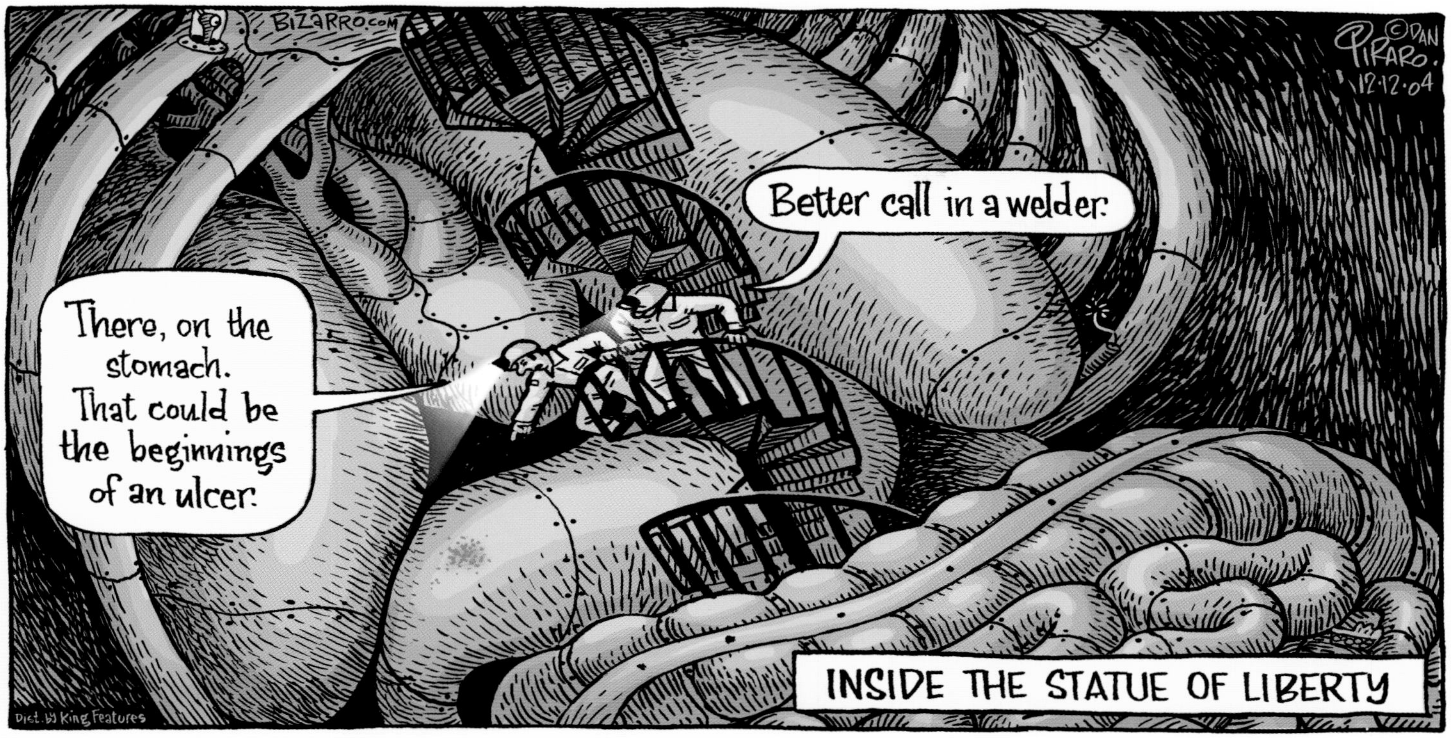
BIZARRO.COM
©DAN PIRARO. 12·12·04
Better call in a welder.
There, on the stomach. That could be the beginnings of an ulcer.
INSIDE THE STATUE OF LIBERTY
Dist. by King Features

I'm happy to say I climbed to the crown of the Statue of Liberty a few years before 9/11, after which it was closed to the public, perhaps for good. I was disappointed to find that it is not as anatomically correct as this cartoon shows. (2004)

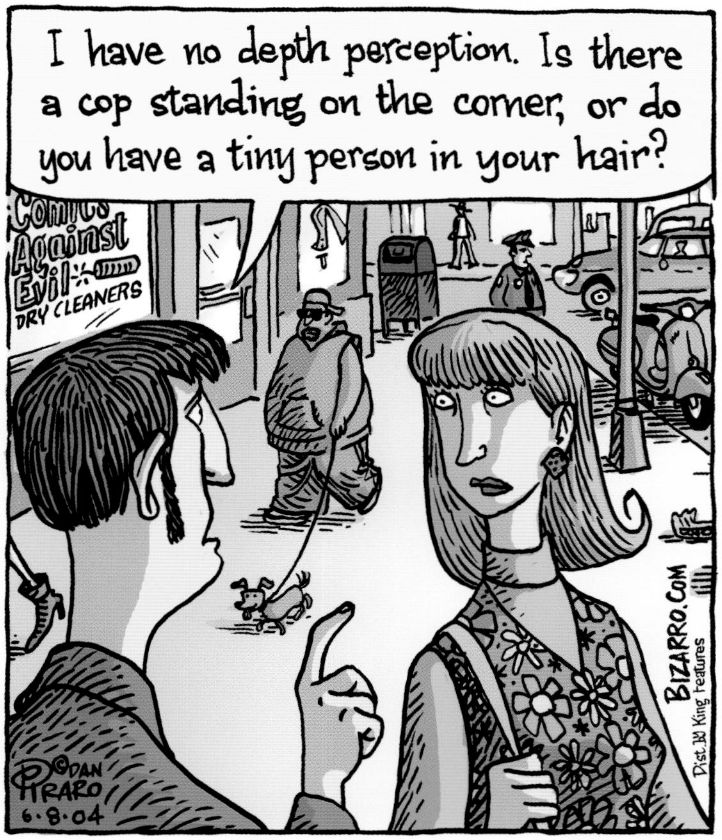
I have no depth perception. Is there a cop standing on the corner, or do you have a tiny person in your hair?
Comics Against Evil
DRY CLEANERS
BIZARRO.COM
Dist. by King Features
©DAN PIRARO 6·8·04

LEFT: In many of my cartoons, this one included, I draw a Vespa scooter in the background. I've been a scooter fanatic since high school, when The Who's album *Quadrophenia* came out and I became aware of the "mod" scooters of 1960s London. I bought a Vespa new in 1980 and have had it ever since. With its ability to slink through traffic jams and park almost anywhere, we find our scooter provides the perfect way for getting around New York City.

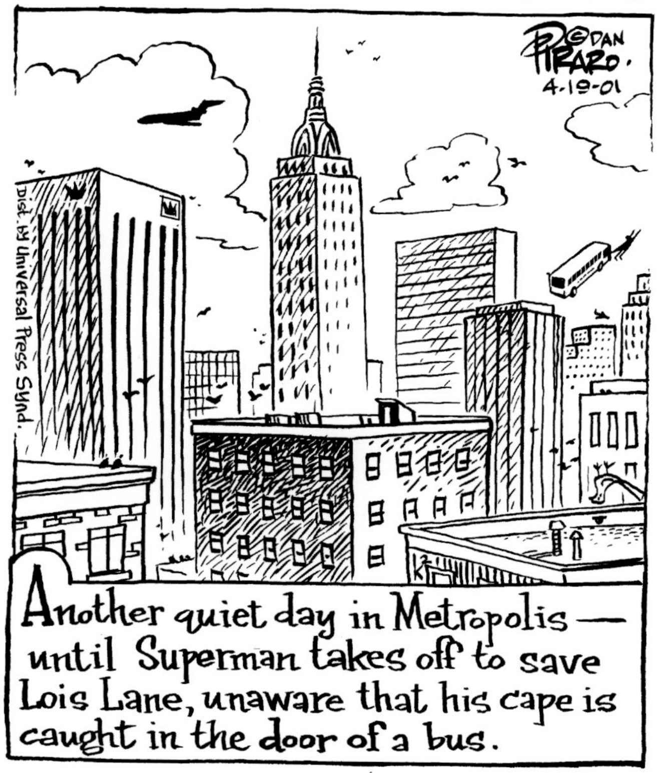
©DAN PIRARO. 4-19-01
Dist. by Universal Press Synd.
Another quiet day in Metropolis — until Superman takes off to save Lois Lane, unaware that his cape is caught in the door of a bus.

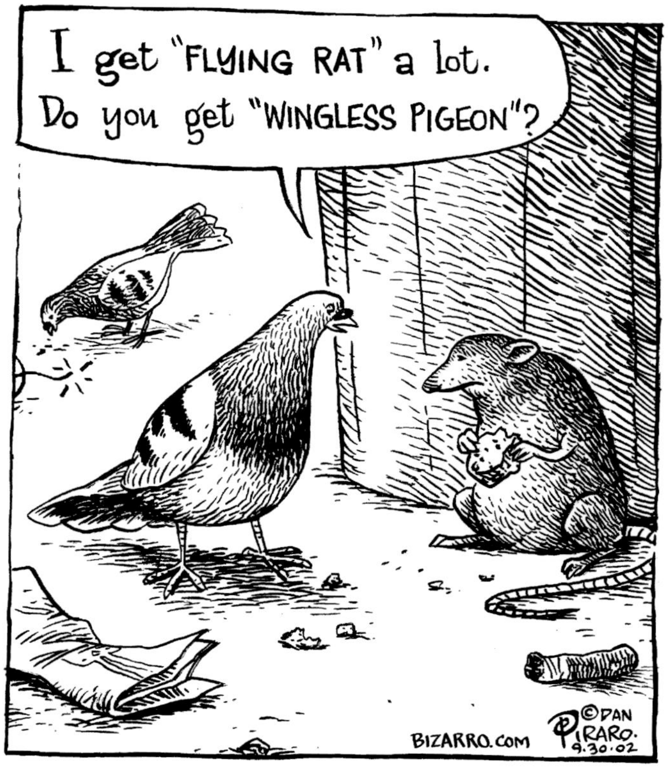
I get "FLYING RAT" a lot. Do you get "WINGLESS PIGEON"?
BIZARRO.COM
©DAN PIRARO. 9.30.02

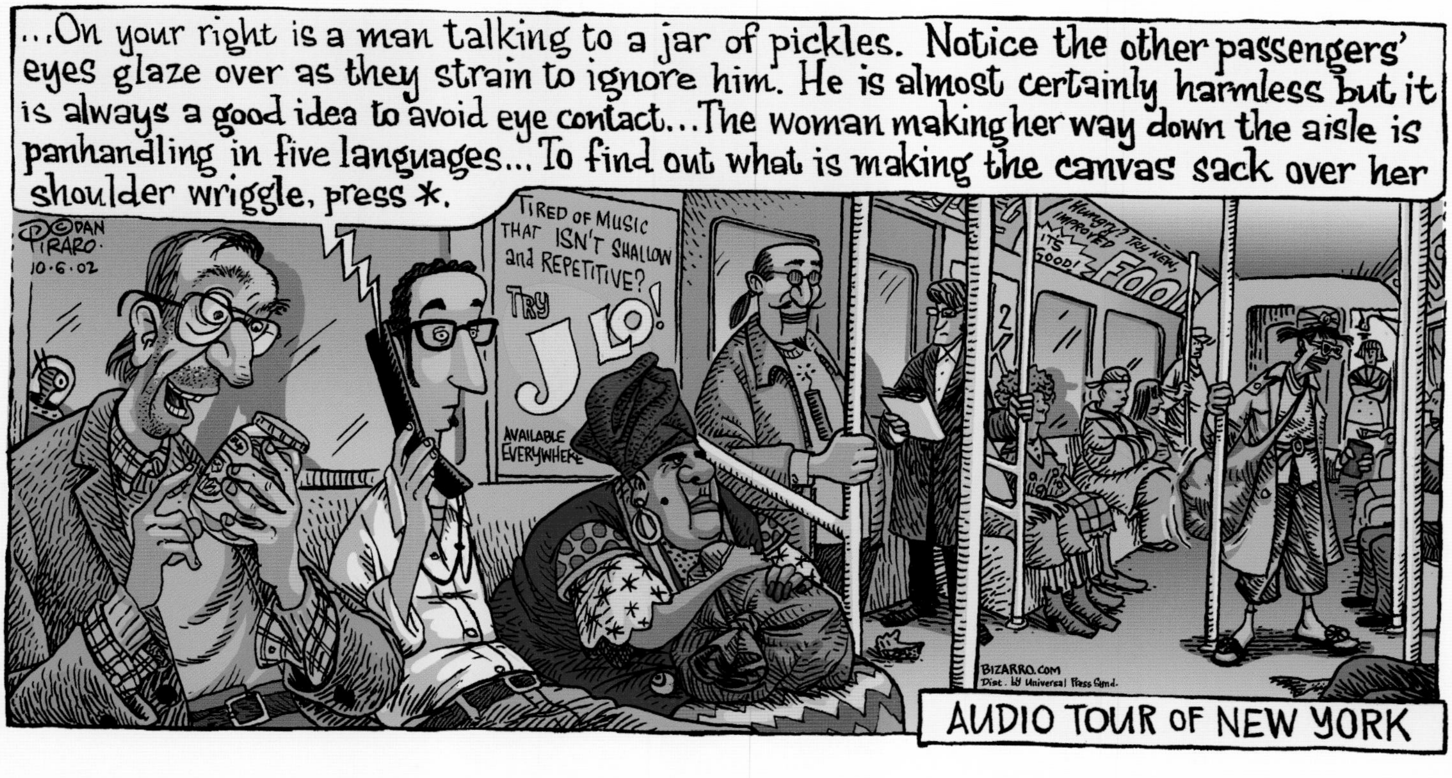
...On your right is a man talking to a jar of pickles. Notice the other passengers' eyes glaze over as they strain to ignore him. He is almost certainly harmless but it is always a good idea to avoid eye contact...The woman making her way down the aisle is panhandling in five languages... To find out what is making the canvas sack over her shoulder wriggle, press *.
©DAN PIRARO. 10.6.02
TIRED OF MUSIC THAT ISN'T SHALLOW and REPETITIVE? TRY J LO! AVAILABLE EVERYWHERE
BIZARRO.COM
Dist. by Universal Press Synd.
AUDIO TOUR OF NEW YORK

OPPOSITE, LEFT: This is the sort of joke I'm known for in which the punch line lies in some small detail that takes a little searching to find. Unfortunately, newspapers are experiencing consistently worsening financial problems and are routinely shrinking comics and expanding ad space in an effort to make ends meet. Already in some markets, my cartoon prints no bigger than a business card—too small for a joke like this to even be seen. (2001)

OPPOSITE, RIGHT: A direct influence of moving to New York City. (2002)

OPPOSITE, BOTTOM: Drawn from experience, a few months after I moved to New York. (2002)

BELOW: Another good sight gag, this time with fun signage in the background. (2004)

The city has been very influential in my cartoons, too. From the superficial—like inspiring me to include more realistic renderings of subways, urban clutter, and pigeons—to the profound, the art and culture I am regularly exposed to has had an impact on my thoughts, themes, and artwork.

I'm very proud to call myself a New Yorker. New York is a microcosm of what America was meant to be. Dozens of different cultures, races, and ethnicities live side by side, harmoniously for the most part, an amazing feat considering the sheer number of people in such a small area. The violent crime rate here is lower per capita than any place I've lived before and the city as a whole doesn't just tolerate diversity and individuality, but embraces and encourages it. Far from the negative impressions that Southerners tend to propagate about "Yankees," I have found New Yorkers to be friendly (except for people who work for the subway), intelligent (except for those who answer the phone at the cable TV company), hard working (except for those at the post office), and well informed about world events. The average cab driver or bartender in New York knows more about American and international politics than most white-collar college grads I knew in the Bible Belt.

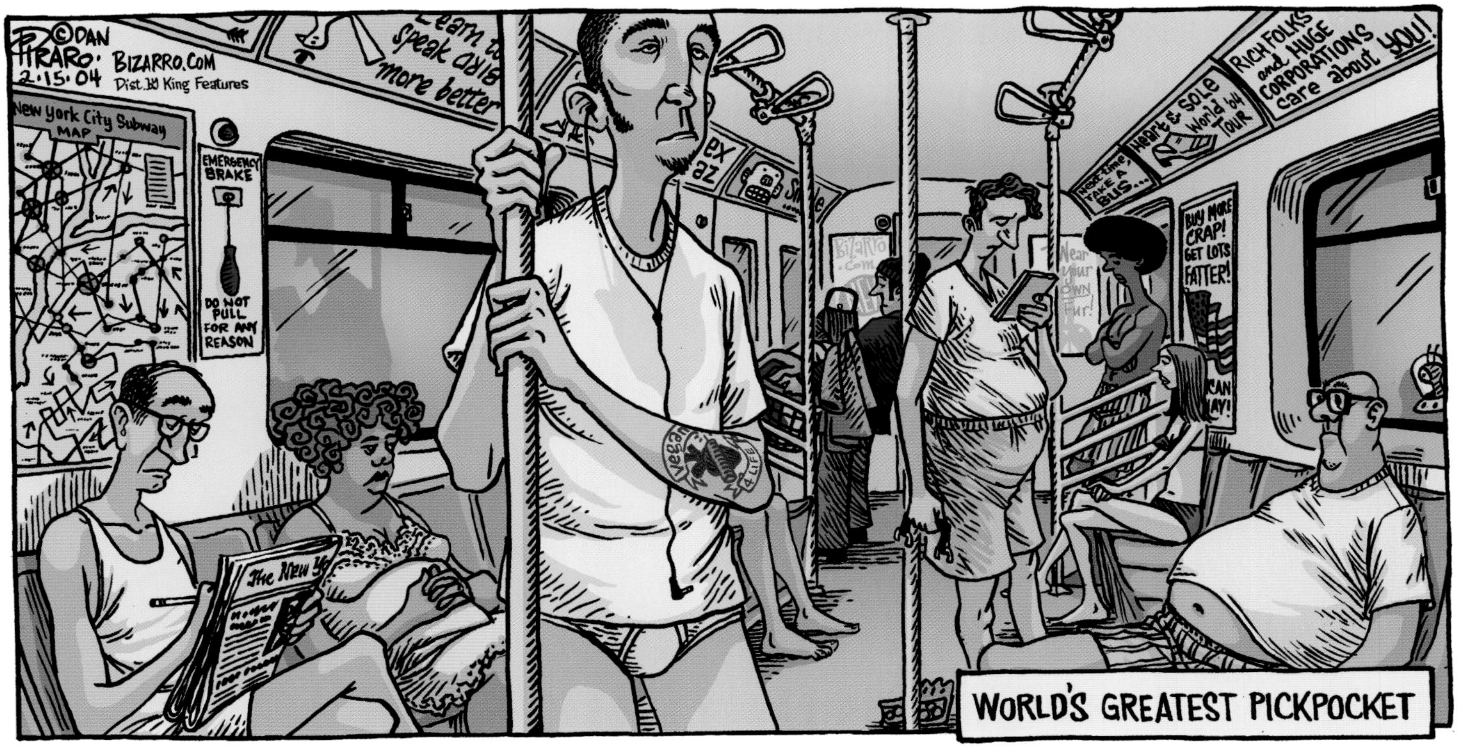
©DAN PIRARO· 2·15·04
BIZARRO.COM
Dist. by King Features
New York City Subway MAP
EMERGENCY BRAKE
DO NOT PULL FOR ANY REASON
Learn to speak gooder more better
Next time, TAKE A BUS...
Heart & Sole World '04 TOUR
RICH FOLKS and HUGE CORPORATIONS care about YOU!
BUY MORE CRAP! GET LOTS FATTER!
Wear your OWN Fur!
WORLD'S GREATEST PICKPOCKET

It's the same in Europe. My theory is that in New York, as in Europe, we live very close to people of nearly every world culture and nationality and are exposed to their lives. Unlike the vast majority of communities in Middle America, so-called minorities aren't in such a minority in New York City; they can't be stored in a small section of town and ignored. Additionally, political decisions made by the U.S. have direct and palpable repercussions around the world, and those of us in New York invariably know people who have been directly affected. In the middle of the country, a war in, oh, say, the Middle East, isn't felt or experienced in any real way unless a person happens to know someone who is serving there. For the most part, the war is just so much patriotic fluff on Fox News. In New York, we are exposed to every side of an issue by people who have been there or have relatives who are there currently.

Amazing people live in New York. You can scarcely leave the house without meeting someone at the top of his or her field, be it law, journalism, art, comedy, television, music, politics, you name it. Sometimes you don't even have to leave the house—you just find them standing in the kitchen or lurking behind a door. They're everywhere. New York City is a very big pond that attracts very big fish. As you might imagine, these well-traveled, well-informed people are fascinating, and conversations with them reveal a great deal about the state of the planet. I love the fact that the dream world of the neocon propaganda machine doesn't work here. Most people just laugh at it.

And possibly the best thing about New York City is that it doesn't have a Wal-Mart. They tried to put one in Queens somewhere, and failed. If they ever succeed I only hope that it's far enough away from Brooklyn and Manhattan so that I can pretend it isn't there. If not, I may consider taking an aerial photo of it and telling Donald Rumsfeld it's a chemical weapons plant.

I have a passion for putting signs and headlines that have nothing to do with the main joke into my cartoons. Here they are the main joke.

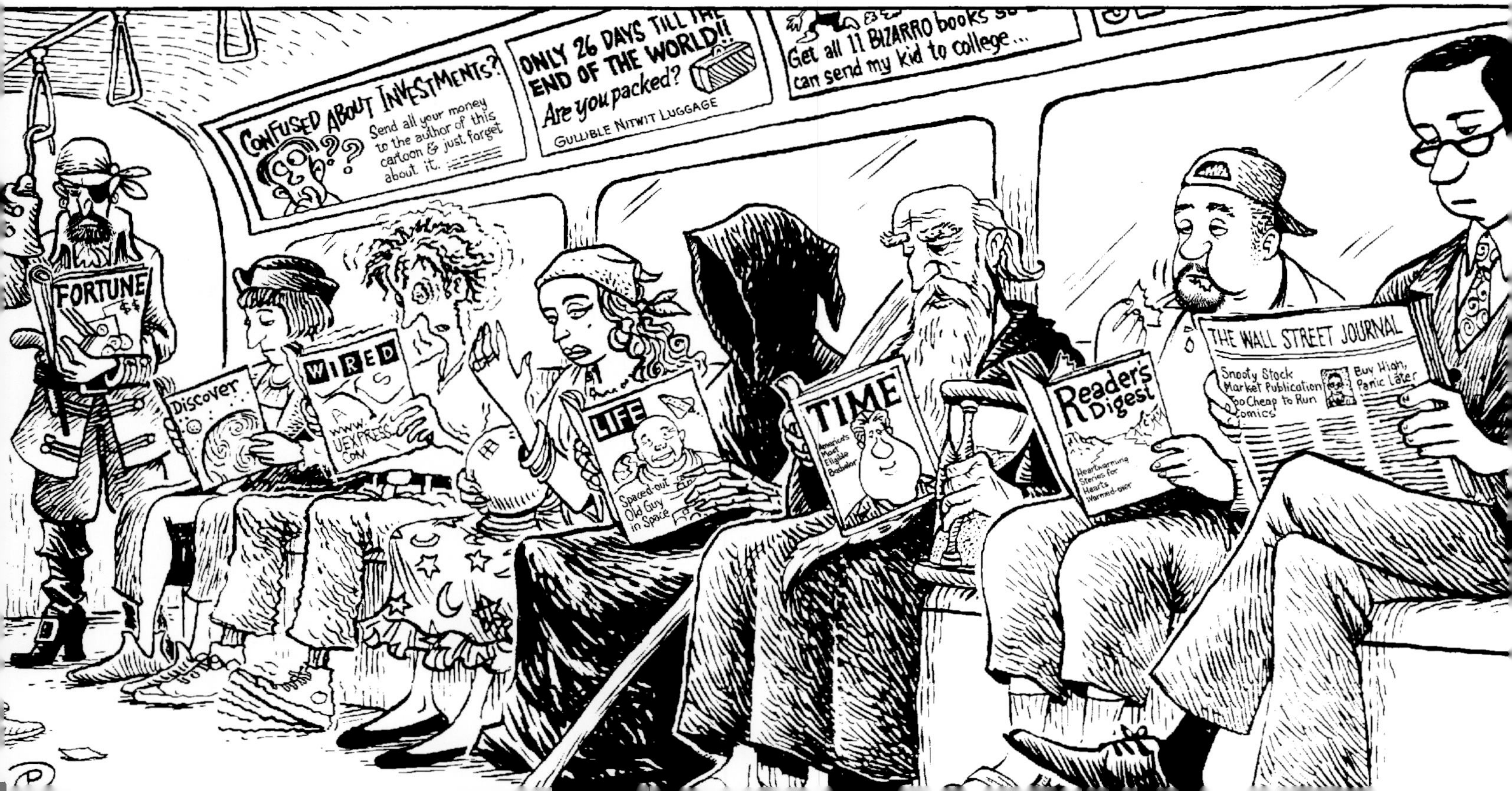

CONFUSED ABOUT INVESTMENTS?
Send all your money to the author of this cartoon & just forget about it.
ONLY 26 DAYS TILL THE END OF THE WORLD!!
Are you packed?
GULLIBLE NITWIT LUGGAGE
Get all 11 BIZARRO books so I can send my kid to college...
FORTUNE
$$
Discover
WIRED
www.UEXPRESS.COM
LIFE
Spaced-out Old Guy in Space
TIME
America's Most Eligible Bachelor
Reader's Digest
Heartwarming Stories for Hearts Warmed-over
THE WALL STREET JOURNAL
Snooty Stock Market Publication Too Cheap to Run Comics
Buy High, Panic Later

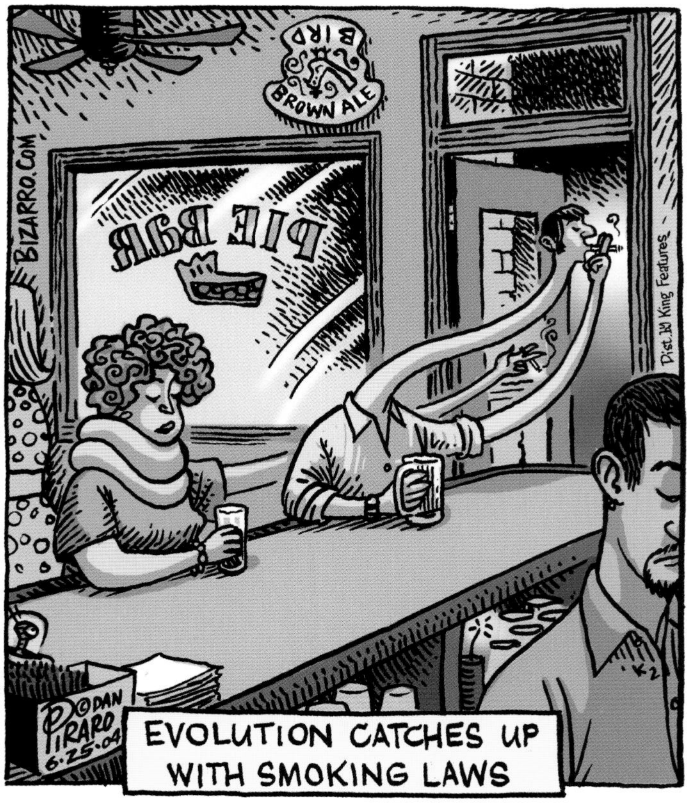
BIRD
BROWN ALE
PIE BAR
BIZARRO.COM
Dist. by King Features
© DAN PIRARO 6.25.04
EVOLUTION CATCHES UP WITH SMOKING LAWS

I never thought New York City would be able to enforce the smoking ban in restaurants and bars that they passed in 2003, but they did. Personally, I love it. I don't find it an infringement on personal rights any more than telling people they can't play their boombox in a restaurant or bar. (2004)

BELOW: This is exactly the way I feel. This drawing is chock full of secret symbols and has a couple of animal rights messages to boot. In the mid-nineties, purely for my own entertainment, I began hiding a little bird with a hat in some of my cartoons. Immediately I began getting feedback from curious readers so I added lots of other symbols, the meanings of which are posted on Bizarro.com under the link "Secret Symbols." (2003)

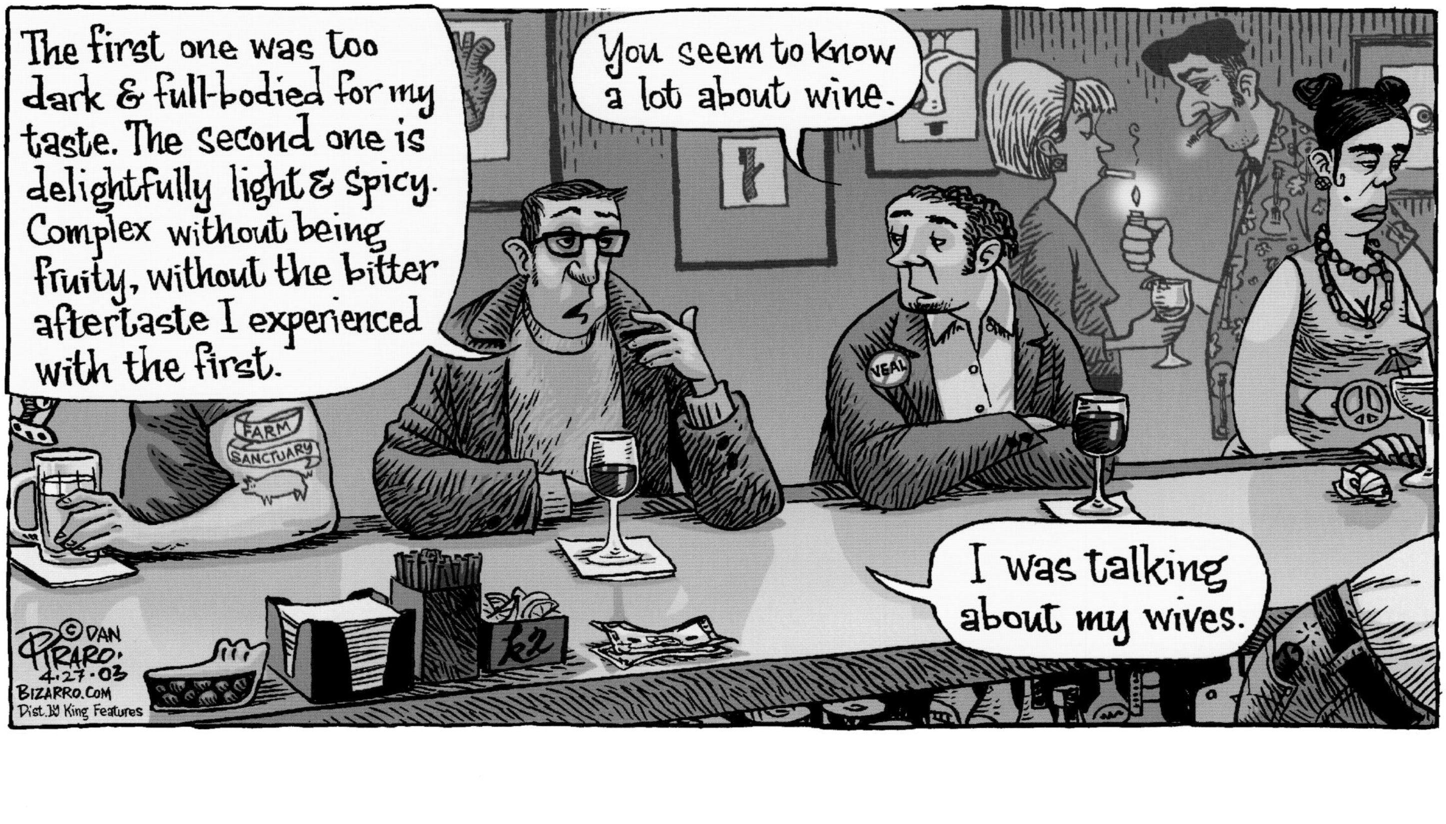
The first one was too dark & full-bodied for my taste. The second one is delightfully light & spicy. Complex without being fruity, without the bitter aftertaste I experienced with the first.
You seem to know a lot about wine.
I was talking about my wives.
FARM SANCTUARY
VEAL
© DAN PIRARO 4.27.03
BIZARRO.COM
Dist. by King Features

All the various influences of New York have nurtured in me a keen interest in two subjects I had not previously given much thought to: politics and animal rights.

Shortly after I began dating my wife, I became aware of the intentionally well-hidden facts about how animals raised for food are treated in modern-day America. Although a story about mad cow disease occasionally hits the headlines and books like *Fast Food Nation* have sold very well, I was completely unaware of animal welfare issues when we met, as the vast majority of Americans still are.

Ashley has been a vegan and animal rights activist since she was a teenager and because she is more inclined to lead by example than to evangelize, she didn't try to indoctrinate me into her belief system. But it was impossible not to soak up a great deal about animal agriculture industries just by being around her and the material she uses in her work.

While I had periodically criticized hunting and the fur industry in *Bizarro* over the years, I must admit I'd always thought of animal rights activists as overly sentimental nuts on the fringe. After all, eating animals and wearing fur were things humans have been doing for millions of years. I was raised to believe that's what they were for. But when I found out about the routine and horrendous abuse countless millions of animals endure daily in our animal-based food industries, I was horrified. I had wrongly assumed there were laws forbidding such cruelty. The sad truth is that animal welfare laws dealing with humane housing specifically exempt livestock, and that humane slaughter laws are shamefully underenforced and completely exempt birds, even though birds account for over 90 percent of the animals killed for food in the United States.

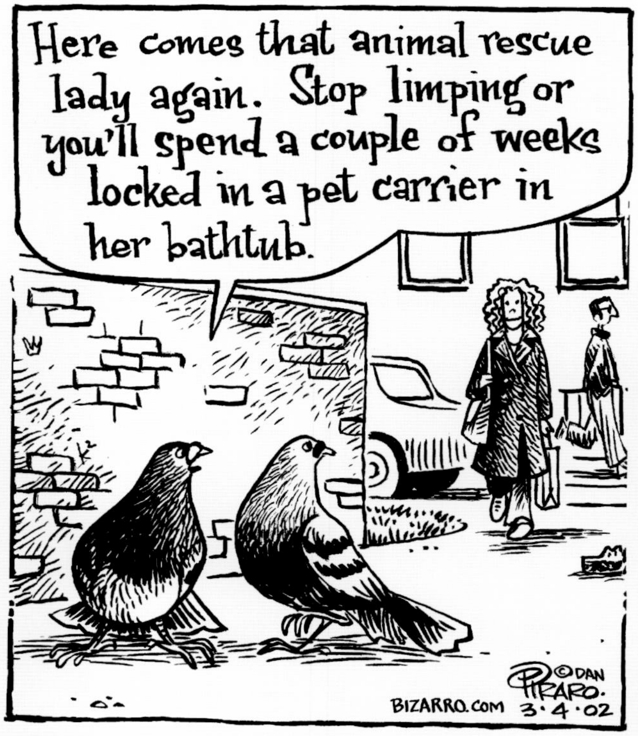
Here comes that animal rescue lady again. Stop limping or you'll spend a couple of weeks locked in a pet carrier in her bathtub.
©DAN PIRARO. 3·4·02
BIZARRO.COM

Drawn shortly after Ashley and I began dating, and inspired by her animal rescue work. The first time I visited her apartment, she had four cats, one dog, and a dozen mice, and there was an injured pigeon in a cat carrier in her bathtub. All were rescues on their way to better lives. We have since housed many dozens of animals. (2002)

The single reason animals are badly treated is to increase profits. You can make more money raising animals in tiny boxes and wire cages, virtually ignoring their medical needs, rarely cleaning their environments, feeding them cheap, fattening, unnutritious food, and operating slaughter lines so fast that animals are often butchered while fully conscious. Conditions are often so wretched, in fact, that many animals die long before they get to the slaughterhouse, and the rest survive only because they are flooded with antibiotics, which, along with steroids and hormones administered to speed up their growth rate, can be found in the blood of those who consume them.

On factory farms, where most animals are now raised, those who die before they reach the slaughterhouse are often left to rot among the living. And those too sick to walk, "downers," are dragged by chains to their deaths. If people treated dogs or cats this way, they could be jailed.

Convinced that animal agriculture was an indefensibly cruel industry that I was unwilling to subsidize, I wondered about the dietary consequences of giving up meat. I did a lot of research and found, to my surprise, that there are only a couple of relatively minor benefits of meat eating, both of which could be easily compensated for by taking inexpensive, readily available supplements. And I discovered several very disturbing disadvantages to regular consumption of animal protein. Numerous large studies have consistently shown that meat eaters have more than twice the chance of developing heart disease than do vegetarians. Moreover, there is growing evidence that several common forms of cancer may also be linked to the consumption of meat. Regular meat eaters also have higher rates of obesity and tend to have a higher incidence of illness of all kinds. While this isn't by any means evidence that vegetarianism is a cure-all, it does make it very difficult to argue from a health standpoint that there is any reason to consume meat, other than that it tastes good. It made me sick to realize that I had been subsidizing torture for the sake of pleasure.

BELOW, LEFT: Hormones that are outlawed in Australia, Canada, and the entire European Union show up in the U.S. milk supply—along with a legally allowable amount of pus, more than twice the amount allowed in Canada and the European Union, believe it or not. (2004)

BELOW, RIGHT: One of the first cartoons I did about the hazards of America's food supply after I'd become a vegan. (2002)

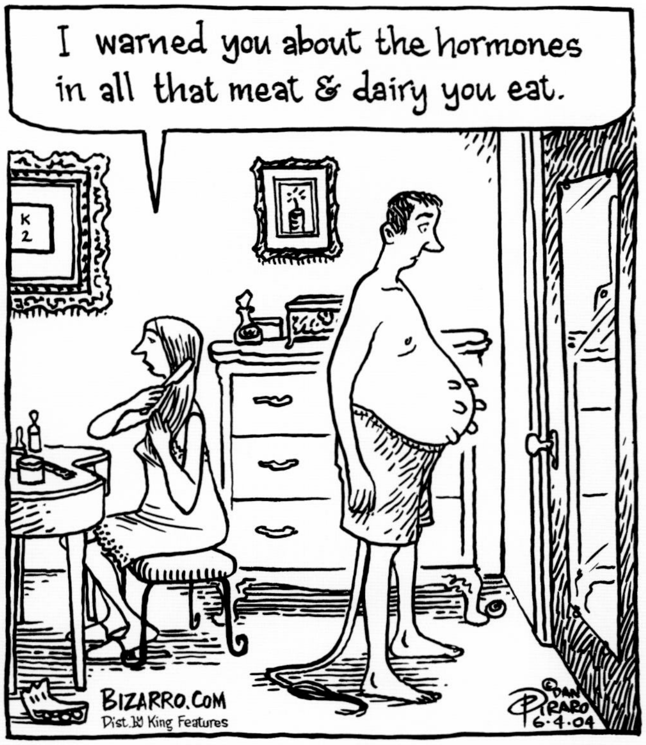
I warned you about the hormones in all that meat & dairy you eat.
BIZARRO.COM
Dist. by King Features
©DAN PIRARO 6-4-04

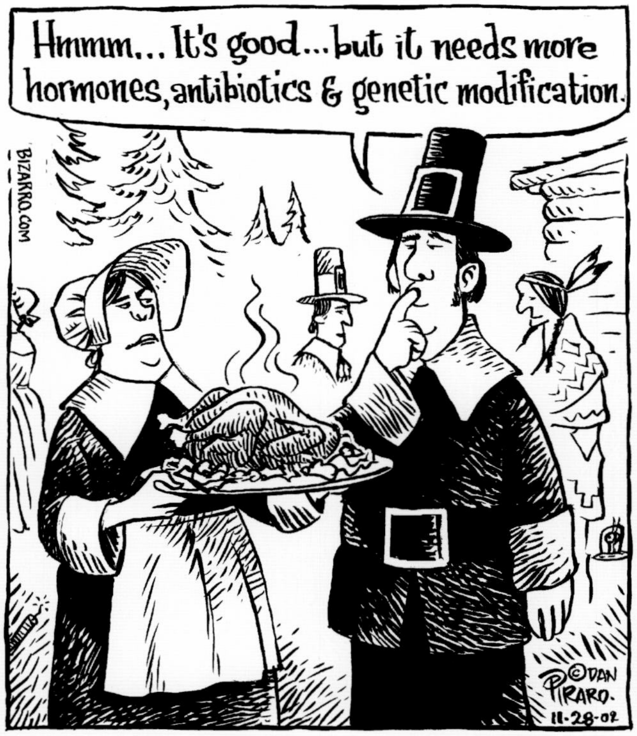
Hmmm... It's good... but it needs more hormones, antibiotics & genetic modification.
BIZARRO.COM
©DAN PIRARO. 11-28-02

My least favorite human trait is the arrogant and small-minded belief that we are the only species that matters.

RIGHT: A favorite of mine that says it all very succinctly. (2004)

BELOW, LEFT: I got this idea from a PETA ad that shows a girl holding up the bloody, skinned carcass of a fox. The headline simply says: "Here's the rest of your fur coat." (2004)

BELOW, RIGHT: A frequently ignored part of animal abuse is the field of entertainment. With the exception of dogs, all animals are miserable when confined and taught to do "tricks." This is a comment only on dogs as a species—it is not to say that some performing dogs are not unhappy or mistreated. In general, I believe forcing anyone or anything to amuse you is wrong. (2004)

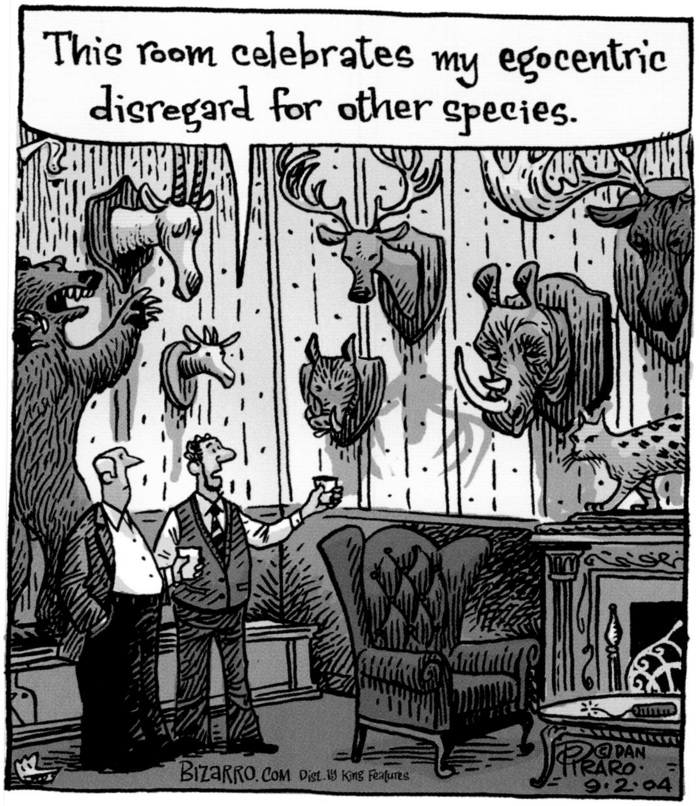
This room celebrates my egocentric disregard for other species.
BIZARRO.COM Dist. by King Features
©DAN PIRARO 9·2·04

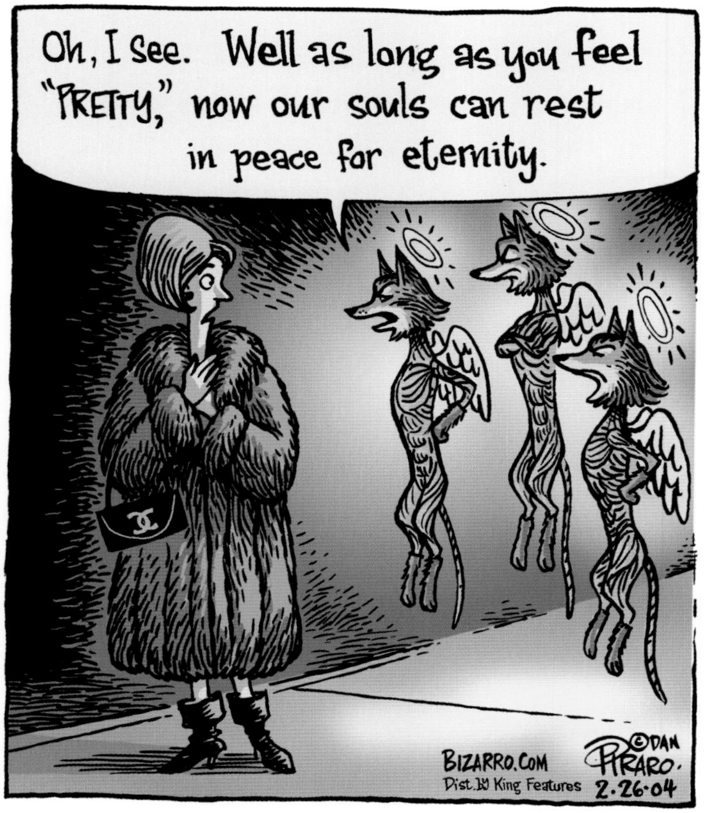
Oh, I see. Well as long as you feel "PRETTY," now our souls can rest in peace for eternity.
BIZARRO.COM Dist. by King Features
©DAN PIRARO. 2·26·04

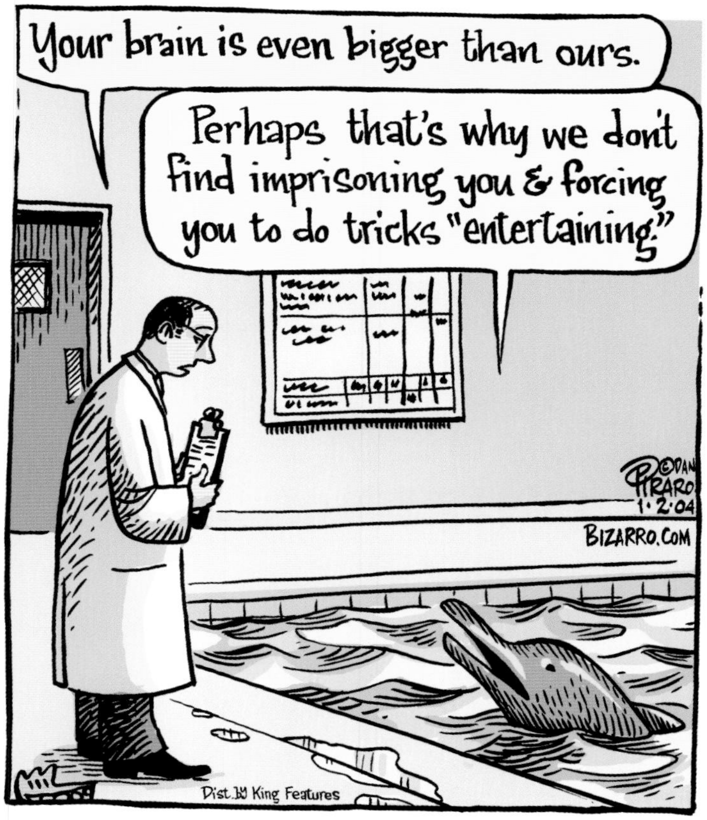
Your brain is even bigger than ours.
Perhaps that's why we don't find imprisoning you & forcing you to do tricks "entertaining."
©DAN PIRARO 1·2·04
BIZARRO.COM
Dist. by King Features

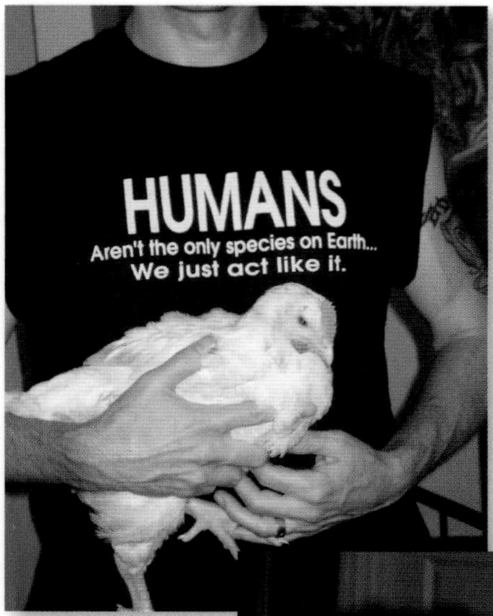
HUMANS
Aren't the only species on Earth...
We just act like it.

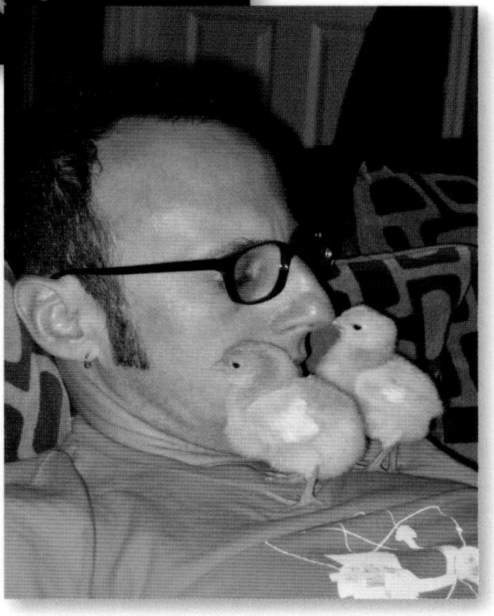

The first chicken we fostered (top), and a couple of chicks that stopped at our place in Brooklyn a year later on their way to a better life via our underground railroad. At factory egg farms, male chicks are useless and are often thrown into grinders alive. Females have their beaks burned off with a hot blade so they can't injure each other in their overcrowded cages.

I became a vegan in August 2002. Vegetarians eat no animals but consume eggs and dairy products because the animal is not killed in gathering them. A vegan consumes no animal products of any kind, including dairy, eggs, and anything containing gelatin or whey. I chose veganism because the dairy and egg industries are arguably the cruelest of them all. Many people don't realize that cows are not just "milk machines," but just like any mammal, don't give milk unless they have young to feed. If you're drinking milk, it means the calves for which it was intended are not. What happens to the calves?

You've likely heard about the horrible way veal calves are treated. Virtually all of them come from the dairy industry. They are taken from their mothers within a couple of days of birth, and most are chained in small boxes so they can't move around. They are fed an iron-deficient diet to keep their flesh pale and then slaughtered after a few months. Their mothers, who fight fiercely to keep their babies and mourn loudly for days after their removal, are often ill treated and commonly suffer from painful udder infections. These infections are routinely left untreated because they don't discernibly affect the quality of the milk. Federal laws regulate the amount of pus from this condition that is allowed in milk. And according to an April 2002 article in a leading dairy industry trade magazine, every single state's milk, on average, is well above that standard. Yum.

And in the end the animals from the dairy and egg industries end up in the same slaughterhouses and are treated as cruelly as ones raised solely for meat. A person who does not want to subsidize animal cruelty *must* give up dairy and eggs. There are many excellent substitutes available in virtually any market.

And don't be fooled by "free range" claims. There is no industry standard for this phrase and as often as not, it means only a slightly less miserable existence for the animals. There is, however, a growing industry of small local farmers hand-raising animals humanely, for meat, milk, and eggs. This is good news, but although they live more comfortable lives, these animals are still sacrificed for our sensory pleasure in the end, and that's something I can no longer abide. And, as in factory dairy farms, if you're drinking cow's milk, a calf is going without. I personally have no problem eating eggs from humanely treated chickens, but without visiting the farm personally, how can one be sure? It has been my experience that when money is involved, people will lie.

Making the decision to become a vegan was scary. It reminded me of when I decided to give up smoking. What sort of misery and denial was I letting myself in for? Would I begin sweating, shaking, and hallucinating as I went through fajita withdrawal? How long before I was sneaking out behind my wife's back to pick up a dime bag of chicken nuggets? And I could only imagine the sort of ridicule I would be receiving from my skeptical friends and relatives behind my back. (Probably the same sort I used to heap on animal rights nuts before I knew anything about it.)

To my great relief, however, the process was easier than I thought it would be, and the rewards have been far greater. This conversion in my diet and beliefs, even more than my resumption of painting several years before, was a true spiritual awakening. With my new knowledge came the desire to educate others, of course, and I eagerly joined my wife's efforts as an activist. I began to look for ways to get this message into *Bizarro* using approaches that my readers would still find entertaining and not too heavy handed. I had no illusions of changing the world but it seemed irresponsible to waste such a large potential audience. I've never been good at keeping quiet when I am aware of an injustice.

Drawing cartoons about animal abuse is like trying to write a comedy routine around pedophilia. The abuse of innocents just isn't funny. But I kept thinking about it and eventually came up with what I consider to be some fairly good efforts. The first one I did was a group of farm pigs building decoy pigs out of tofu as they plan to escape. I later realized that this cartoon inadvertently perpetuates the myth that food animals are still raised outdoors on bucolic farms. But it was only my first attempt.

It took me a long time to find ways to do cartoons about animal abuse issues. Living beings as victims of torture isn't a naturally funny topic.

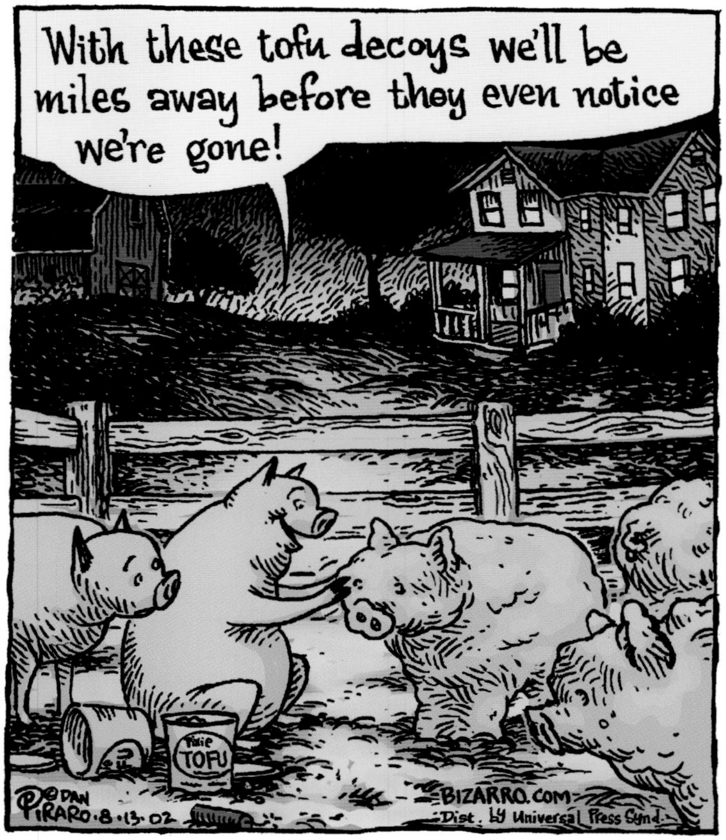
With these tofu decoys we'll be miles away before they even notice we're gone!
TOFU
©DAN PIRARO·8·13·02
BIZARRO.COM
Dist. by Universal Press Synd.

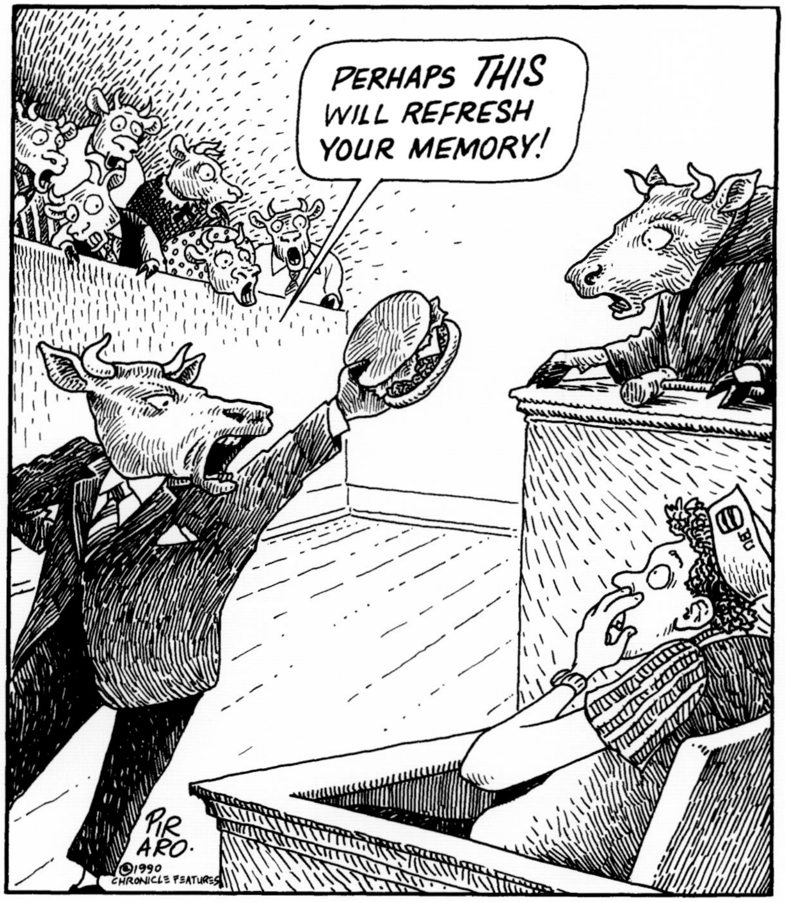
PERHAPS THIS WILL REFRESH YOUR MEMORY!
PIRARO
©1990 CHRONICLE FEATURES

When I drew this cartoon in 1990, I still thought animal rights people were nuts. Little did I know...

BELOW, LEFT: Almost as soon as I sent this cartoon in I wished I'd used a pig as the ghost and had Scrooge eating a traditional ham dinner. It's so obvious. Why am I so stupid? (Kids, the previous comment was written by a professional humorist for humorous effect. Self criticism is a dangerous habit and should not be tried at home without adult supervision.) (2002)

BELOW: Even before I became an animal rights activist, I found pet birds to be particularly sad. No matter how much your parrot appears to love you, it would rather be flying, plain and simple. Why not remove its wings and legs entirely, put a harness on it, and wear it around your neck like a pendant?

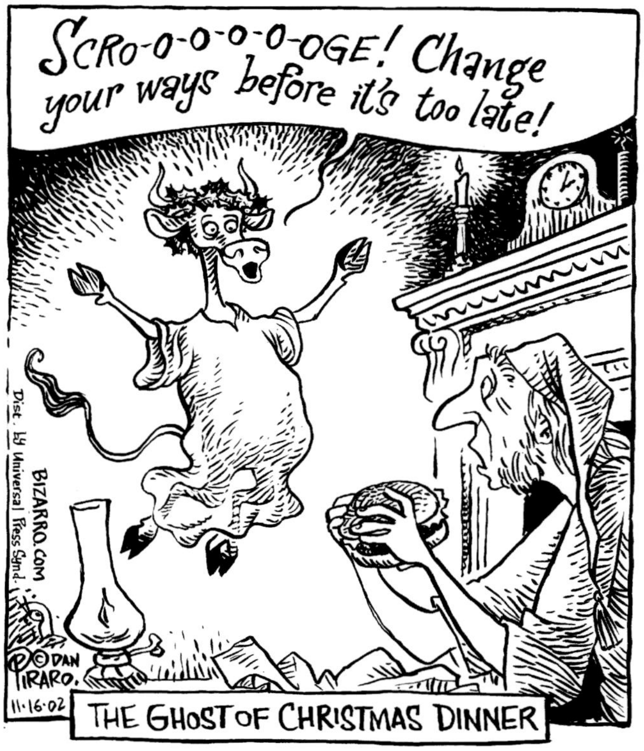
SCRO-O-O-O-O-OGE! Change your ways before it's too late!
BIZARRO.COM
Dist. by Universal Press Synd.
©DAN PIRARO 11-16-02
THE GHOST OF CHRISTMAS DINNER

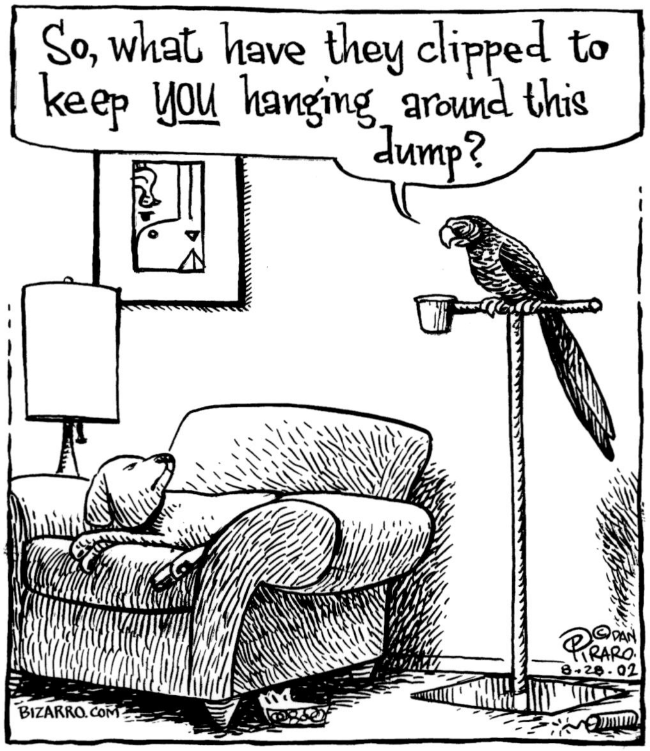
So, what have they clipped to keep YOU hanging around this dump?
©DAN PIRARO 8-28-02
BIZARRO.COM

RIGHT: Pretty much any idiot knows it's wrong to shove a metal tube down a bird's throat several times a day and force-feed it far more than it would normally eat until its liver becomes huge and it explodes. But some folks don't know this is how that pricey treat in restaurants is produced. (2004)

BELOW: Sadly, after the arduous journey to the slaughterhouse, many cattle are too weak and dehydrated to escape even if they were given the chance. (2003)

OPPOSITE: Not a particularly big problem in this country, but a good gag I thought. (2004)

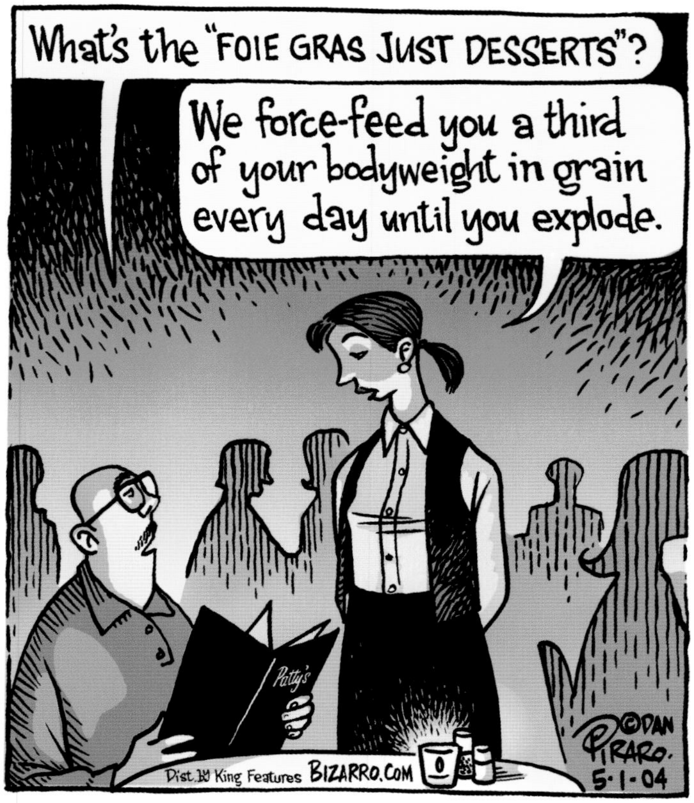
What's the "FOIE GRAS JUST DESSERTS"?
We force-feed you a third of your bodyweight in grain every day until you explode.
Patty's
Dist. by King Features BIZARRO.COM
©DAN PIRARO 5-1-04

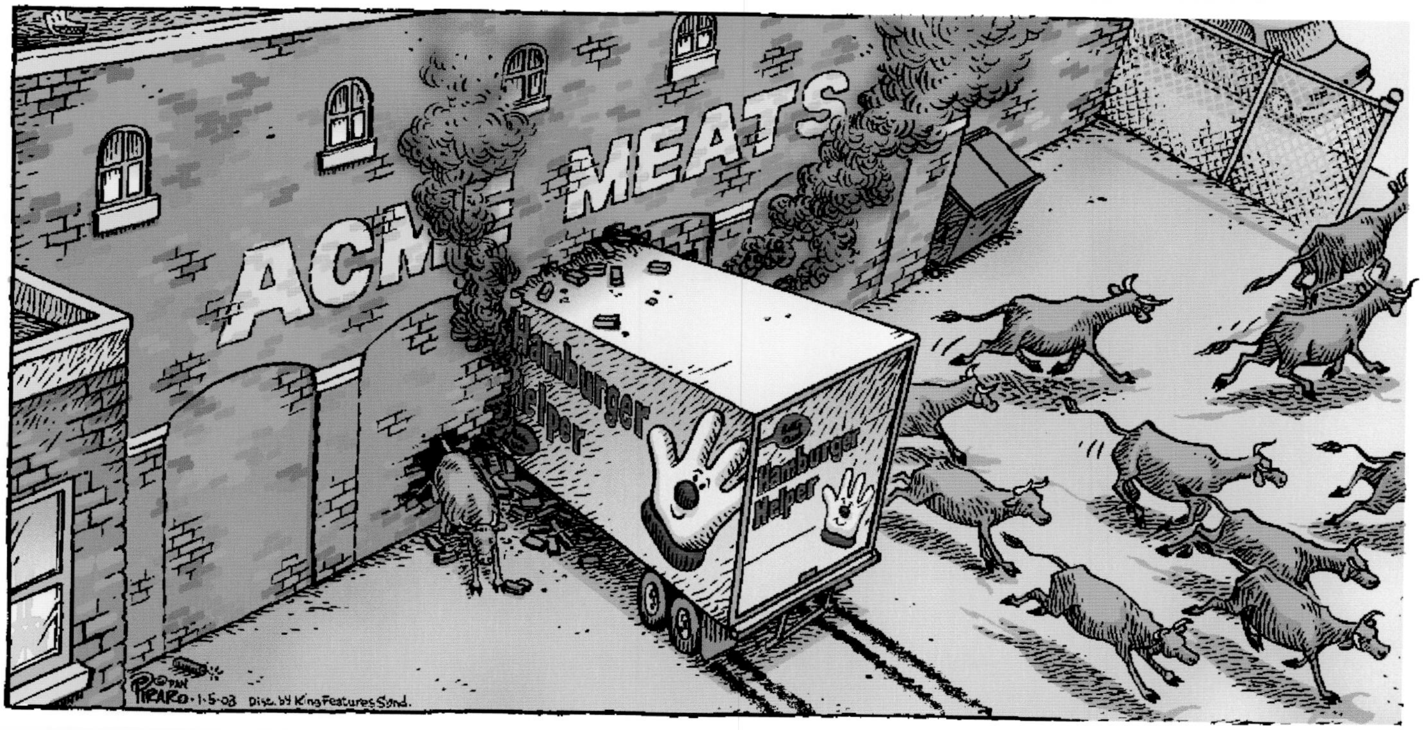
ACME MEATS
Hamburger Helper
Hamburger Helper
©DAN PIRARO 1-5-03 Dist. by King Features Synd.

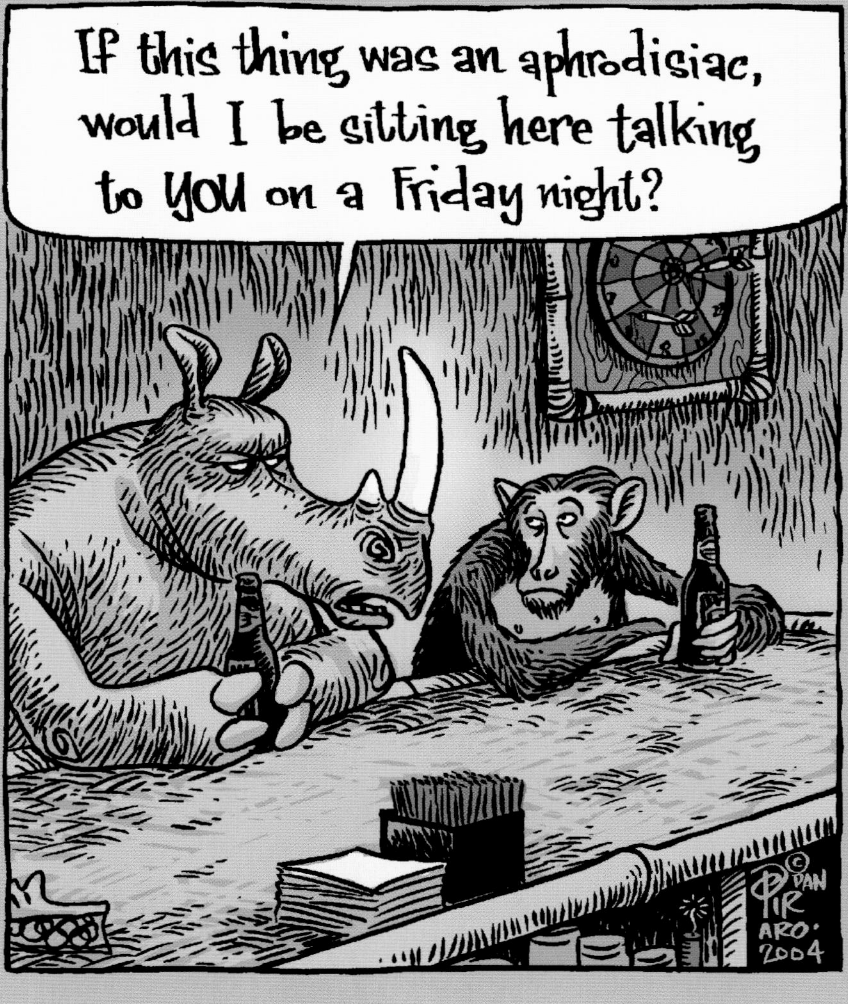
If this thing was an aphrodisiac, would I be sitting here talking to YOU on a Friday night?
© DAN PIRARO · 2004

Over the past few years, I've published dozens of cartoons about this issue, some funnier than others, some just poignant. But all of them fall within my guidelines for a cartoon that delivers a serious message but also has the potential to appeal to those not already on board with the cause.

A personal favorite is one I did at Christmas featuring the ghost of a turkey speaking to a reindeer outside Santa's Workshop. His admonition, "I'm just saying watch your back. I was a holiday icon, too, and look what happened to me," is an attempt to point out what has become a regular theme for me: the innate hypocrisy in revering some animals or species while wantonly abusing others for our own pleasure. From my point of view, few things are more blatantly hypocritical than a person dressed in a fur coat walking a pampered pooch on a leash. Unfortunately, this image is a staple of the Manhattan winter cityscape and I always wish I were able to approach such a person and say something. Instead, I said it in *Bizarro* (opposite).

Another personal favorite is a caged lab chimp asking the scientist, "Hey, Einstein, how about coming up with a cure for insensitivity to other species?" Most people assume, as I did until recently, that while medical experiments on other species may be cruel, they are necessary to our safety and health. In fact, much lab cruelty exists solely because there is so much money in it. As new drugs are developed, often to replace perfectly good drugs that no longer make money for a drug company because their patent has run out, animals are used in testing. And plenty of universities survive on government grants for research whether or not that research is aimed at saving human lives.

LIBERATION
LIBERATION

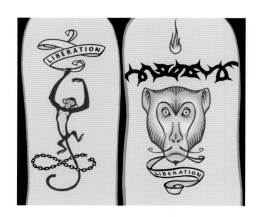

I designed these tattoos for my wife and me in 2003. (The larger arm is mine.) The rough sketch of the black "crown of thorns" strip above the head is a band I already had around my upper arm. The mustache and beard were added because I used to wear ones like that. The broken chain in my wife's design is in the shape of the mathematical symbol for infinity, to express the hope for the eventual end of animal slavery.*

**Free advice: If you get a tattoo, always be certain the artist has excellent taste and superior hand skills. Never use a fat, bald guy over fifty with a long beard who rides a Harley, unless you've personally seen his work and love it.*

Dist. by King Features
Next.
LUCKY
BIZARRO.COM
©DAN PIRARO 11·8·03
WHEN PENGUINS GET DRUNK

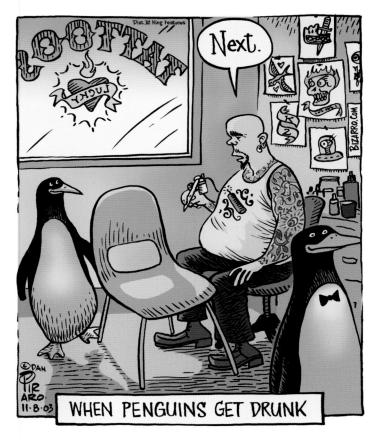

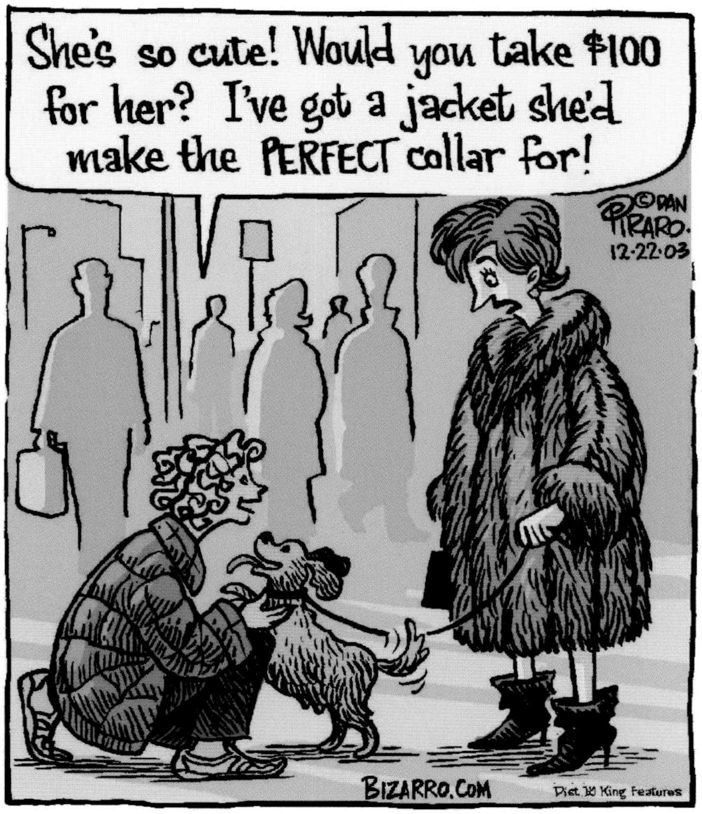
She's so cute! Would you take $100 for her? I've got a jacket she'd make the PERFECT collar for!
©DAN PIRARO. 12·22·03
BIZARRO.COM
Dist. by King Features

Few people know that all medical research isn't to save lives and that all lab animals aren't rats and mice. Much of the research is purely for profit, and many tens of thousands of dogs and cats are tortured and killed each year in laboratories.

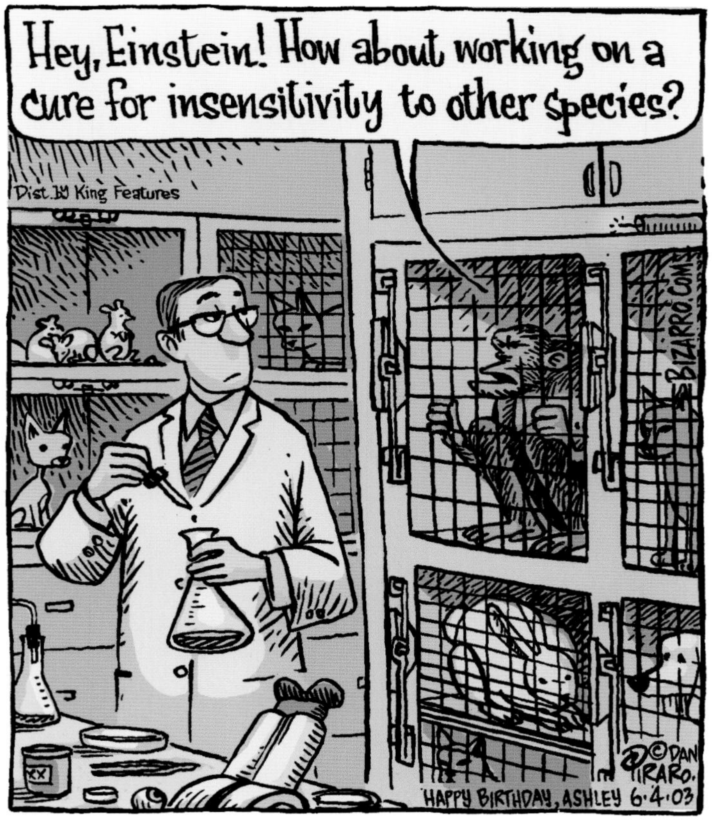
Hey, Einstein! How about working on a cure for insensitivity to other species?
Dist. by King Features
BIZARRO.COM
©DAN PIRARO.
HAPPY BIRTHDAY, ASHLEY 6·4·03

I included dogs and cats in this cartoon since few people realize how many dogs and cats (in addition to guinea pigs, rabbits, nonhuman primates, and other animals) are used in laboratory testing. Some puppies and kittens are raised for this specific purpose. In 2002, the most recent year from which test data is available, 68,253 dogs and 24,222 cats were used in research in the United States. Hundreds of thousands of animals are used annually to test the safety of household chemicals and cosmetics—to find out what side effect you might expect if you should happen to accidentally pour bleach into your eye, or poke a hole in your cornea with a mascara wand. These animals are rarely afforded the expense of anesthetics. If this bothers you, you can stop rewarding companies that test on animals with your consumer dollars.

For more information on this subject, check out the website for the Physicians Committee for Responsible Medicine (pcrm.org). PCRM is a group of physicians and laypeople working to promote compassionate and effective medical research (no animal testing) and practice. They know what they're talking about. And they aren't crystal-worshiping animal rights hippies living in VW vans.

The truly grand hypocrisy of this whole practice is that as a society we are saying, "We test on animals because they are so like us, but it is morally acceptable to test on them because they are *not* like us." This "not as good as us" argument has been used countless times through history when people have wanted to exploit not only other species but also each other: blacks, Jews, women, children, the physically and mentally disabled. Nowadays, most people agree that human exploitation is clearly wrong, but that we must draw a line between humans and other animals. But the only substantive biological difference between humans and many other species is our degree of intelligence. If disparity in IQ is a license to abuse, why not eat the mentally handicapped?

I got some mail from people who felt sorry for Roy Horn, the goofball Las Vegas magician who was attacked by one of his tigers a couple of weeks before this cartoon ran. My sympathy immediately went to the tiger. Of the two beings involved, only Horn was there by choice. I've often thought of marketing a squeaky cat toy that looks like him, but it's probably too late now. I'm sure I'm not the only person to have thought of it. (2003)

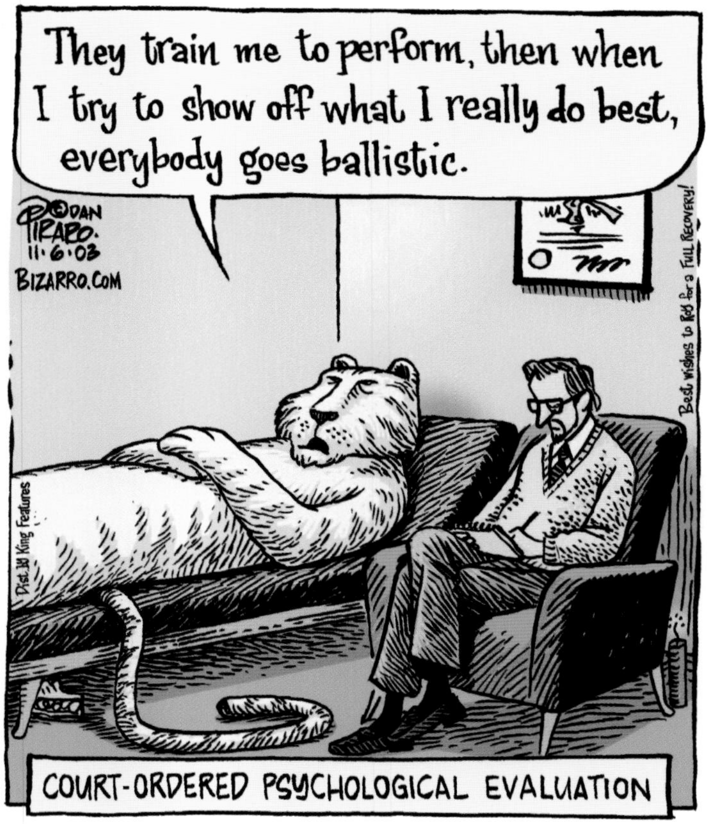
They train me to perform, then when I try to show off what I really do best, everybody goes ballistic.
©DAN PIRARO 11·6·03
BIZARRO.COM
Dist. by King Features
COURT-ORDERED PSYCHOLOGICAL EVALUATION

In human development, a baby's first awareness is only of herself. Very quickly, her awareness expands to include her mother and father. As a toddler, her growing circle of compassion ideally includes her siblings, close friends, relatives, and neighbors. Through the years she is encouraged to widen her compassion to include people she cannot see—her community, the residents of her city, state, and country. A well-rounded adult has compassion for all people worldwide. My assertion is that expanding one's compassion to include all thinking, feeling beings is a natural progression of intelligence, and one that I hope one day becomes a common feature of our social evolution.

At this point in the debate, people often bring in religious beliefs, citing the possession of a soul as defining our moral superiority over our fellow mammals. Putting other obvious difficulties with that argument aside, I will say only that that very argument was used for centuries by white people against blacks. If we are morally superior to other species, why then do we not rise above our animal nature and stop exploiting others for our own pleasure? One would think that having a soul would first and foremost incline one to spare other creatures from unnecessary suffering. If God created animals for our exploitation and sanctions our indifference to their suffering, why did he give them the ability to feel pain? An excellent book by a Christian (and Republican, of all things) that deals with this very contradiction is *Dominion: The Power of Man, the Suffering of Animals, and the Call to Mercy* by Matthew Scully.

Another famous argument is that we've been eating animals for tens of thousands of years, thus making it "natural." We've also been taking slaves, waging war, polluting our planet, and abusing women and children since the beginning of time. Precedence is a poor excuse for abuse.

Physical evidence—the shape of our teeth and jaws, the length of our digestive tract, the chemical makeup of our saliva and stomach, our poor night vision, and our natural revulsion at the smell of a dead animal—shows us clearly to have begun as herbivores. Some argue that while we started as vegetarians, we have "evolved" to eat meat. Biologically speaking, we haven't changed at all in this regard. You might as well say we've evolved to smoke tobacco. We've been doing it for centuries and we enjoy it, but we haven't developed a natural need for it, or a defense against its ill effects.

Injecting these themes and ideas into *Bizarro* was gratifying, but I wanted to be able to say more than I was able to in a cartoon. So I've begun putting my strongest feelings about animal cruelty into paintings. The first I did was called *Champion Cat Rescuer Shares Chicken Recipe* (see page 96). It challenges those who champion cats and dogs while their lifestyle subsidizes the routine abuse of so many other equally sentient animals. It's amazing to me, but many animal welfare crusaders are not vegetarians and sometimes even serve meat at their fund-raisers. Though I used to be a meat-eating champion of dogs and cats myself, from my current perspective, I find this astounding. Having worked with farm animals personally, I can assure you that they are just as personable as any dog or cat. It is absurd to think of them suffering horribly on factory farms and then being brutally butchered to provide appetizers for pet rescue fund-raisers.

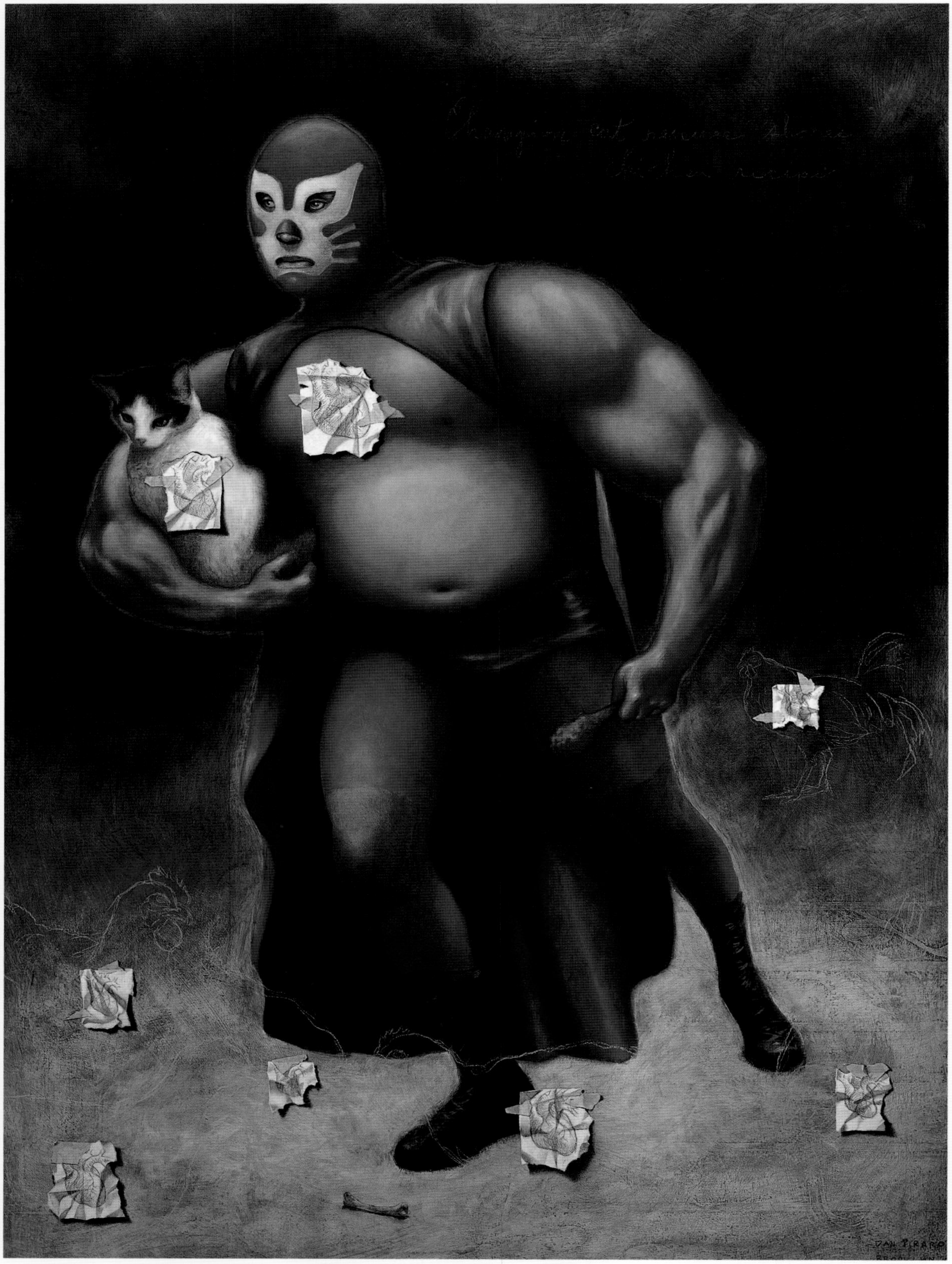
DAN PIRARO

OPPOSITE: *Champion Cat Rescuer Shares Chicken Recipe* (2004, oil on canvas, 40" x 30"). My first animal rights–themed painting, based on the hypocrisy of dedicating your life to rescuing dogs and cats but subsidizing the abuse of other species by eating meat.

LEFT: *Champion Cat Rescuer* (detail). The hearts represent the similarities among all species, which far outweigh our differences.

BELOW: *Delicious Possessions #3* (2004, oil on canvas, 12" x 12"). This is my favorite of a series of paintings of pet heads on plates. Our presumed "ownership" of other animals leads to contradictions in the way we treat them.

As a result of overfishing and pollution, life is disappearing from our oceans at an alarming rate and many scientists believe we have already passed the point of no return. Hundreds of thousands of seals are being mercilessly slaughtered annually in Canada because fishermen convinced the government they were serious competition for the few remaining fish in their waters.

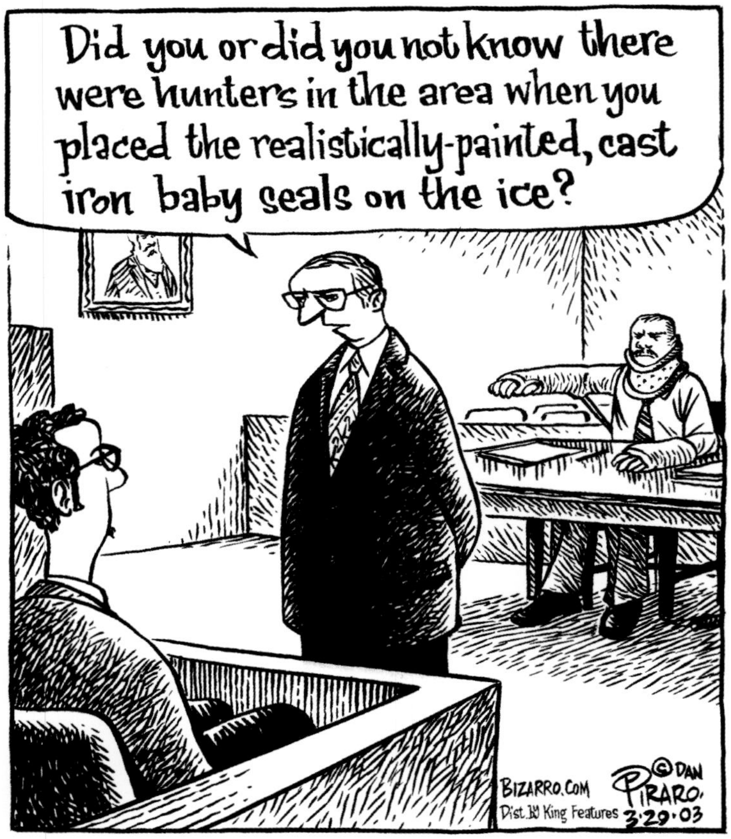
Did you or did you not know there were hunters in the area when you placed the realistically-painted, cast iron baby seals on the ice?
BIZARRO.COM
Dist. by King Features
© DAN PIRARO. 3·29·03

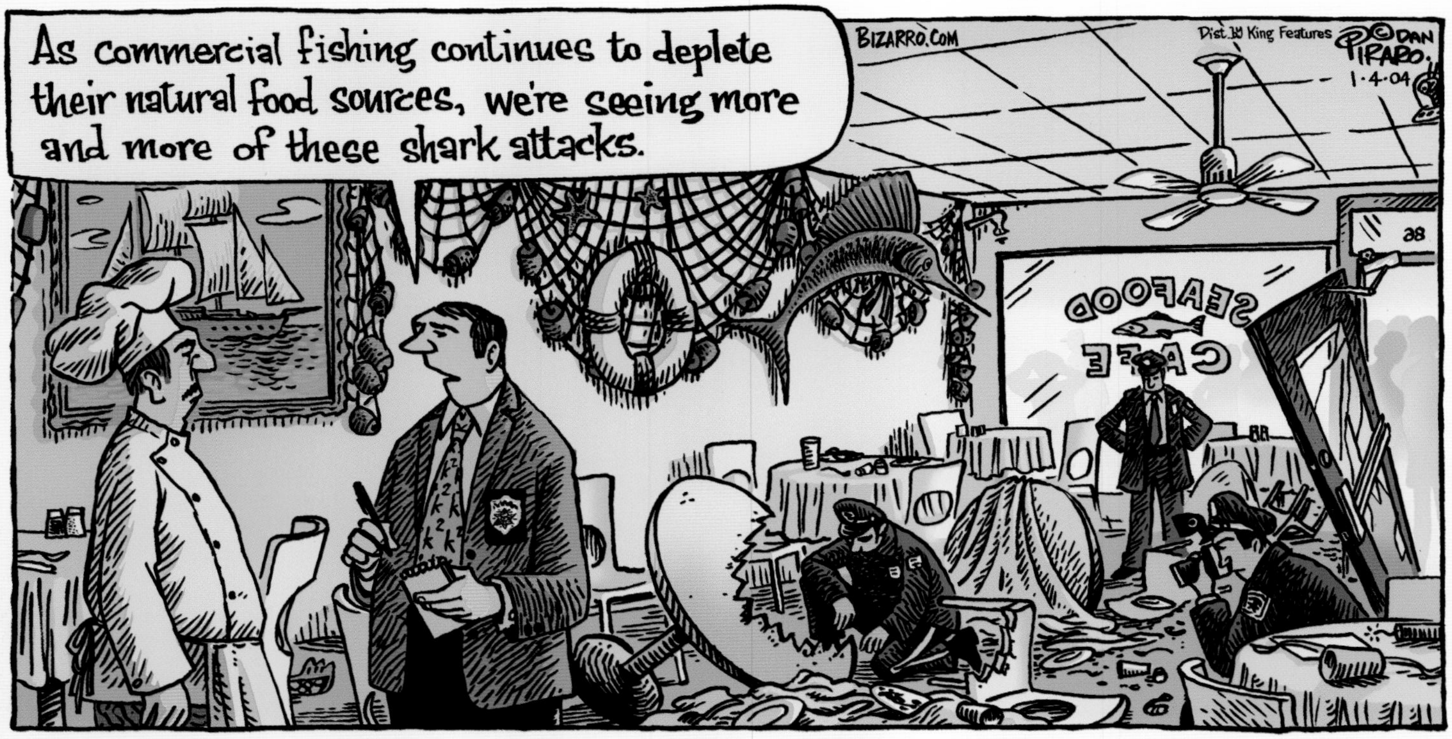
As commercial fishing continues to deplete their natural food sources, we're seeing more and more of these shark attacks.
BIZARRO.COM
Dist. by King Features
© DAN PIRARO. 1·4·04
SEAFOOD CAFE

My animal activism led to some startling revelations about the environmental damage huge factory farms cause. Even more devastating is the impact on the oceans of fish farms and commercial fishing. Our irresponsible use and abuse of the planet goes well beyond animal abuse in a connected series of activities and industries that has led to chain reactions in the environment that are close to being irreversible. According to a recent issue of *National Geographic* dedicated to the subject of global warming, we'll likely see major effects on our communities and our health within a generation.

Should we really care about this stuff or is it just some far-distant science-fiction monster that we'll figure out how to kill moments before it eats Chicago? Will some science egghead come up with a magical fix at the last minute? *National Geographic* reports that even if we stopped all our damaging behavior today (yeah, that's likely), it would be another lifetime before the planet could return to what we called normal even ten years ago.

This is the sort of information that makes me want to run screaming into the streets to warn people, like that guy at the end of *Invasion of the Body Snatchers.* But instead, I include these ideas in my work. At least when half the world is underwater and nobody's kid can leave the house without an asthma inhaler and safety glasses for all three sets of eyes, it won't be because I didn't warn them with silly drawings and a handful of paintings.

These two cartoons go along with my favorite saying: "Humans aren't the only species on Earth. We just act like it." (2004, 2005)

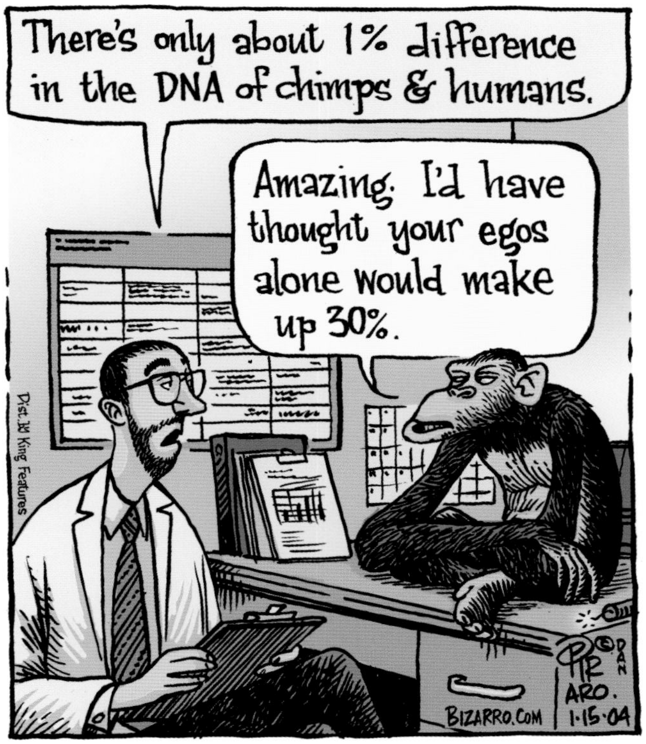
There's only about 1% difference in the DNA of chimps & humans.
Amazing. I'd have thought your egos alone would make up 30%.
Dist. by King Features
BIZARRO.COM
©DAN PIRARO. 1·15·04

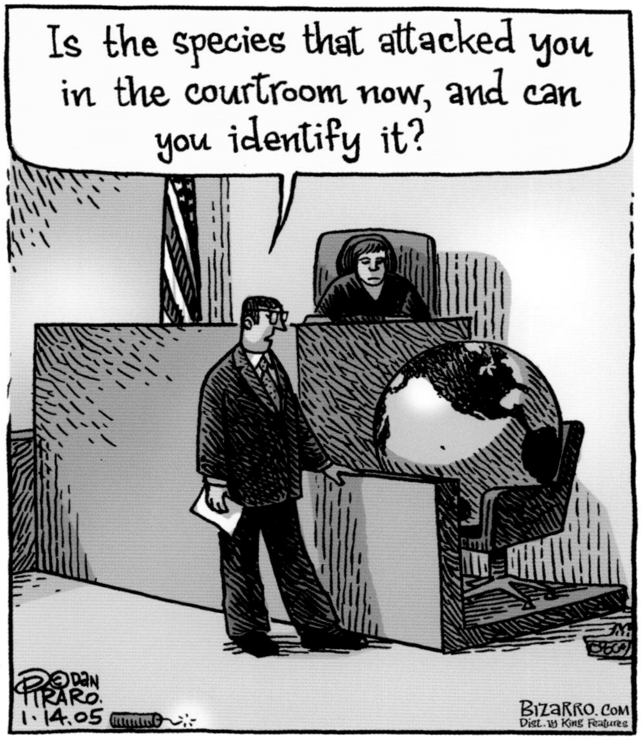
Is the species that attacked you in the courtroom now, and can you identify it?
©DAN PIRARO. 1·14·05
BIZARRO.COM
Dist. by King Features

I created these four illustrations for my website. They were later used on T-shirts and cards as fund-raisers for Farm Sanctuary, PETA, and other animal rescue groups.

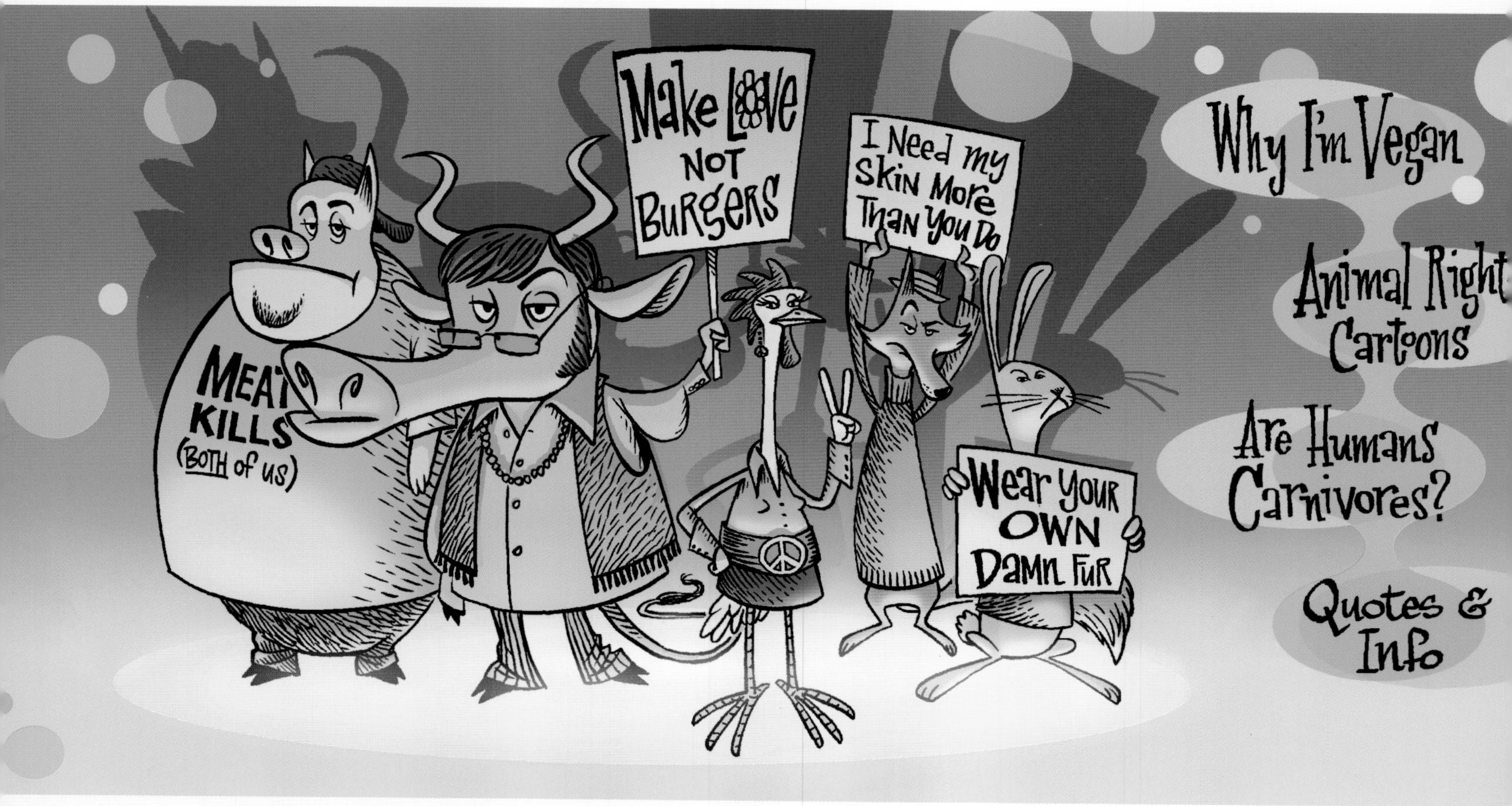

MEAT KILLS (BOTH of us)
Make Love NOT BURGERS
I Need my SKIN More Than You Do
Wear Your OWN Damn Fur
Why I'm Vegan
Animal Right Cartoons
Are Humans Carnivores?
Quotes & Info

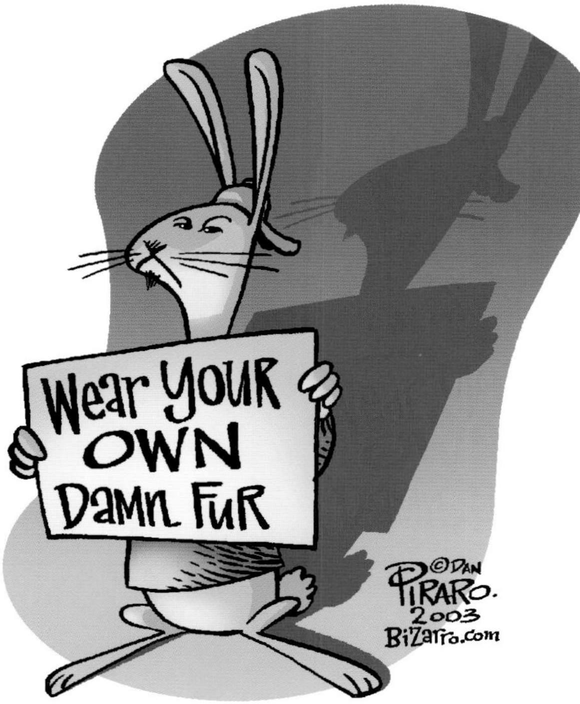
Wear YOUR OWN Damn Fur
©DAN PIRARO. 2003 BiZarro.com

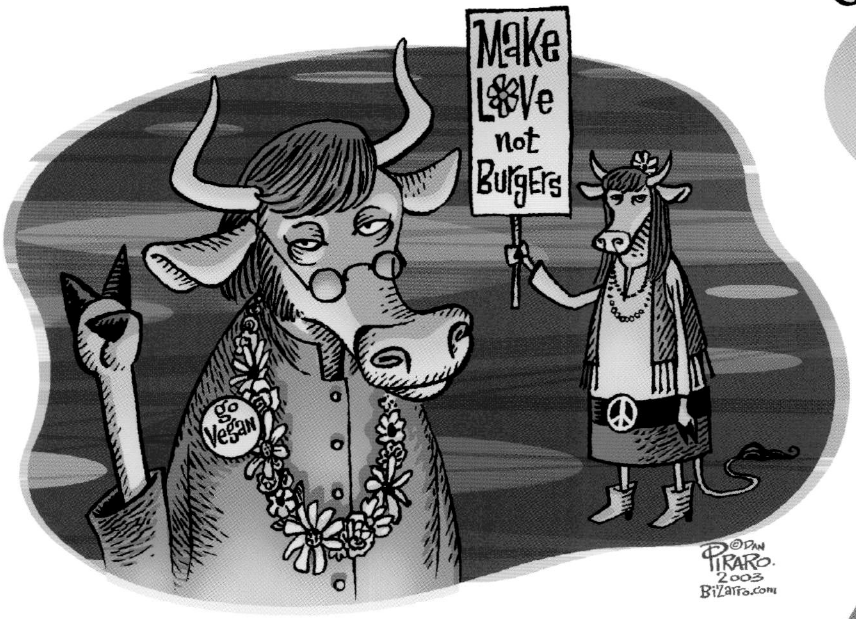
Make Love not Burgers
go Vegan
©DAN PIRARO. 2003 BiZarro.com

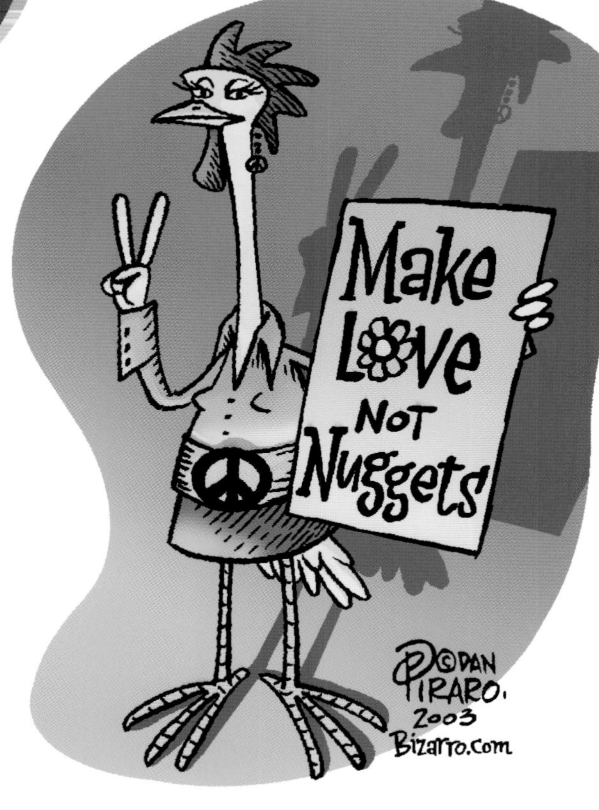
Make Love NOT Nuggets
©DAN PIRARO. 2003 Bizarro.com

Pirates, vikings, and cowboys

When I was a very young boy, many television shows and movies were about the Old West, as the industry had not yet gotten into the sci-fi phase of the late sixties. My earliest career aspiration was to be a cowboy. Growing up in Oklahoma and Texas cured me of that, but I still love doing cartoons about it. Other popular fantasy characters for me were Vikings and pirates.

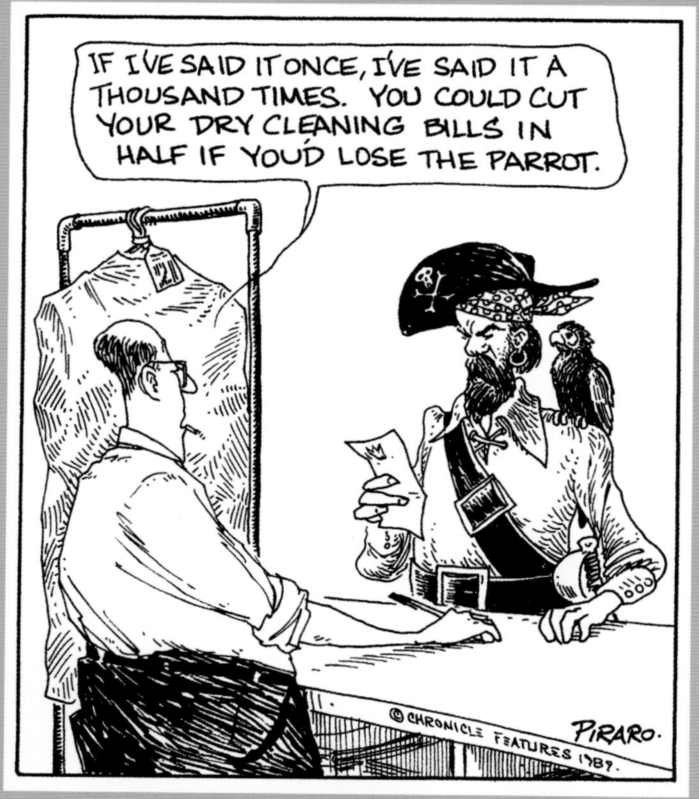
IF I'VE SAID IT ONCE, I'VE SAID IT A THOUSAND TIMES. YOU COULD CUT YOUR DRY CLEANING BILLS IN HALF IF YOU'D LOSE THE PARROT.
© CHRONICLE FEATURES 1987.
PIRARO.

My favorite jokes are ones that look like one thing, but the punch line leads you in a completely different direction. Being fooled like that always makes me laugh. (1998)

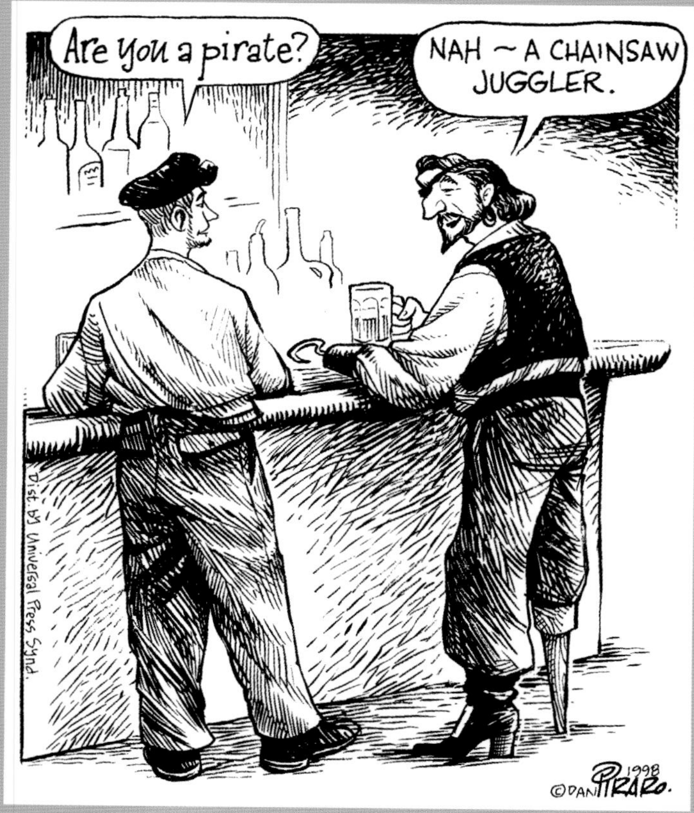
Are you a pirate?
NAH ~ A CHAINSAW JUGGLER.
Dist. by Universal Press Synd.
©DAN PIRARO. 1998

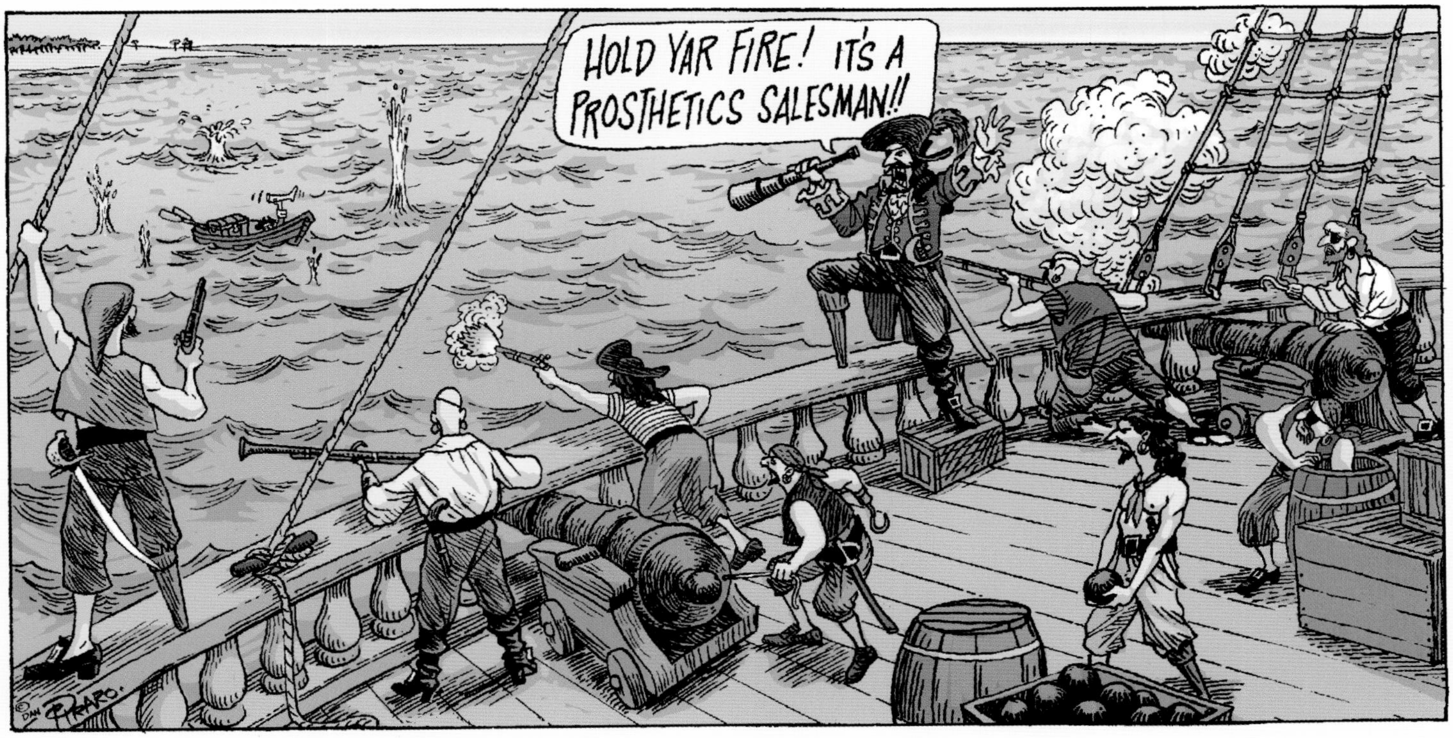
HOLD YAR FIRE! IT'S A PROSTHETICS SALESMAN!!

I got a couple of complaints from able-bodied people about the insensitivity of this cartoon, but several letters of thanks from amputees who thought it was great. A company that makes prosthetic limbs licensed it for T-shirts to give to clients. (1995)

My cartoons have experienced a fair amount of popularity in Sweden and Norway and I've been there twice for promotional reasons. I found both countries and their people to be wonderful and their history to be rich in cartoon opportunities. Vikings have almost as much cartoon fertility as pirates. My cartoons have been published there in a monthly magazine called *Bizarro*, filled mostly with my work but also including a few other American syndicated features and work by a couple of Scandinavian cartoonists.

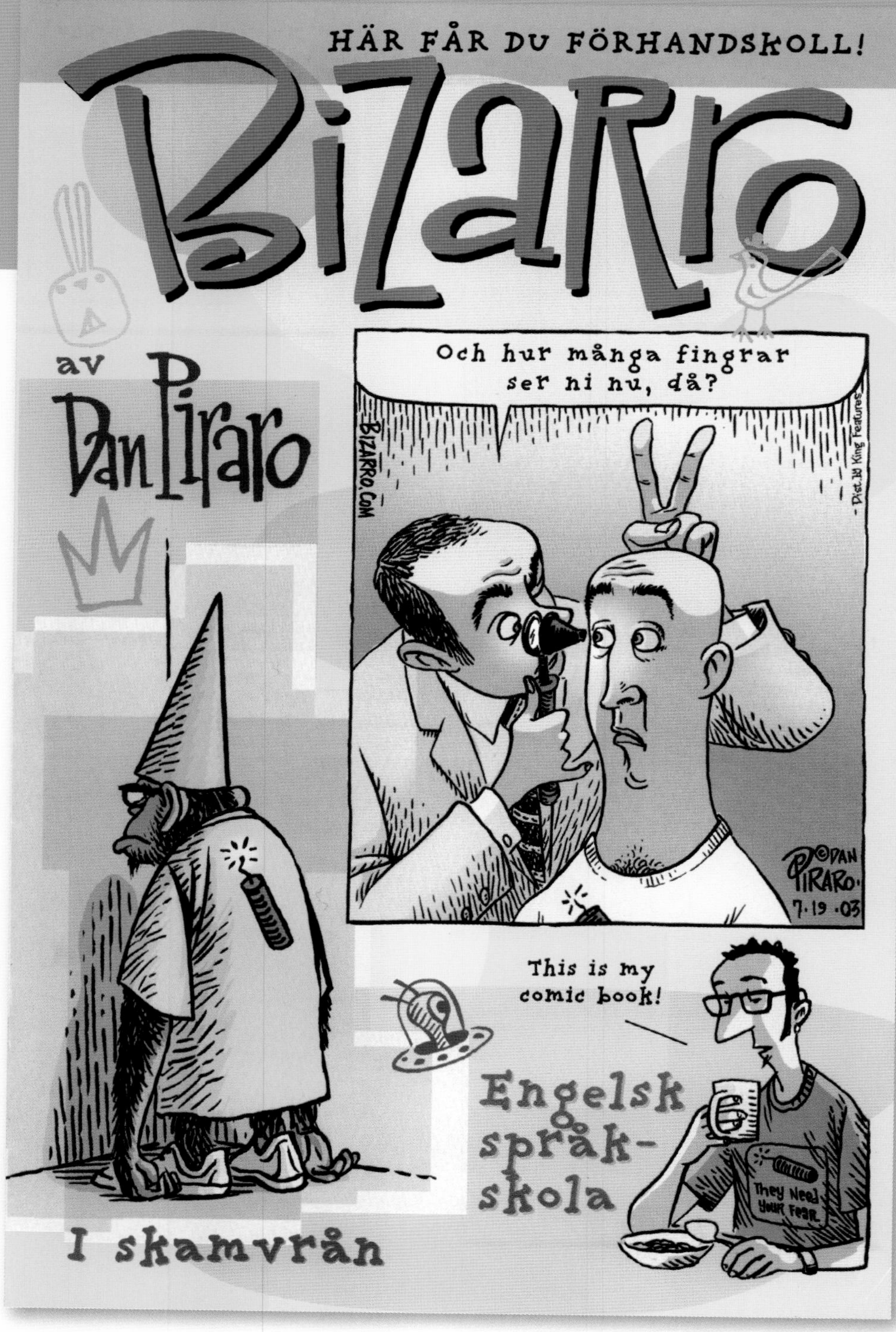

HÄR FÅR DU FÖRHANDSKOLL!
Bizarro
av Dan Piraro
Och hur många fingrar ser ni nu, då?
BIZARRO.COM
Dist. by King Features
©DAN PIRARO 7.19.03
This is my comic book!
Engelsk språk-skola
They Need Your Fear
I skamvrån

This is the cover of *Bizarro* monthly magazine in Norway or Sweden, not sure which. I can't tell their languages apart, frankly. People often ask me if I translate them myself. "*Ja*," I respond. I also operate the printing presses, drive the distribution trucks, stock the shelves, and make change.

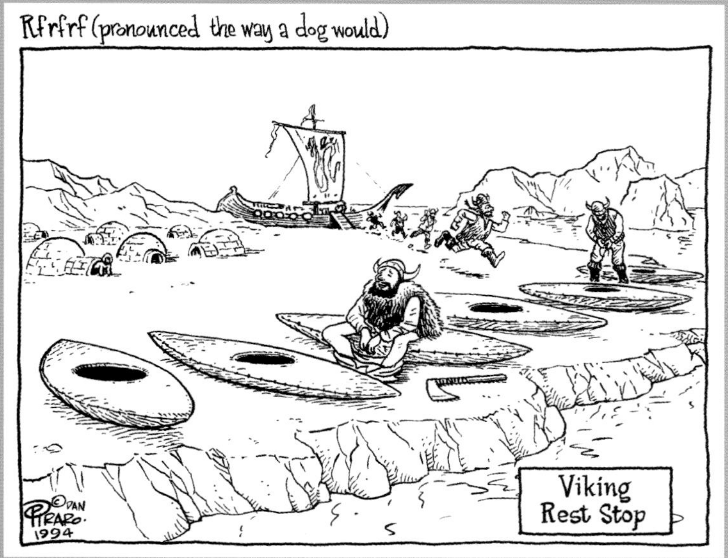
Rfrfrf (pronounced the way a dog would)
Viking Rest Stop
©DAN PIRARO. 1994

Because Scandinavians aren't as puritanical as Americans, I sent them cartoons that I couldn't put in American newspapers. They published them in a special feature called *Rfrfrf* (pronounced the way a dog would), which was a page of three or four adult cartoons in each issue.

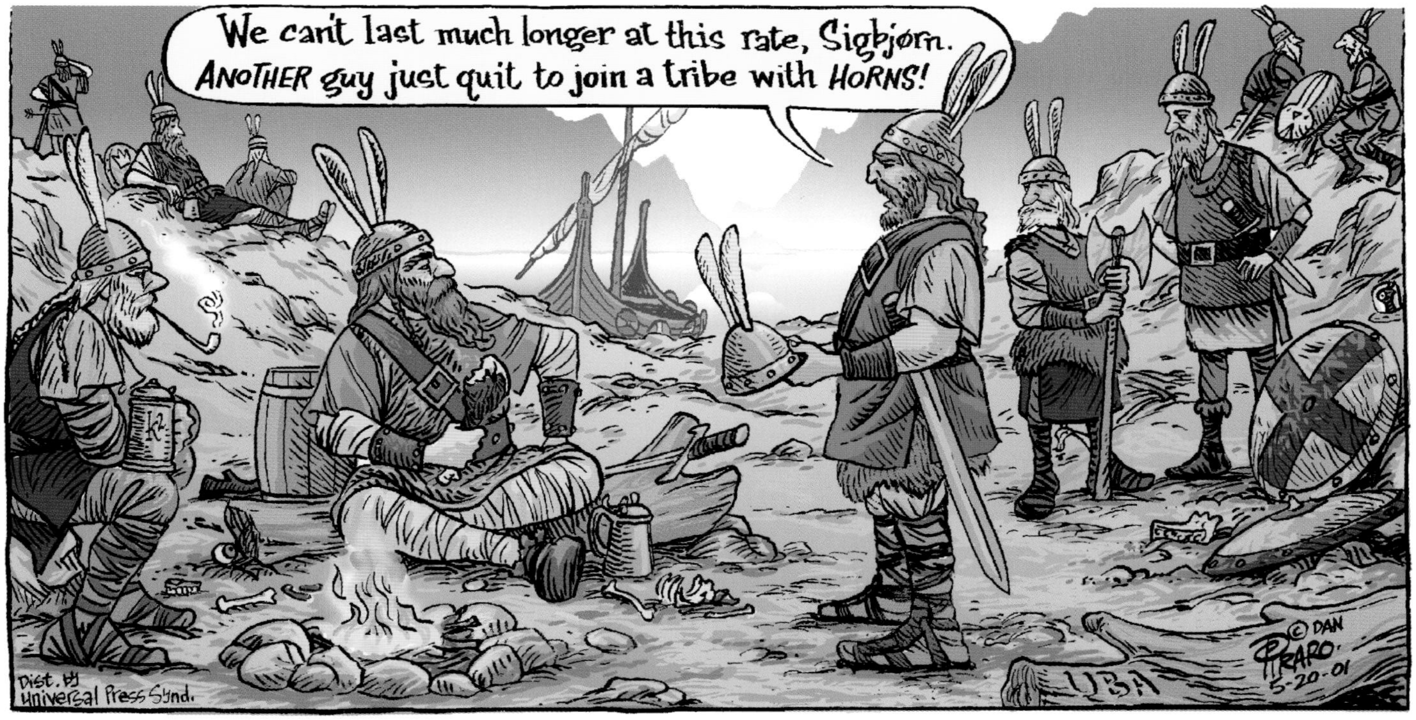
We can't last much longer at this rate, Sigbjørn. ANOTHER guy just quit to join a tribe with HORNS!
Dist. by Universal Press Synd.
© DAN PIRARO. 5-20-01

Since I was born eight years before *Star Trek's* TV debut, my early memories are filled with cowboy TV shows and movies. Though I loved the space shows when they began popping up, to this day I still do more cowboy cartoons than outer-space ones. Never underestimate the power of those formative years.

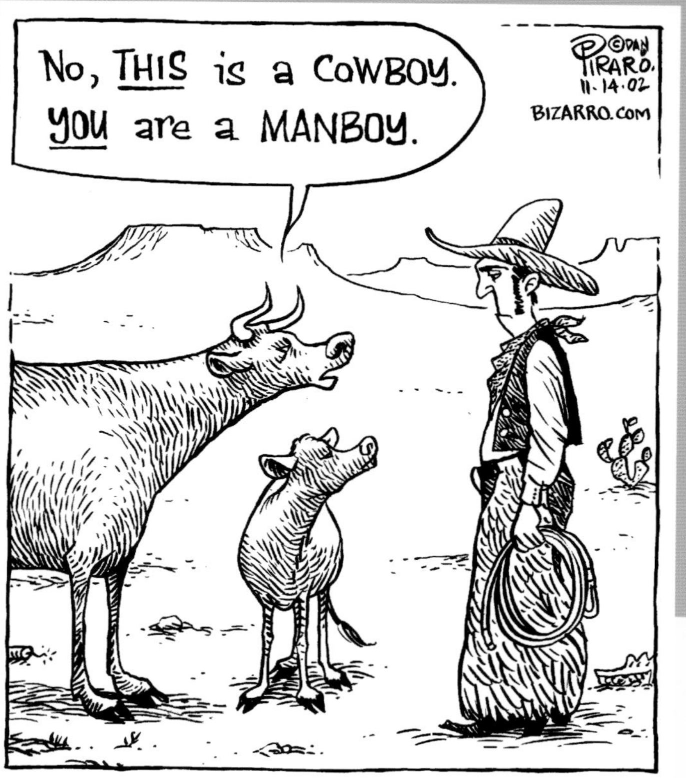
No, THIS is a COWBOY. YOU are a MANBOY.
©DAN PIRARO. 11.14.02
BIZARRO.COM

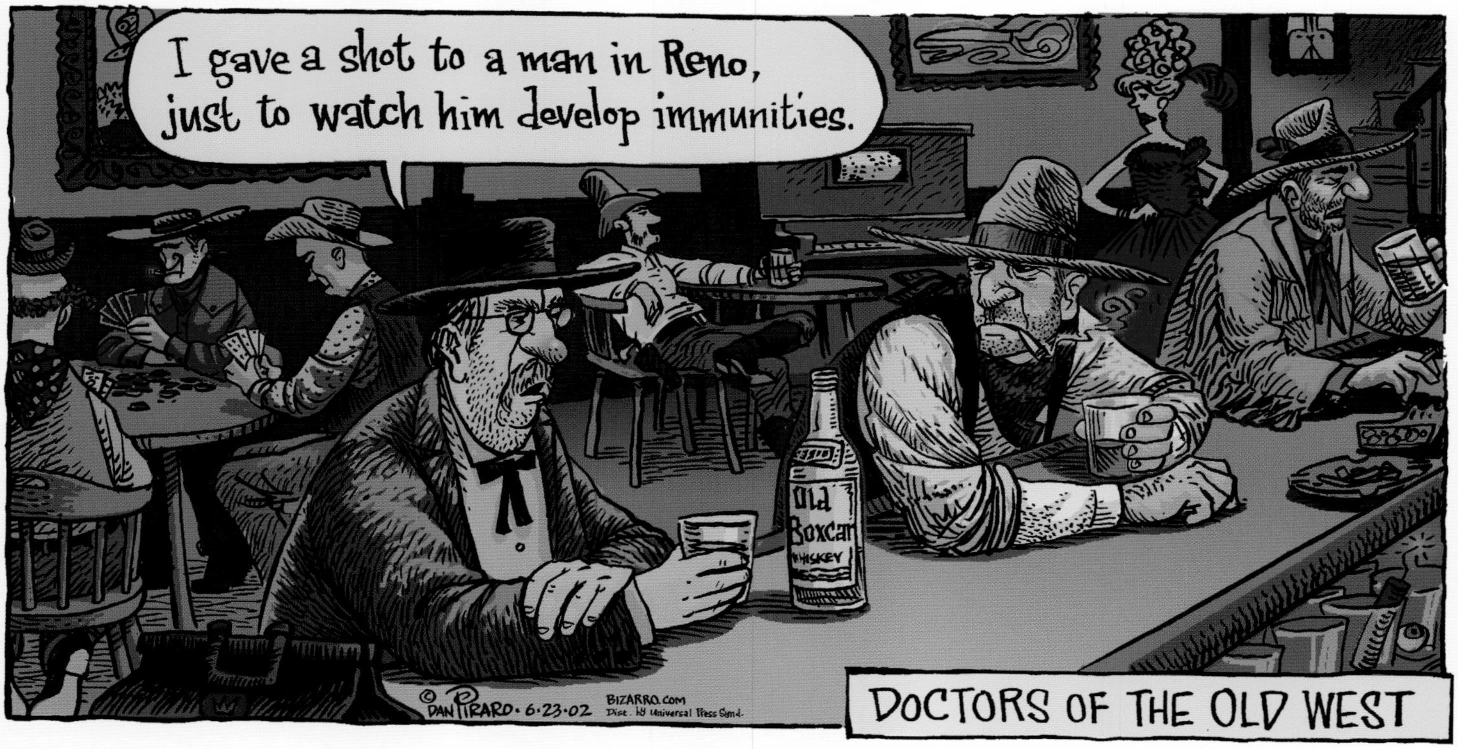
I gave a shot to a man in Reno, just to watch him develop immunities.
Old Boxcar Whiskey
©DAN PIRARO. 6.23.02
BIZARRO.COM
DOCTORS OF THE OLD WEST

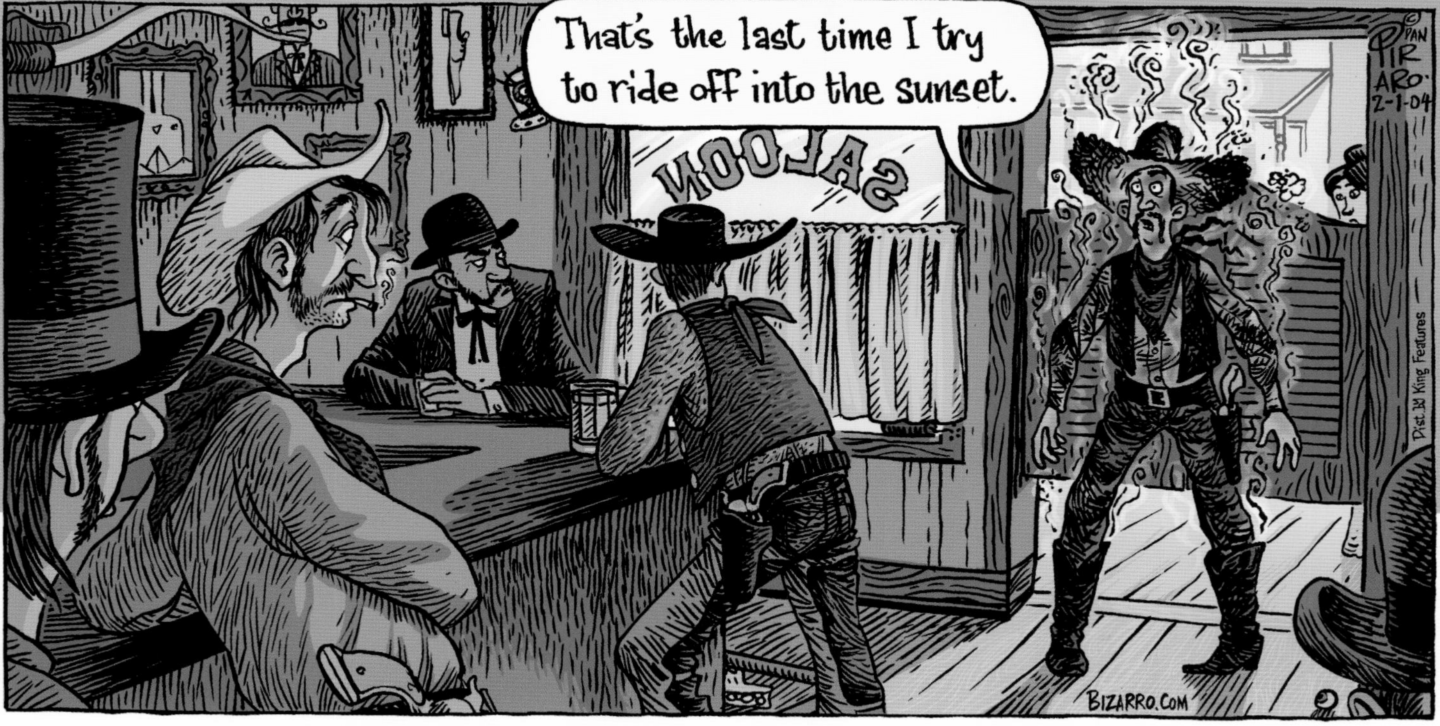
That's the last time I try to ride off into the sunset.
SALOON
©DAN PIRARO 2-1-04
Dist. by King Features
BIZARRO.COM

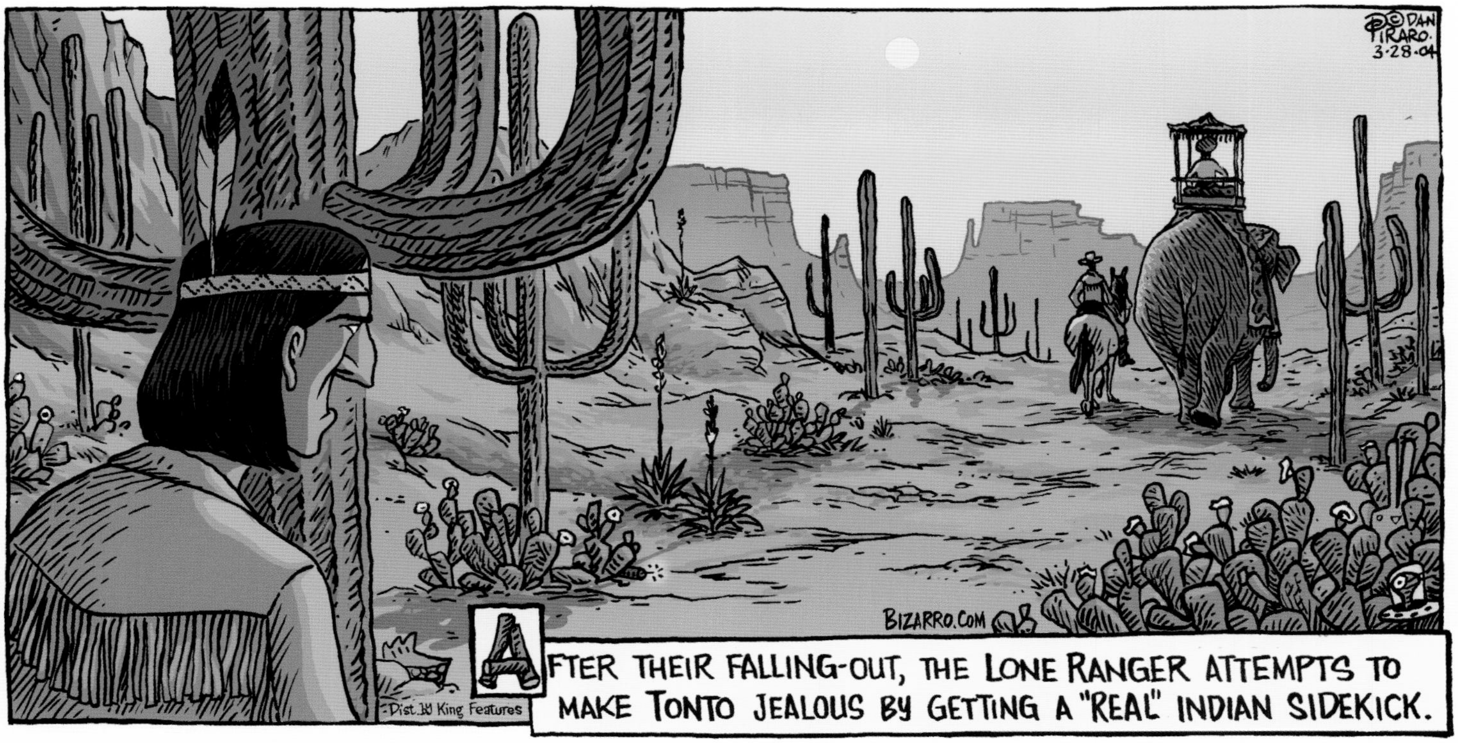
©DAN PIRARO 3-28-04
BIZARRO.COM
Dist. by King Features
AFTER THEIR FALLING-OUT, THE LONE RANGER ATTEMPTS TO MAKE TONTO JEALOUS BY GETTING A "REAL" INDIAN SIDEKICK.

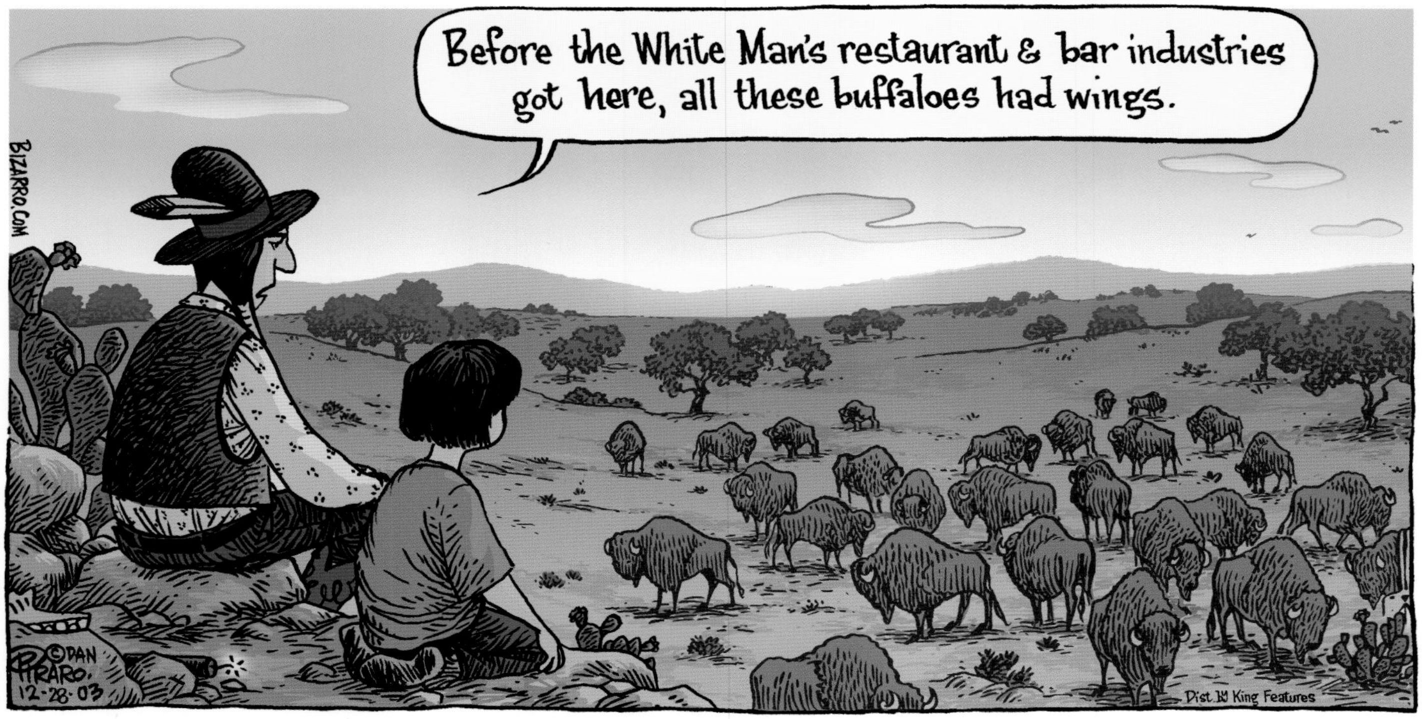
Before the White Man's restaurant & bar industries got here, all these buffaloes had wings.
BIZARRO.COM
©DAN PIRARO. 12-28-03
Dist. by King Features

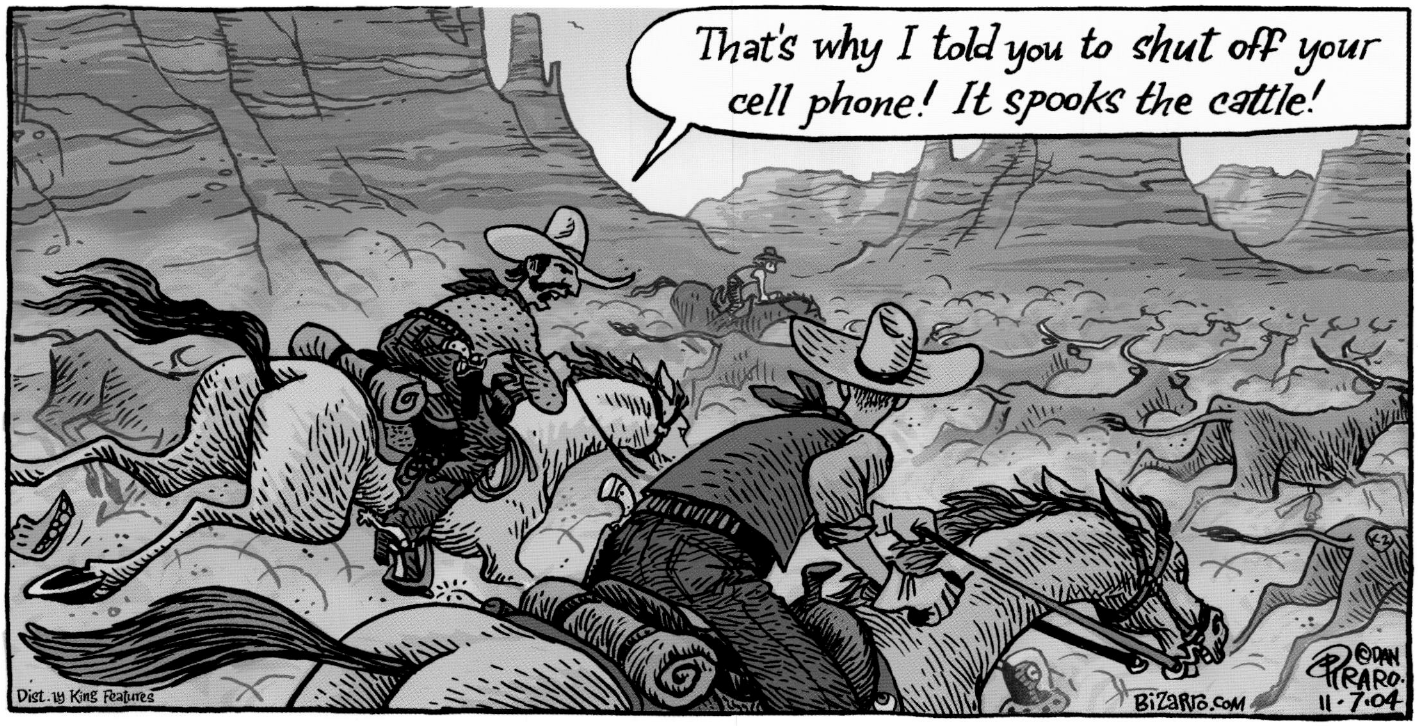
That's why I told you to shut off your cell phone! It spooks the cattle!
Dist. by King Features
BIZARRO.COM
©DAN PIRARO. 11-7-04

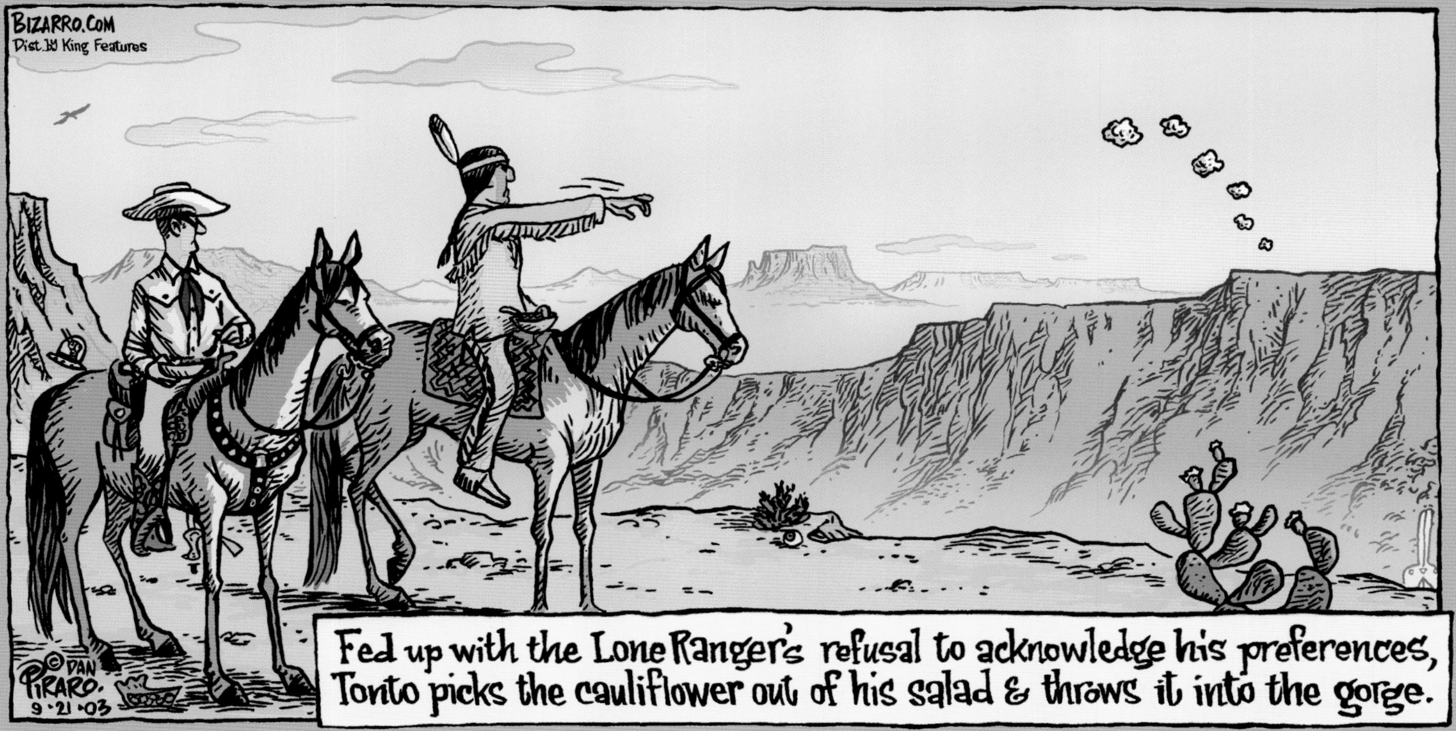
BIZARRO.COM
Dist. by King Features
© DAN PIRARO. 9·21·03
Fed up with the Lone Ranger's refusal to acknowledge his preferences, Tonto picks the cauliflower out of his salad & throws it into the gorge.

Every now and then I happen across an idea that meets all my requirements for a great cartoon: humor, surprise, absurdity, cool art. This is one of those rare creations. It was especially satisfying after so many years of doing cartoons that spoof the smoke signals motif. (2003)

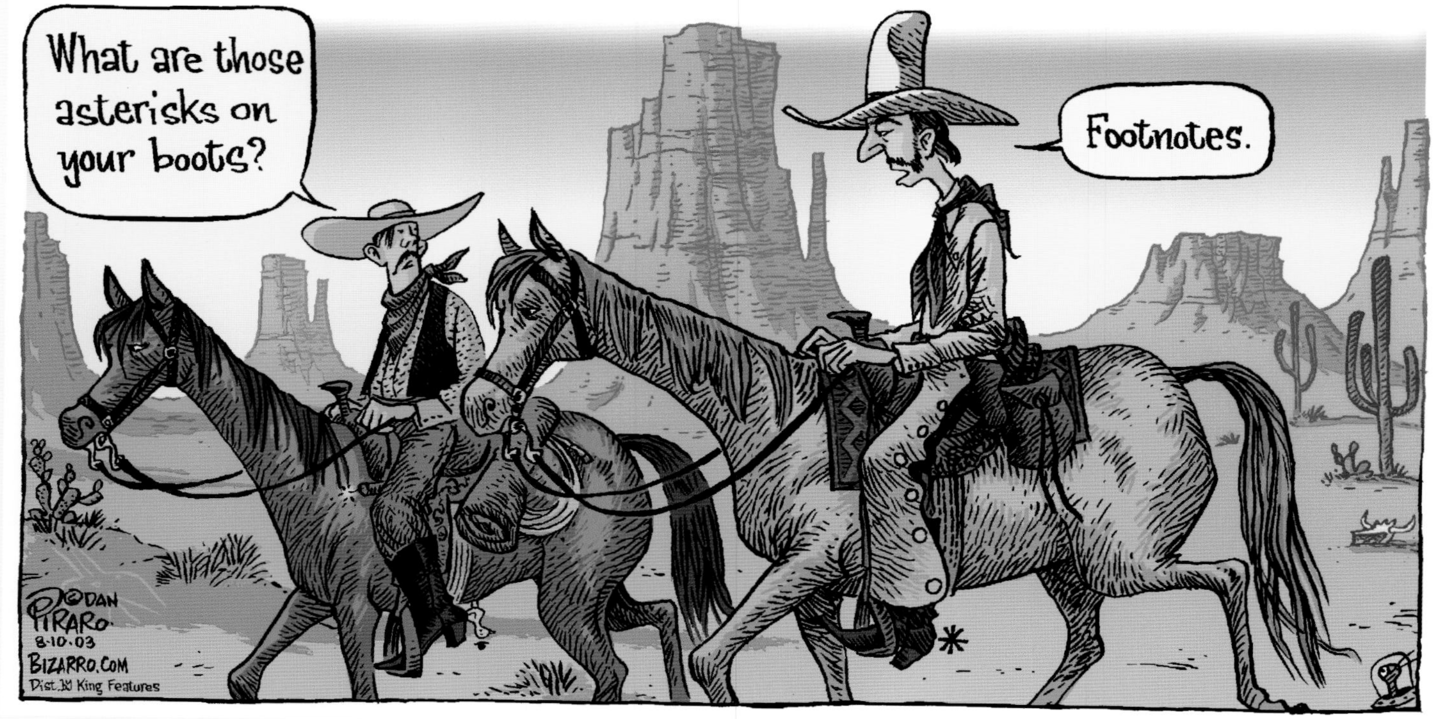
What are those asterisks on your boots?
Footnotes.
©DAN PIRARO 8-10-03
BIZARRO.COM
Dist. by King Features

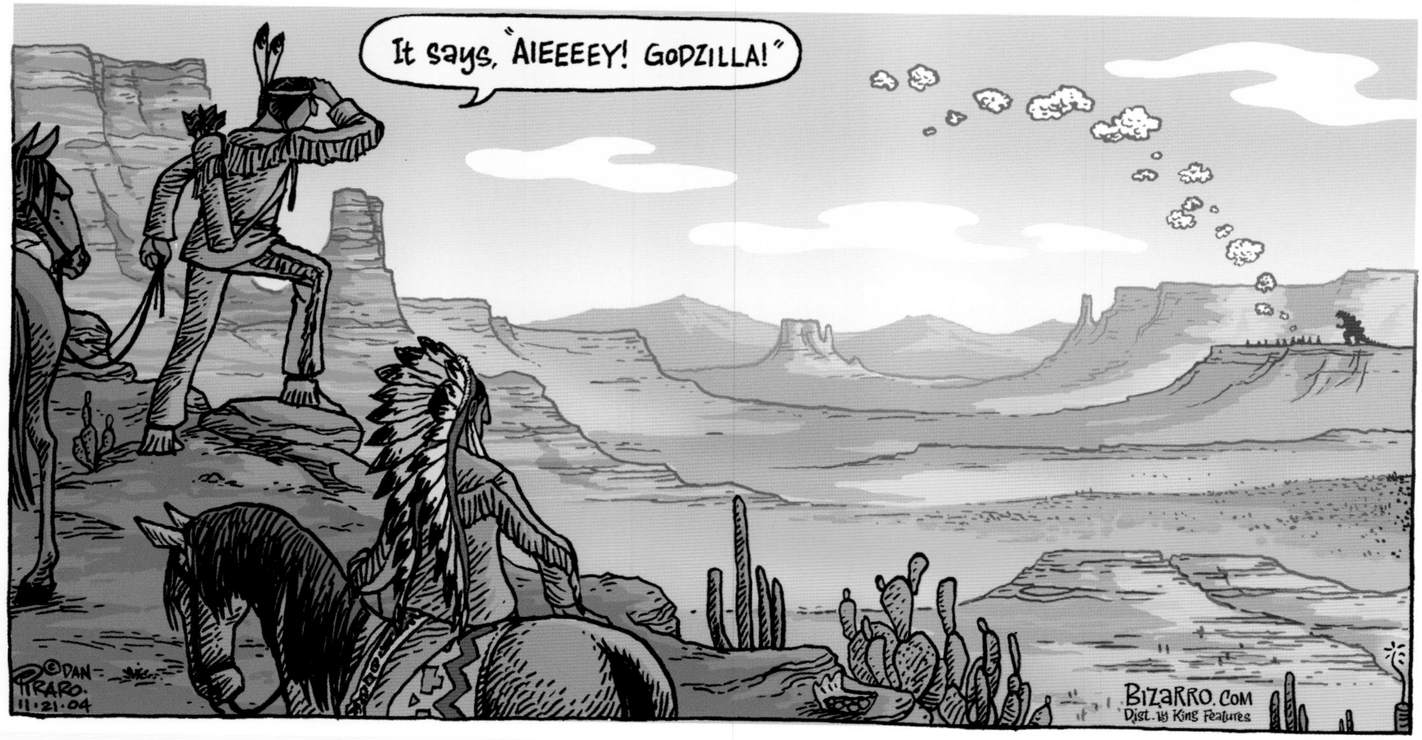
It says, "AIEEEEY! GODZILLA!"
©DAN PIRARO 11-21-04
BIZARRO.COM
Dist. by King Features

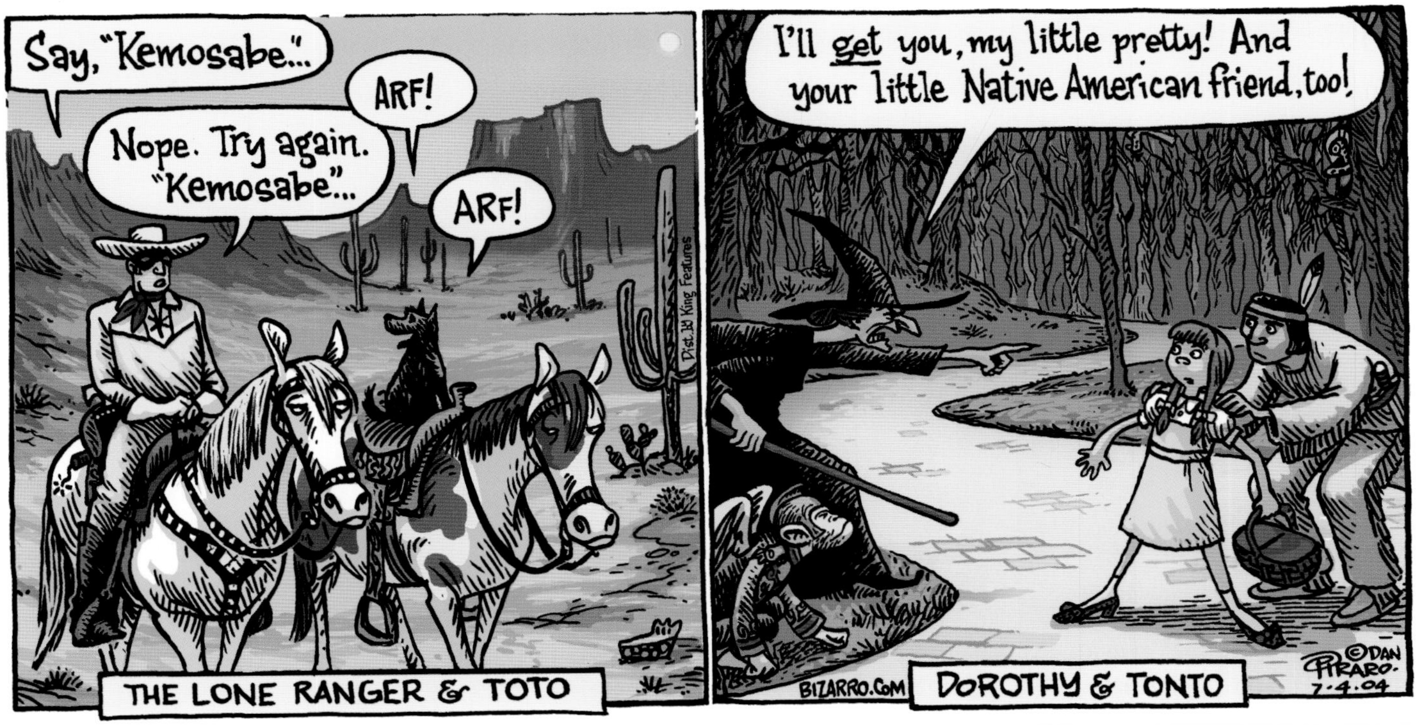
Say, "Kemosabe."...
Nope. Try again. "Kemosabe."...
ARF!
ARF!
Dist. by King Features
THE LONE RANGER & TOTO
I'll get you, my little pretty! And your little Native American friend, too!
BIZARRO.COM
DOROTHY & TONTO
©DAN PIRARO. 7.4.04

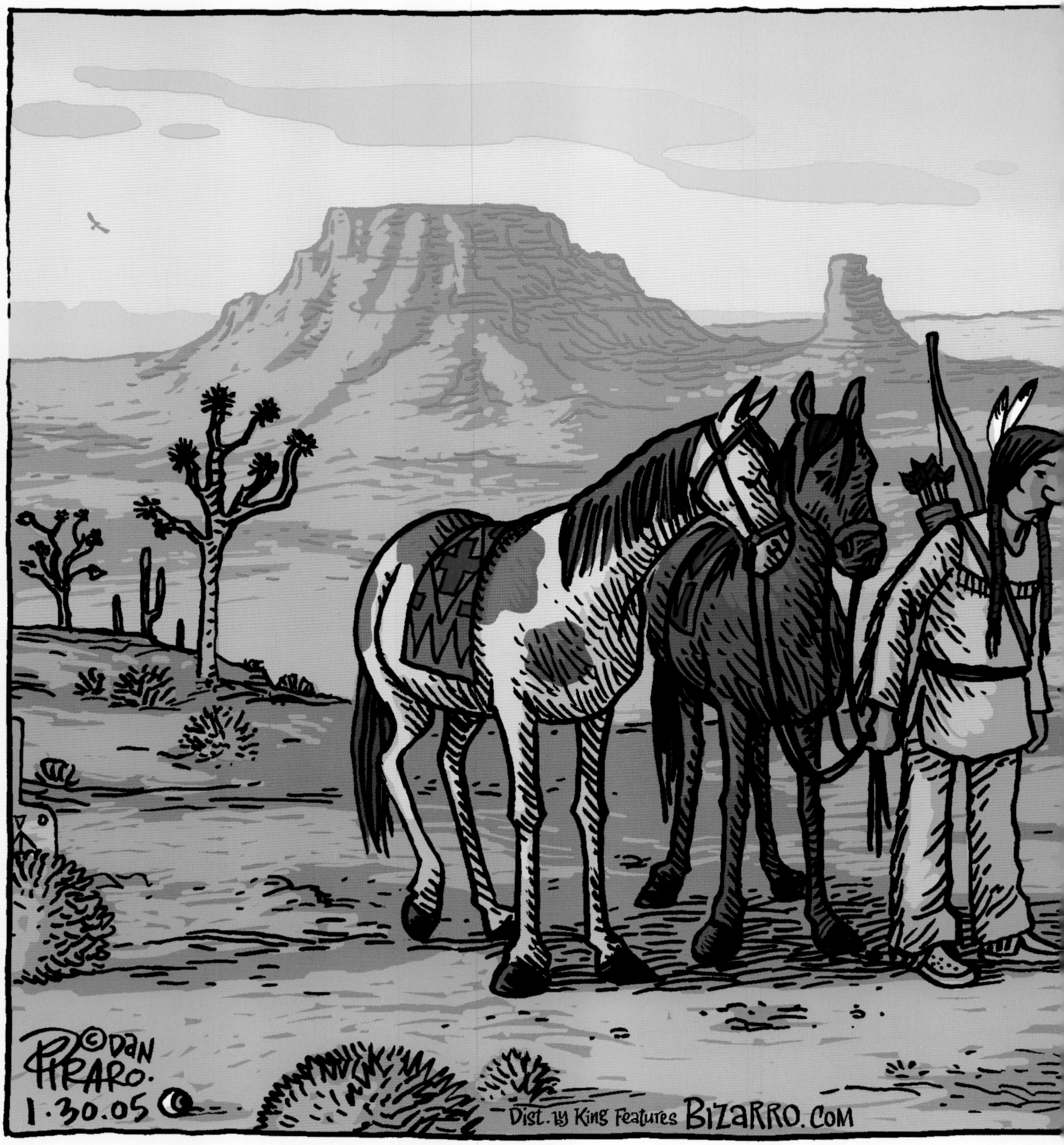

© DAN PIRARO. 1.30.05
Dist. by King Features BIZARRO.COM

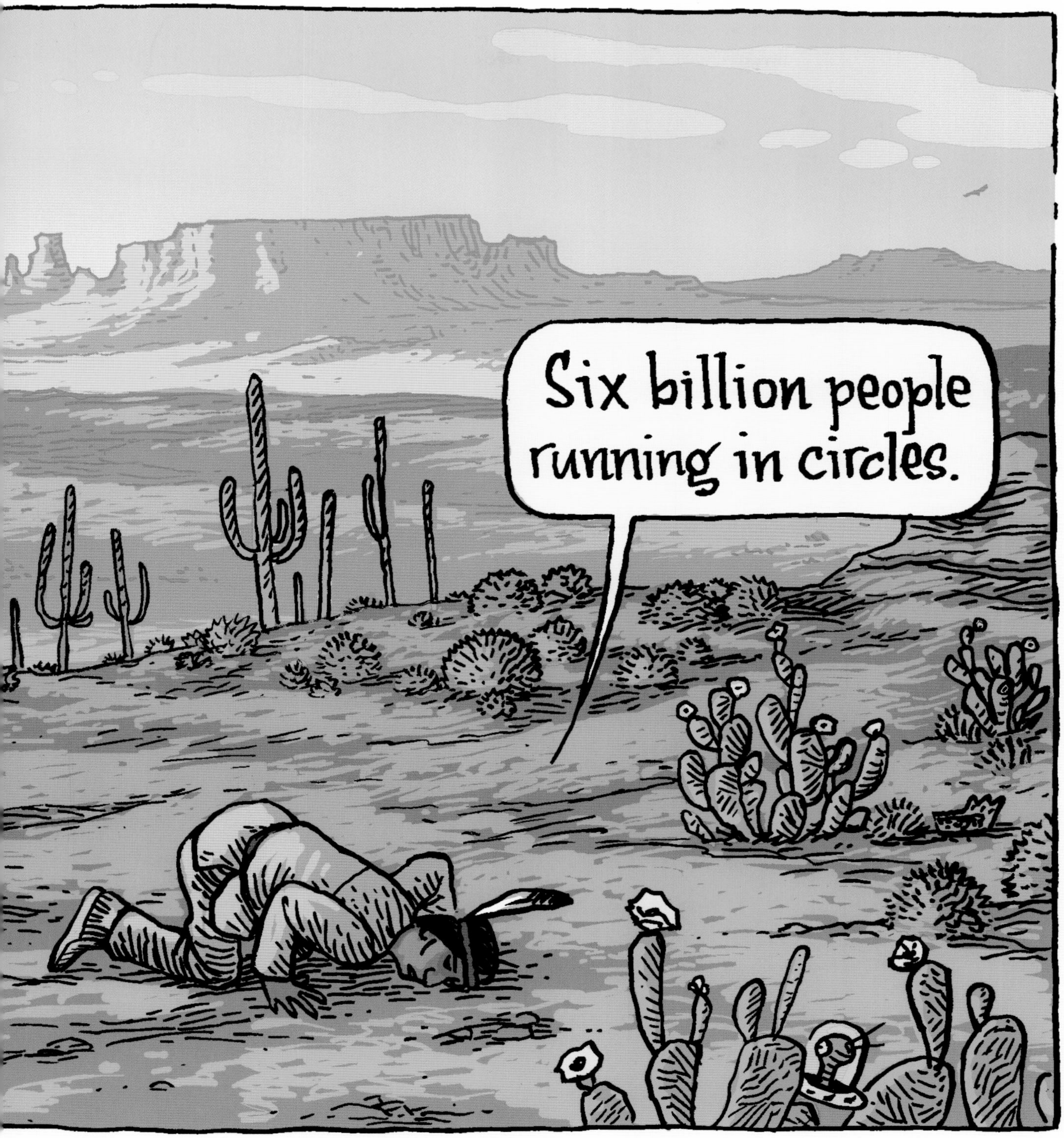
Six billion people running in circles.

Part of my fascination with American Indians is their respect for the earth and animals. The country could use a good dose of that now. (2005)

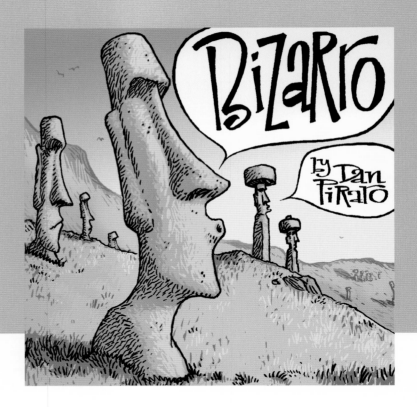

Easter Island

Easter Island is a virtually inexhaustible subject for cartoons. The square panel was the title panel for the rectangular one in a Sunday cartoon.

Bizarro
by Dan Piraro

Virginia! The tourguide specifically said, "NO SPELUNKING"!
Dist. by Universal Press Synd.
10-11 © Dan Piraro 1998

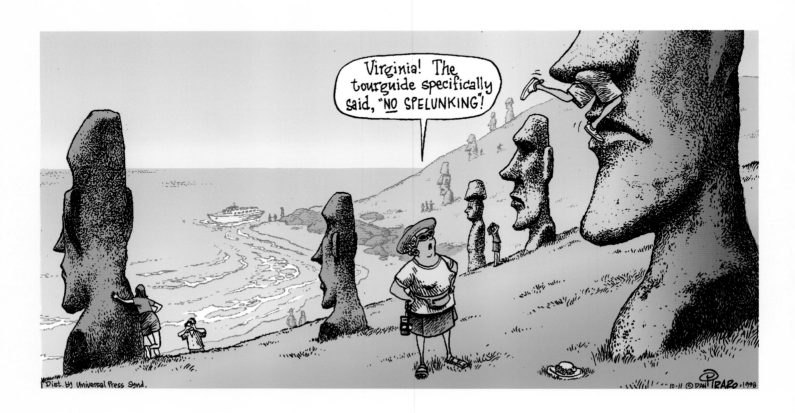

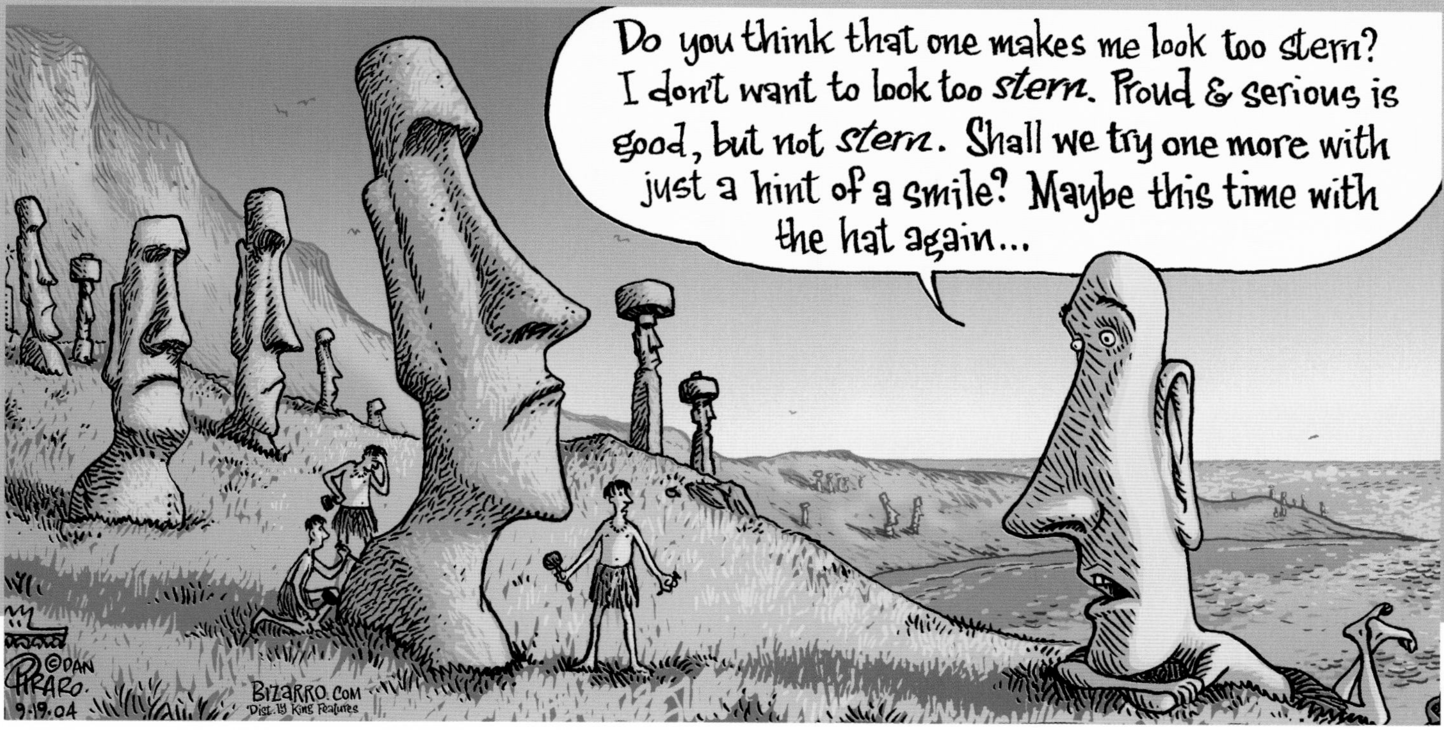
Do you think that one makes me look too stern? I don't want to look too stern. Proud & serious is good, but not stern. Shall we try one more with just a hint of a smile? Maybe this time with the hat again...
©DAN PIRARO. 9-19-04
BIZARRO.COM
Dist. by King Features

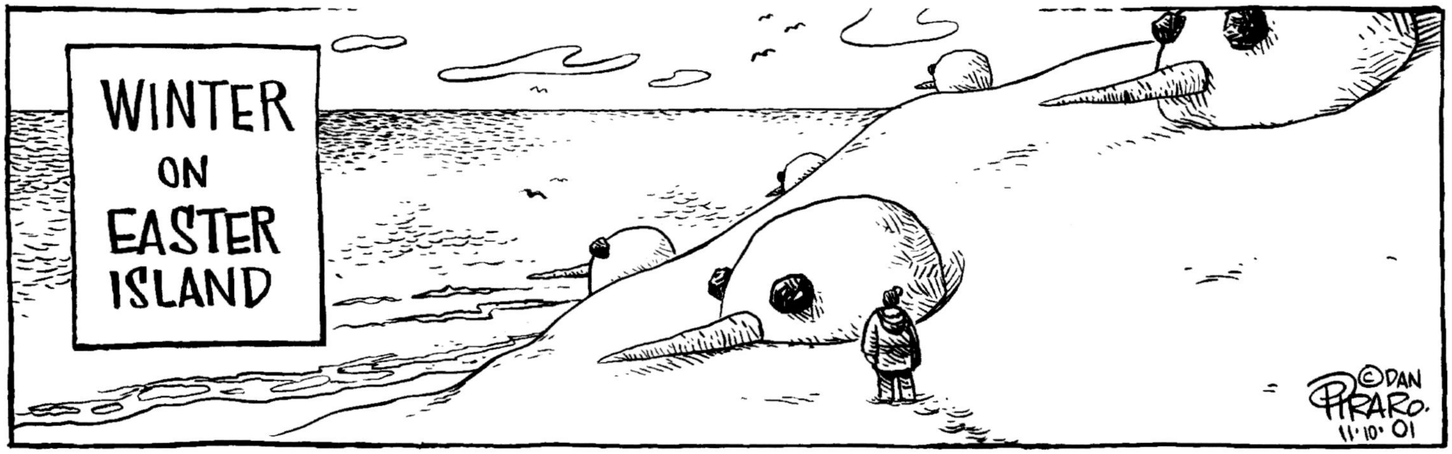
WINTER ON EASTER ISLAND
©DAN PIRARO. 11-10-01

Guatemala

In 1986 or so, I published a cartoon that featured a person being awarded the "Albert G. Thompson Award." To the recipient's surprise, the award is Albert G. Thompson himself, packed and ready to move in. Soon after the cartoon appeared in the papers, I received a letter from a faculty member at Marquette named Albert G. Thompson (a name I thought I'd made up) wondering if I had been one of his students. He was a very witty and charismatic fellow, we exchanged a few humorous letters, and I gave him the original art to the cartoon. He was very grateful, and I assumed that was the end of the story.

In 1996, some ten years later, I got an email from his adult son, Chris. Chris informed me that his parents had retired and now lived on a small coffee plantation they'd built in rural Guatemala. Chris and his family had just returned from one of their many visits there. He saw my cartoon hanging in a prominent place in his father's "bodega," the small building where he processed their coffee, and asked him about it. When Al mentioned how much joy he'd gotten out of the cartoon over the years, showing it to friends and tourists passing through, Chris asked him if he'd ever considered inviting me to visit. He said he had thought about it, but never acted on it because he didn't think I'd come.

When Chris returned home, he looked me up on the Internet and saw that I had been touring the country and staying with fans (as I recounted in *Bizarro among the Savages*) and he called his dad and said, "He'll *definitely* come. You've got to ask him!" He agreed and Chris extended the invitation to what he called "the Garden of Eden." On my book tour I had stayed in far stranger places, so I jumped at the chance.

Albert's wife, Carolyn, designed and had local artisans build their home, which is beautiful, as are the grounds. Everyone I've met in Guatemala has been wonderful, and the Thompsons themselves are amazing people with whom I became instant family. I have been back to visit them almost yearly ever since. Al and Carolyn are what I aspire to be: always learning, always open, always living life to its fullest. And Al is as irreverent and mischievous today as he must have been as a schoolboy. Meeting them is one of the greatest unexpected fringe benefits of my career.

Far left is Chris Thompson, who invited me down the first time, with his children, Matthew and Beth; his wife, Anne; and Al and Carolyn. (2003)

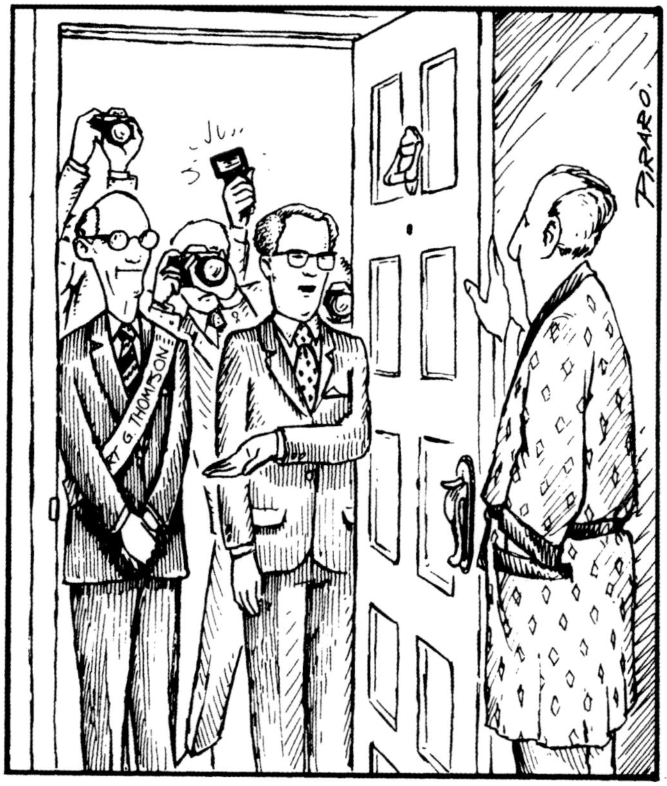
PIRARO

"Dr. Simms, you are this year's recipient of the coveted 'Albert G. Thompson Award'. And here, for your personal enrichment for one full year, is Albert G. Thompson."

Lovely wife and crazy Al in the "Garden of Eden." (2004)

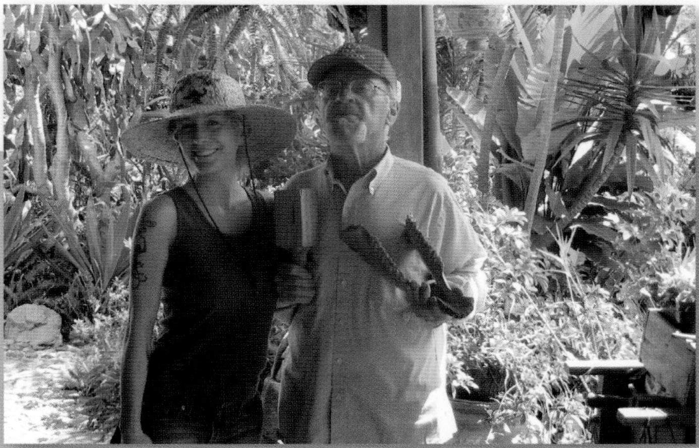

In Guatemala, preparing to slay an army with the jawbone of an ass. (2004)

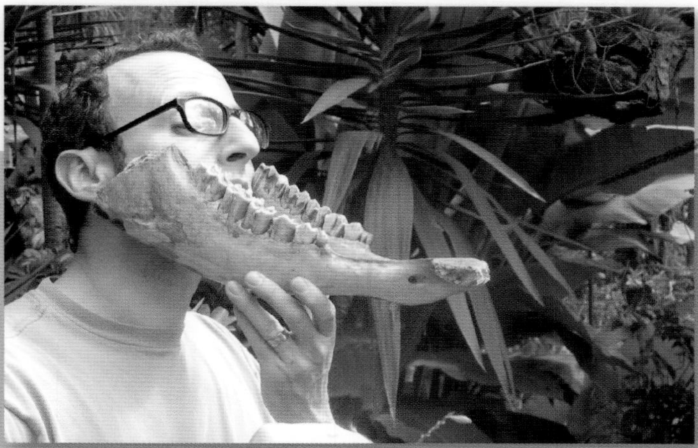

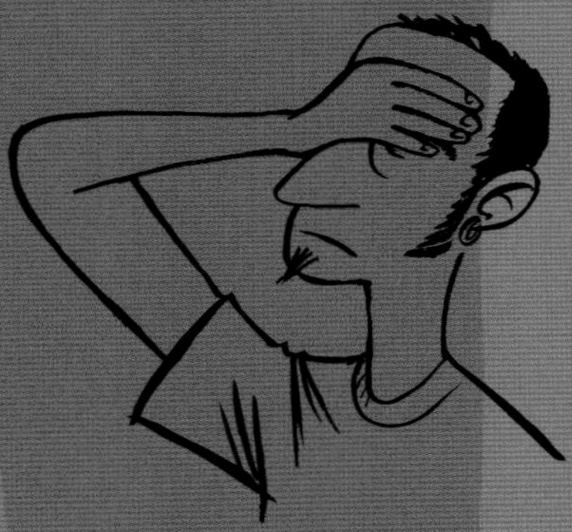

Chapter four

It verges on the criminal

From the subject of environmental damage, it is a short hop to the politics that make that destruction possible and profitable. And that leads pretty clearly to the neoconservative hold on power and the George W. Bush White House. Few would argue that any president has had a worse environmental record. Second place isn't even close. When you consider the long-term effects of Bush's policies, it verges on the criminal.

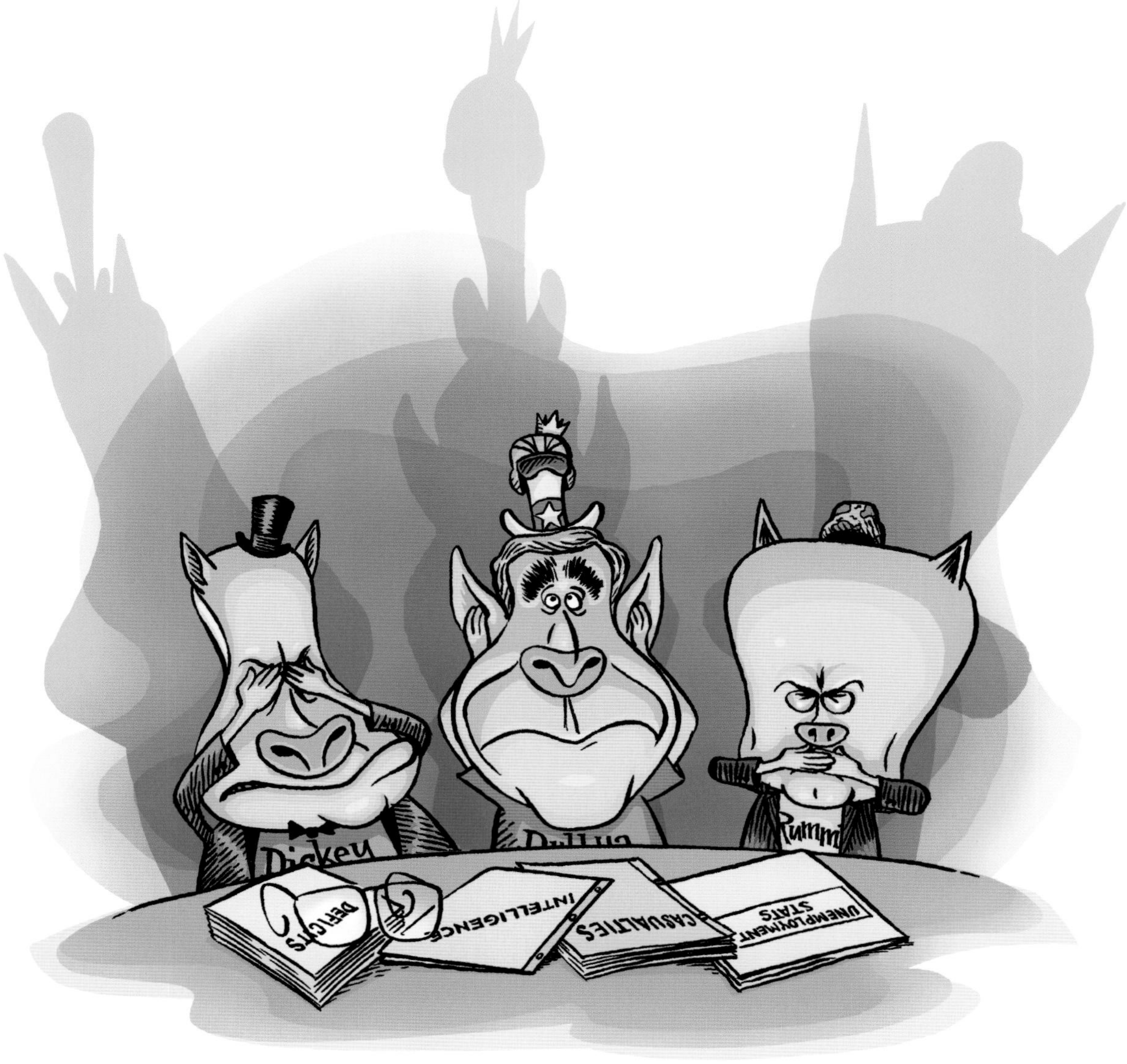
Dickey
Rumm
DEFICITS
INTELLIGENCE
CASUALTIES
UNEMPLOYMENT STATS

Until 2000 I didn't have much interest in politics. It always seemed to me to be too complicated if you didn't follow it closely, and reading about it every day seemed way too much like homework. Like most Americans, I followed world events via TV headlines, which don't tell you enough to make an informed decision about anything. The Lewinsky affair was much more interesting than NAFTA, so that's what they put on TV and that's what I knew most about. Like the vast majority of voters, I voted for president based on which candidate gave me the best "vibes." (For the record, I voted for Al Gore in 2000, even though the vibes he gave me were questionable—but Bush actually sucked the vibes right out of me, leaving me with nothing but the willies.)

But when I realized that America was rather clearly on the way up Shit Creek and Bush had given all our paddles away to his rich friends, I started following the news more carefully. Nothing motivates a mammal like fear, so I found myself climbing with great interest deeper and deeper into the world of politics as one smoking gun led to another. One fact became blatantly obvious: George W. Bush's presidency has been among the most incompetent and irresponsible in history in virtually every area of government. In fact, it verges on the criminal. Behind every move the neocons make is a scheme that shifts more power and wealth to the rich and powerful at the expense of the middle and lower class, public health and safety, and the environment. It really is that simple. So this, too, began to find its way into *Bizarro*—and not always to favorable reviews.

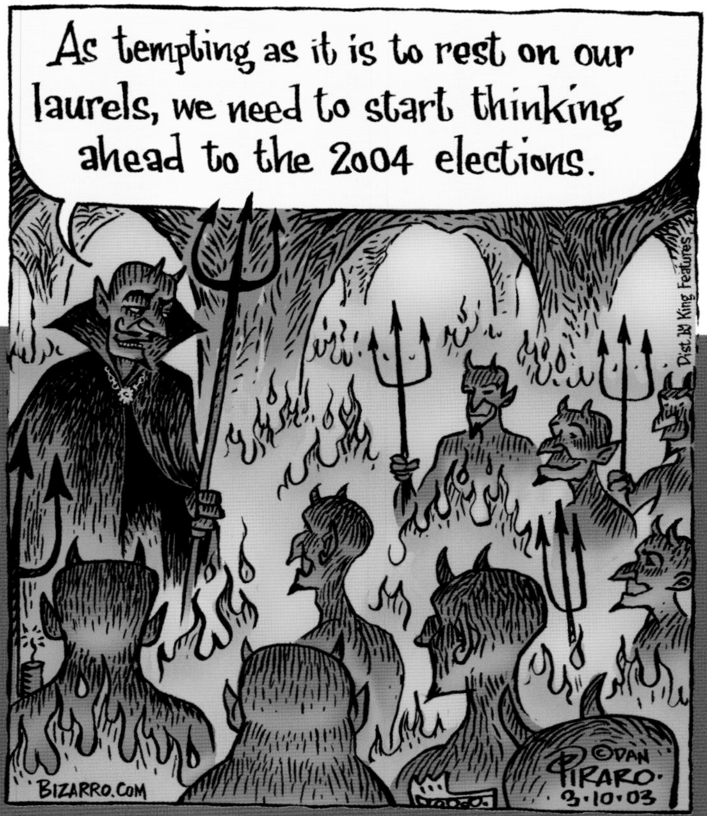
As tempting as it is to rest on our laurels, we need to start thinking ahead to the 2004 elections.
Dist. by King Features
BIZARRO.COM
©DAN PIRARO 3·10·03

Little did I know when I wrote this how prophetic it would turn out to be. (2003)

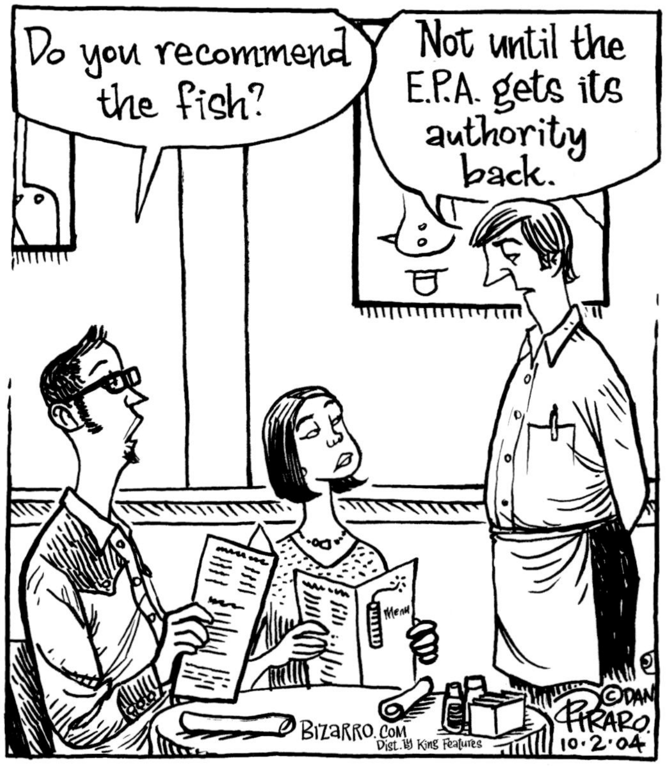
Do you recommend the fish?
Not until the E.P.A. gets its authority back.
BIZARRO.COM
Dist. by King Features
©DAN PIRARO 10·2·04

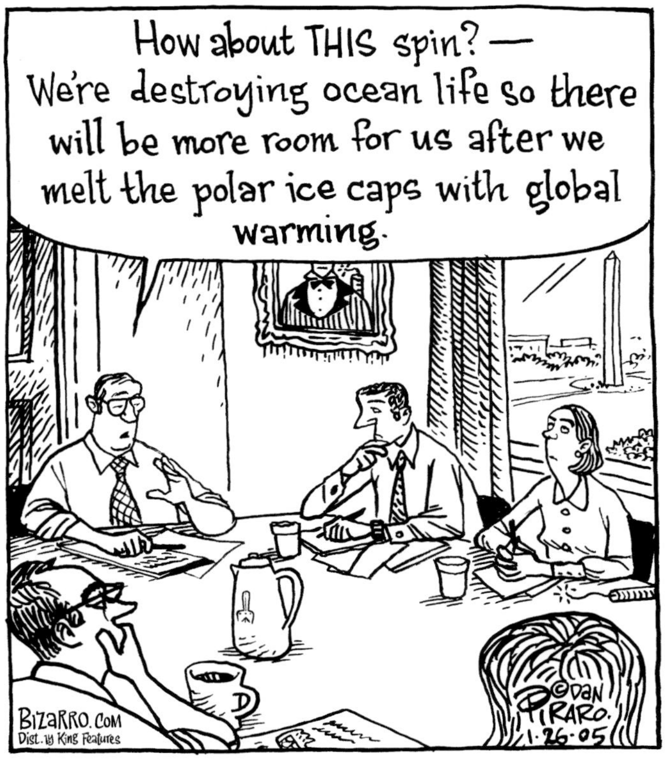
How about THIS spin? — We're destroying ocean life so there will be more room for us after we melt the polar ice caps with global warming.
BIZARRO.COM
Dist. by King Features
©DAN PIRARO 1·26·05

Two examples of the crossover between animal rights and politics. Most Americans think animal rights activists are flakes, but our legislative goals would make America's food, air, and water supply safer and feed the poor more efficiently. (2004, 2005)

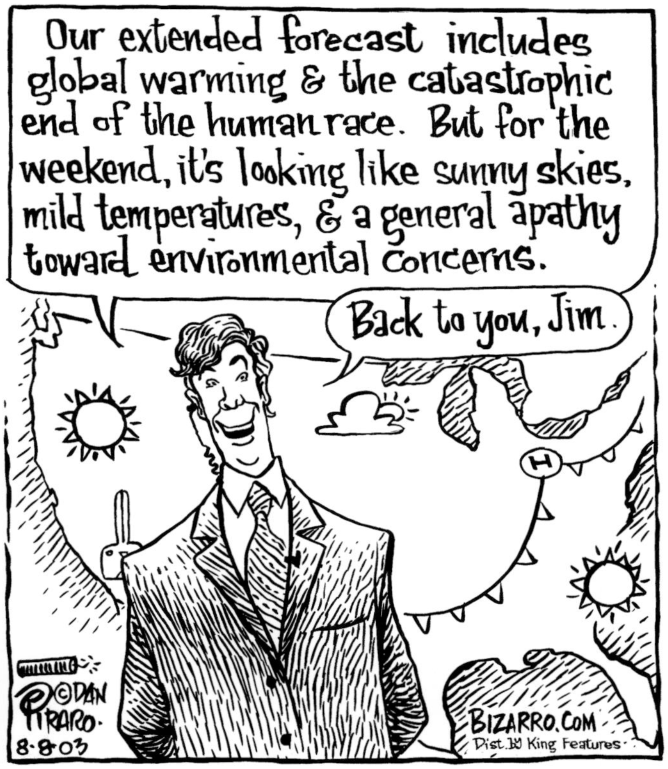
Our extended forecast includes global warming & the catastrophic end of the human race. But for the weekend, it's looking like sunny skies, mild temperatures, & a general apathy toward environmental concerns.
Back to you, Jim.
©DAN PIRARO 8·8·03
BIZARRO.COM
Dist. by King Features

Ignorance is bliss, and shortsightedness is rapture. (2003)

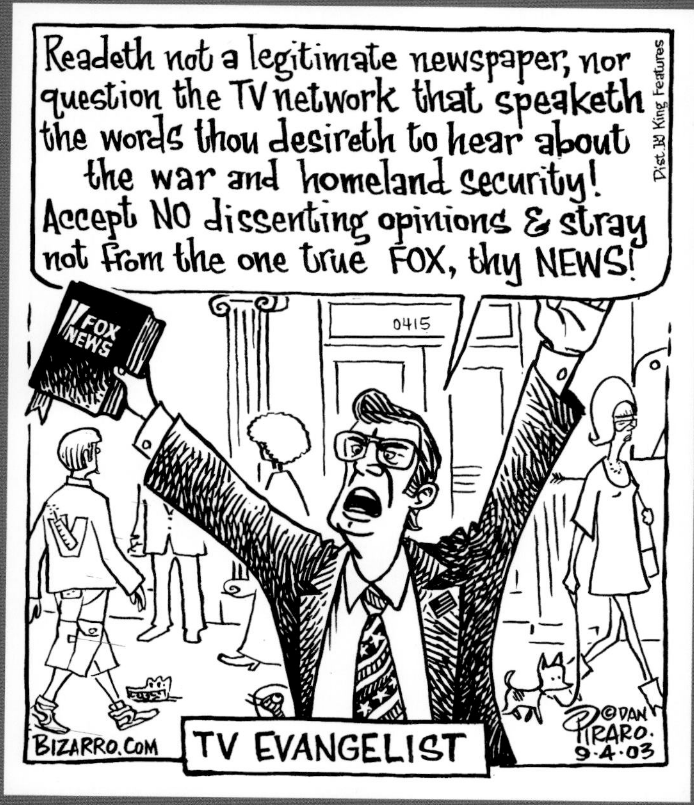
Readeth not a legitimate newspaper, nor question the TV network that speaketh the words thou desireth to hear about the war and homeland security! Accept NO dissenting opinions & stray not from the one true FOX, thy NEWS!
FOX NEWS
0415
Dist. by King Features
BIZARRO.COM
TV EVANGELIST
©DAN PIRARO. 9·4·03

Welcome back to the Dark Ages.

It amazes me how many Americans think Fox News is a real news channel. Have there always been this many intellectually challenged people in America, or have the neocons been slipping something into the meat supply? Is this the same affliction that causes people to think professional wrestling is real? (2003)

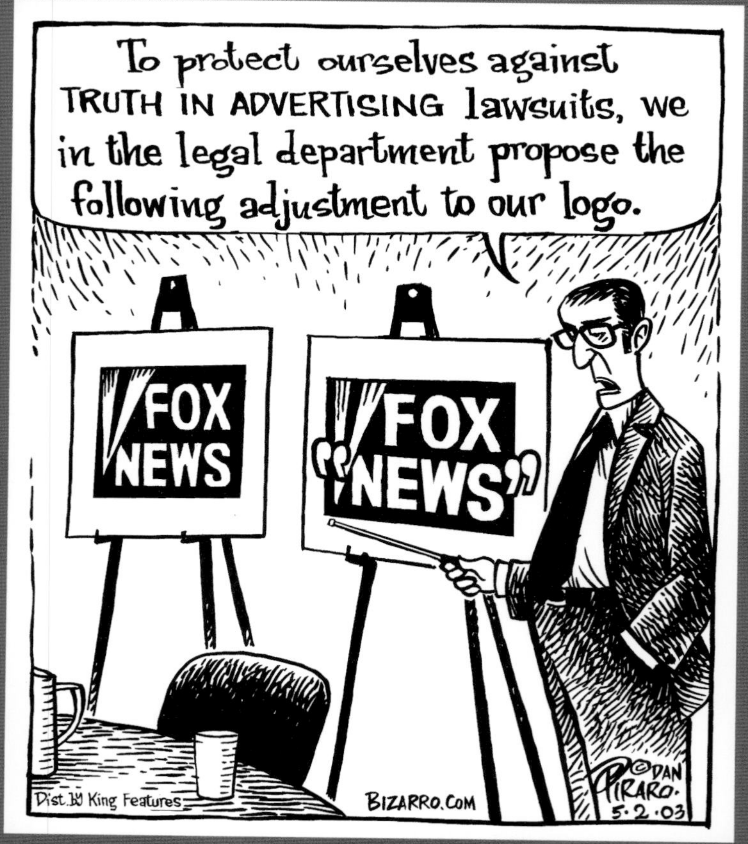
To protect ourselves against TRUTH IN ADVERTISING lawsuits, we in the legal department propose the following adjustment to our logo.
FOX NEWS
FOX "NEWS"
Dist. by King Features
BIZARRO.COM
©DAN PIRARO. 5·2·03

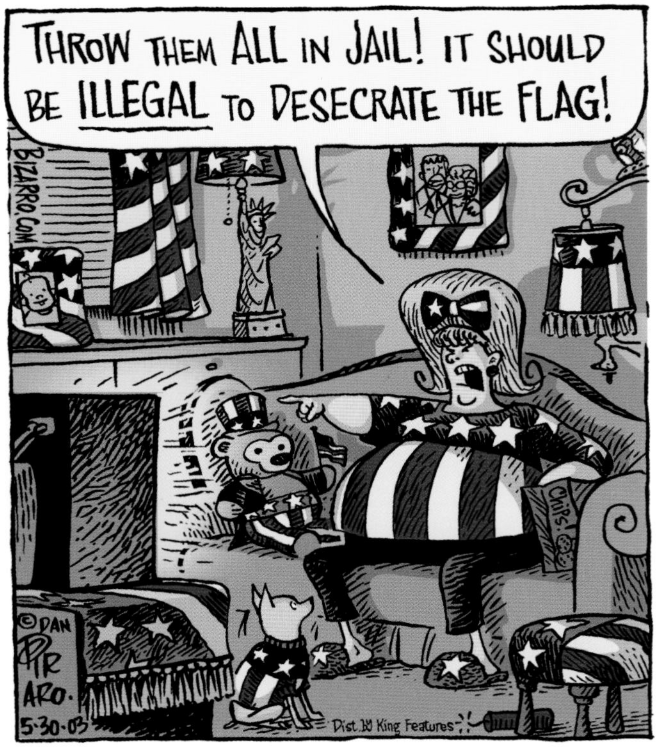
THROW THEM ALL IN JAIL! IT SHOULD BE ILLEGAL TO DESECRATE THE FLAG!
BIZARRO.COM
CHIPS
©DAN PIRARO. 5-30-03
Dist. by King Features

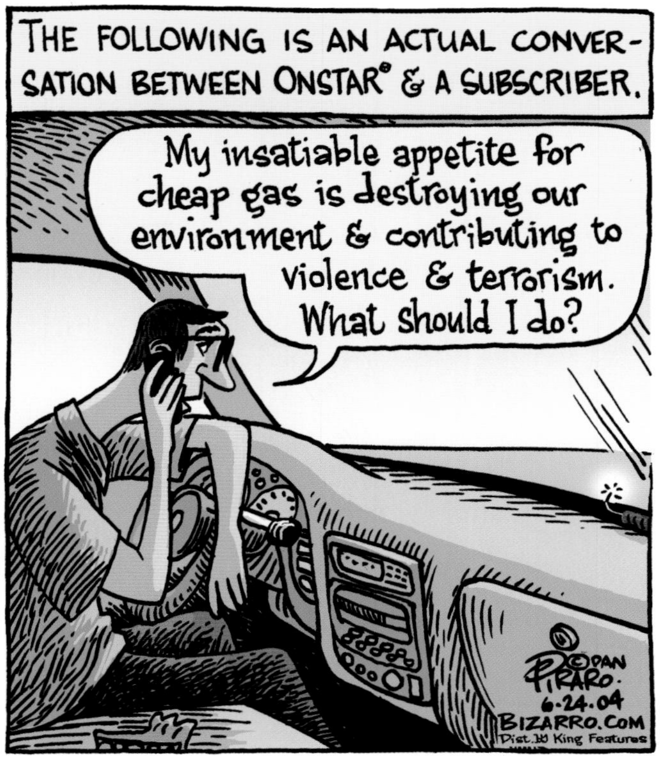
THE FOLLOWING IS AN ACTUAL CONVERSATION BETWEEN ONSTAR® & A SUBSCRIBER.
My insatiable appetite for cheap gas is destroying our environment & contributing to violence & terrorism. What should I do?
©DAN PIRARO. 6-24-04
BIZARRO.COM
Dist. by King Features

How about read a legitimate newspaper and wake up?

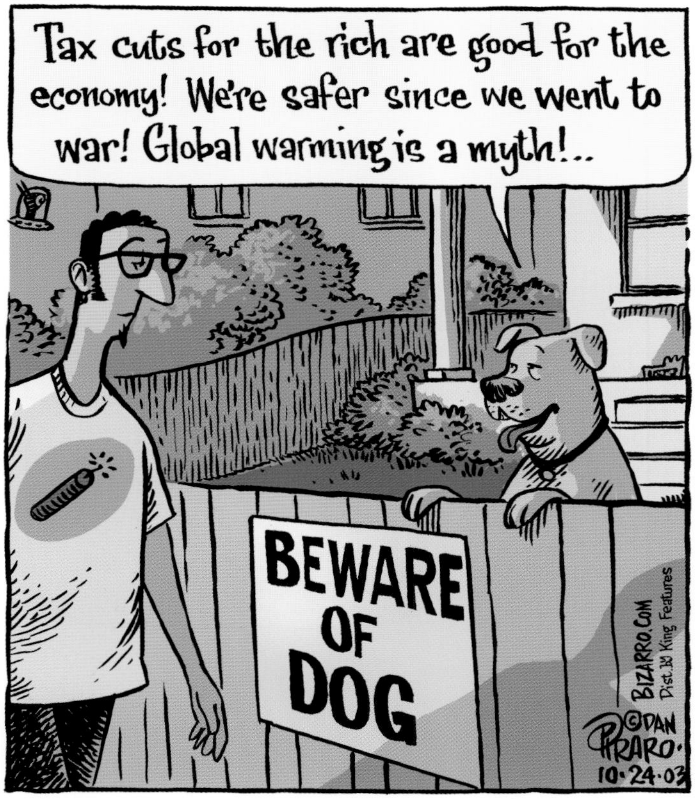
Tax cuts for the rich are good for the economy! We're safer since we went to war! Global warming is a myth!...
BEWARE OF DOG
BIZARRO.COM
Dist. by King Features
©DAN PIRARO
10-24-03

Beware, but vote for him anyway? (2003)

ABOVE, RIGHT: Of course, the boom of the nineties was a delayed reaction to Reagan's tax cuts, and the slump in the early–mid 2000s was due to the Clinton/Lewinsky scandal. I suppose if Bush ends up starting World War III, it will be because of Kennedy's race to the moon. (2004)

RIGHT: This one got so much vicious hate mail I almost bought a flak jacket to wear when I left the house. A surprising number of people included in their letter something like, "May I remind you HE IS STILL ALIVE!" Were they worried I had the power to change that with my cartoon? (2003)

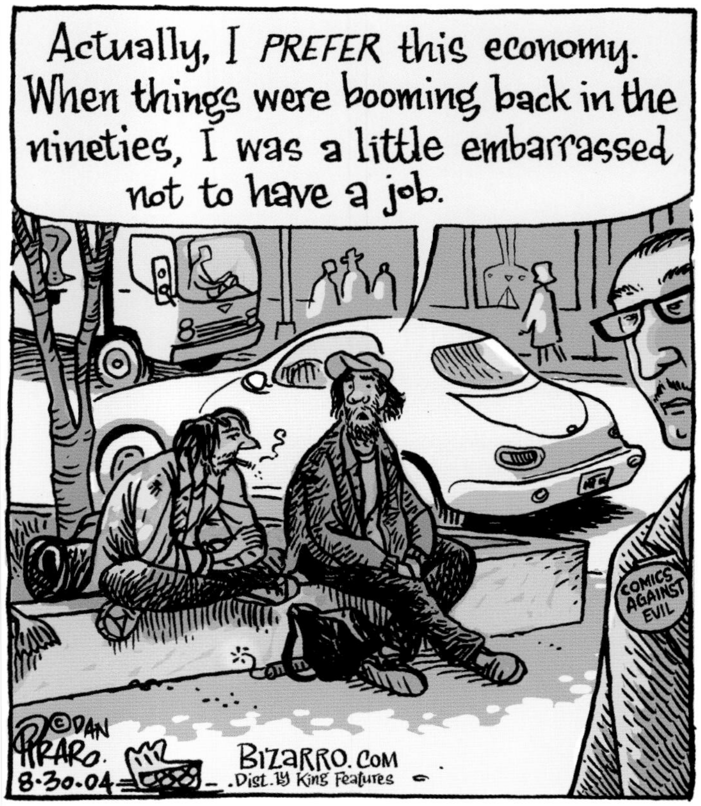
Actually, I *PREFER* this economy. When things were booming back in the nineties, I was a little embarrassed not to have a job.
COMICS AGAINST EVIL
©DAN PIRARO
8-30-04
BIZARRO.COM
Dist. by King Features

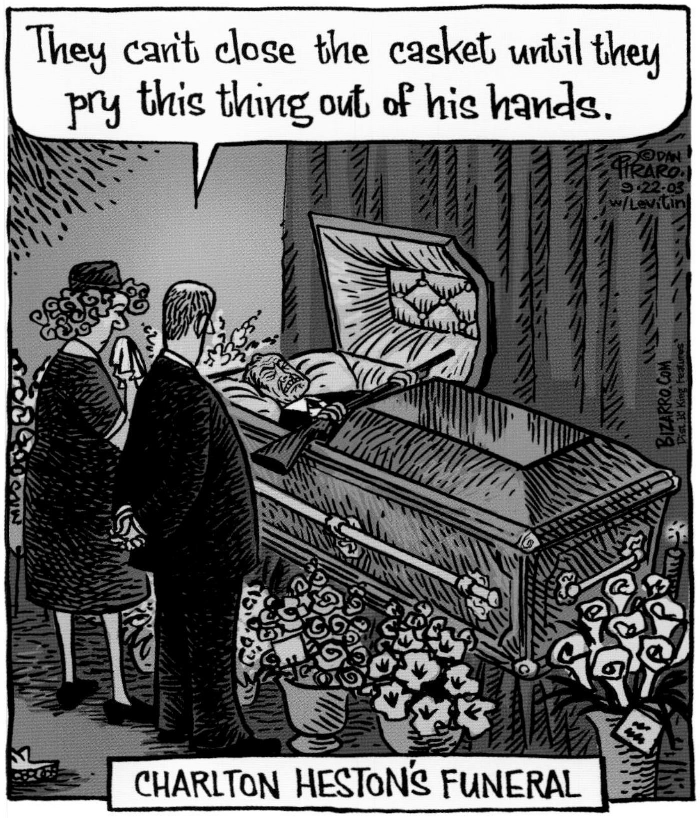
They can't close the casket until they pry this thing out of his hands.
©DAN PIRARO
9-22-03
w/Levitin
BIZARRO.COM
Dist. by King Features
CHARLTON HESTON'S FUNERAL

Objectively study any issue or agenda the neocons push forward and you will begin to see this trend clearly. Even their so-called family values issues—abortion, stem-cell research, gay marriage—are a part of this paradigm. These issues boil down to faith, one of the precious few things that will get people sufficiently emotionally involved to get to the polls. And this minority of Bible-waving, witch-hunting voters is just enough to maintain the slim lead that keeps the neocons in power. "If we elect the wrong person, we may get hit again," as Dick Cheney said during the 2004 campaign, is a comical and indefensible ploy, but it scares the hell out of anyone with small children.

I contend that the neocons' declared passion for family values is nothing more than another empty campaign tool. If they really cared about "family values," would they be trying to systematically dismantle Social Security and Medicare? Is making it legal for corporations and utility companies to poison our country's water, land, and air pro-family? What about economic policies that shift the tax burden away from multi-billion-dollar corporations and the extremely wealthy and onto the shoulders of the average working family—is that something families value? If they really wanted to promote a "culture that values life," would they have let the assault weapons ban expire? Assault weapons kill stem cells, too. *Big* groups of stem cells. Ones with arms and legs and hearts and brains and families and hairdos and college plans.

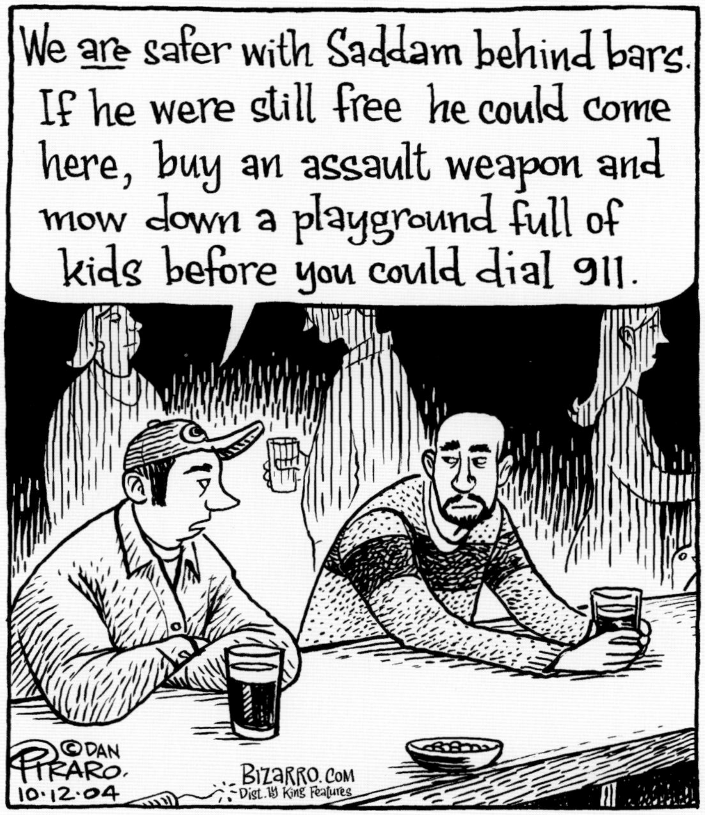
We are safer with Saddam behind bars. If he were still free he could come here, buy an assault weapon and mow down a playground full of kids before you could dial 911.
©DAN PIRARO. 10·12·04
BIZARRO.COM Dist. by King Features

This cartoon was published very soon after Bush let the assault weapons ban expire. Concurrently, I began using a variation of this line in my political stand-up comedy act. One night, as soon as I'd finished the punch line, a woman in the audience said, "Well, so could we." Unable to come up with a clever retort, I blurted, "Yeah. That's the point." (2004)

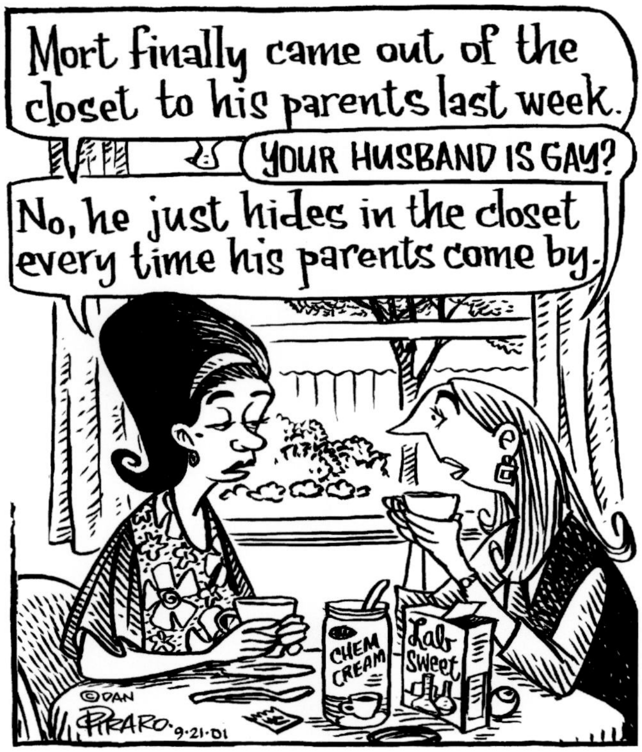
Mort finally came out of the closet to his parents last week.
YOUR HUSBAND IS GAY?
No, he just hides in the closet every time his parents come by.
CHEM CREAM
Lab Sweet
©DAN PIRARO 9-21-01

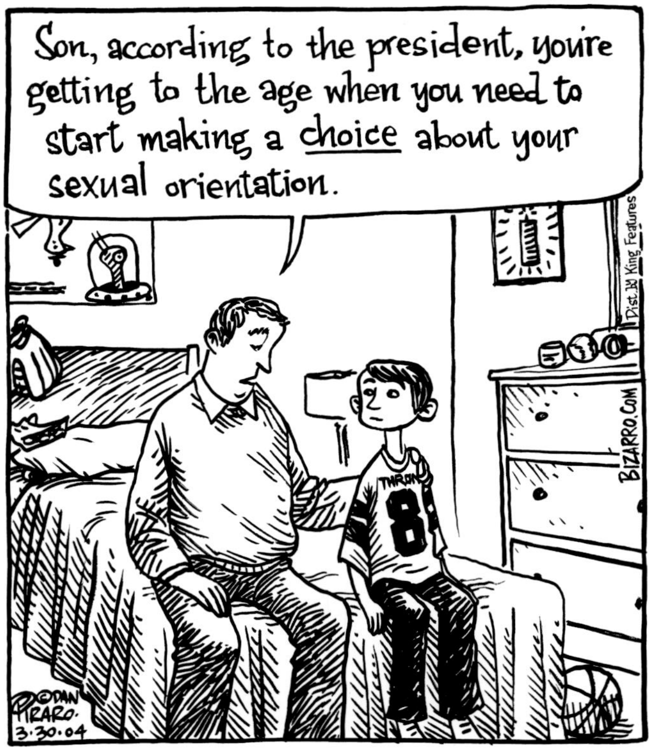
Son, according to the president, you're getting to the age when you need to start making a choice about your sexual orientation.
BIZARRO.COM
Dist. by King Features
©DAN PIRARO 3-30-04

Not specifically about gay rights, but I believe that including the subject in casual and common places like the comics pages helps to normalize it, thus making future generations less likely to persecute them as freaks. (2001)

ABOVE, RIGHT: The idea that sexual orientation is a choice is so funny I can hardly stand it. Does this mean that Dubya and Jerry Falwell and Rick Santorum chose to be heterosexual but could just as easily have been gay? That would explain why this issue gets them so riled up. (2004)

RIGHT: How could anyone make a bigger mockery of marriage than heterosexuals already have? (2004)

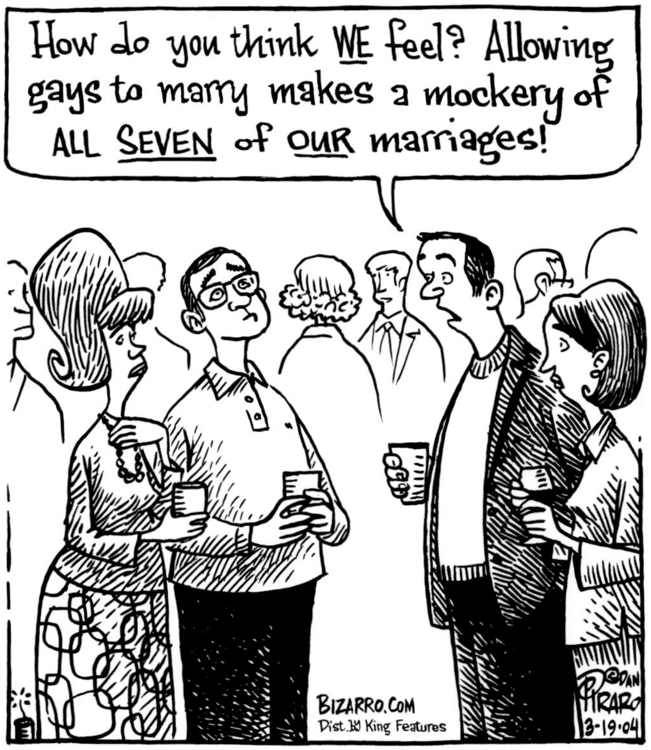
How do you think WE feel? Allowing gays to marry makes a mockery of ALL SEVEN of OUR marriages!
BIZARRO.COM
Dist. by King Features
©DAN PIRARO 3-19-04

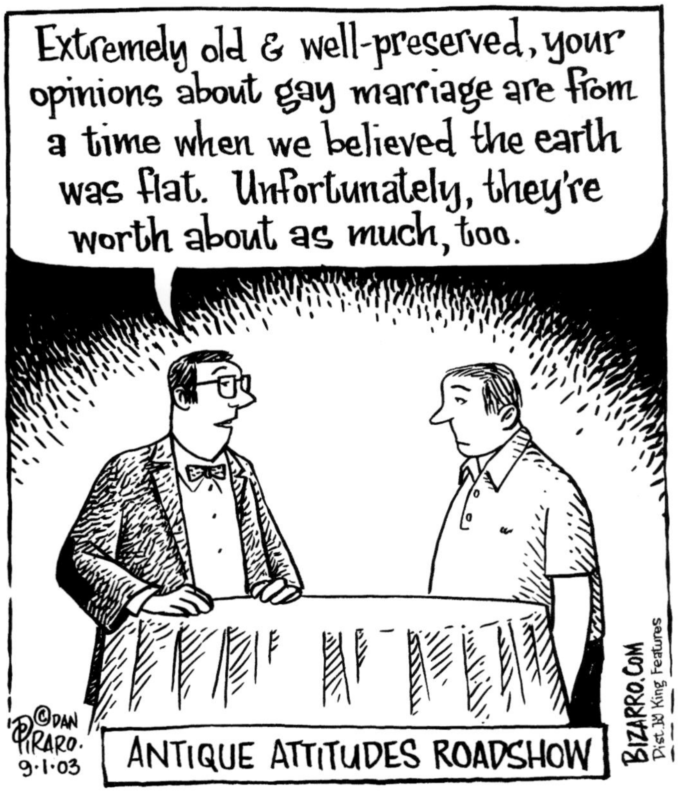
Extremely old & well-preserved, your opinions about gay marriage are from a time when we believed the earth was flat. Unfortunately, they're worth about as much, too.
©DAN PIRARO. 9·1·03
ANTIQUE ATTITUDES ROADSHOW
BIZARRO.COM
Dist. by King Features

Conservative Bible Belt states have a higher rate of divorce than the rest of the country, but they are the ones who scream the loudest about protecting "traditional marriage." Cartoons about gay rights get me almost as much hate mail as ones about gun control. Probably from the same readers.

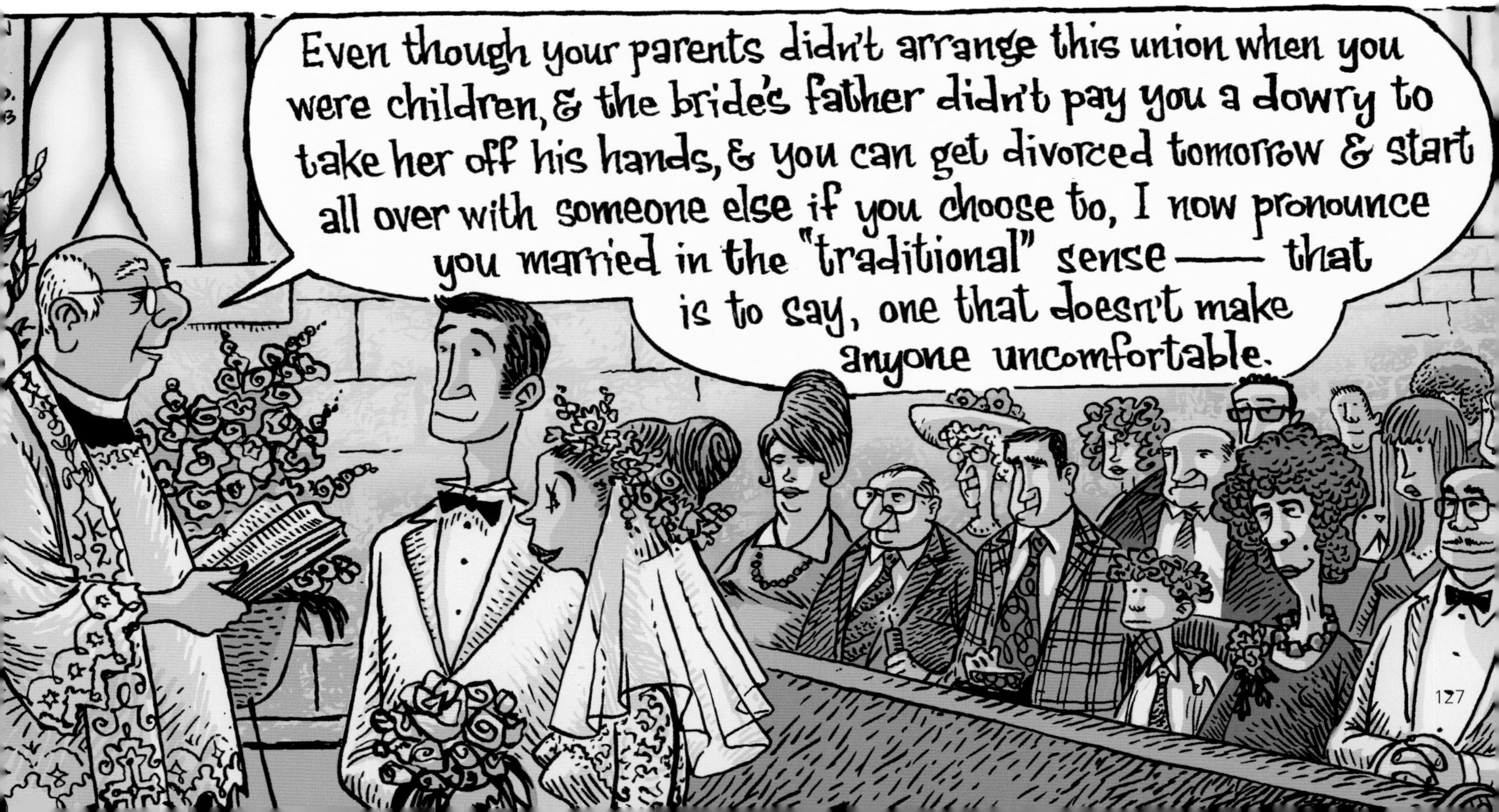
Even though your parents didn't arrange this union when you were children, & the bride's father didn't pay you a dowry to take her off his hands, & you can get divorced tomorrow & start all over with someone else if you choose to, I now pronounce you married in the "traditional" sense —— that is to say, one that doesn't make anyone uncomfortable.

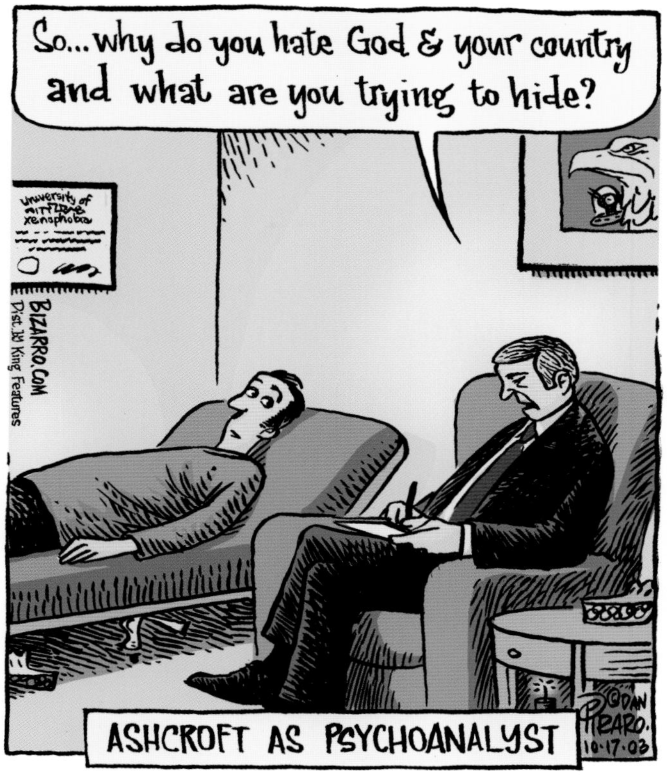
So...why do you hate God & your country and what are you trying to hide?
University of Xenophobia
BIZARRO.COM
Dist. by King Features
©DAN PIRARO. 10-17-03
ASHCROFT AS PSYCHOANALYST

Our generation's Joe McCarthy. If this guy's actions weren't enough to land him in jail, his singing and songwriting certainly are. (See *Fahrenheit 9/11*.) (2003)

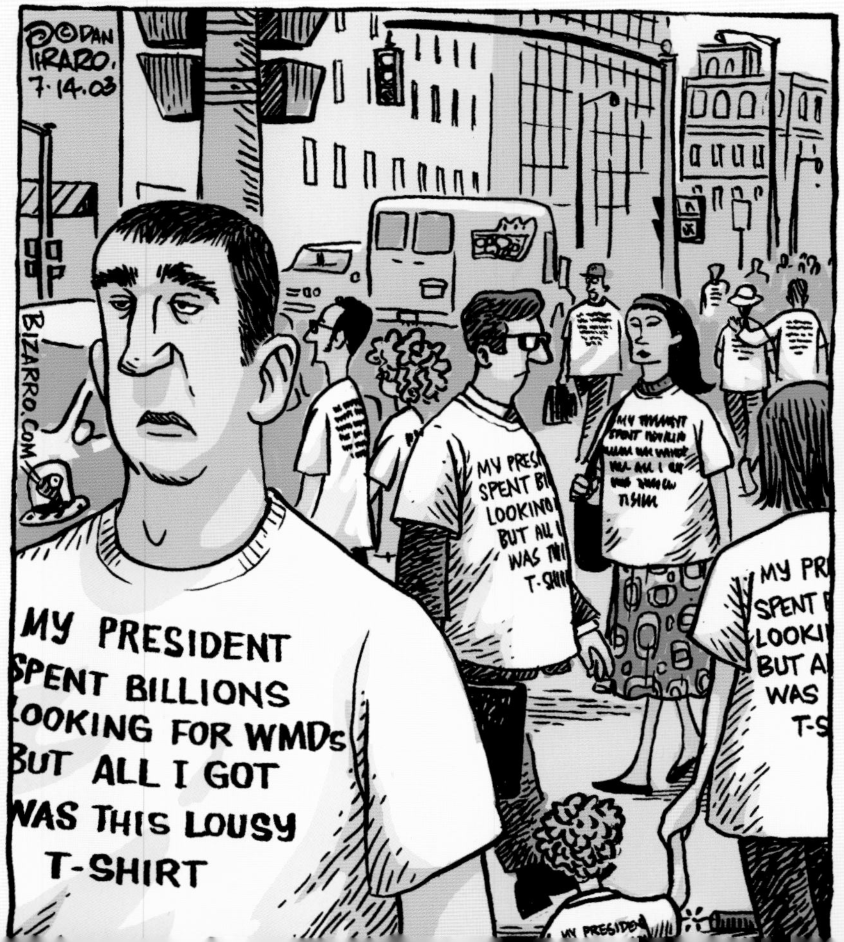
©DAN PIRARO. 7-14-03
BIZARRO.COM
MY PRESIDENT SPENT BILLIONS LOOKING FOR WMDs BUT ALL I GOT WAS THIS LOUSY T-SHIRT

I made up a batch of these T-shirts and sold them after my political comedy shows. (2003)

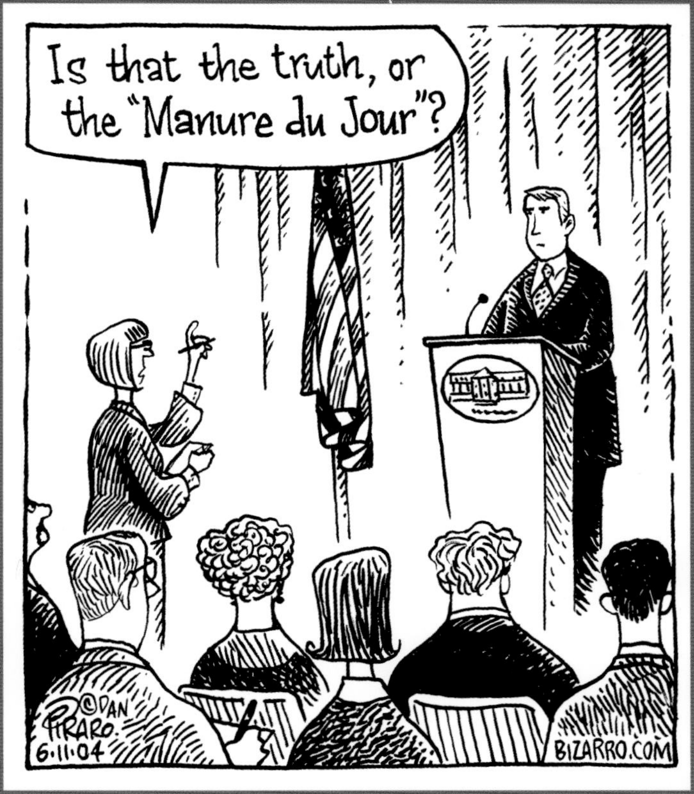
Is that the truth, or the "Manure du Jour"?
©DAN PIRARO 6.11.04
BIZARRO.COM

It was decided that this cartoon would be tantamount to saying the president was full of shit and would lead to cancellations, so it was never published. (2004)

BELOW, LEFT: Our homeland security efforts are obviously designed to make people feel better without spending much money. Always a step behind the latest attempt. (2003)

BELOW: The T-shirt I'm wearing in this panel is something I saw as graffiti in San Francisco. (2003)

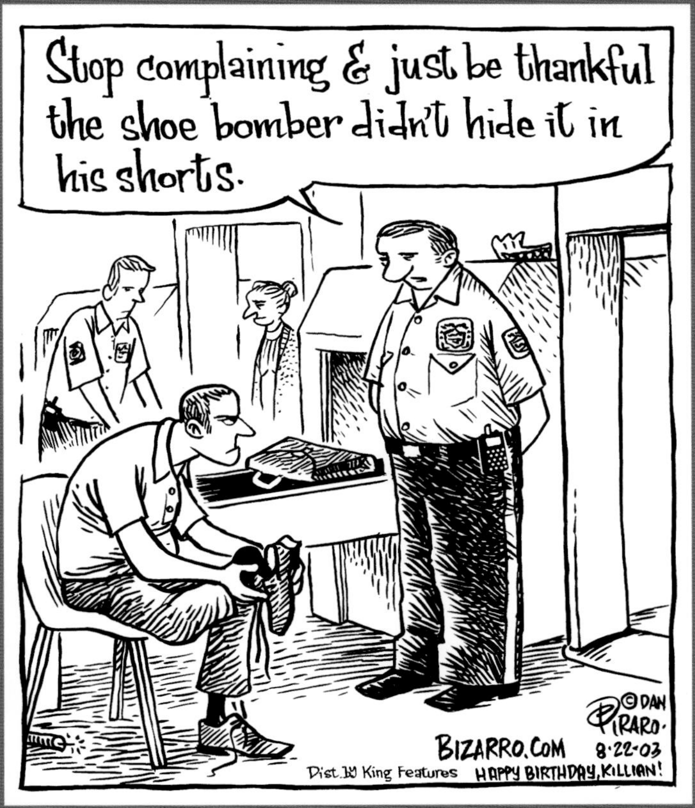
Stop complaining & just be thankful the shoe bomber didn't hide it in his shorts.
©DAN PIRARO 8·22·03
BIZARRO.COM
Dist. by King Features
HAPPY BIRTHDAY, KILLIAN!

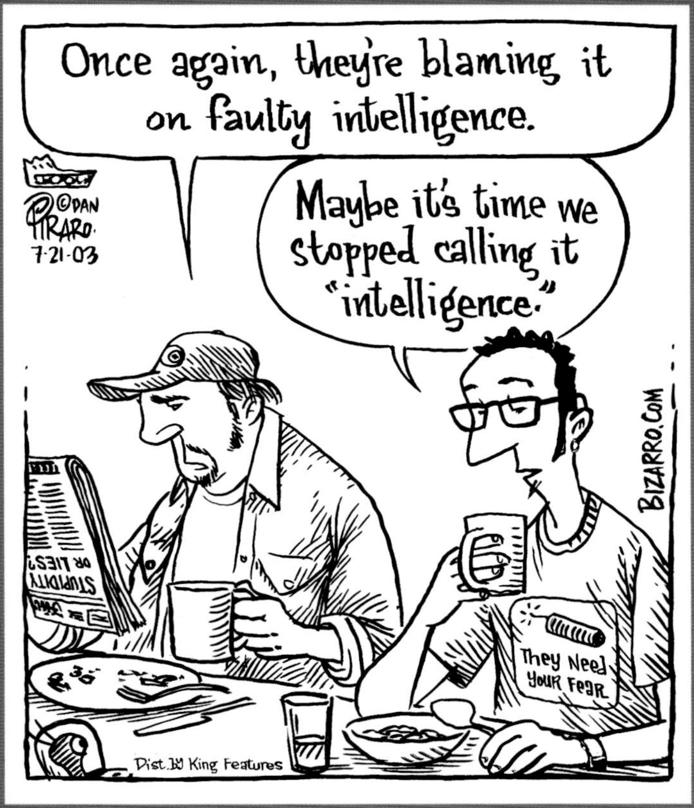
Once again, they're blaming it on faulty intelligence.
Maybe it's time we stopped calling it "intelligence."
©DAN PIRARO 7·21·03
STUPIDITY OR LIES?
They Need Your Fear.
BIZARRO.COM
Dist. by King Features

Once they gained power, every single issue of substance the neocons have advanced, including the war in Iraq, is about shifting money toward the top.

The vast majority of people in the world find the motives behind this war ludicrously transparent. The Bush administration consists of mostly former (and current) petroleum and utility executives and a few lawyers. They lied and exaggerated to get us to conquer and occupy the country with the second-largest oil reserves in the world and are attempting to rebuild it as a Western-style democracy (which virtually all leading experts on the Middle East have warned will never happen). Is it coincidental that if this scheme should work, American petroleum companies would be assured colossal profits for decades to come? Why haven't we dethroned any of the dozens of cruel dictators who *aren't* sitting on oceans of oil?

Few terrorism experts would disagree that there are far more efficient ways to fight "terror" than by invading a country that had much less to do with international terror than any number of other countries in that region and around the world and nothing to do with 9/11. Combine that with the Bush administration's nonexistent attention to terrorism before 9/11 and their tragically lax homeland security efforts, and you've got a smoking gun that only Bill O'Reilly could ignore. Yes, you guessed it. It verges on the criminal.

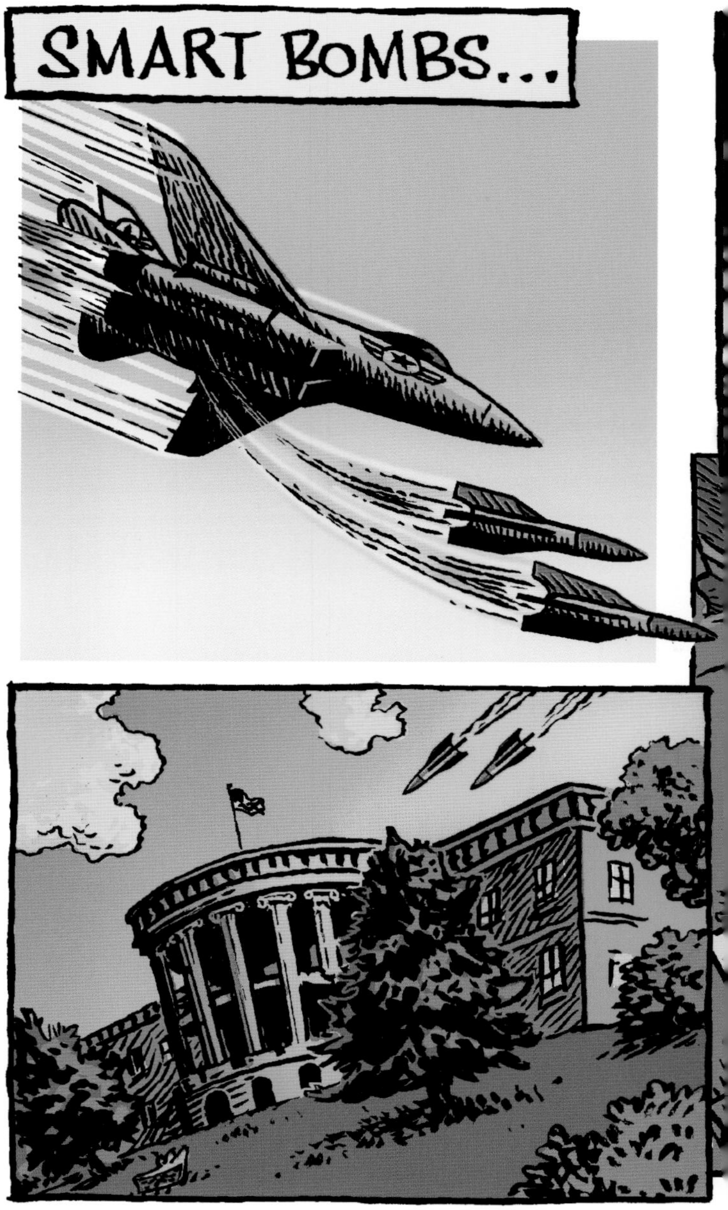
SMART BOMBS...

One of my first overtly anti-Bush cartoons. (2003)

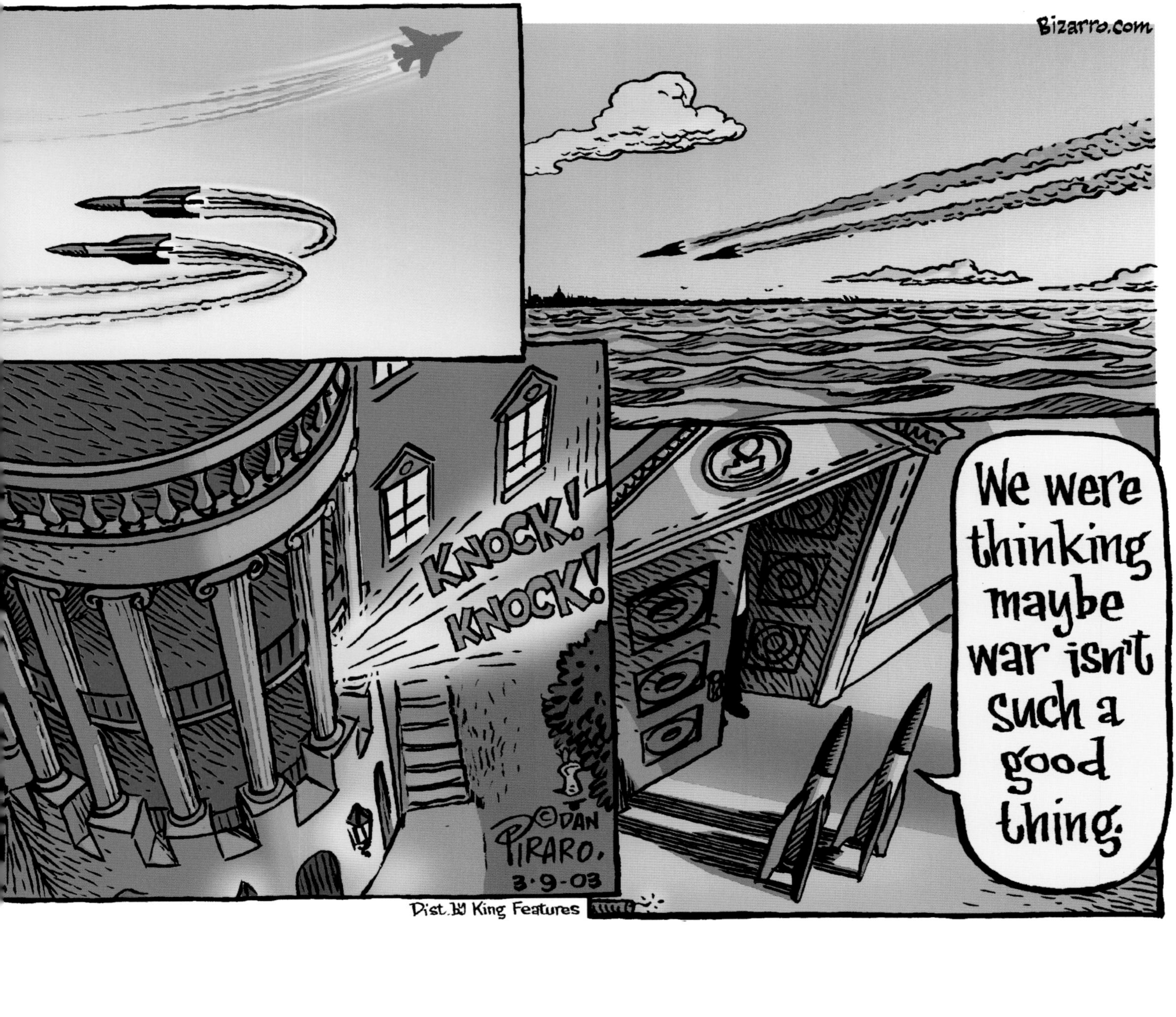
Bizarro.com
KNOCK! KNOCK!
We were thinking maybe war isn't such a good thing.
©DAN PIRARO. 3-9-03
Dist. by King Features

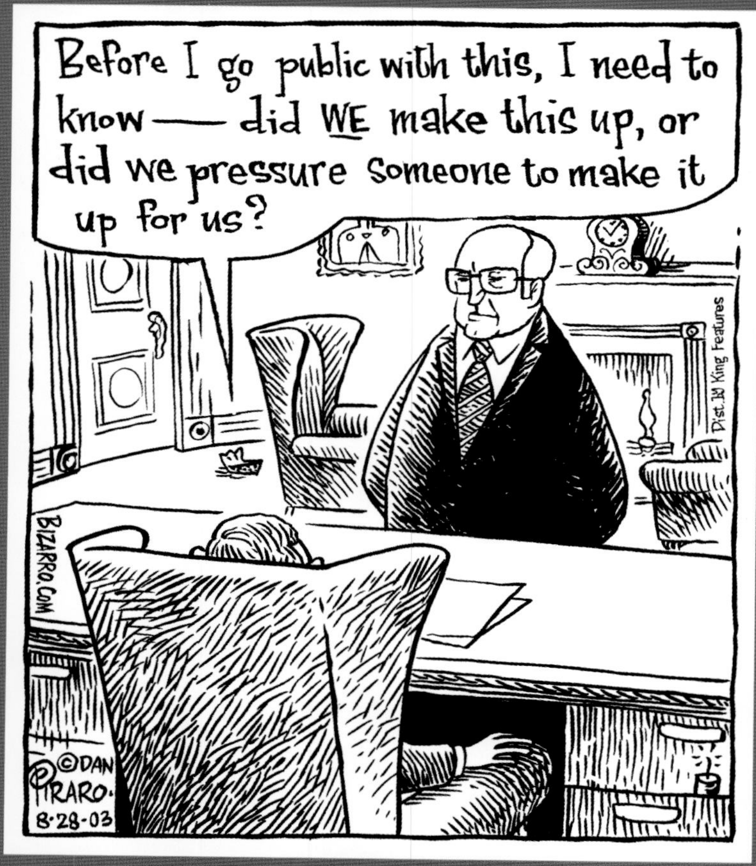
Before I go public with this, I need to know — did WE make this up, or did we pressure someone to make it up for us?
Dist. by King Features
BIZARRO.COM
©DAN PIRARO 8-28-03

The answer is probably "both." (2003)

For those readers not skilled at Wheel of Fortune, the answers to the questions at right are "pot," "Bible," and "Iraq." For those not familiar with pop culture crimes against good taste, the doll below was actually marketed.

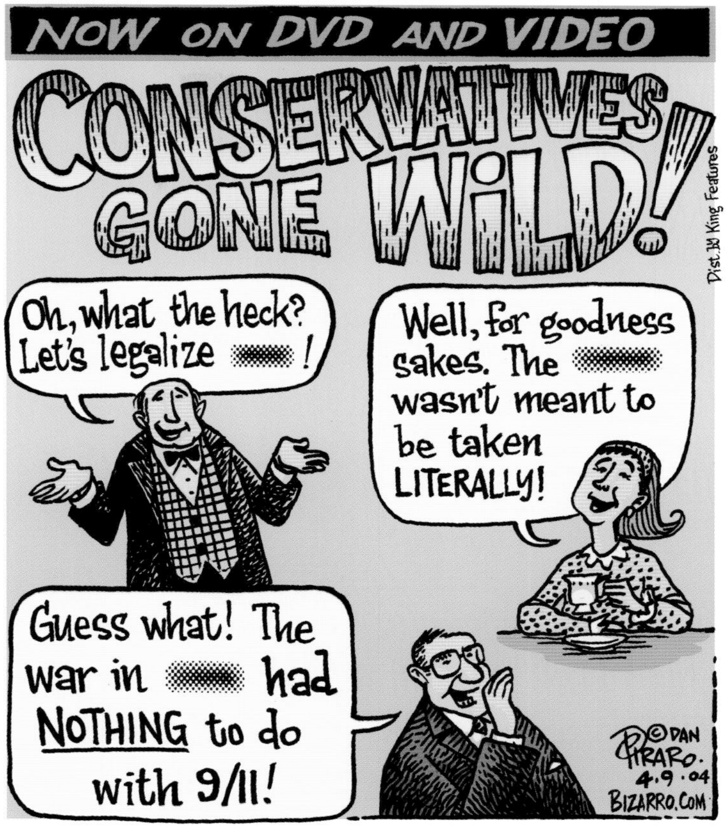

NOW ON DVD AND VIDEO
CONSERVATIVES GONE WILD!
Oh, what the heck? Let's legalize !
Well, for goodness sakes. The wasn't meant to be taken LITERALLY!
Guess what! The war in had NOTHING to do with 9/11!
©DAN PIRARO. 4.9.04
BIZARRO.COM
Dist. by King Features

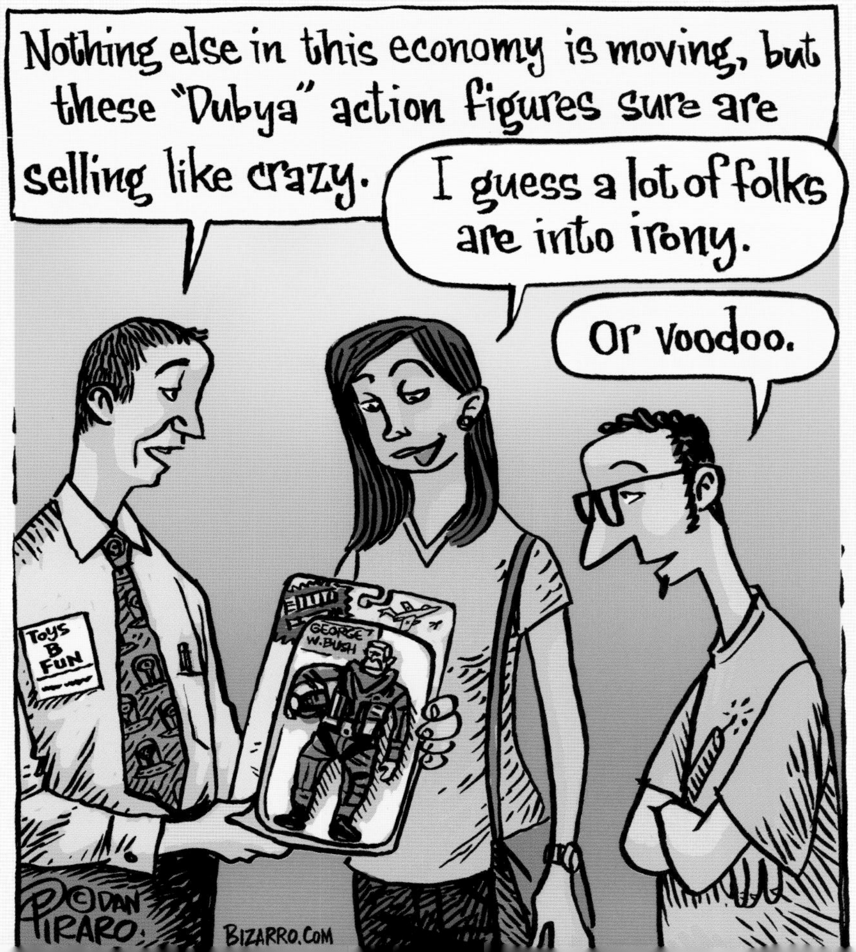

Nothing else in this economy is moving, but these "Dubya" action figures sure are selling like crazy.
I guess a lot of folks are into irony.
Or voodoo.
Toys R Fun
GEORGE W. BUSH
©DAN PIRARO
BIZARRO.COM

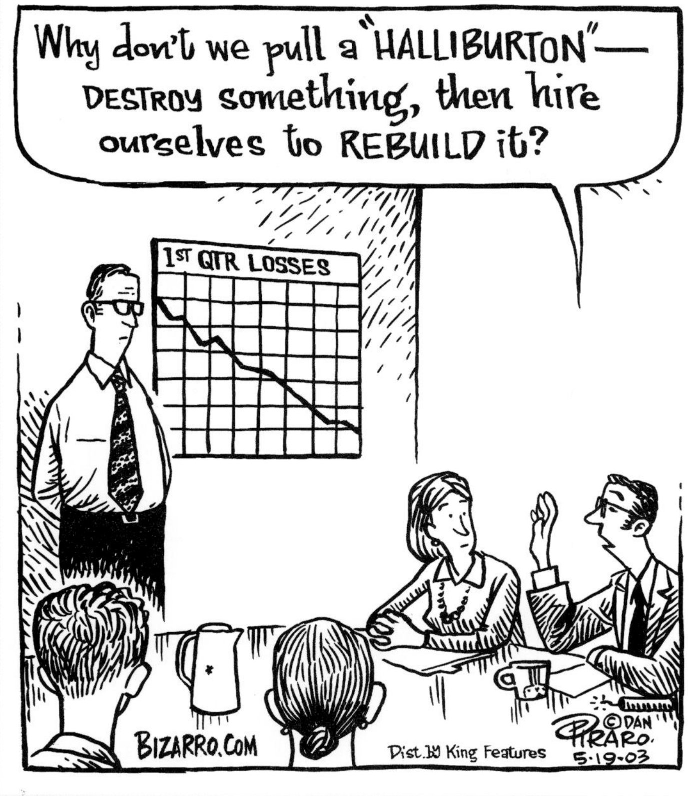
Why don't we pull a "HALLIBURTON"— DESTROY something, then hire ourselves to REBUILD it?
1ST QTR LOSSES
BIZARRO.COM
Dist. by King Features
©DAN PIRARO. 5-19-03

Could the connection between big oil and the Bush administration's policy decisions be any more transparent? But add fear into the mix, and you've got a political juggernaut. (2003)

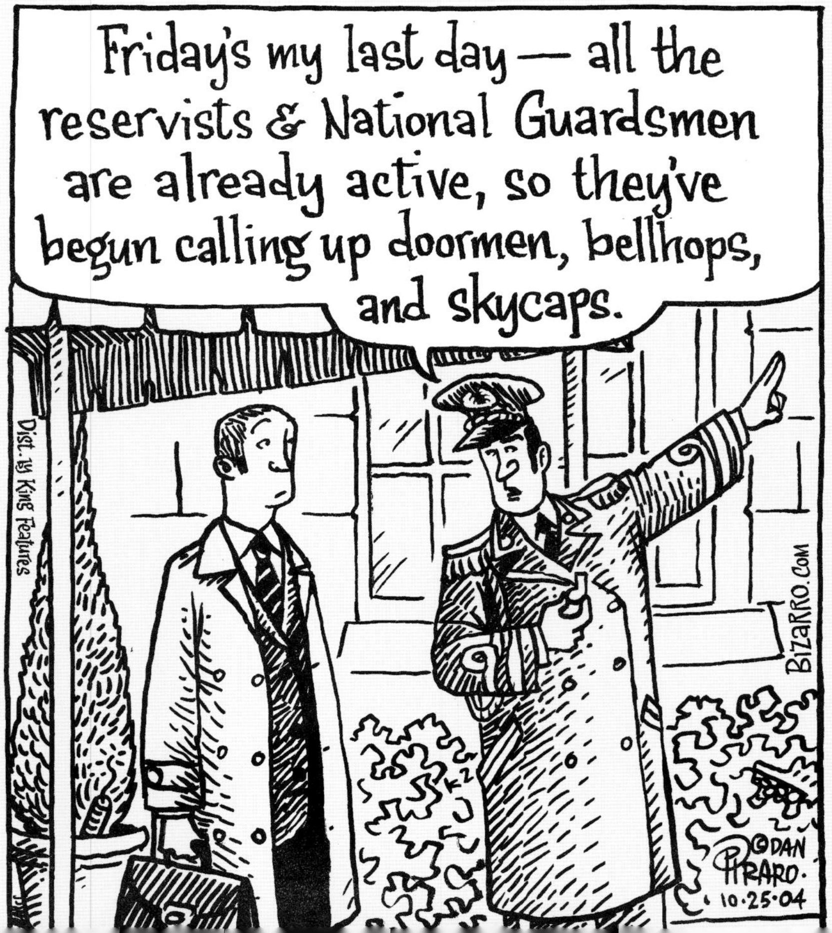
Friday's my last day — all the reservists & National Guardsmen are already active, so they've begun calling up doormen, bellhops, and skycaps.
Dist. by King Features
BIZARRO.COM
©DAN PIRARO. 10-25-04

Cheney and Rumsfeld objected to Nixon's attempts to make peace with the Soviets and trumped up the existence of weapons of mass destruction in the USSR to fuel the Cold War under Ford and Reagan. These guys never grew out of playing army. Maybe if either of them had ever seen combat (Cheney never even served), they'd have lost their adolescent view of heroism and patriotism. (2004)

To this day I am astounded by the Republican propaganda machine being able to make a war hero into a villain and a spoiled, sissy, combat-dodging rich kid into a war hero.

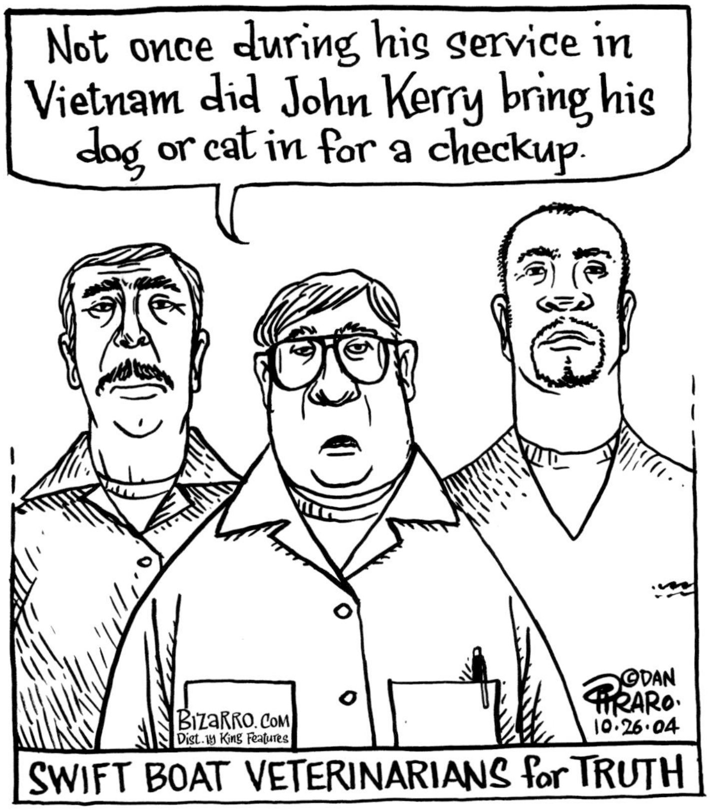
Not once during his service in Vietnam did John Kerry bring his dog or cat in for a checkup.
BIZARRO.COM Dist. by King Features
©DAN PIRARO. 10·26·04
SWIFT BOAT VETERINARIANS for TRUTH

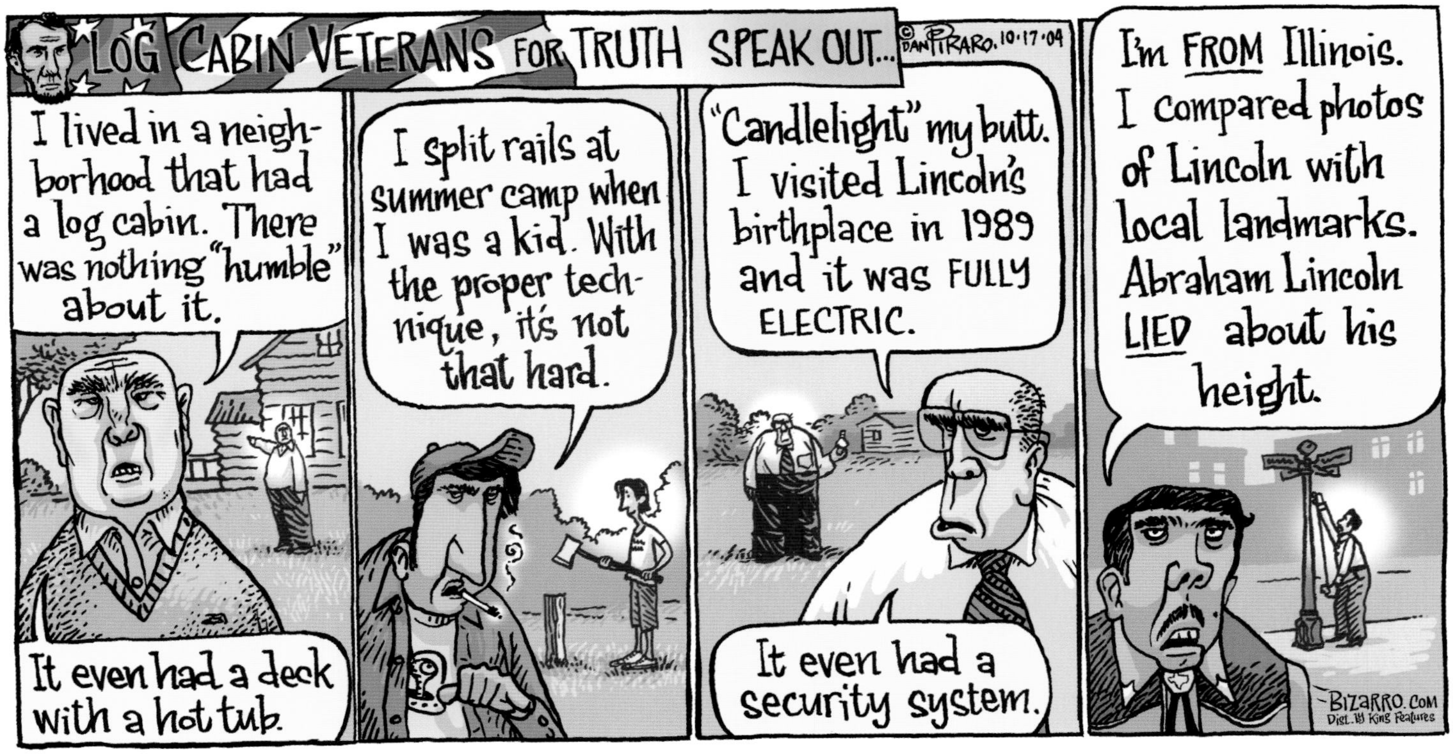
LOG CABIN VETERANS FOR TRUTH SPEAK OUT...
© DAN PIRARO. 10·17·04
I lived in a neighborhood that had a log cabin. There was nothing "humble" about it.
It even had a deck with a hot tub.
I split rails at summer camp when I was a kid. With the proper technique, it's not that hard.
"Candlelight" my butt. I visited Lincoln's birthplace in 1989 and it was FULLY ELECTRIC.
It even had a security system.
I'm FROM Illinois. I compared photos of Lincoln with local landmarks. Abraham Lincoln LIED about his height.
BIZARRO.COM Dist. by King Features

As with the fight against animal abuse, I felt impelled to bring some of these political issues to the public. As corny as it may sound, it wasn't an attempt to remake America to my liking, but to do my small part to help save the country from what I perceive to be a very selfish and irresponsible regime. To my mind, this is everyone's patriotic duty—much more so than plastering flags and ribbon magnets all over your gas-guzzling SUV and declaring the infallibility of the president regardless of the evidence to the contrary. Nor was it an attempt to draw attention to myself and further my own career aspirations. In fact, putting my political beliefs in *Bizarro* was a risky thing to do.

Here's why: when newspaper editors buy a cartoon to run in their papers, they expect it not to change. At least it should remain in the same category. If you bought *Family Circus* for your paper because you wanted a wholesome cartoon about family life, and two years later it became a pointed social commentary on the injustice of current marijuana laws, you might reconsider your decision.

Such was the case with some editors when *Bizarro* became political in the last couple of years of the first George W. Bush administration. *Bizarro* is sold as a surreal joke-a-day feature, not as a political feature. Some editors were not sure they wanted to deal with the waves of phone calls, letters, and emails they would get from readers who had accepted the president as their personal savior when I would suggest that he might actually be a mortal. And not a particularly good one.

Not long after 9/11 I began railing against the average American's response to the attacks. These cartoons are aimed at the sort of people who confuse the flag with the principles behind it and imagine they can defeat the resentment of untold millions of people all across the world without doing anything more than plastering their possessions with flags and backing the politician with the most convincing macho facade. Incidentally, fascist governments always encourage this behavior. It keeps them in power and the people afraid to dissent. (2001)

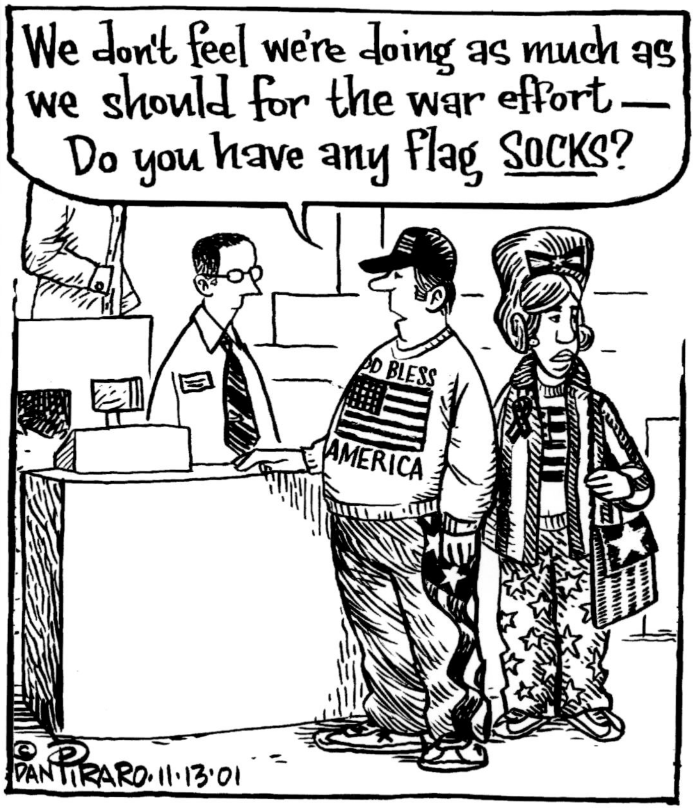
We don't feel we're doing as much as we should for the war effort — Do you have any flag SOCKS?
D BLESS AMERICA
© DAN PIRARO · 11 · 13 · 01

This is my favorite time—the 3 years, 11 months & 29 days between presidential elections when I don't have to pay attention.
©DAN PIRARO 12-6-04
BIZARRO.COM
Dist. by King Features

Me likes president because he talk so smart like us do.
©DAN PIRARO 5-31-04
BIZARRO.COM
Dist. by King Features

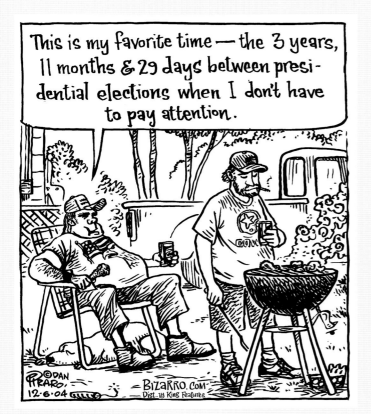

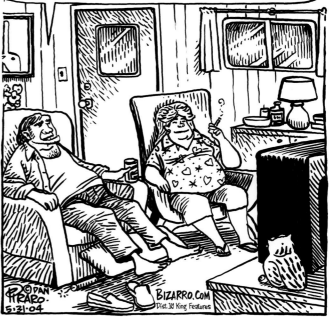

It is terrifying that people who know nothing of politics or history can decide an election, but that's democracy. As Churchill said, it's the worst form of government on earth, except for all the rest. Call me an elitist, but I think you should have to pass a simple intelligence and current events test to earn the right to vote. If you don't pass, you can't vote. If you can't vote, you can't be elected. Several birds with one stone. (2004)

ABOVE RIGHT: This panel provoked some (poorly written) hate mail. (2004)

WWJD?
WAP!
© Dan Piraro 2004

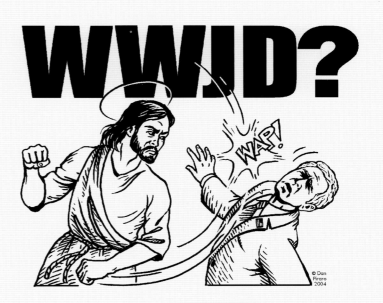

T-shirt design I sold at comedy clubs. If you're fortunate enough to be unacquainted with fundamentalist lingo, WWJD stands for "What would Jesus do?" After studying the Bible quite a bit from both a religious and a secular point of view, I am thoroughly convinced that this image is dead-on accurate.

I certainly had no desire to be canceled but I did not want to abandon my opinions, either. So I discussed it with a few concerned editors from around the country and decided to try to walk a thin line. I limited the frequency of my political cartoons and attempted to cloak them with enough ambiguity so that they were comments on current conditions and attitudes more than open indictments of anyone in particular. The one exception in my policy of ambiguity was the week before the 2004 presidential election when I did eight political jokes in a row, from the previous Monday to election Tuesday (not counting Sunday). I endured a storm of complaints—especially about the one concerning Karl Rove and Plato (below)—but thankfully, the only cancellation was from a paper in a small Southern town with a military base. It amazes me that no matter how much a president abuses his troops, they can't bear to believe he isn't right in doing so.

OPPOSITE: This cartoon was way too far left for *D* (and way too true) and the publisher almost filled his pants when he saw it. The only reason it made it into the magazine was that he happened to be out of town when it went to press. Maybe there is a god. If there is, I'm damn sure he/she isn't a right-winger.

These two cartoons printed the week before the 2004 election were a last-ditch effort to wake people up.

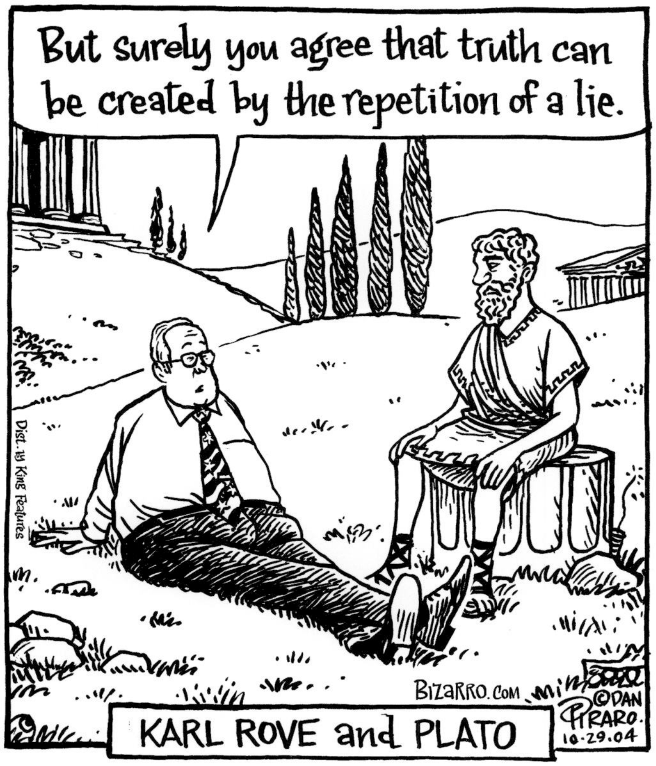
But surely you agree that truth can be created by the repetition of a lie.
BIZARRO.COM
©DAN PIRARO. 10·29·04
KARL ROVE and PLATO

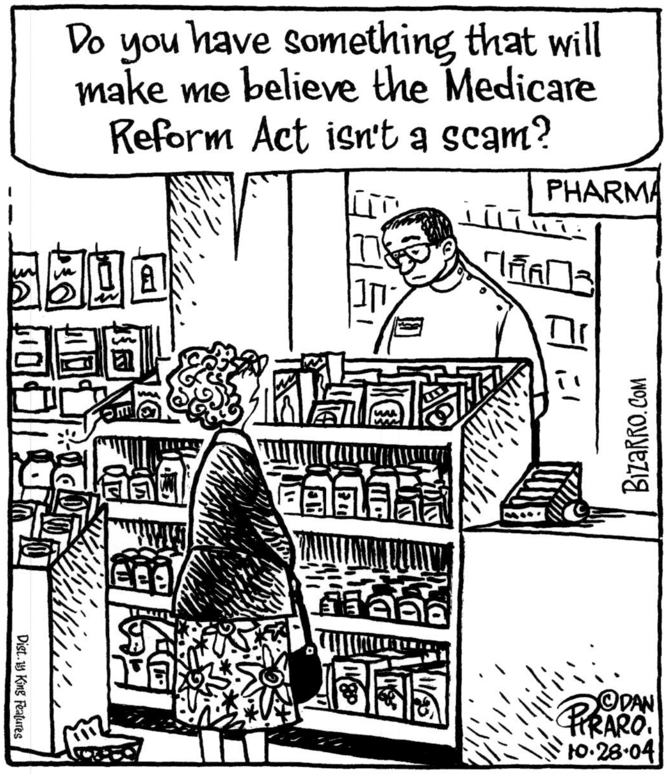
Do you have something that will make me believe the Medicare Reform Act isn't a scam?
PHARMA
BIZARRO.COM
©DAN PIRARO. 10·28·04

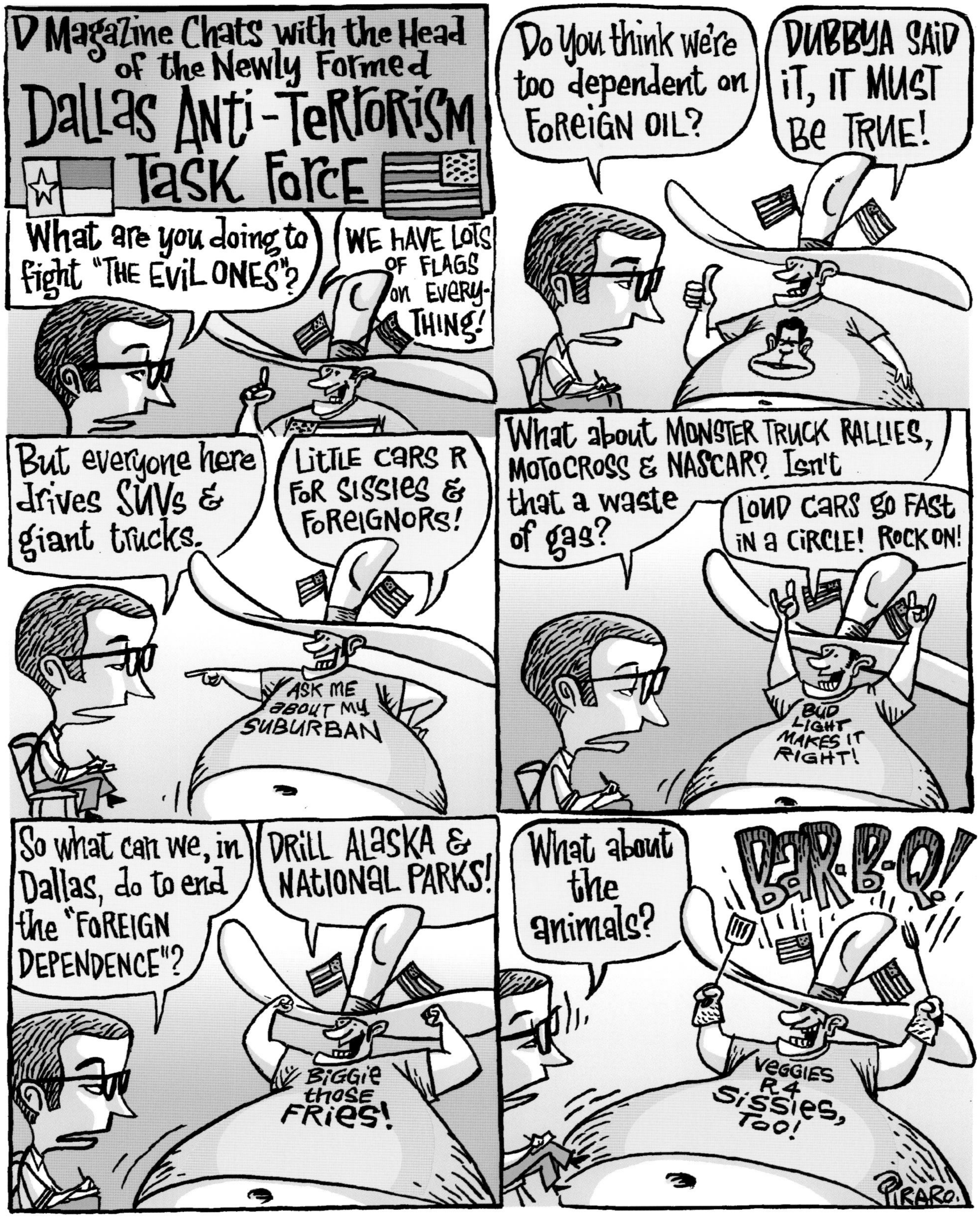
D Magazine Chats with the Head of the Newly Formed
Dallas Anti-Terrorism Task Force
What are you doing to fight "THE EVIL ONES"?
WE HAVE LOTS OF FLAGS on EVERY-THING!
Do you think we're too dependent on Foreign oil?
DUBBYA SAID IT, IT MUST Be TRUE!
But everyone here drives SUVs & giant trucks.
LITTLE CARS R FOR SISSIES & FOREIGNORS!
ASK ME ABOUT MY SUBURBAN
What about MONSTER TRUCK RALLIES, MOTOCROSS & NASCAR? Isn't that a waste of gas?
LOUD CARS go FAST IN A CIRCLE! ROCK ON!
BUD LIGHT MAKES IT RIGHT!
So what can we, in Dallas, do to end the "FOREIGN DEPENDENCE"?
DRILL ALASKA & NATIONAL PARKS!
BiGGIE those FRIES!
What about the animals?
BAR-B-Q!
VEGGIES R 4 SISSIES, TOO!
PIRARO

This anticancellation dance left me with ideas and energy to spare, so in late 2003, I began working on a mock children's book called *The Three Little Pigs Buy the White House*. In my version, the title characters are Dickey (Cheney), Rummy (Rumsfeld), and Dubya. They inherit a country made of bricks and immediately begin to give the bricks away to their rich friends, replacing them with mud and straw. While they're counting their millions, the Big Bad Wolf blows down a couple of big buildings and the other animals in the land insist that the pigs do something about it. Unable to find the Big Bad Wolf who's responsible, they set their sights on another one, one they hate and know would be easier to catch. They convince everyone that he has WMDs (winds of mass destruction). Meanwhile, most of the country is falling apart—people are out of work, millions have no health care or are homeless—and people start to question the pigs' policies. The surprise ending is one I had hoped would occur in November '04, but alas, between computerized machines with no paper trail, disenfranchised voters, a glaring lack of voting machines in Democratic areas, and myriad other tactics by Republican-run election boards across the nation, Bush squeaked by for another term.

The cover of my political satire. (2004)

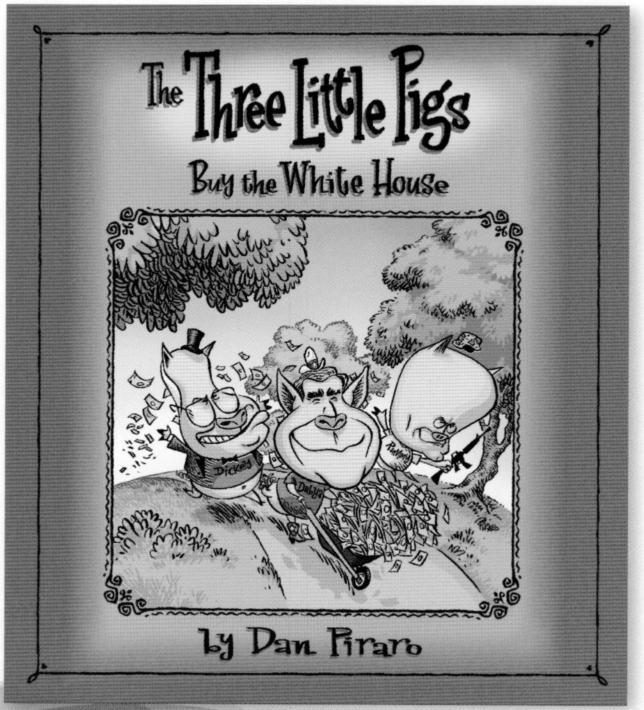
The Three Little Pigs
Buy the White House
by Dan Piraro

The title page art. I'm not particularly experienced with caricatures, so I was pretty happy with these. (2004)

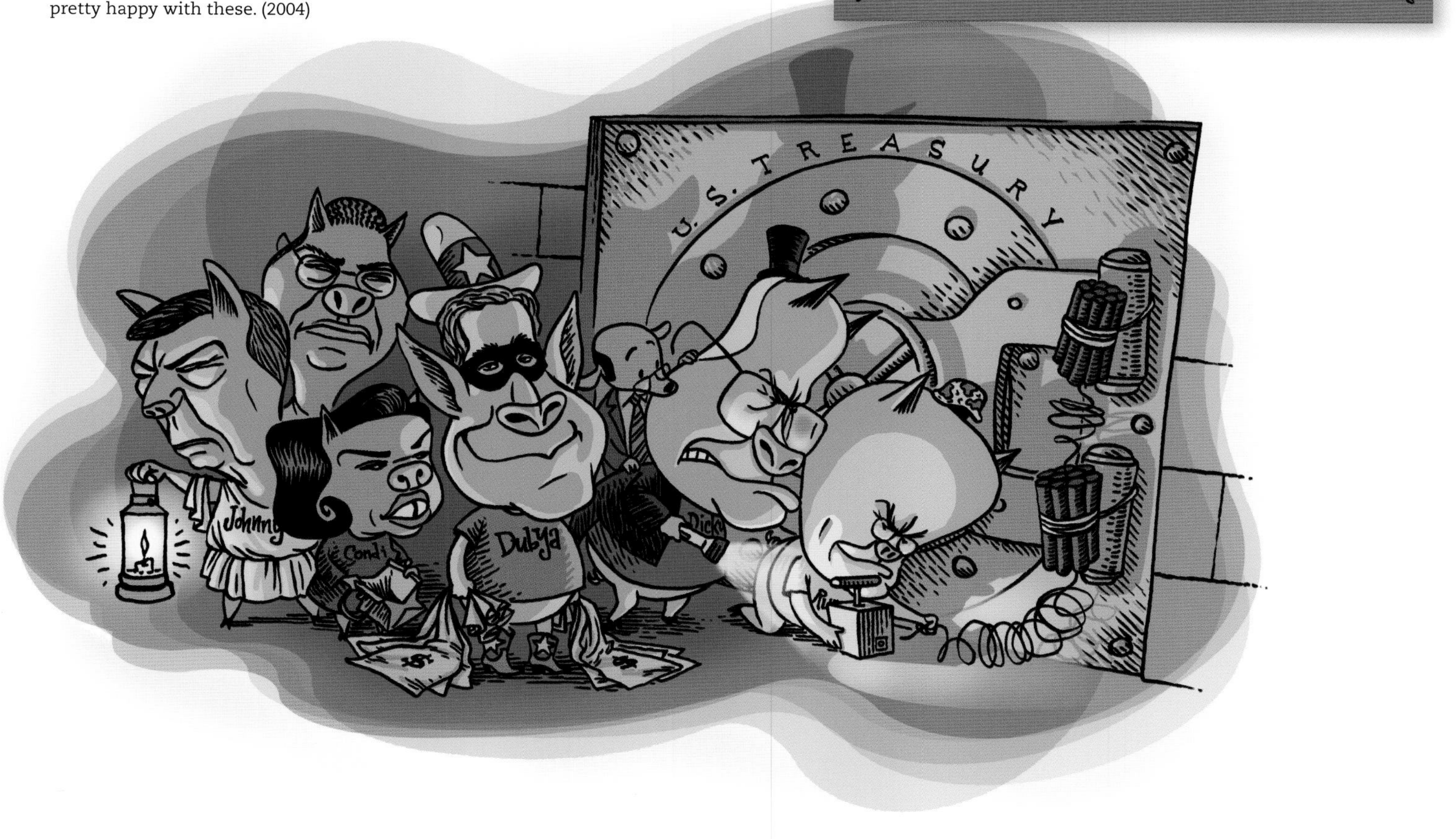
U.S. TREASURY
Johnny
Condi
Dubya
Dick

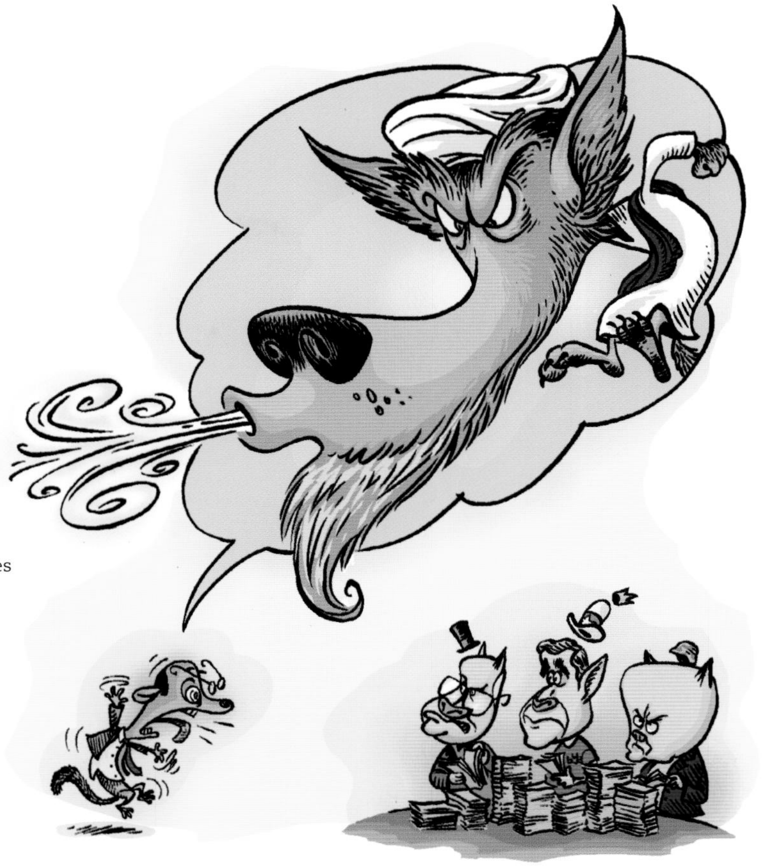

Press Secretary Ari the Weasel announces that the Big Bad Wolf has blown down some big buildings. (2004)

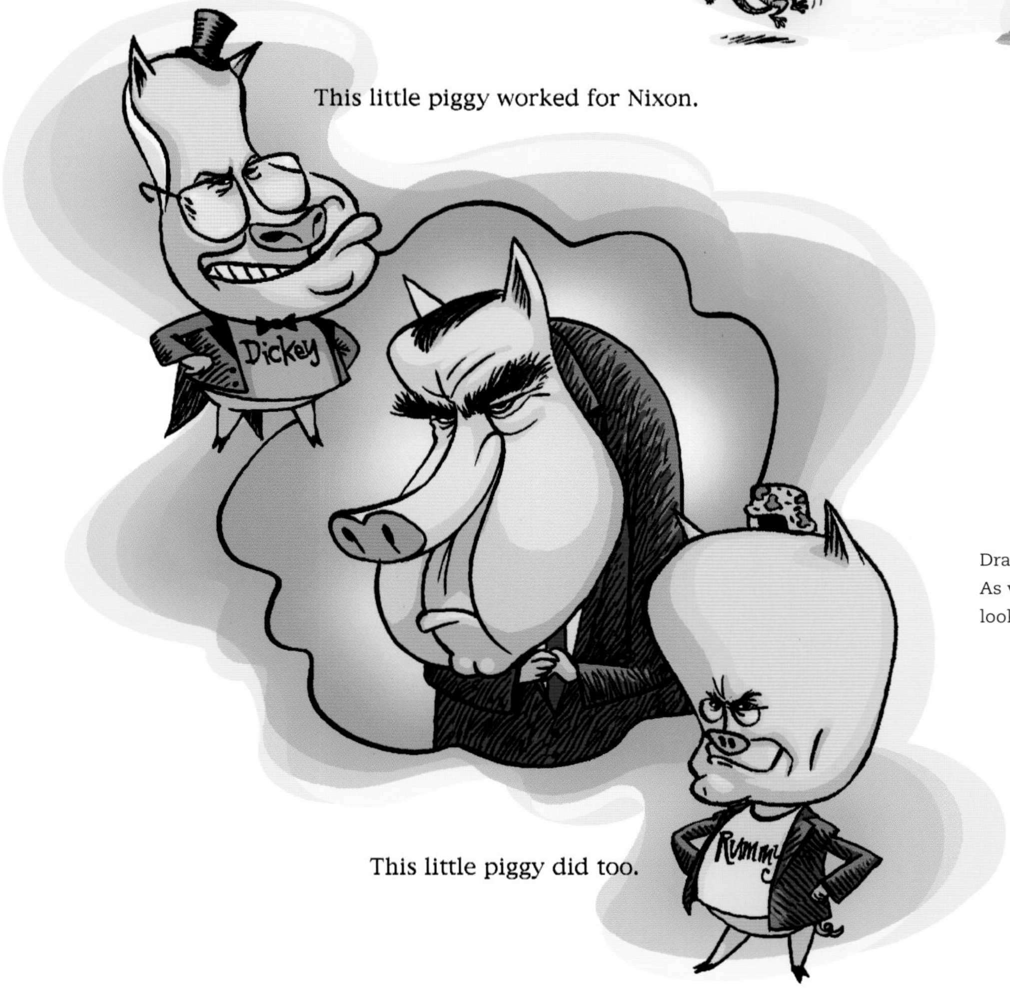
This little piggy worked for Nixon.
Dickey
Rummy
This little piggy did too.

Drawing Nixon as a pig was alarmingly easy. As wicked as he was, the neocons make him look like Mother Teresa on Valium. (2004)

This book sold quite well by my standards, and I am very proud of it. If Bush had been defeated, sales would have come to an abrupt stop, so it was in my financial best interest for him to win a second term. Yet, like a true Democrat, I put the good of the people ahead of my own financial gain and campaigned relentlessly against Genghis Bush and his Millionaire Marauders. To this end, I put the Bizarro Bologna Show on hiatus and enlisted three stand-up comics and formed a political comedy show called *Bizarro*'s Politicomedy-A-Go-Go. Beginning in April 2004, we toured the country playing comedy clubs and small theaters all over the U.S. By Election Day, we had done thirty-five shows in nineteen cities.

Keeping up with the tour schedule and my regular *Bizarro* deadlines nearly burned a hole in my cerebral cortex. The tour was conducted on a shoestring budget, so we spent a lot of time piled into a small rental car, driving all day, doing a show that night, sleeping on someone's couch, then starting all over again the next morning. You often hear rock stars complaining about the rigors of touring. This was just like that but without the adulation, money, groupies, or drugs.

A promo poster for one of our political comedy shows in San Francisco.

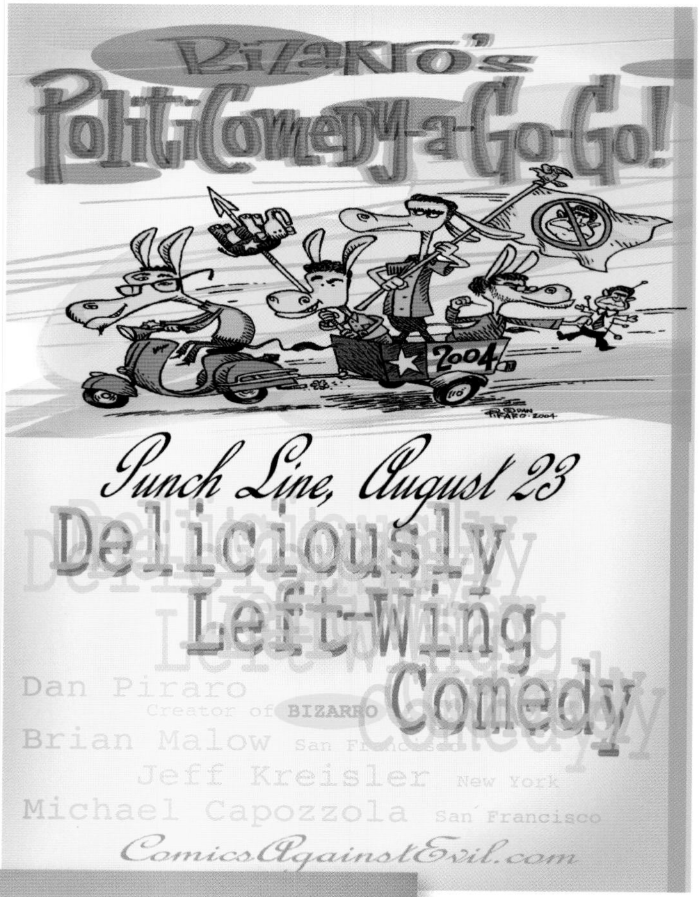
Bizarro's
PolitiComedy-a-Go-Go!
2004
Punch Line, August 23
Deliciously
Left-Wing
Comedy
Dan Piraro
Creator of BIZARRO
Brian Malow San Francisco
Jeff Kreisler New York
Michael Capozzola San Francisco
ComicsAgainstEvil.com

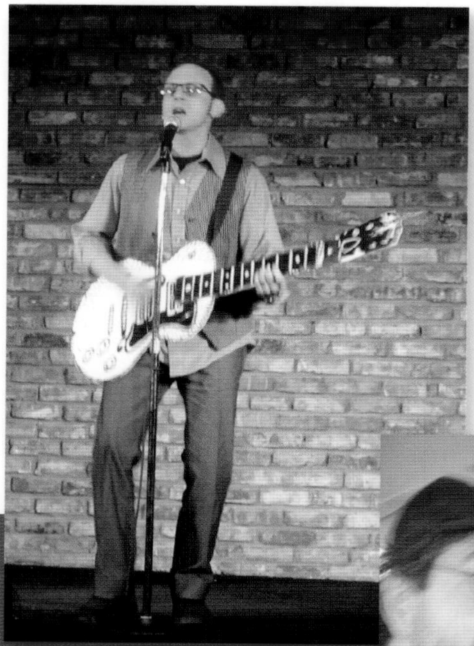

On stage at an improv club. Most people are surprised at how well I play cardboard guitar. (2004)

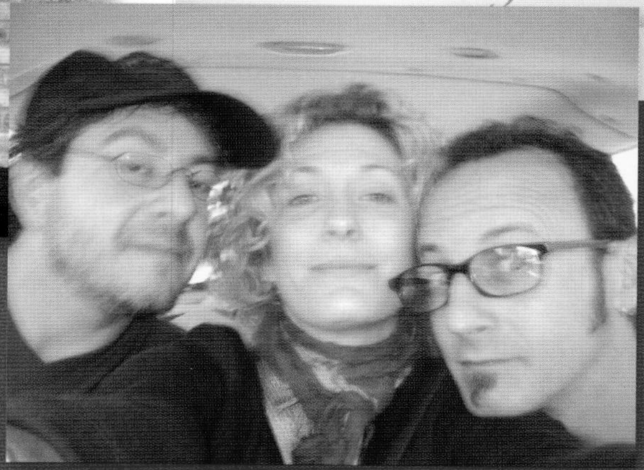

RIGHT: Crammed into a rental car on the road with fellow comedian Brian Malow and my wife, Ashley Lou Smith. (2004).

The webpage I designed for our political comedy tour. The blank, greenish areas were full of info and links. (2004)

CENTER: Back in the mid-eighties, I was a Big Brother to this guy. He was five years old then and about one-eighth this size. He showed up at one of my comedy shows in Texas. By the look on his face, he may have regretted it. (2004)

BELOW: I was interviewed before one of the shows in Austin by a documentary film director, Craig Duff. Some footage of our 9/11 material was included in a Discovery Channel show about homeland security. (2004)

BELOW, RIGHT: The cast in the green room at an improv club. From left: A much-too-happy Jeff Kreisler, a concerned Brian Malow, Michael Capozzola, Liz Taylor. (2004)

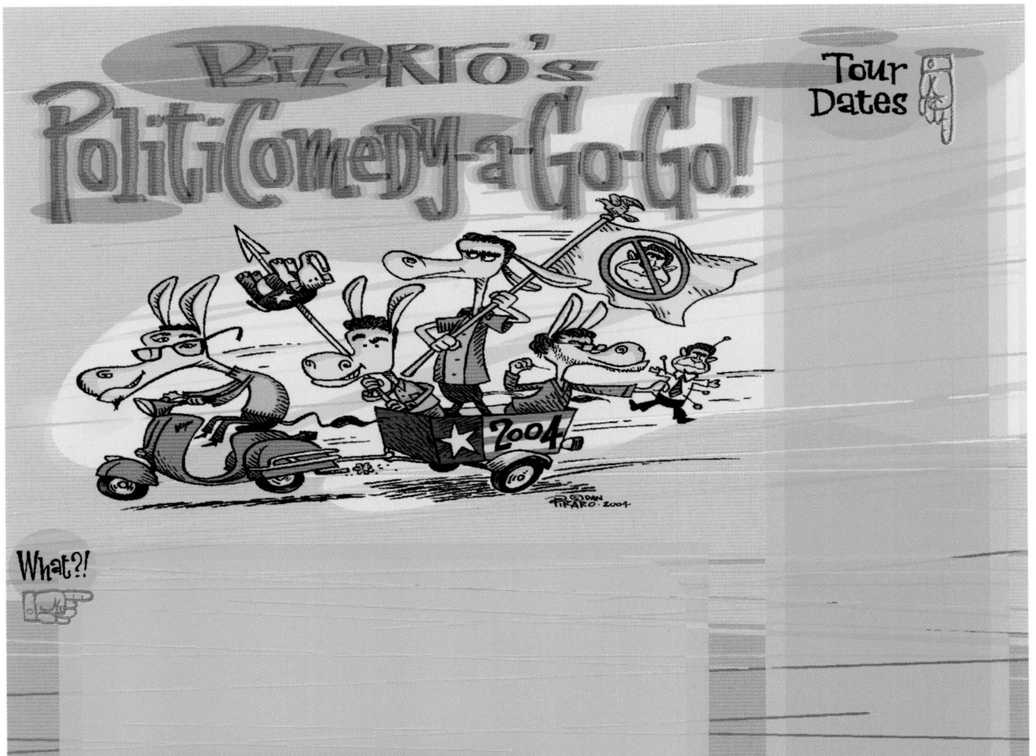

Piraro's
PolitiComedy-a-Go-Go!
Tour Dates
2004
What?!

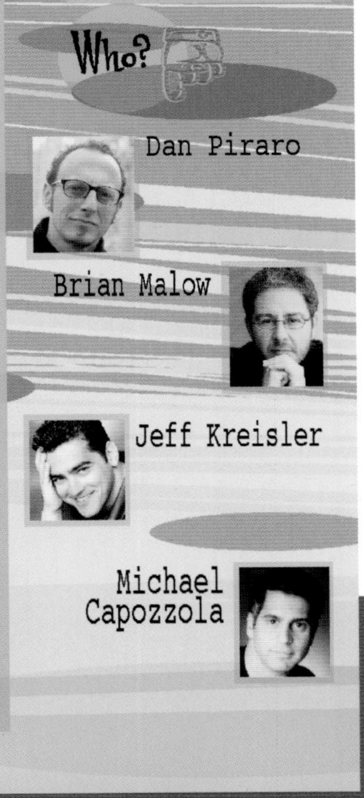

Who?
Dan Piraro
Brian Malow
Jeff Kreisler
Michael Capozzola

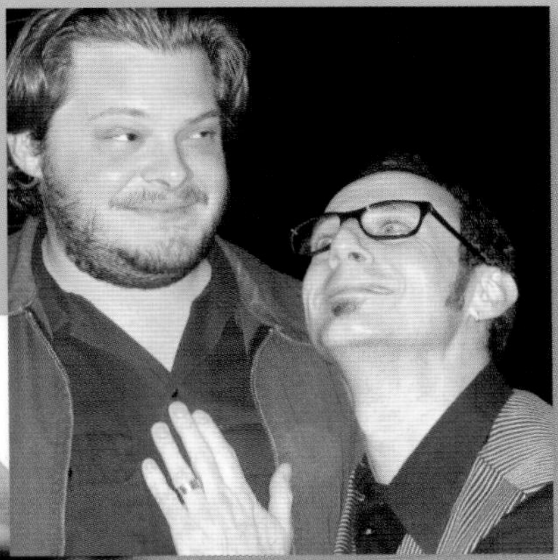

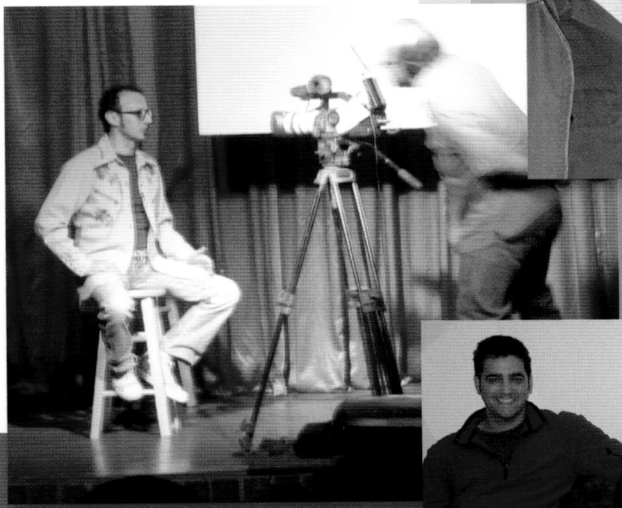

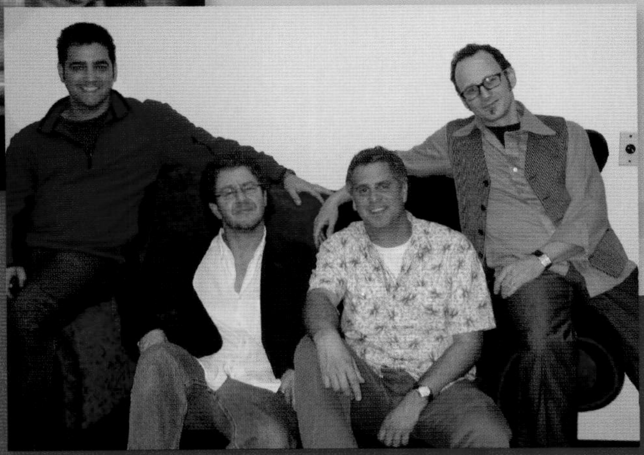

A little help from my friends

I get hundreds of ideas for cartoons each year from readers and friends but I use only a very small handful of them. A couple of friends who have contributed more than their share are Michael Capozzola, one of the stand-up comics on the PolitiComedy tour and David Levitin, a psychology professor in Montreal. These are a few of my favorites from them.

Michael Capozzola is a working stand-up comic by trade and a cartoonist in his spare time. He publishes some of his work in a San Francisco weekly and recently sold a couple of things to MAD magazine. He also sells his work on greeting cards and magnets (see www.capozzola.com).

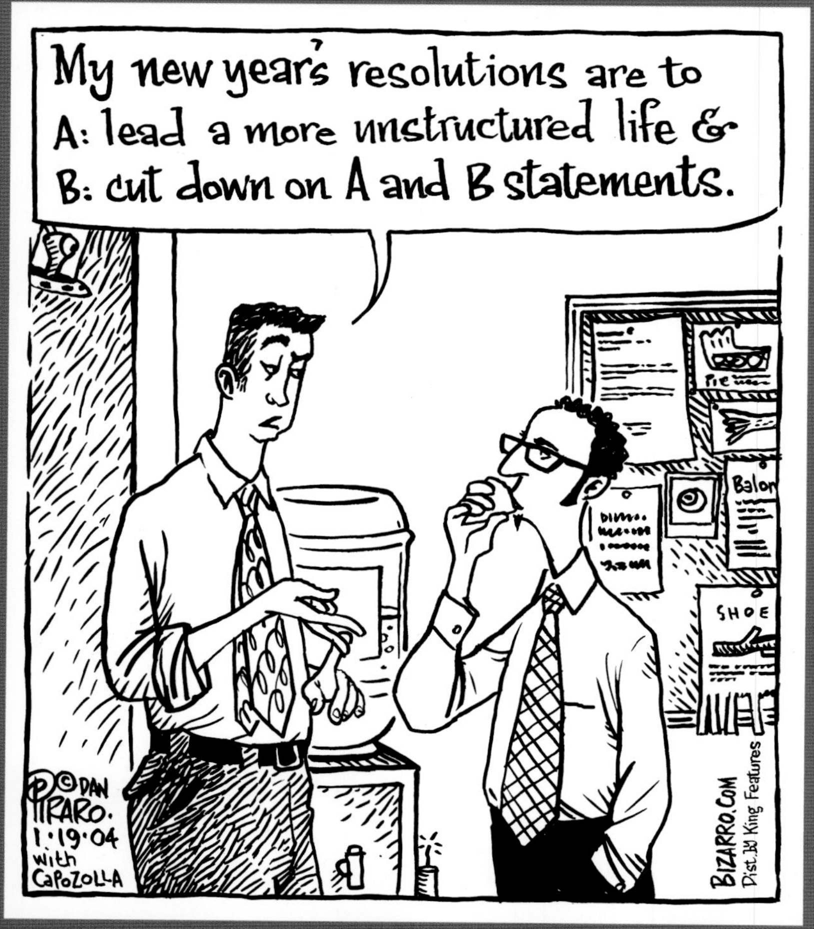
My new year's resolutions are to A: lead a more unstructured life & B: cut down on A and B statements.
©DAN PIRARO. 1·19·04 with CAPOZOLLA
BIZARRO.COM Dist. by King Features
SHOE

This is a rough caricature of Michael and me, with Mike delivering his own line. (2004)

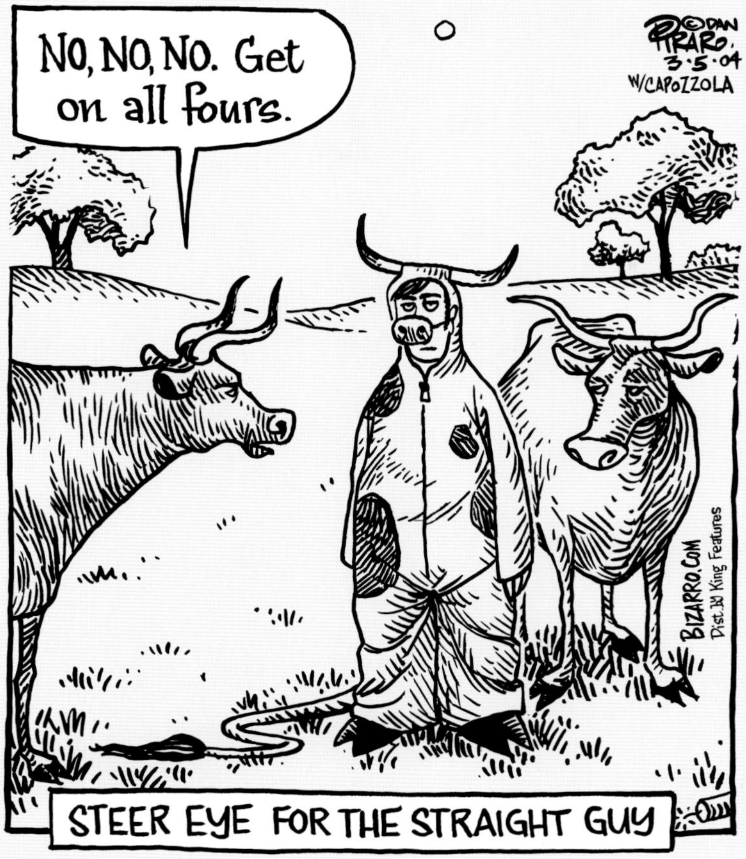
NO, NO, NO. Get on all fours.
©DAN PIRARO. 3·5·04 W/CAPOZZOLA
BIZARRO.COM Dist. by King Features
STEER EYE FOR THE STRAIGHT GUY

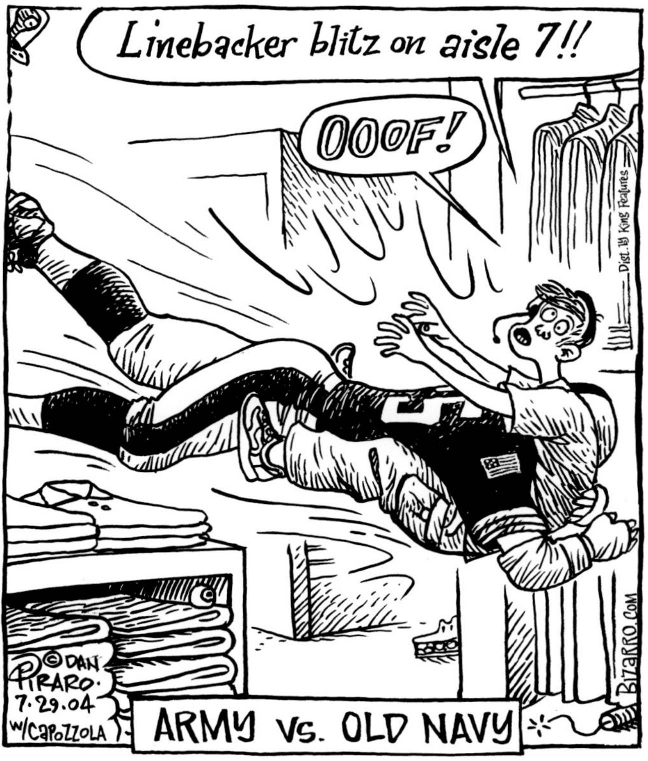
Linebacker blitz on aisle 7!!
OOOF!
Dist. by King Features
BIZARRO.COM
©DAN PIRARO. 7·29·04 W/CAPOZZOLA
ARMY VS. OLD NAVY

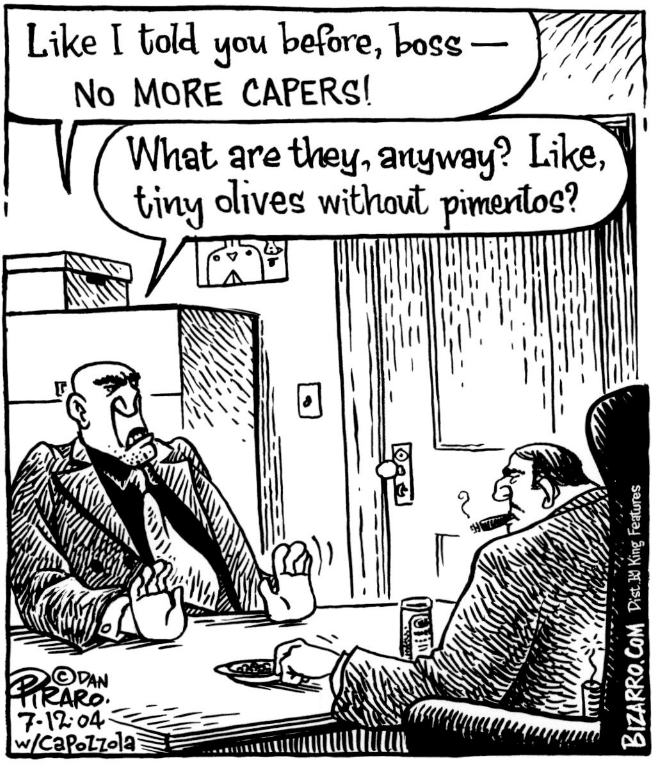
Like I told you before, boss — No MORE CAPERS!
What are they, anyway? Like, tiny olives without pimentos?
©DAN PIRARO. 7·12·04 w/CAPOZZOLA
BIZARRO.COM Dist. by King Features

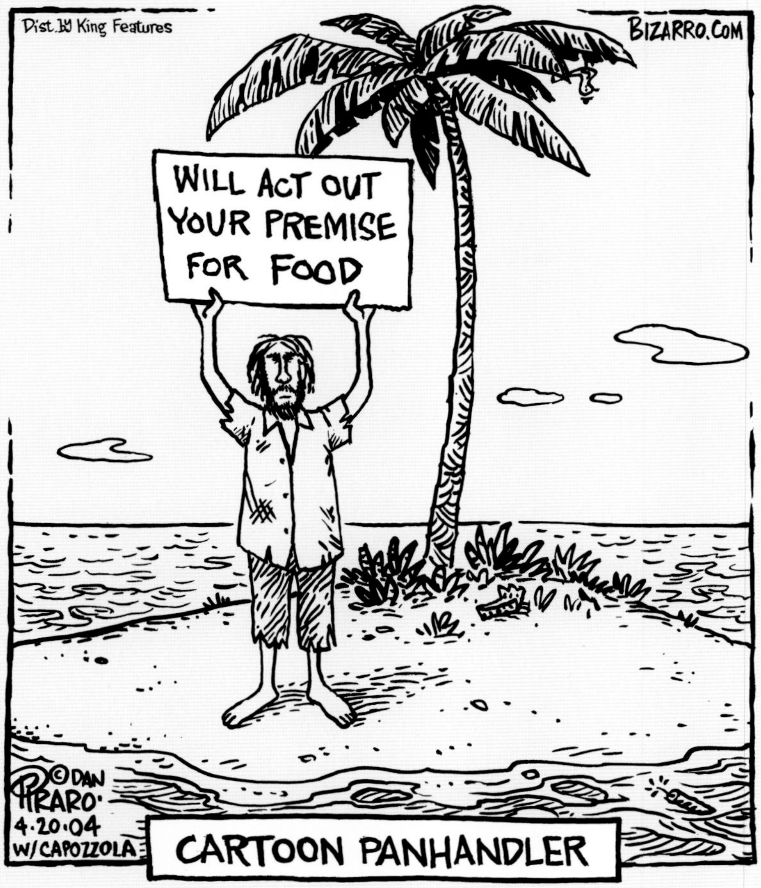
Dist. by King Features
BIZARRO.COM
WILL ACT OUT YOUR PREMISE FOR FOOD
©DAN PIRARO 4.20.04 W/CAPOZZOLA
CARTOON PANHANDLER

An interesting take on one of the most popular cartoon premises of the twentieth century. (2004)

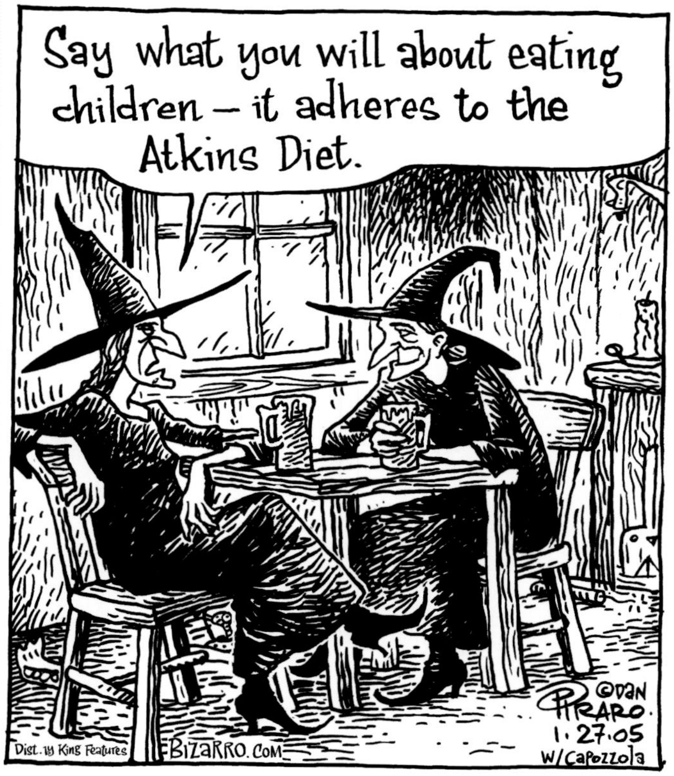
Say what you will about eating children – it adheres to the Atkins Diet.
©DAN PIRARO. 1.27.05 W/CAPOZZOLA
Dist. by King Features
BIZARRO.COM

With his permission, I gave one of the lines from Michael's stand-up act a different slant. His line is: "I was watching a Discovery Channel show the other night about a primitive tribe and say what you will about cannibalism..." As an animal-rights guy, I despise the meat-heavy Atkins Diet. Lots of cardiologists are building summer homes because of it, however. (2005)

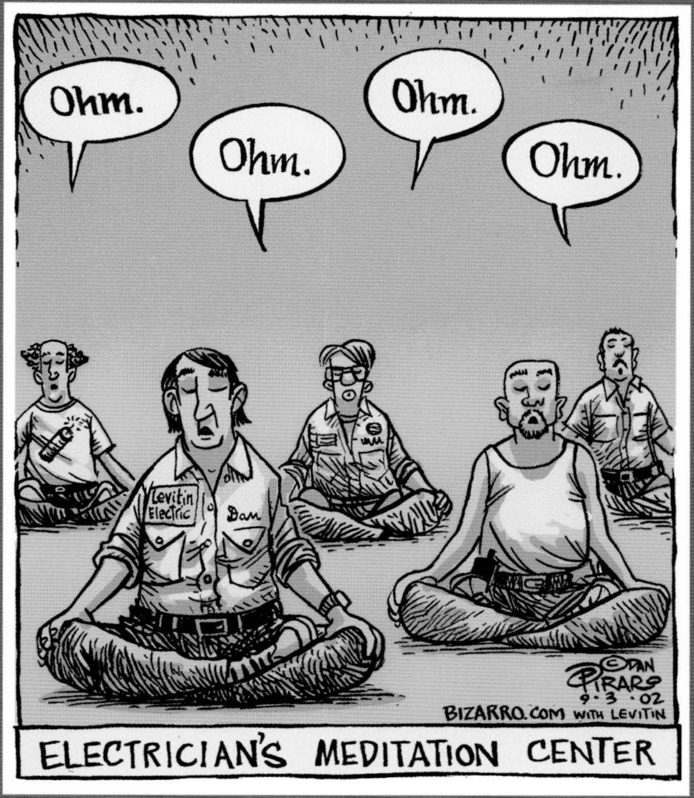
Ohm.
Ohm.
Ohm.
Ohm.
Levitin Electric
Dan
©DAN PIRARO 9·3·02
BIZARRO.COM WITH LEVITIN
ELECTRICIAN'S MEDITATION CENTER

Before Dan Levitin's current gig as a college professor, he did stand-up comedy and was successful as a music journalist and record producer, actually garnering several gold records.

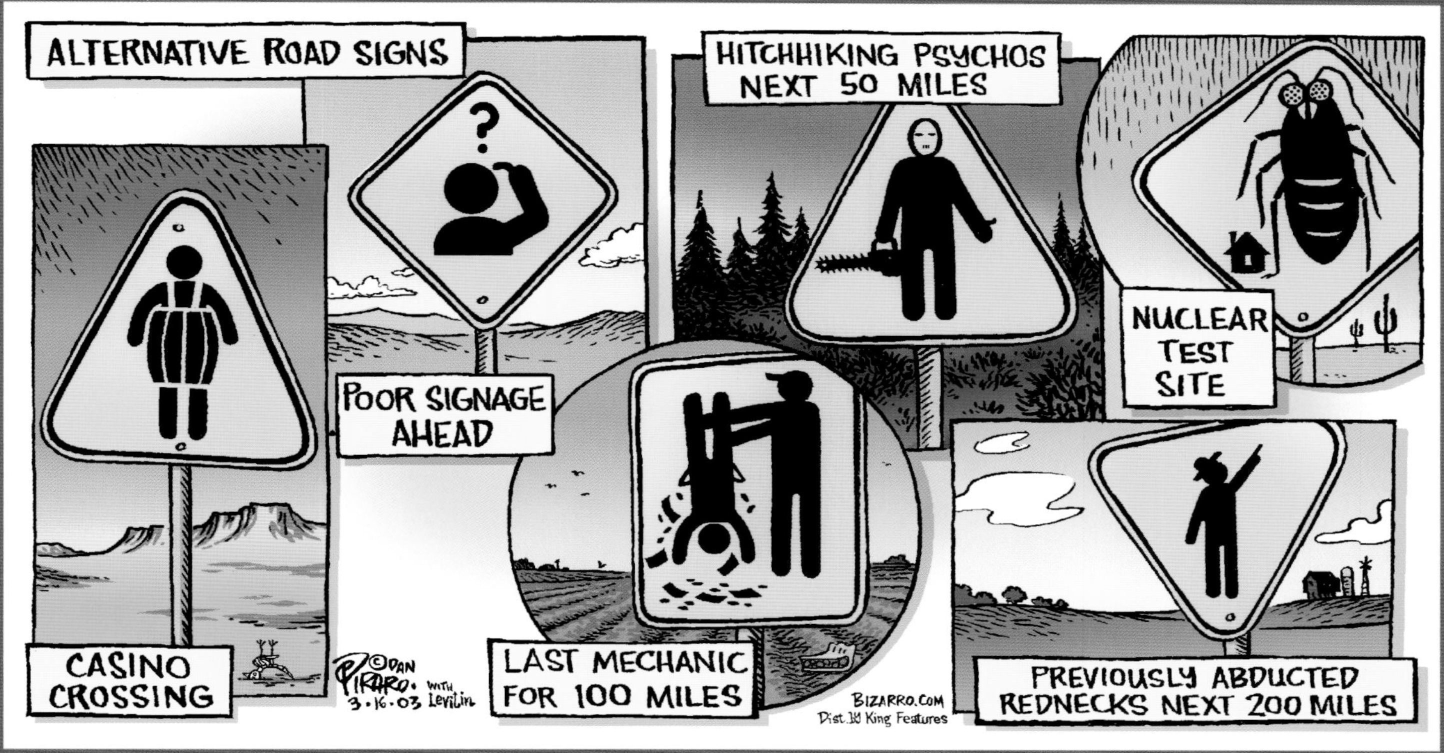
ALTERNATIVE ROAD SIGNS
HITCHHIKING PSYCHOS NEXT 50 MILES
NUCLEAR TEST SITE
POOR SIGNAGE AHEAD
CASINO CROSSING
©DAN PIRARO. WITH Levitin 3·16·03
LAST MECHANIC FOR 100 MILES
BIZARRO.COM Dist. By King Features
PREVIOUSLY ABDUCTED REDNECKS NEXT 200 MILES

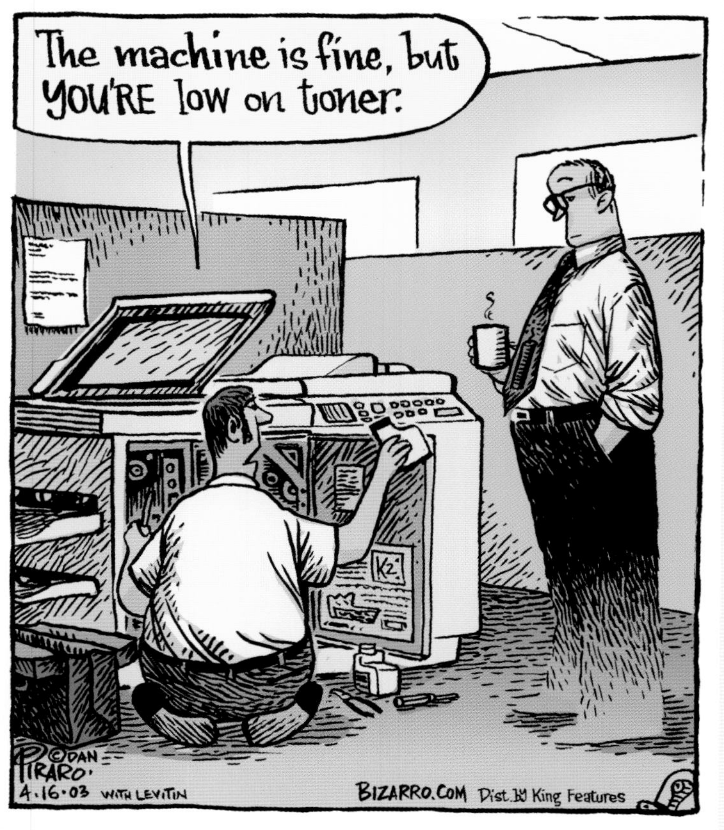
The machine is fine, but YOU'RE low on toner.
©DAN PIRARO 4.16.03 WITH LEVITIN
BIZARRO.COM Dist. by King Features

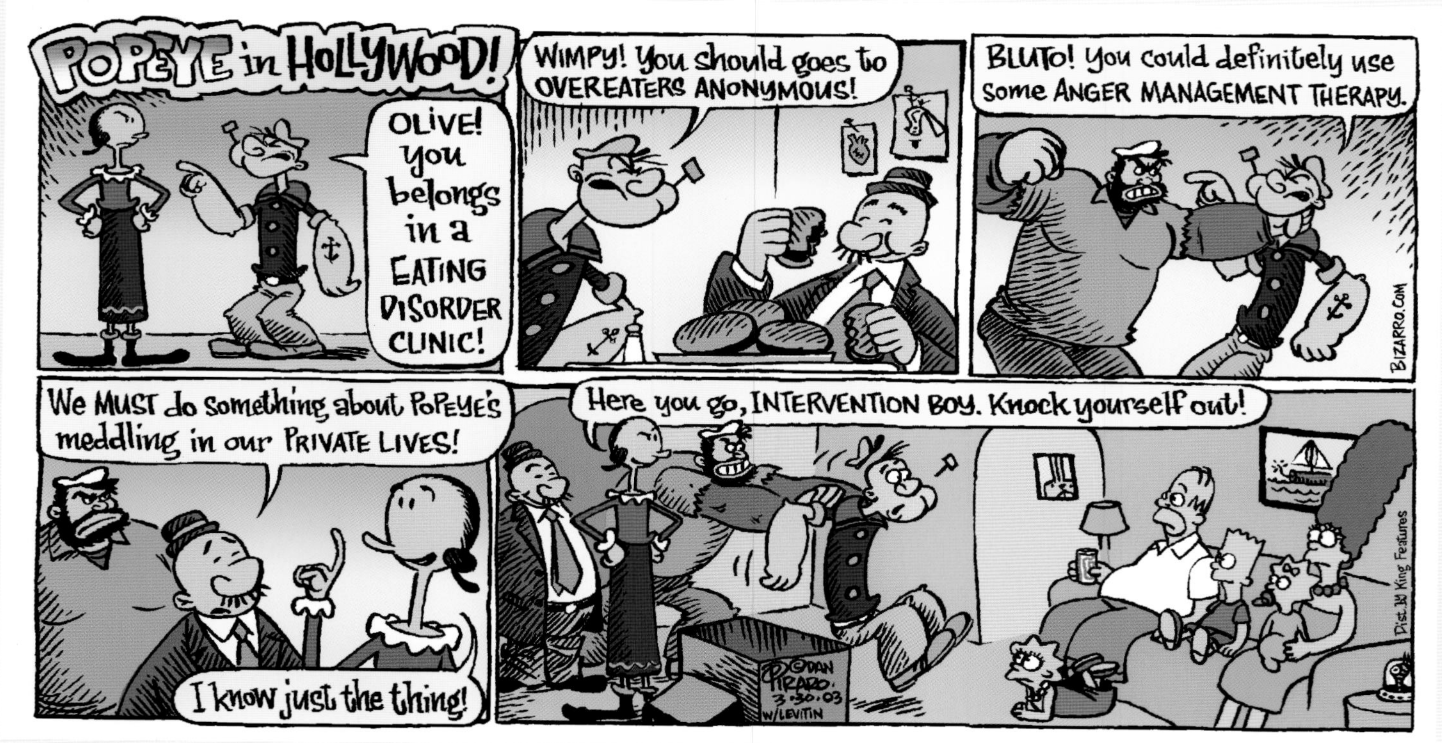
POPEYE in HOLLYWOOD!
OLIVE! you belongs in a EATING DISORDER CLINIC!
WIMPY! You should goes to OVEREATERS ANONYMOUS!
BLUTO! You could definitely use some ANGER MANAGEMENT THERAPY.
BIZARRO.COM
We MUST do something about POPEYE'S meddling in our PRIVATE LIVES!
I know just the thing!
Here you go, INTERVENTION BOY. Knock yourself out!
©DAN PIRARO 3.30.03 W/LEVITIN
Dist. by King Features

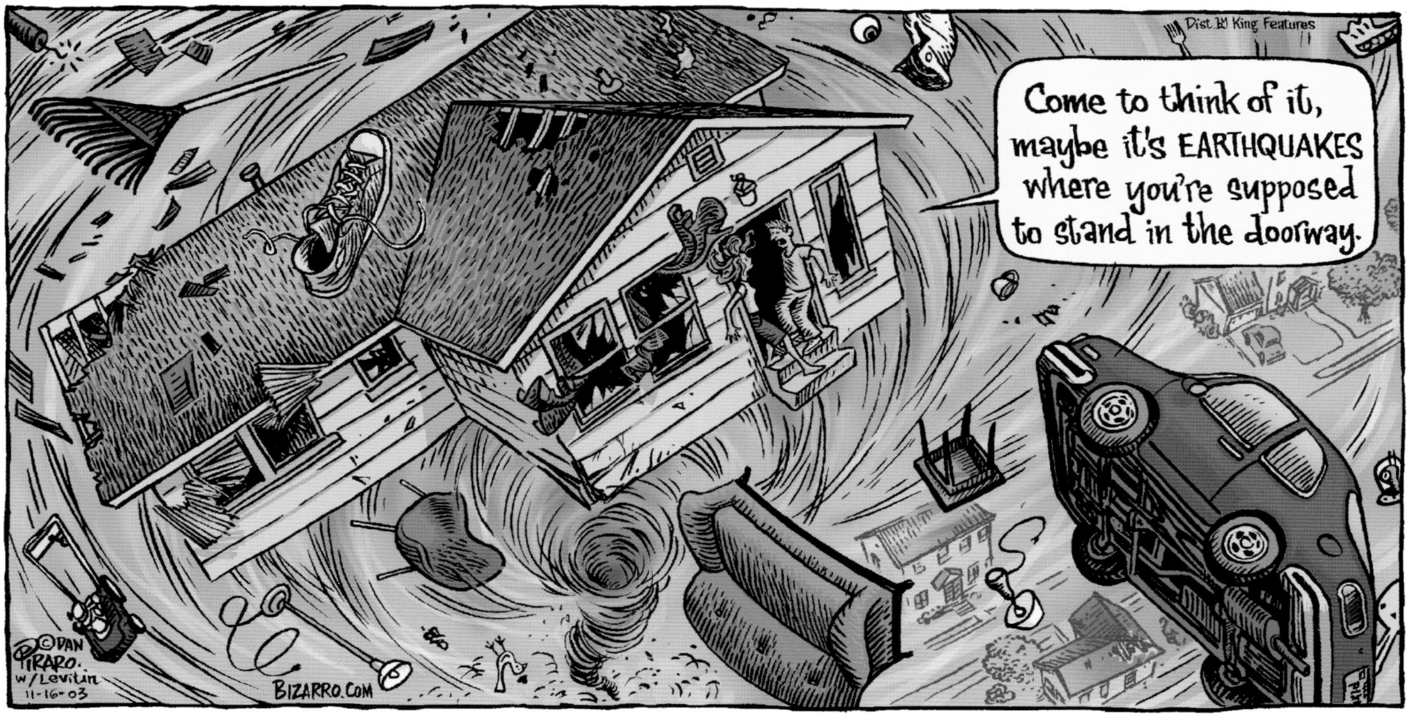
Dist. by King Features
Come to think of it, maybe it's EARTHQUAKES where you're supposed to stand in the doorway.
©DAN PIRARO. w/Levitin 11-16-03
BIZARRO.COM

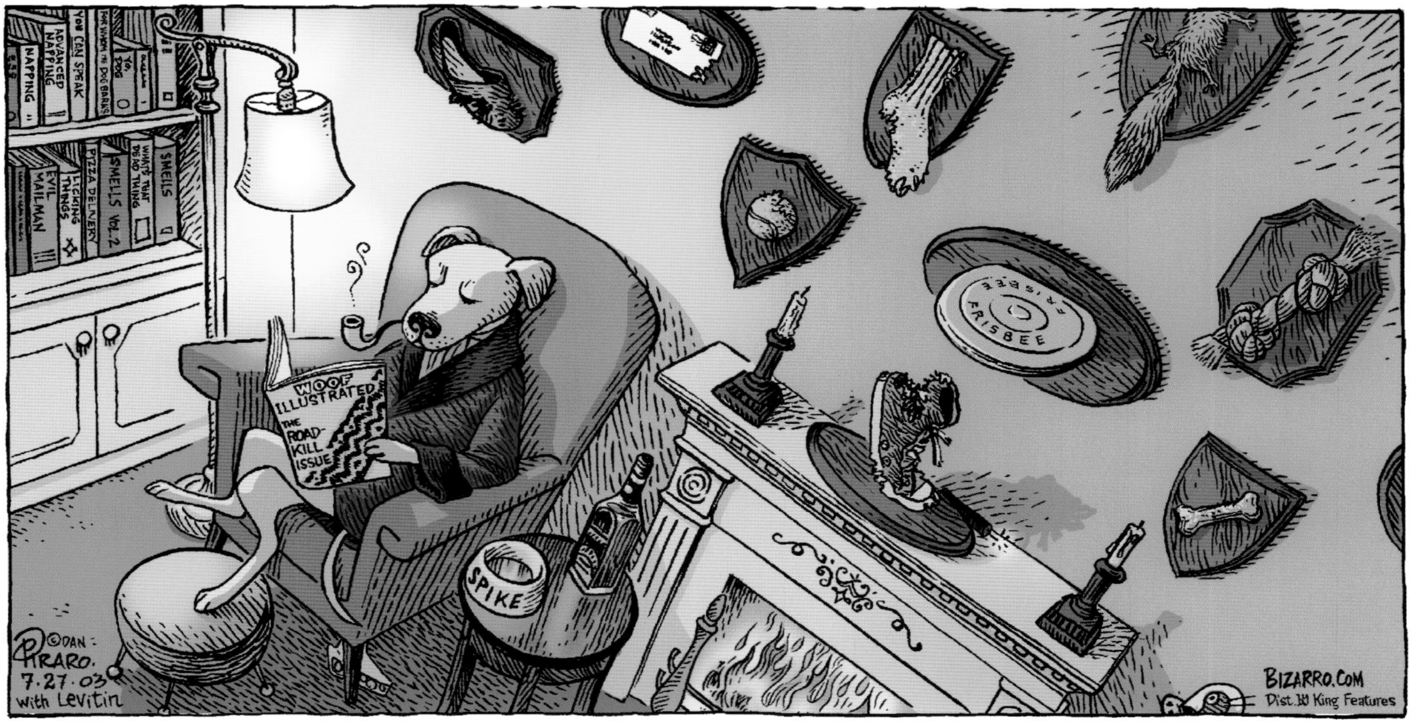
YOU CAN SPEAK
ADVANCED NAPPING
SMELLS
EVIL MAILMAN
LICKING THINGS
PIZZA DELIVERY
SMELLS Vol. 2
WHAT'S THAT DEAD THING
WOOF ILLUSTRATED
THE ROAD-KILL ISSUE
FRISBEE
SPIKE
©DAN PIRARO. 7.27.03 with Levitin
BIZARRO.COM
Dist. by King Features

I've always tried to make decisions based on my personal beliefs rather than financial considerations. I've come to believe that working for causes you believe in is the secret of happiness (if there is such a secret). Contrary to common business sense, I've steadfastly refused to develop regular characters to license (don't get me wrong, I have nothing against licensing or making money—I just don't think *Bizarro* would work well with regular characters) or to steer clear of subjects I think are important but will make many readers and editors uncomfortable. Jokes about the NRA or gay rights always put me on a number of major shit lists and under a cascade of hate mail. All these factors combined, I don't make a lot of money but I'm proud of my work and look forward to getting out of bed in the morning. I've always found pride in a creative endeavor more satisfying than owning a new Hummer, anyway. A few cartoonists get to have both pride in their work *and* a fabulous fortune (Groening, Larson) but most of us have to choose.

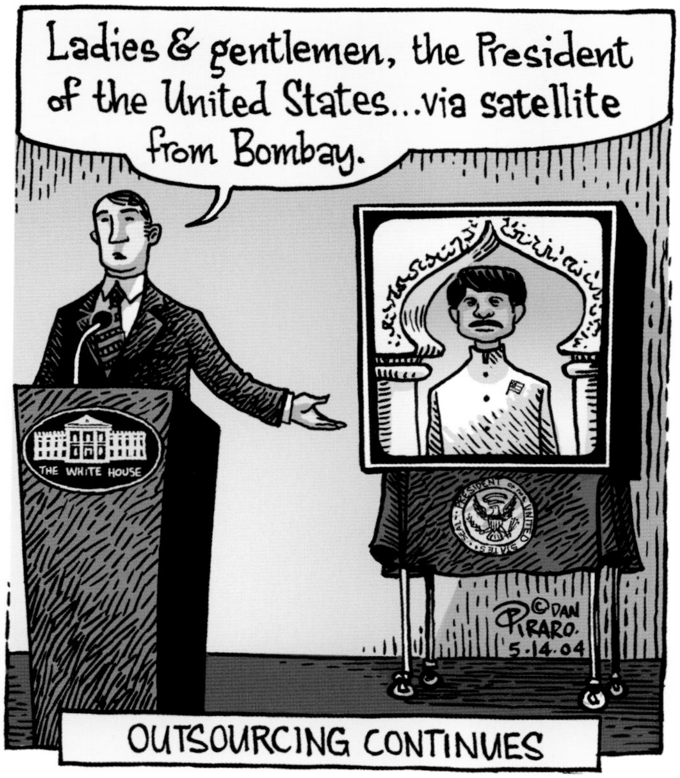
Ladies & gentlemen, the President of the United States...via satellite from Bombay.
THE WHITE HOUSE
©DAN PIRARO 5-14-04
OUTSOURCING CONTINUES

If only. (2004)

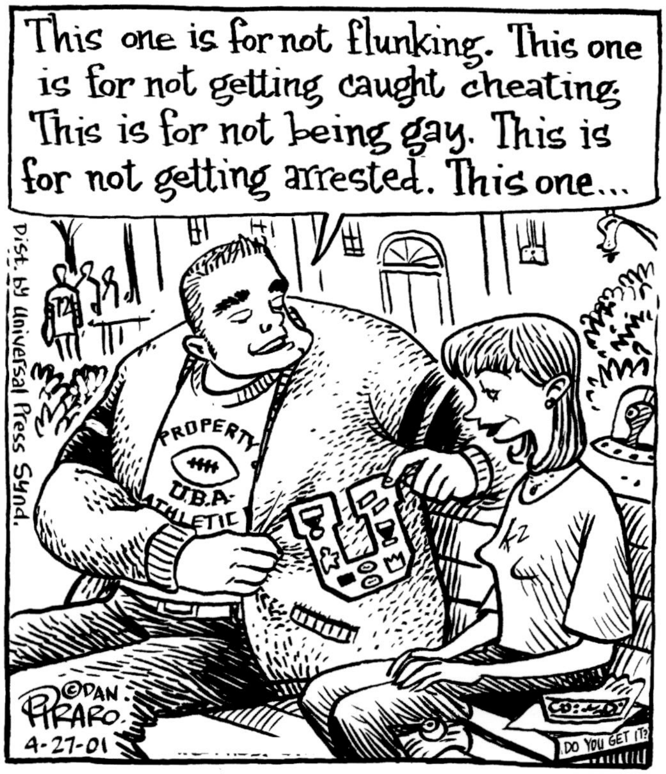
This one is for not flunking. This one is for not getting caught cheating. This is for not being gay. This is for not getting arrested. This one...
Dist. by Universal Press Synd.
PROPERTY
U.B.A.
ATHLETIC
©DAN. PIRARO. 4-27-01
DO YOU GET IT?

The subject that elicits the second-greatest amount of hate mail is homosexuality, frequently from both sides of the issue. A few gay people will write thinking I'm making fun of them. When I explain I'm in favor of gay rights and that my cartoons are actually making fun of homophobia, not homosexuals, they graciously apologize and say they're just so used to being bashed that they've become defensive. Most of the mail, however, is from right-wing wackos who want me to keep this sort of content out of the funny pages. They seem to think if their children even know what homosexuality is they will choose it. God forbid. (2001)

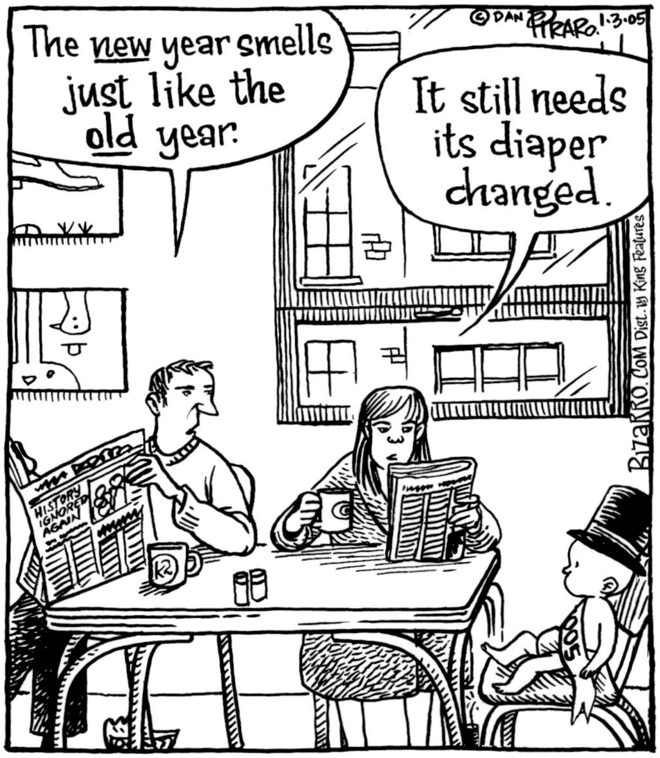
The new year smells just like the old year.
It still needs its diaper changed.
HISTORY IGNORED AGAIN
2005
©DAN PIRARO. 1·3·05
BIZARRO.COM Dist. by King Features

This one got me canceled from a paper in a small town in Texas. Even though they won the election, I guess they'd finally had enough of my smart mouth. (2005)

BELOW, LEFT: Of all the controversial subjects I've touched on, the one that consistently gets the most hate mail is anything against the NRA. Especially if you mention Charlton Heston. Apparently, that guy is their messiah. (2002)

BELOW: I wrote this cartoon shortly after 9/11, but waited a year before I thought the country was ready for a joke about the Taliban. (2002)

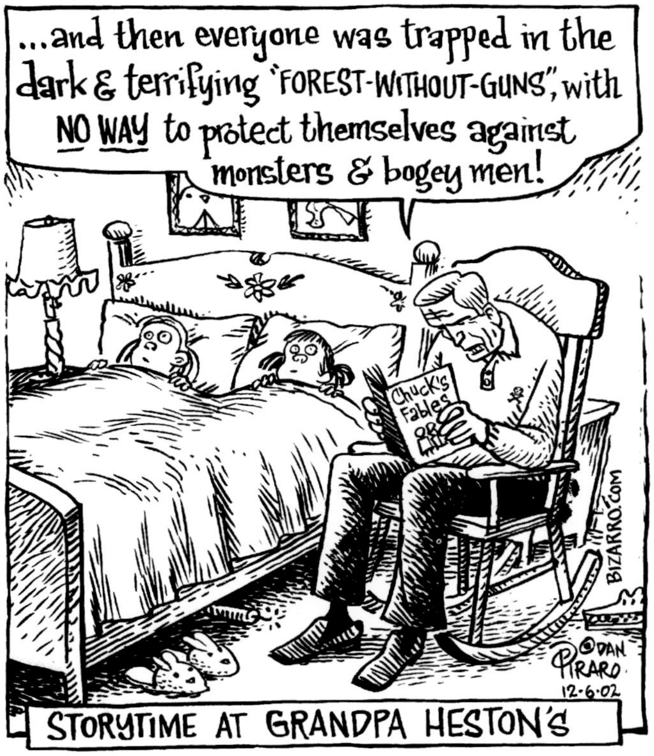
...and then everyone was trapped in the dark & terrifying "FOREST-WITHOUT-GUNS", with NO WAY to protect themselves against monsters & bogey men!
Chuck's Fables
BIZARRO.COM
©DAN PIRARO 12·6·02
STORYTIME AT GRANDPA HESTON'S

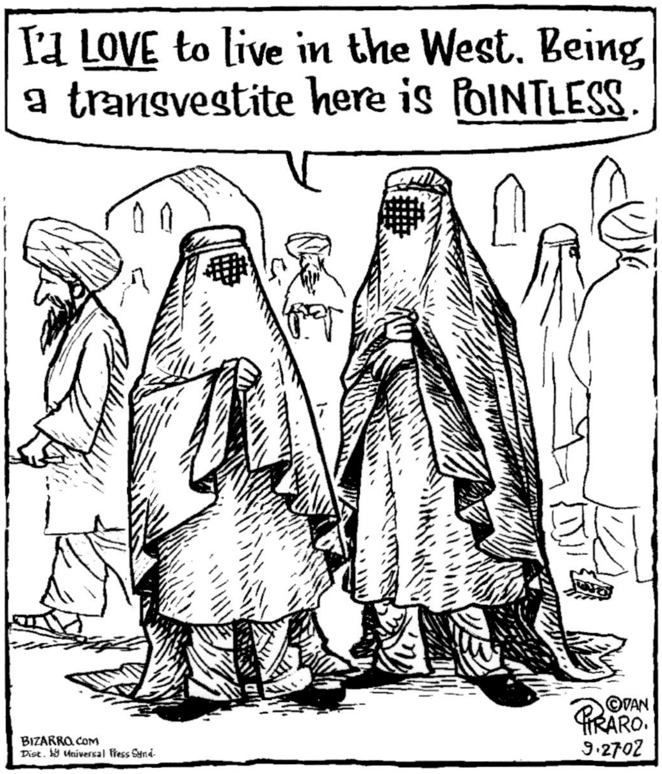
I'd LOVE to live in the West. Being a transvestite here is POINTLESS.
BIZARRO.COM
Dist. by Universal Press Synd.
©DAN PIRARO. 9·27·02

Sex and other adult humor

The mischievous little boy in me can't help occasionally looking for ways to legally subvert newspapers' strict decency rules, but occasionally I get ideas that are too "adult" to print in *Bizarro*. I've published them in Scandinavian publications from time to time and have in recent years sold a few to *Playboy*. I'm proud that most of my adult cartoons don't include nudity. Not because I think there's anything wrong with it, but because it's a sort of challenge, like being funny onstage without profanity.

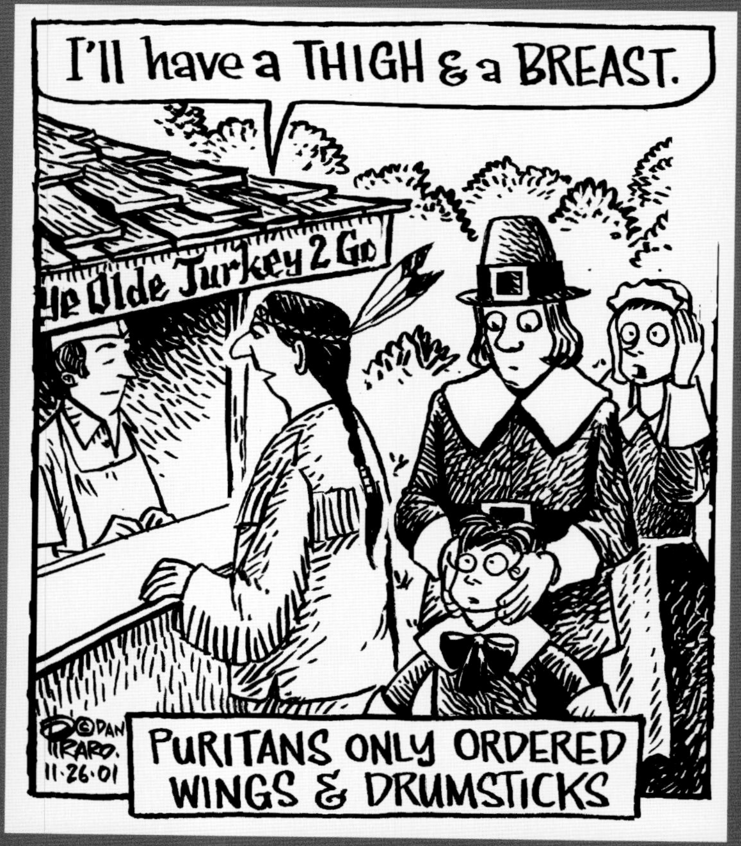
I'll have a THIGH & a BREAST.
Ye Olde Turkey 2 Go
©DAN PIRARO. 11·26·01
PURITANS ONLY ORDERED WINGS & DRUMSTICKS

It's amazing how little things have changed in America since the days of the Pilgrims. (2001)

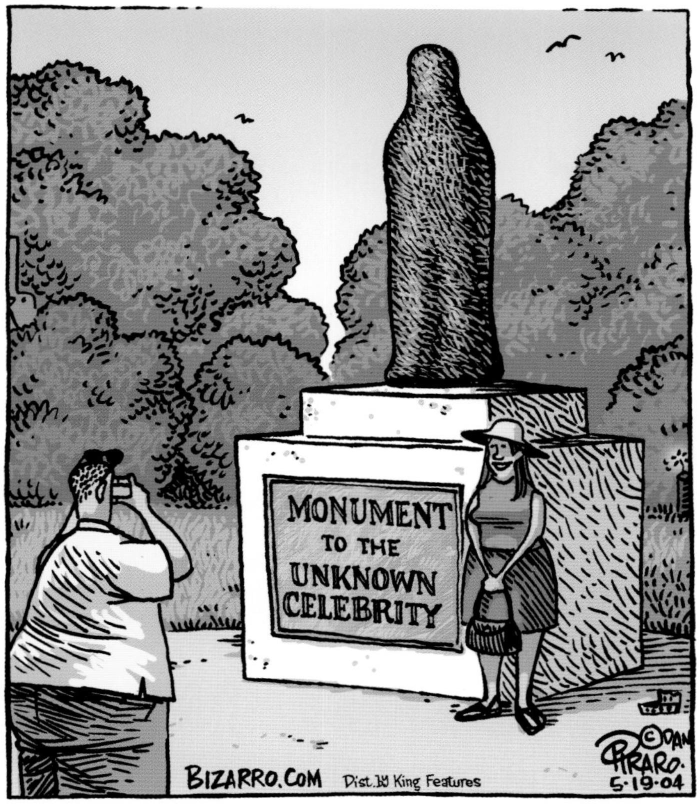
MONUMENT TO THE UNKNOWN CELEBRITY
©DAN PIRARO. 5-19-04
BIZARRO.COM Dist. by King Features

A newspaper editor forwarded a letter to me from someone complaining about seeing a drawing of a condom in the funny pages. I guess it's my fault, but that interpretation never would have occurred to me. (2004)

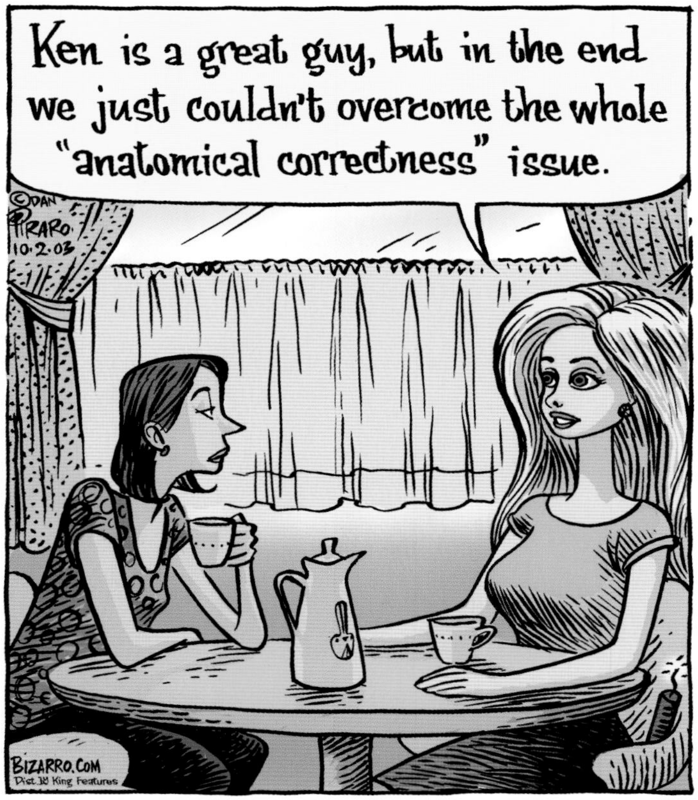
Ken is a great guy, but in the end we just couldn't overcome the whole "anatomical correctness" issue.
©DAN PIRARO 10-2-03
BIZARRO.COM Dist. by King Features

Believe it or not, this is very close to crossing the line, according to the unspoken puritanical decency code of newspaper comics. (2003)

A rough sketch submitted to *Playboy*, but not bought. (2003)

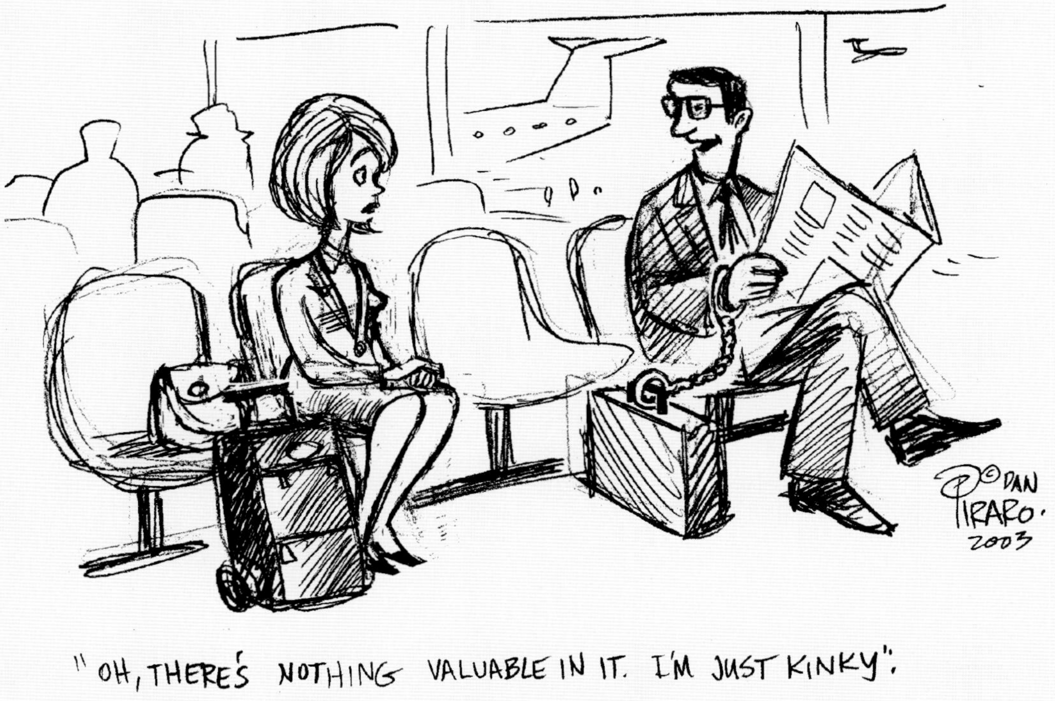
©DAN PIRARO. 2003
"OH, THERE'S NOTHING VALUABLE IN IT. I'M JUST KINKY".

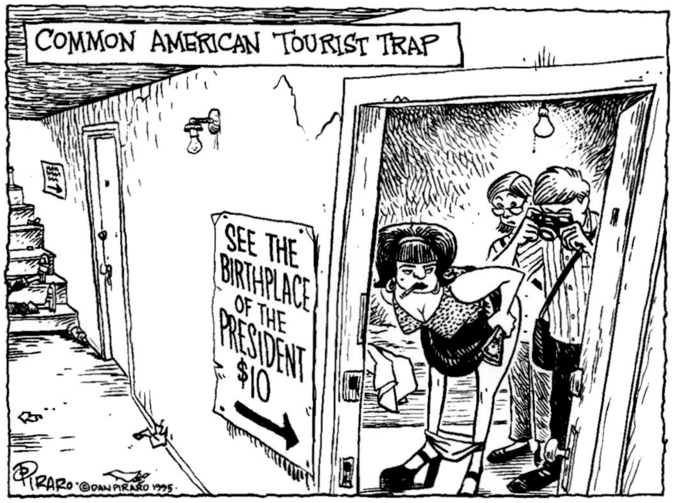
COMMON AMERICAN TOURIST TRAP
SEE THE BIRTHPLACE OF THE PRESIDENT $10
PIRARO ©DAN PIRARO 1995

LEFT: Perhaps the crudest cartoon I ever drew, but it still makes me laugh. I hope my mother never sees this book. (1994)

BELOW: I love this picture and can't understand why *Playboy* rejected it. I'm sure I could find another publication for it, but I'm too lazy to look. (2004)

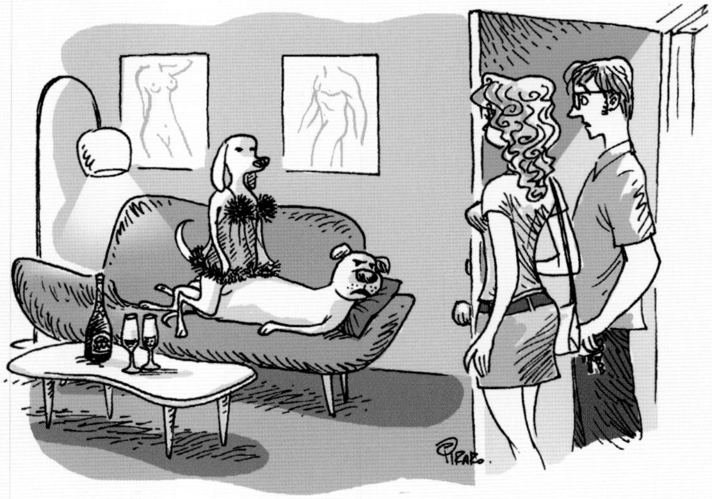
PIRARO.

"What's the big deal? YOU guys do it DOGGY style."

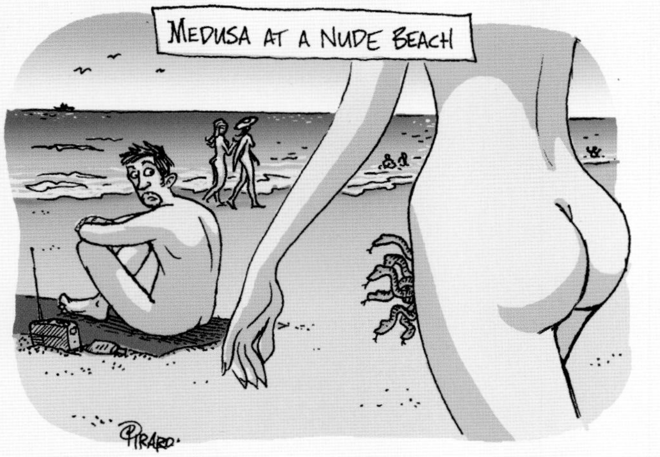
MEDUSA AT A NUDE BEACH
PIRARO.

ABOVE: This is a quick sketch of a cartoon that I think is one of my best. I show it in stage shows and it always kills. For some reason, *Playboy* didn't want this one. Maybe it creeped out Hef. (1998)

RIGHT: Another rough sketch *Playboy* turned down. The cartoon editor there loved it, but Hef didn't, for some reason. I can't help but wonder what makes a person turn down a good cartoon. Perhaps he didn't want readers to think that *Playboy* doesn't endorse blow jobs from strangers. (2003)

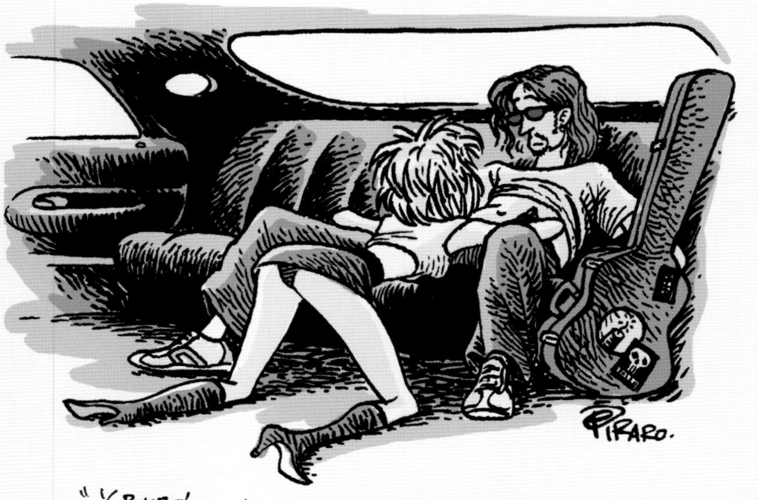
PIRARO.

"'GROUPIE' IS NO LONGER POLITICALLY CORRECT. I PREFER TO BE CALLED 'MORALLY CHALLENGED.'"

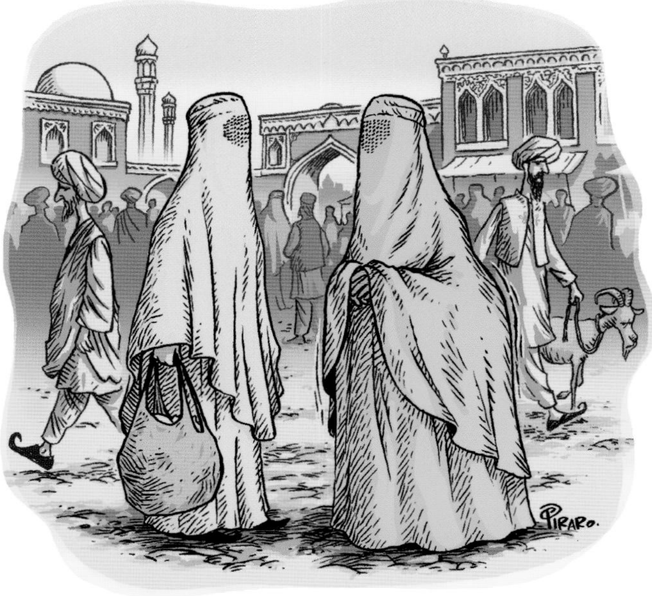
PIRARO.

"What my husband doesn't know is that Rashid, the grocer, is under here with me."

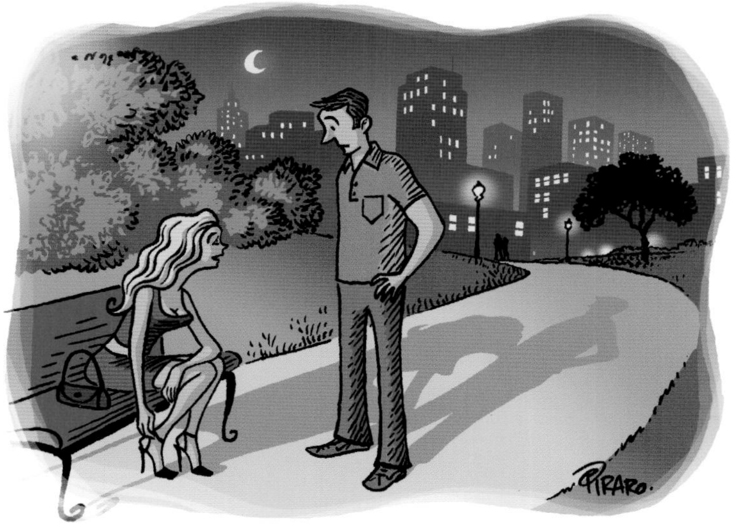
PIRARO.

"Shall we head back to my place, or are we just going to let our shadows have all the fun?"

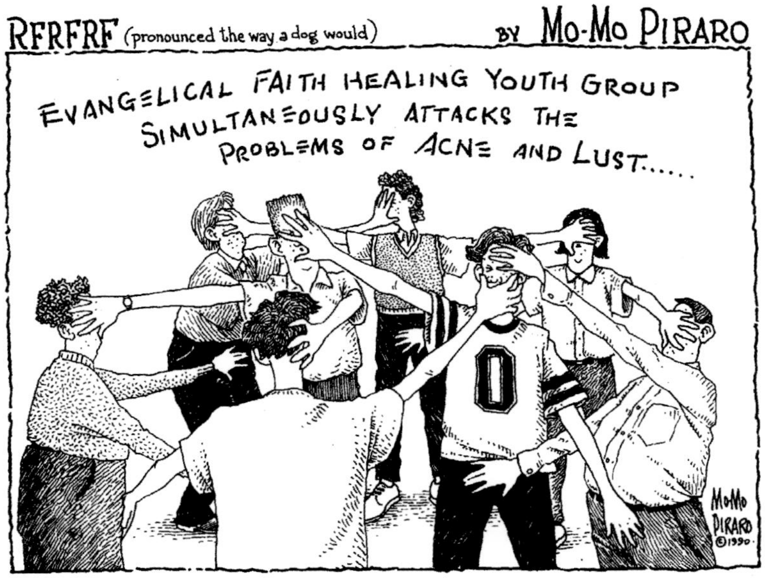
RFRFRF (pronounced the way a dog would)
BY MO-MO PIRARO
EVANGELICAL FAITH HEALING YOUTH GROUP SIMULTANEOUSLY ATTACKS THE PROBLEMS OF ACNE AND LUST.....
0
MOMO PIRARO ©1990.

Death

Through the ages, humor has been a tool for dealing with subjects that frighten us. I think that's why death has been such a common subject for me and so many others. These cartoons are my way of "whistling past the graveyard."

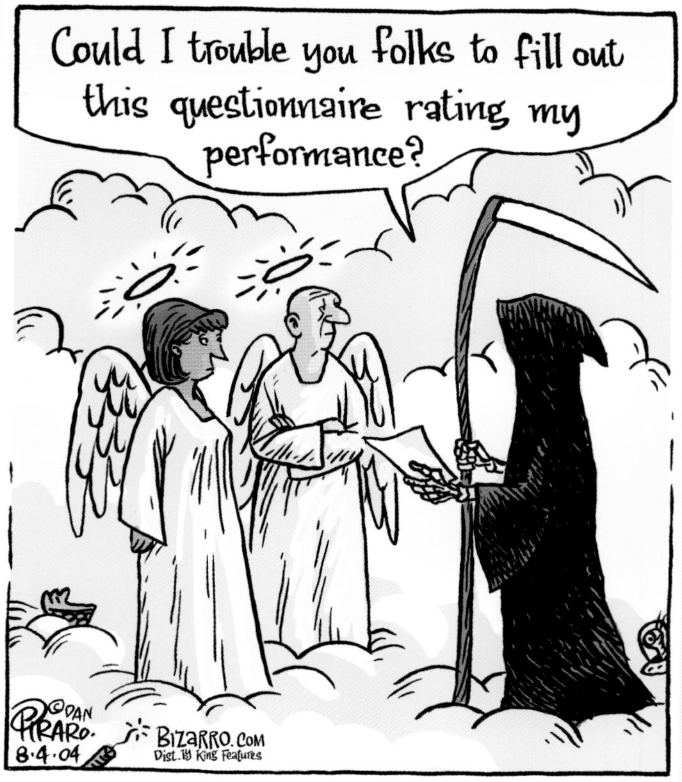
Could I trouble you folks to fill out this questionnaire rating my performance?
©DAN PIRARO. 8·4·04
BIZARRO.COM
Dist. by King Features

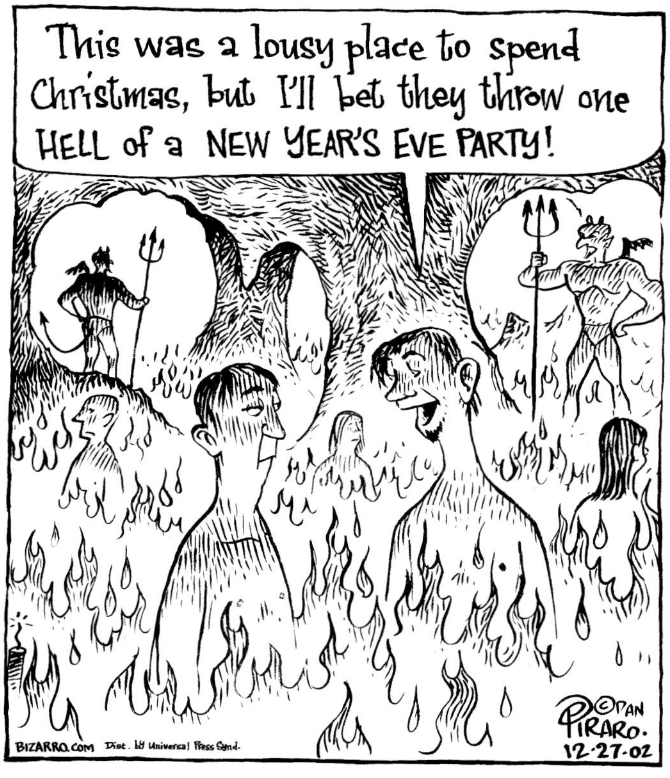
This was a lousy place to spend Christmas, but I'll bet they throw one HELL of a NEW YEAR'S EVE PARTY!
BIZARRO.COM Dist. by Universal Press Synd.
©DAN PIRARO. 12·27·02

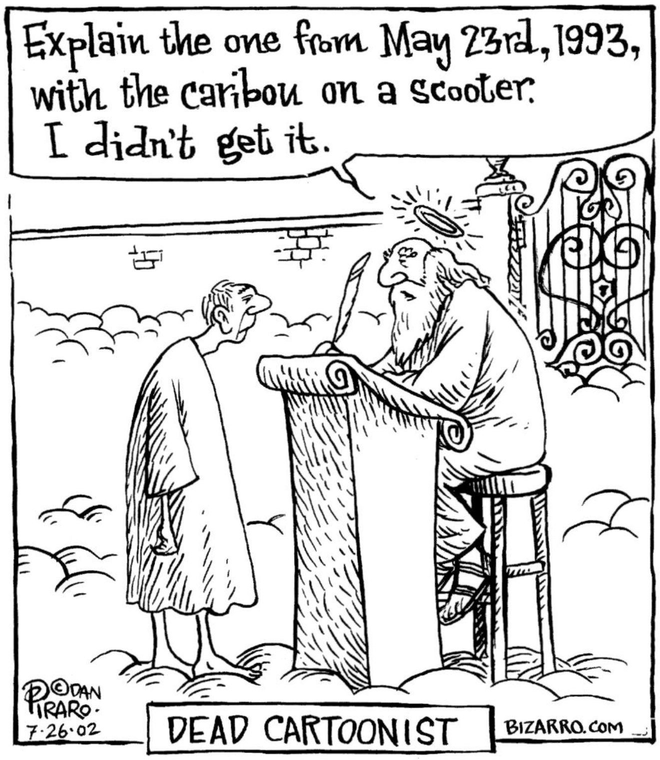
Explain the one from May 23rd, 1993, with the caribou on a scooter. I didn't get it.
©DAN PIRARO· 7·26·02
DEAD CARTOONIST
BIZARRO.COM

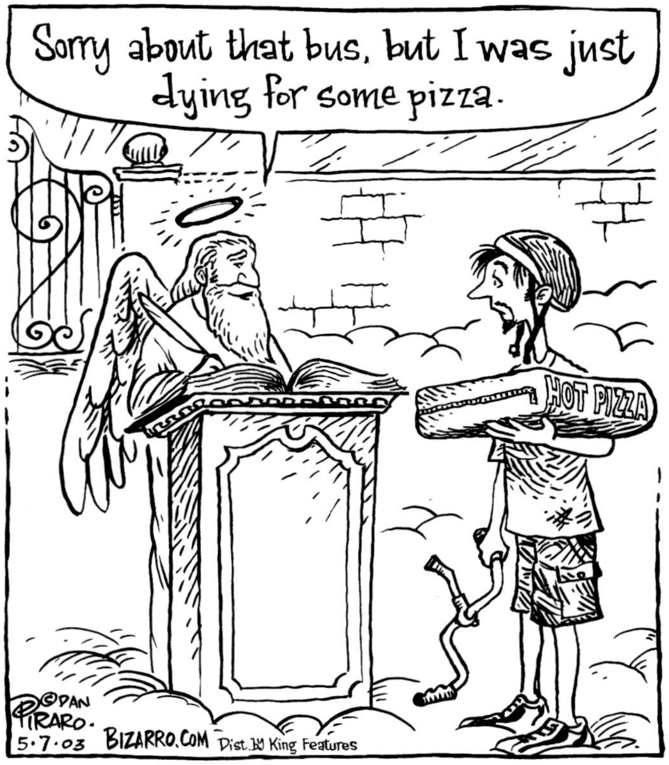
Sorry about that bus, but I was just dying for some pizza.
HOT PIZZA
©DAN PIRARO· 5·7·03
BIZARRO.COM
Dist. by King Features

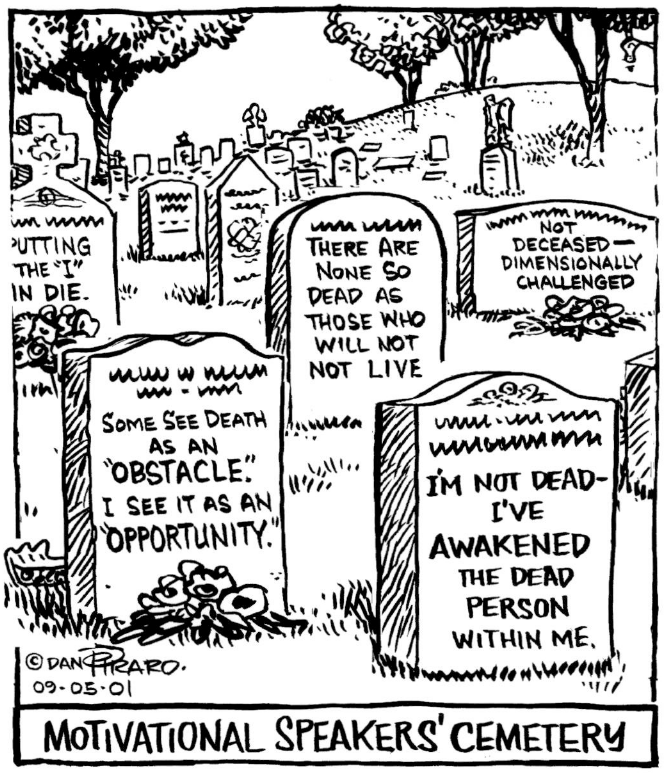
PUTTING THE "I" IN DIE.
THERE ARE NONE SO DEAD AS THOSE WHO WILL NOT NOT LIVE
NOT DECEASED— DIMENSIONALLY CHALLENGED
SOME SEE DEATH AS AN "OBSTACLE." I SEE IT AS AN "OPPORTUNITY."
I'M NOT DEAD- I'VE AWAKENED THE DEAD PERSON WITHIN ME.
©DAN PIRARO· 09-05-01
MOTIVATIONAL SPEAKERS' CEMETERY

Sometimes dark humor backfires. The day before the above cartoon appeared in the paper, a prominent cyclist in a major U.S. city was killed by a car. I got angry letters from a few readers who thought I was commenting on it. What they didn't know is that newspaper cartoons, with the exception of editorial ones, are sent in at least four weeks ahead of publication. All cartoonists cross their fingers when they turn in an earthquake or hurricane gag.

Chapter five

Mr. Know-It-All moves on

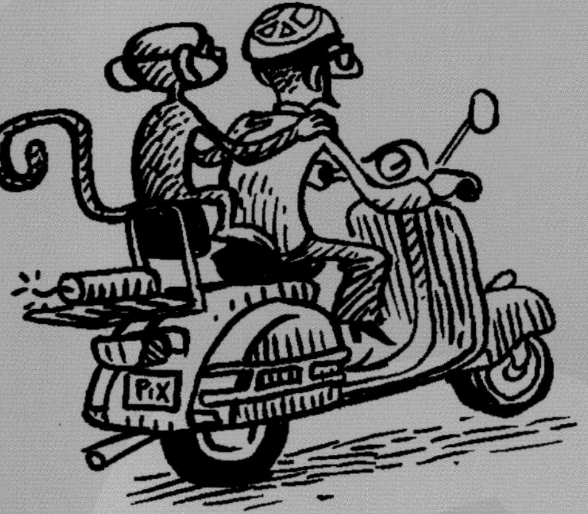
PIX

I would like to retire from cartooning one day (no time soon; I can't afford it) and spend my remaining years painting. To do that, I'll somehow need to either earn a hell of a lot more from *Bizarro*, or begin to make decent money from my fine art. But I am confident that one way or another I'll be primarily a painter in the second half of my life. People in my family tend to live well past life expectancy, no matter how badly they abuse their bodies, so I figure with regular exercise and my vegan diet, I should live well into the next century. Surely by the time I'm 150 I will be able to support myself as a painter.

These days my paintings mostly deal with political, animal, and environmental issues and I'm looking forward to mounting a show when I'm ready.

Since I began painting again in the early nineties, I have favored large canvases (three feet by four feet, or so) in oil, although I also enjoy making smaller watercolor pieces. In both mediums, I've begun scribbling or writing on top of the paint with pencils and pens of different sorts, oil pastels, litho crayons, or anything else that is stick shaped. Another fun new approach for me has been adding the title to the composition itself so it becomes an integral part of the painting. This combination of painting, drawing, and writing is likely to play a major role in my future work. The piece at right is an intentionally ridiculous example of this approach of adding text. Its title is as overstated and absurd as the so-called journalism on Fox News.

In terms of subject matter, this is a big change. Until relatively recently my art dealt primarily with the spiritual, social, and psychological aspects of religion. After I spent my first six years in Catholic school and attending mass on a schedule worthy of a guilt-ridden obsessive-compulsive serial killer (an hour-long mass every morning before school and another with the folks on Sunday), these images seemed to ooze out of my subconscious whether I liked it or not. It seemed so natural to me that it never occurred to me what someone looking at my paintings might make of them. Then, during my "dating around" period after my divorce, a friend introduced me to a Jewish woman she thought I might hit it off with. After the woman visited my house, my friend reported that the woman was worried that I was a religious fanatic. I laughed out loud. As completely logical as it was, it had never crossed my mind that people would make such an assumption.

So, "Jewish woman I might hit it off with," if you're still wondering, I'm not particularly religious. At least not in any traditional sense. But I've always been fascinated with religion, its effect on individuals and societies, and its intersection of heroes and hypocrisy. One culture's religion is another's mythology, and vice versa. Some of the greatest heroes and most loathsome villains have been devoted followers of the same religion.

Fox News Special Report—Giant, Hairy, One-eyed, Atheist, Flag-Burning, Socialist, Godless, Jesus-Hating, Lying, Alcoholic, Terrorist-Sympathizing, Deceitful, Tree-Hugging, Liberal, Sin-Loving, Heathen, Intellectual, French, Condescending, Abortion-Supporting, Peacenik, Illegal Alien-Loving, ACLU Member, Hateful, Name-Calling, Transvestite, Communist, Drug-Addicted, AIDS-Carrying, Pot-Smoking, Child-Molesting, Baby-Stealing, Tax-Raising, Buggering Homos to Invade Red States (2004, watercolor, 13" x 18"). The first painting I did after the tragic "elections" of 2004. Virtually all of the epithets listed in the title and written on the painting are ones I've heard used by right-wingers against Democrats. And they call us "hateful." The rest of the words are ones I presume they would have used if they'd known what they meant.

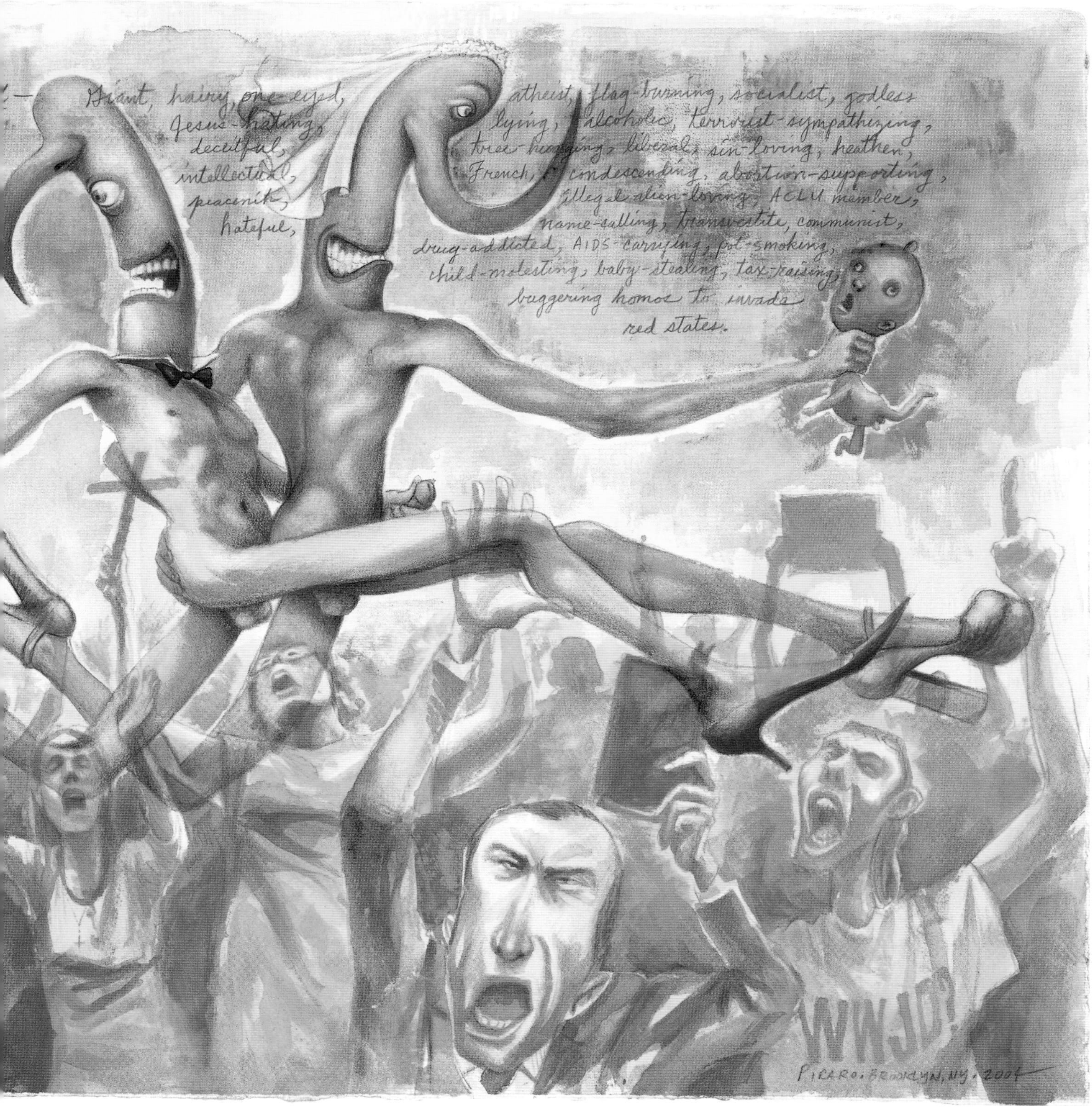
Giant, hairy, one-eyed,
Jesus-hating,
deceitful,
intellectual,
peacenik,
hateful,
atheist, flag-burning, socialist, godless
lying, alcoholic, terrorist-sympathizing,
tree-hugging, liberal, sin-loving, heathen,
French, condescending, abortion-supporting,
illegal alien-loving, ACLU member,
name-calling, transvestite, communist,
drug-addicted, AIDS-carrying, pot-smoking,
child-molesting, baby-stealing, tax-raising,
buggering homos to invade
red states.
WWJD?
PIRARO. BROOKLYN, NY. 2004

MoMo PIRARO.
If Jesus had died in the electric chair....
©1994 PIRARO.

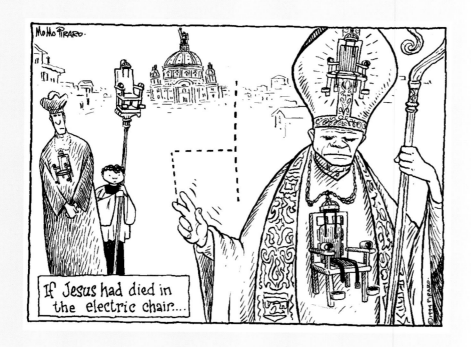

Published in Scandinavia. They love Catholic humor there. (1995)

BELOW: When I show this cartoon on stage, audiences always laugh first, then sadly say "Awwww." (2001)

For the LAST TIME! You kids get OUT of here with that phoney TUNNEL OF LIGHT!!
OLD GUY
713
OTHER OLD GUY
uCOMICS.COM
© DAN PIRAARO. 8-12 2001
Dist. by Universal Press Synd.

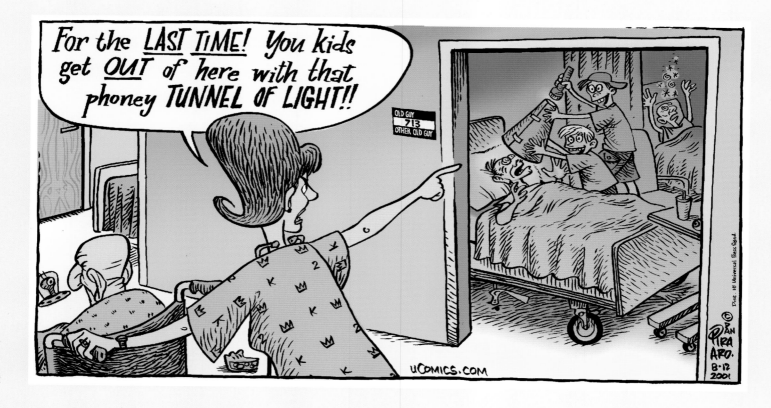

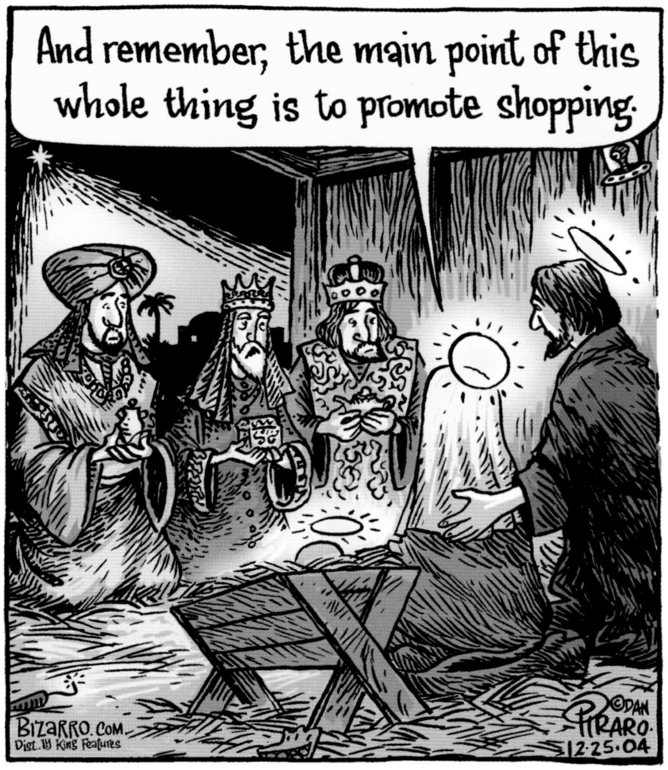

And remember, the main point of this whole thing is to promote shopping.
BIZARRO.COM
Dist. By King Features
©DAN PIRARO
12-25-04

This cartoon, of course, drew lots of criticism from religious types who possess no understanding of irony. “The Lord’s mother would never have said something like that!” I was told. And my personal favorite: “Why do all people in the media hate Christians and Christianity?” (2004)

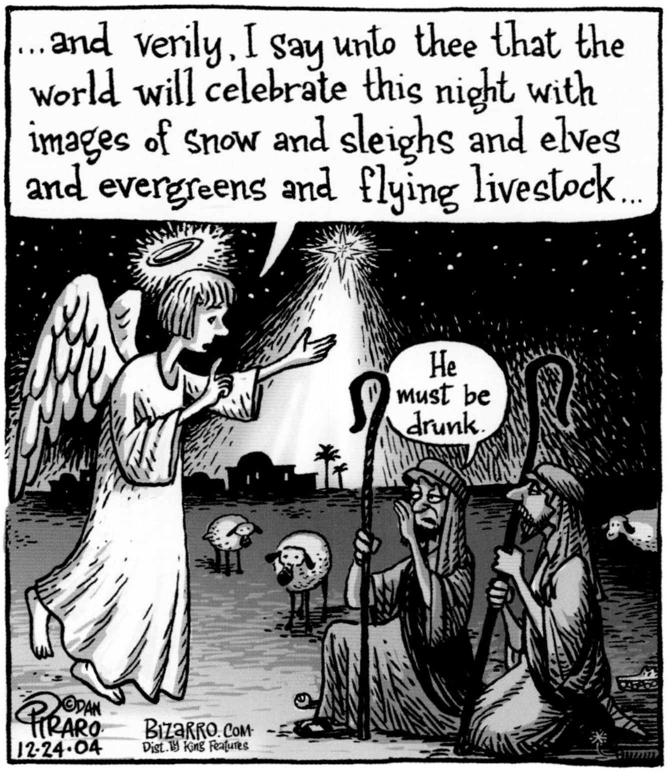

...and verily, I say unto thee that the world will celebrate this night with images of snow and sleighs and elves and evergreens and flying livestock...
He must be drunk.
©DAN PIRARO
12-24-04
BIZARRO.COM
Dist. By King Features

Verily, modern-day American Christmas makes me want to vomit. My wife and I avoid it like the matching sweatsuit sets at Wal-Mart. (2004)

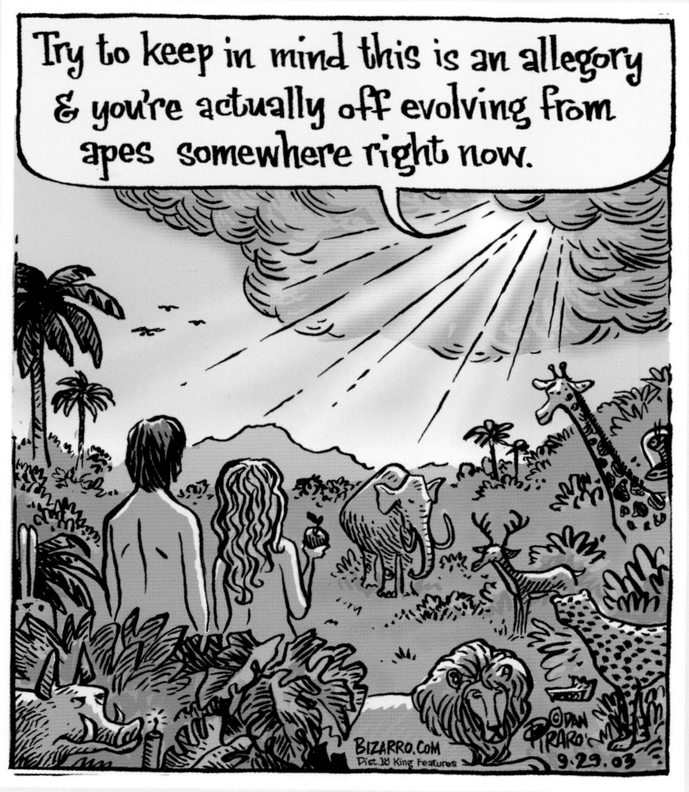
Try to keep in mind this is an allegory & you're actually off evolving from apes somewhere right now.
BIZARRO.COM
Dist. by King Features
©DAN PIRARO
9.29.03

Some fun hate mail from the Bible Belt came in on this cartoon—just another fringe benefit of the job. Believing in creationism is fine, I suppose, but to be angry enough to write a complaint letter to everyone who doesn't is amusing. (2003)

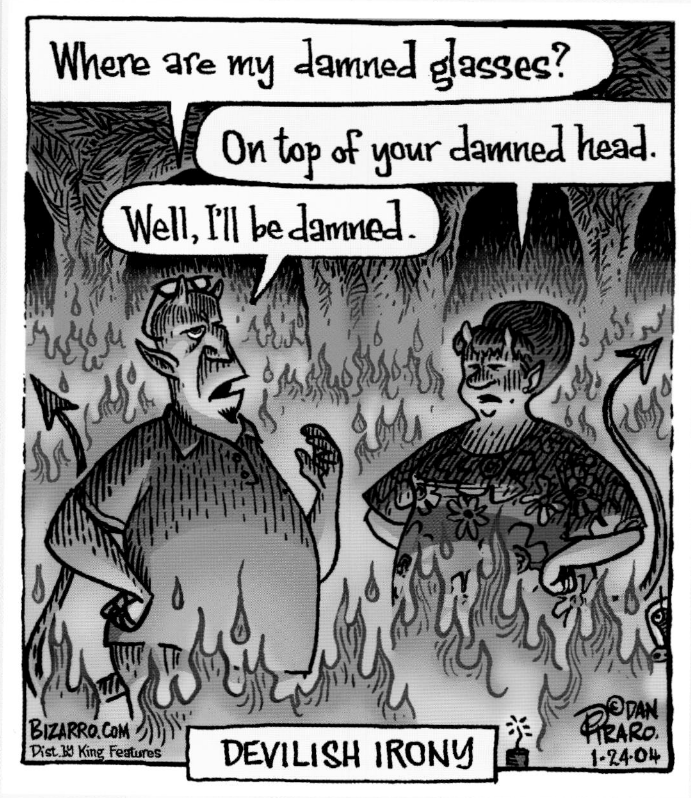
Where are my damned glasses?
On top of your damned head.
Well, I'll be damned.
BIZARRO.COM
Dist. by King Features
DEVILISH IRONY
©DAN PIRARO
1-24-04

The mischievous little boy in me can't help occasionally looking for ways to legally subvert newspapers' strict decency rules. These same lines would likely be censored if the couple were in their own kitchen. (2004)

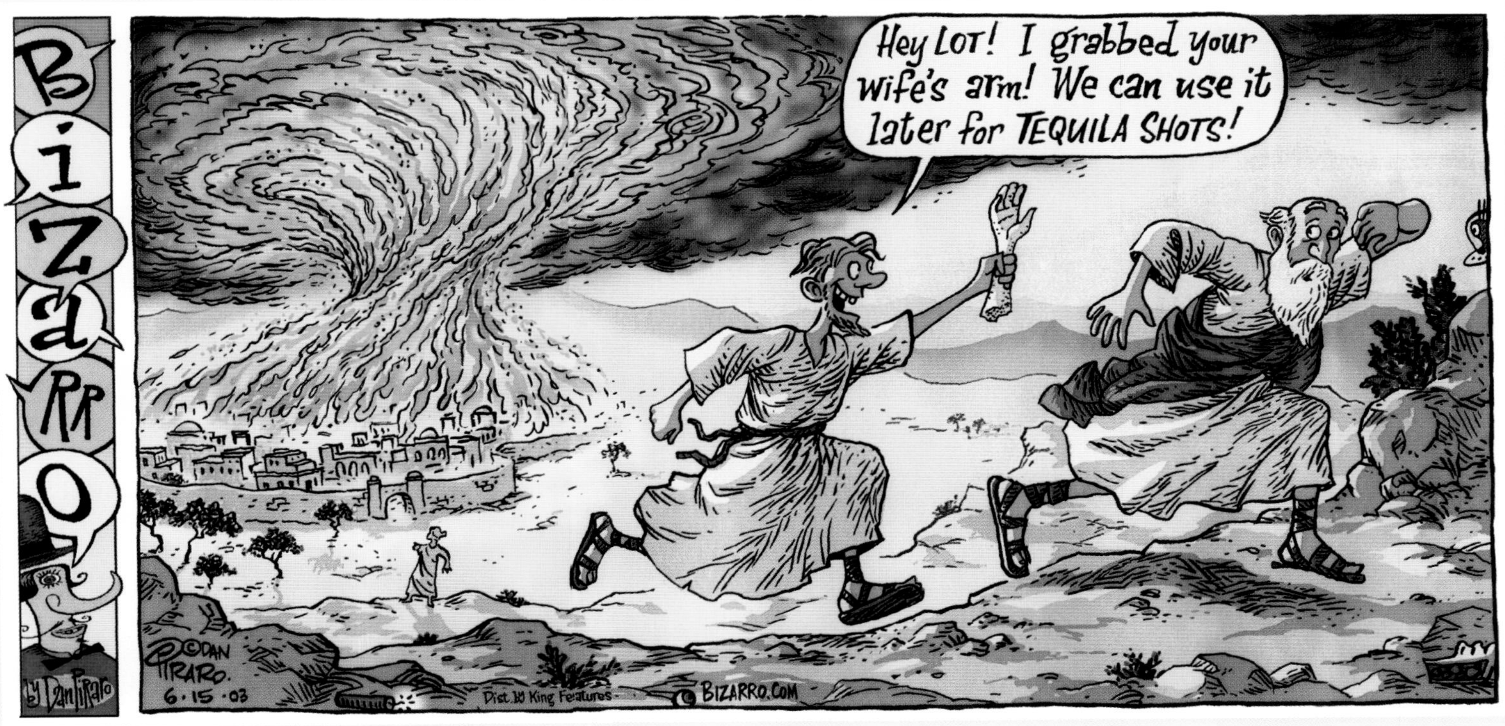

Hey LOT! I grabbed your wife's arm! We can use it later for TEQUILA SHOTS!
BIZARRO
by Dan Piraro
©DAN PIRARO. 6·15·03
Dist. by King Features
© BIZARRO.COM

The idea for this cartoon was given to me by fellow cartoonist Todd Clark, who writes the syndicated strip *Lola*. I think it's brilliant. My editors talked me out of publishing it, however. The combination of an Old Testament Bible story and tequila was feared to be too much for the American Sunday comics-reading public. (2003)

History is full of regrettable political actions executed in the name of religious faith, and we tend to think of the "olden days" as being less enlightened than today. But even now, many Americans don't differentiate between faith and fact and are still arguing in courts over Old Testament creationism vs. Darwinian evolution, or whether a person's sexual orientation is chosen or innate and whether it is condemned by God. Even though I was born and raised in the middle of the Bible Belt, this preference for ancient allegory over common sense, evidence, and logic still astounds me, and I enjoy creating both fine art and cartoons about it. More thoughtful and mature attitudes toward spirituality interest me, too—ones that are based on individual discovery and the belief that God would not have given us such powerful minds if we were not to ask questions. All these themes are explored in my religious-looking paintings, but not in ways that are necessarily obvious to the casual observer.

As a result, I am regularly asked to explain my paintings. I always refuse. This is partly because there are few things in the world that annoy me more than "artist's statements." For those of you who don't haunt art galleries, these are the often long-winded, pompous paragraphs that accompany exhibitions, in which the artist is supposed to explain his or her intent and influences, and so on. While some are fine, most of them go something like this:

My work is an investigation of conceptually based sociopolitical themes deconstructing the American Dream juxtaposed against gender roles and the fragility of the underlying threads of domestic violence, eating disorders, and the culture of mediocrity and the mundane in the current day. I achieve this with a minimalistic approach to unifying elements of overembellished and disparate themes using non-site-specific installations combined with traditional techniques that utilize clues to our common social underpinnings.

This sort of language reminds me of an athlete's self-conscious overanalysis of the big game. Watching the game is fun. Watching a sweaty guy tell you what you just saw is a drag.

On the rare occasions I have shown my work I have refused to provide an artist's statement. If they insist, I use this:

These are some paintings I did to express some things.

I'm not trying to be a snob—quite the opposite. I just don't believe that a verbal explanation of art is essential to viewing it. I know that not everyone will see in an artwork exactly what the artist was thinking when he or she created it. But to my mind that's one of the great things about art—viewers bring a lot of themselves to the process. Don't get me wrong. I'm not against artists providing historical or biographical information that tells you where they came from or what situations led to the creation of a body of work. That can be as informative as any historical information about anything. But I strongly believe that a work of art in any field should stand on its own without a lot of mumbo jumbo to justify it.

Four Clerics Ignoring a Vision (1994, oil on canvas, 40" x 40"). This painting uses images of sexuality and religion to suggest our age-old battle to deny our animal nature and become something different, "more important." I'm perfectly happy calling myself an animal and have never felt that lessened my worth as a human.

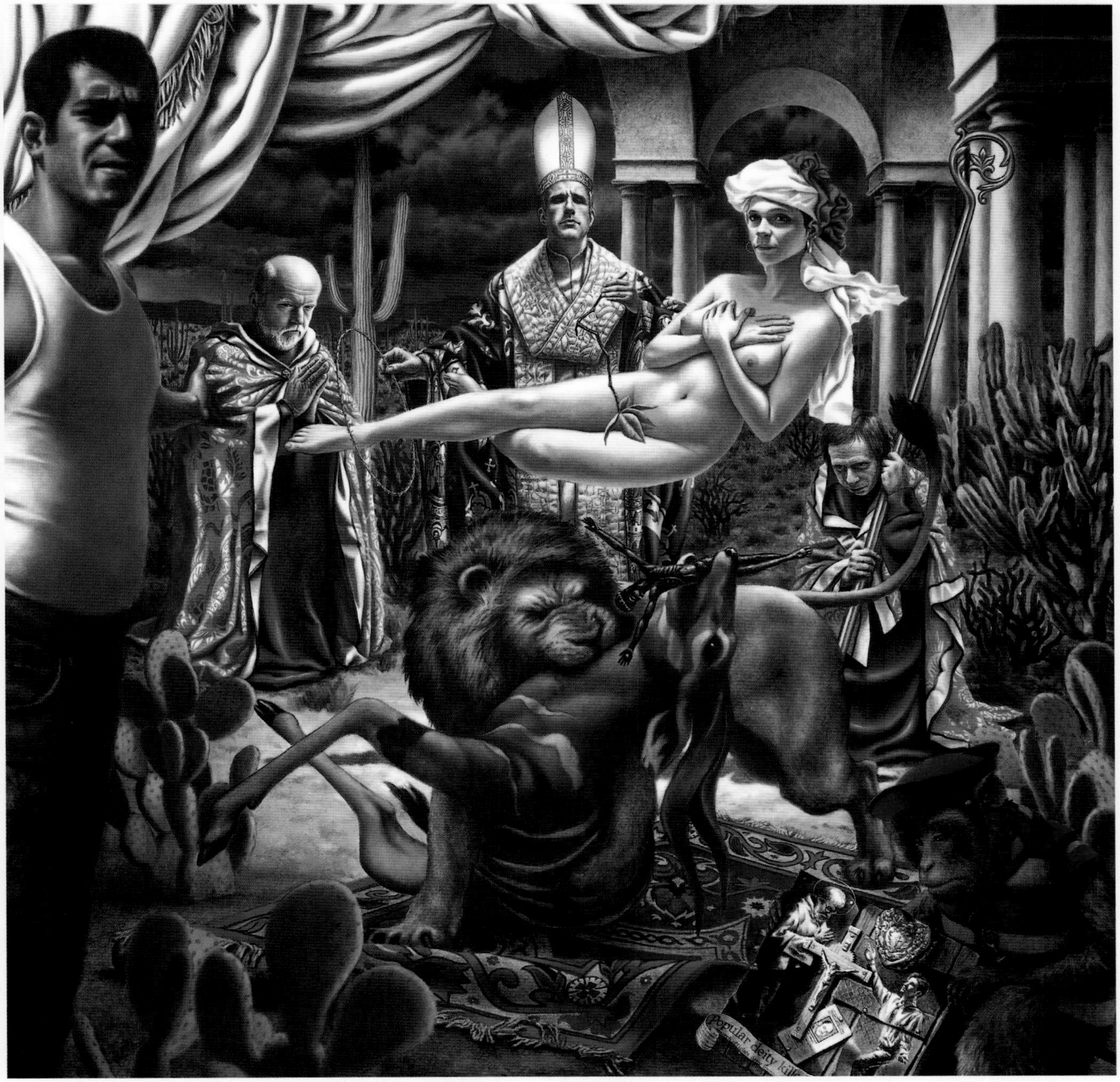
Popular deity

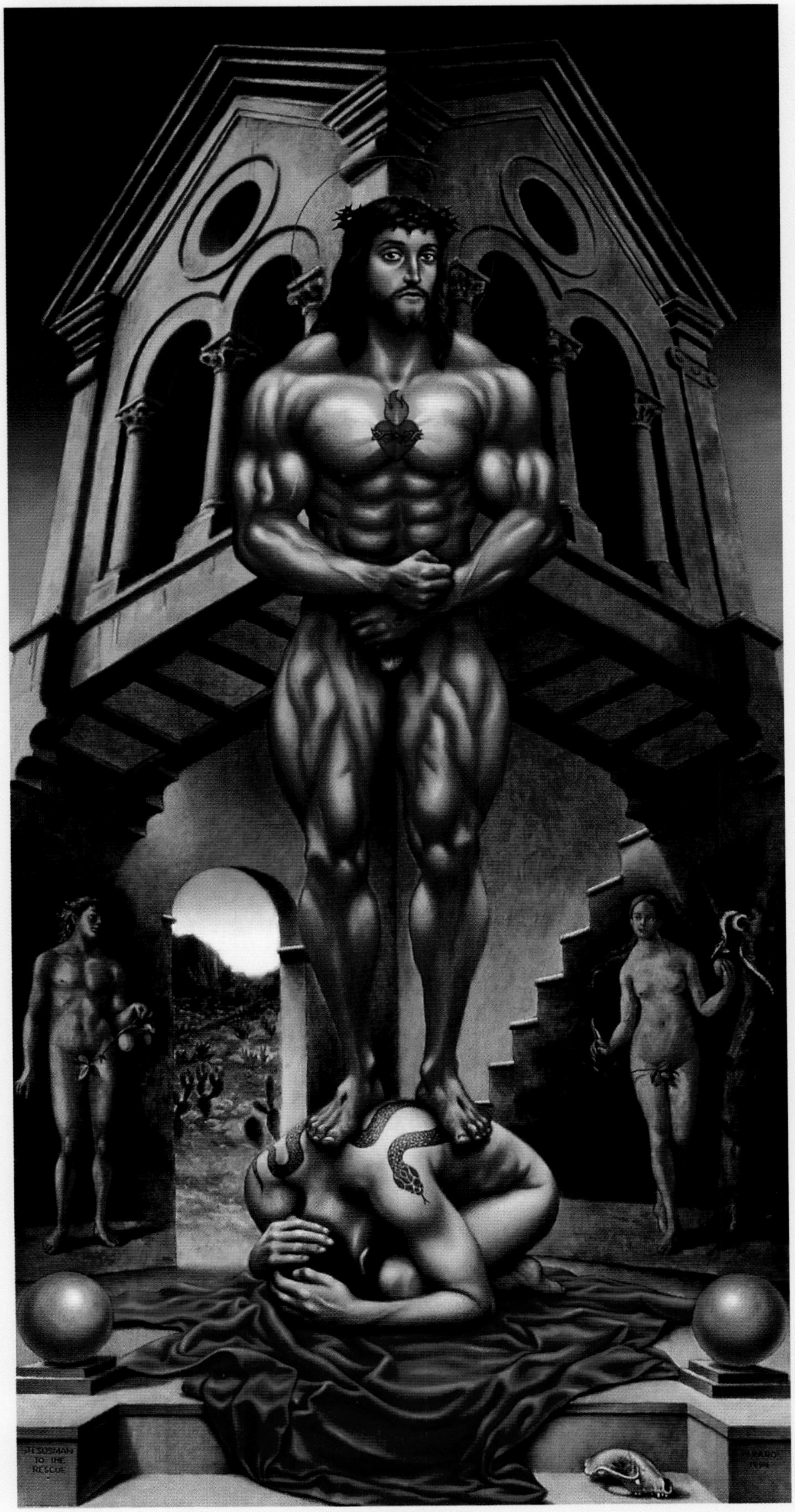
JESUSMAN
TO THE
RESCUE

RIGHT: *Jesusman to the Rescue* (1994, oil on linen, 40" x 20"). A painting dealing with religion and heroes. One of my wittier friends dubbed it Jesus Schwarzenegger.

OPPOSITE: *Starts Today* (1995, watercolor and colored pencil, 12" x 18"). Honestly, I am not sure what this painting is about. It combines medieval versions of Jesus and Mary, cartoon aliens from outer space, and the Hollywood movie-ad phrase "Starts today." This combo interests me somehow, but I can't explain why. That indescribable connection is one of the best things about making and viewing art.

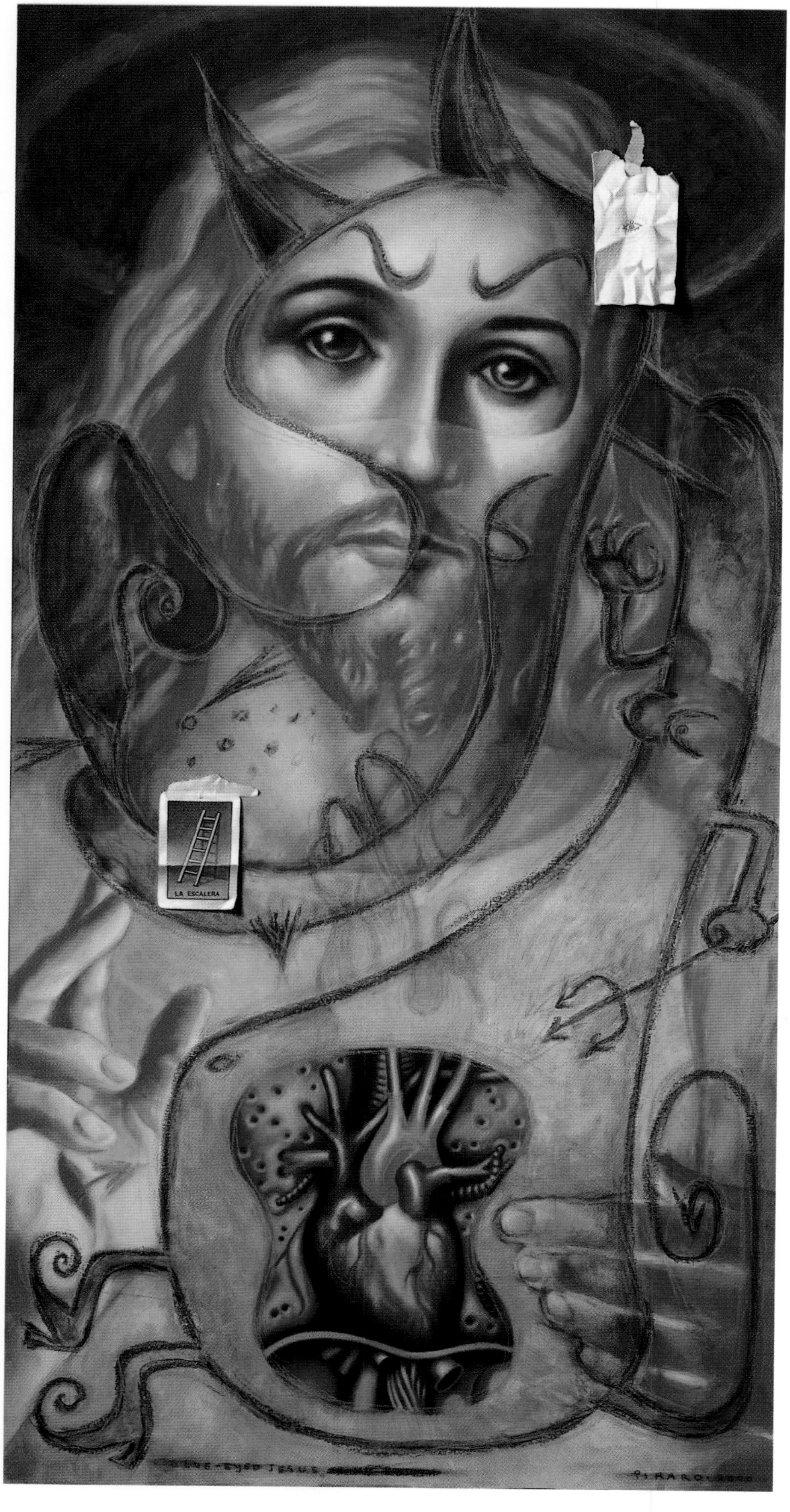
LA ESCALERA
BLUE-EYED JESUS

Blue-Eyed Jesus (1999, oil on linen, 40" x 20"). In this painting, the same set of eyes are used for Jesus and a devil-dog character. Jesus, the Christian son of God, has a human heart. Good/evil, God/mortal. What's it all mean? I don't know. That's why I make paintings about it. This was the first painting in which I used trompe-l'oeil to paint things that looked to be taped to the surface of the painting. When the painting is lit to match the painted shadows, these pass as real from three or four feet away. I love that.

OPPOSITE: *Girls! Girls! Girls!* (2000, oil on linen, 40" x 20"). A companion to *Blue-Eyed Jesus*.

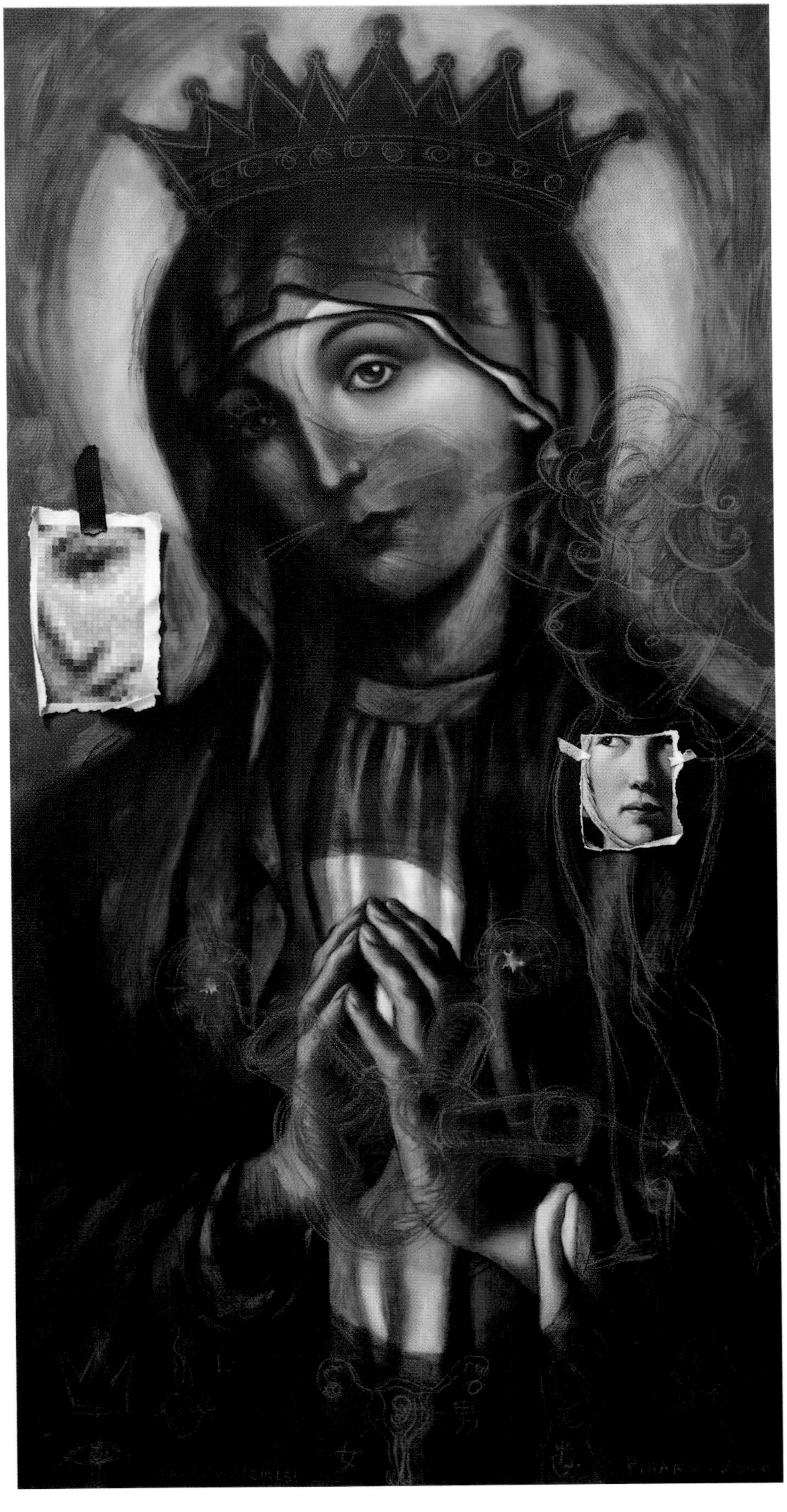

Yes, I can be a bit of a curmudgeon at times. In the privacy of your own home, you may even call me a "dick" if you wish. I wish you wouldn't say it to my face, though, because it would hurt my feelings.

And what's the deal with stuff like Mark Rothko's work? How does a person become so famous painting big rectangles? A series of very famous Rothko paintings consists of a black rectangle above a gray rectangle. In fact, most of his most famous stuff is a colored rectangle above another one of a different color. Go to Google, click the "images" link and type in "Rothko." Look at the page that comes up and explain to me why it's an important body of work.

Now if you're a knowledgeable art-history sort, you're going to say that Rothko's place in art history has a lot to do with what he was trying to say about representational art and distilling forms down to the essence of shape and color and juxtaposing conceptually explored deconstructivized something or other. And if I were the sophisticated *artiste* I pretended to be when I was younger, I'd understand what you were talking about and be fully prepared to discuss it until well past midnight over martinis at a bar painted completely black. But the truth is that the nicest thing I can say about Rothko's work is that the red and yellow one might look cool in the spare bedroom with that campy rug we bought at Ikea. And I'm serious about that, it would. I'd spend $50 on it and hang it there and be really happy with it for years. I just wouldn't spend $50,000. Perhaps it's just over my head.

It says here he painted it "after staring out the window of a Paris bar at night."
WHICH IS WHY FRIENDS SHOULDN'T LET FRIENDS PAINT DRUNK.
©DAN PIRARO. 7-15-02
BIZARRO.COM

Dang. That thing sat in a vacant lot in my neighborhood for two years & I never saw the potential.
©DAN PIRARO. 5-6-04
BIZARRO.COM
Dist. by King Features

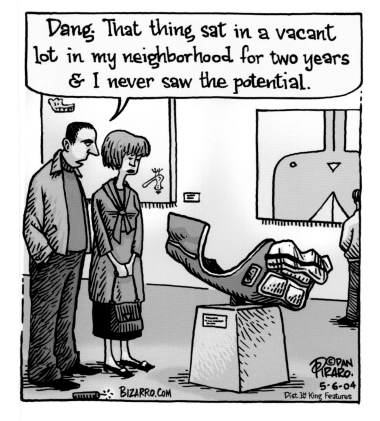

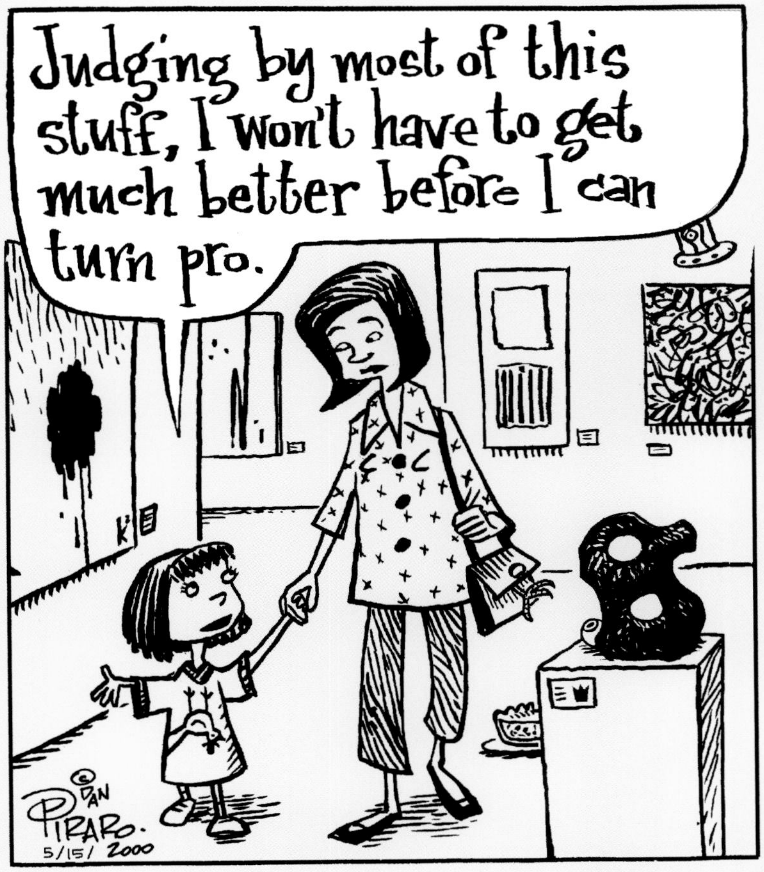
Judging by most of this stuff, I won't have to get much better before I can turn pro.
©DAN PIRARO. 5/15/2000

This is an example of what my mother calls my "ax-grinding cartoons." She's right, of course. (2000)

BELOW, LEFT: Doing art projects is a terrific way to deal with your feelings. I get to do it every day in the newspaper. (2004)

BELOW: I know that readers with little knowledge of art history won't get this, but I fantasize that they look up René Magritte and figure it out. More likely, they say "Hmmm," and move on to Zippy the Pinhead. (2004)

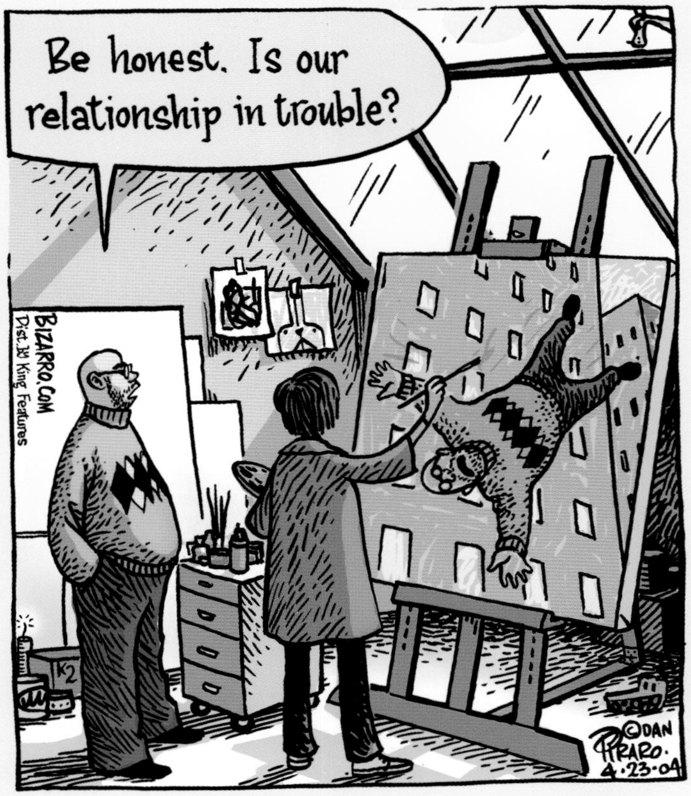
Be honest. Is our relationship in trouble?
BIZARRO.COM Dist. by King Features
©DAN PIRARO. 4.23.04

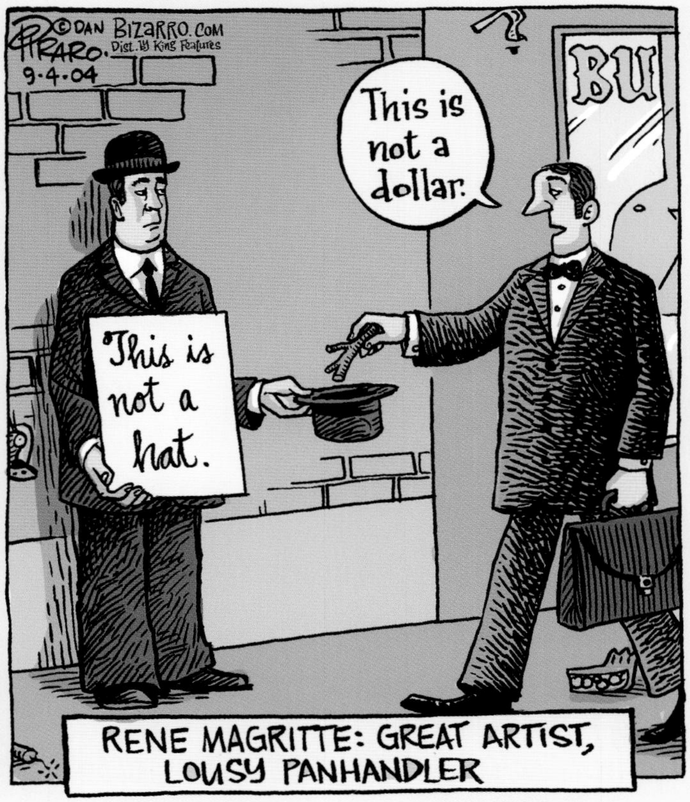
©DAN BIZARRO.COM PIRARO. Dist. by King Features 9.4.04
BU
This is not a dollar.
This is not a hat.
RENE MAGRITTE: GREAT ARTIST, LOUSY PANHANDLER

On the other hand, I don't disparage all nonrepresentational art. I have a great deal of affection and respect for Andy Goldsworthy's work. He walks out into the woods and spends hours pinning leaves together with tiny thorns to form gradually shifting patterns and colors. Or he breaks icicles into small pieces and holds them together in loopy shapes until the cold air refreezes them together. Or he stacks rocks or sticks in circles to make igloo- or egg-shaped monuments. Most of his work is temporary, sometimes lasting less than a day, though some, like his stone walls, will last indefinitely. He photographs his creations for a permanent record but for the most part his art is about creating something new from nature that is as ephemeral as the natural forms themselves. A beautiful documentary about Goldsworthy called *Rivers and Tides* gives a lot of insight into the man and his work.

Does this all sound exactly like the sort of mumbo jumbo that I just criticized in the previous paragraph? Have I contradicted myself completely? Perhaps, but that's what I mean about the interaction of art and what a person brings to it. To Goldsworthy's work I bring a lifelong appreciation of the natural beauty of the world and see human artistic efforts as some attempt to connect with or comment on that beauty. To Rothko's work I seem only to bring a rug from Ikea. Your results may vary.

In spite of my bitchy attitude toward work that I don't understand, I love the fact that the art world has no rules or regulations. And I certainly would never presume to criticize an artist's work to his or her face, no matter what a piece looked like. I adamantly defend Rothko's—and everyone else's—right to create and display anything they want for any reason. My objection is the veneration of certain work by the mainstream art world.

As far as I can tell, this doesn't happen in any other field of creativity. Can you imagine an author receiving wealth and critical acclaim for publishing a series of books with nothing but blank pages? What about a musician who only plays one note on every track of a CD? Would you pay to see a blank film at the theater or a play with an empty stage and no actors? Styles vary widely in any art form, but in the visual arts I believe many have made careers from a lack of content. Rothko's work is no different to me than a song with only two notes.

Another favorite art peeve of mine is the habit of people listing "mixed media" on the label next to their artwork. "Oil," "watercolor," "charcoal"—these all tell me something meaningful. "Mixed media" tells me nothing. Why not just put "art supplies" or "matter"?

Now that I've revealed myself to be a bourgeois boob, I shall pontificate about my own recent artwork. I will, however, maintain my facade of superiority by avoiding use of the word "juxtapose."

My work has changed quite a lot over the years. Since I've never had any commercial success as a fine artist, this hasn't been a problem for me. All my work has been entirely to please myself, and it has always tended toward having a message. I sometimes enjoy nonrepresentational art by others, but the art that I enjoy creating the most is the sort that expresses an idea of some sort through the use of reasonably recognizable elements. Pure design is a beautiful thing to behold, but it doesn't arouse my passion as much as representational art does.

Funereal Weekend (1991, oil on canvas, 48" x 24"). A self-portrait I made after my grandfather and a close friend of mine died in the same week. I spent the weekend going to wakes and funerals. These were the first two loved ones I lost.

When I was young, I bought into what I now see as the Emperor's New Clothes attitude of the contemporary art world and was ashamed of my tendencies toward message and realism. I often struggled to get away from it with looser and vaguer compositions. As I have matured, however, I've come to believe that the best thing any artist can do is to be true to him- or herself. For whatever reason, I enjoy expressing my thoughts and feelings in my art and I am thrilled by realism when used in a creative way. So that's what I now do.

This basic "to thine own self be true" principle is at work behind all forms of art, music, literature, cartoons, whatever. Great art is always a result of an honest expression of something within the artist, not a calculated effort to reach a demographic. If it excites *you*, you've succeeded. Aiming at some hypothetical audience is a great way to create contrived, commercial crap. Of course, that's not to say that what you create for yourself won't also be crap, but at least you'll be pleased with it.

The pieces of mine that I find most satisfying are the ones in which I can combine realism with looser, abstract cartoon images. In the past few years I've gravitated heavily toward a relatively realistic character surrounded by cartoon scribbles with a few bits of trompe-l'oeil on top. I suppose you could say a similar pattern can be seen in my cartoons as well. When I'm just drawing in a sketchbook for fun, I create exaggerated, abstracted images and characters and I really enjoy that sort of thing in other people's work. But my cartoons tend more toward exaggerated, surreal things happening in mostly realistic settings. It just seems to be the way my mind works when I have a specific message to convey.

When I'm on the phone I doodle mindlessly and sometimes jot down notes about the phone call. I save these drawings because they come from a place in my head that I can't get to intentionally. Sometimes I keep the same pieces of paper around until they are full; other times I find scraps lying around that I've doodled on and paste them into my sketchbook.

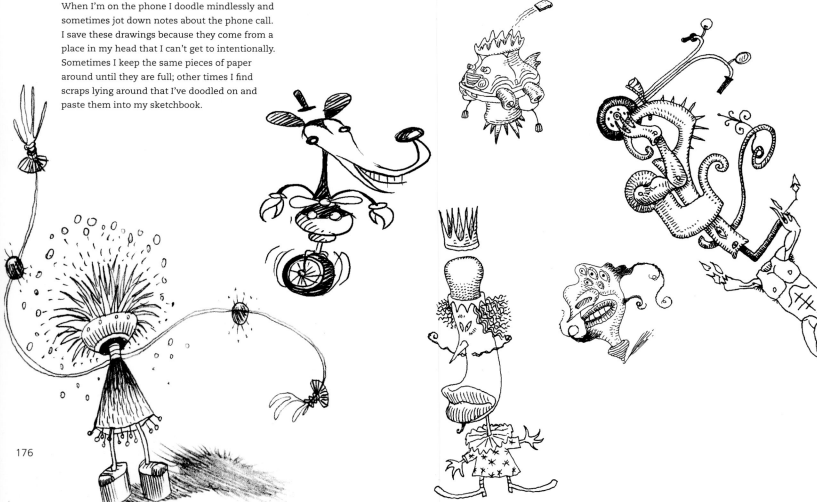

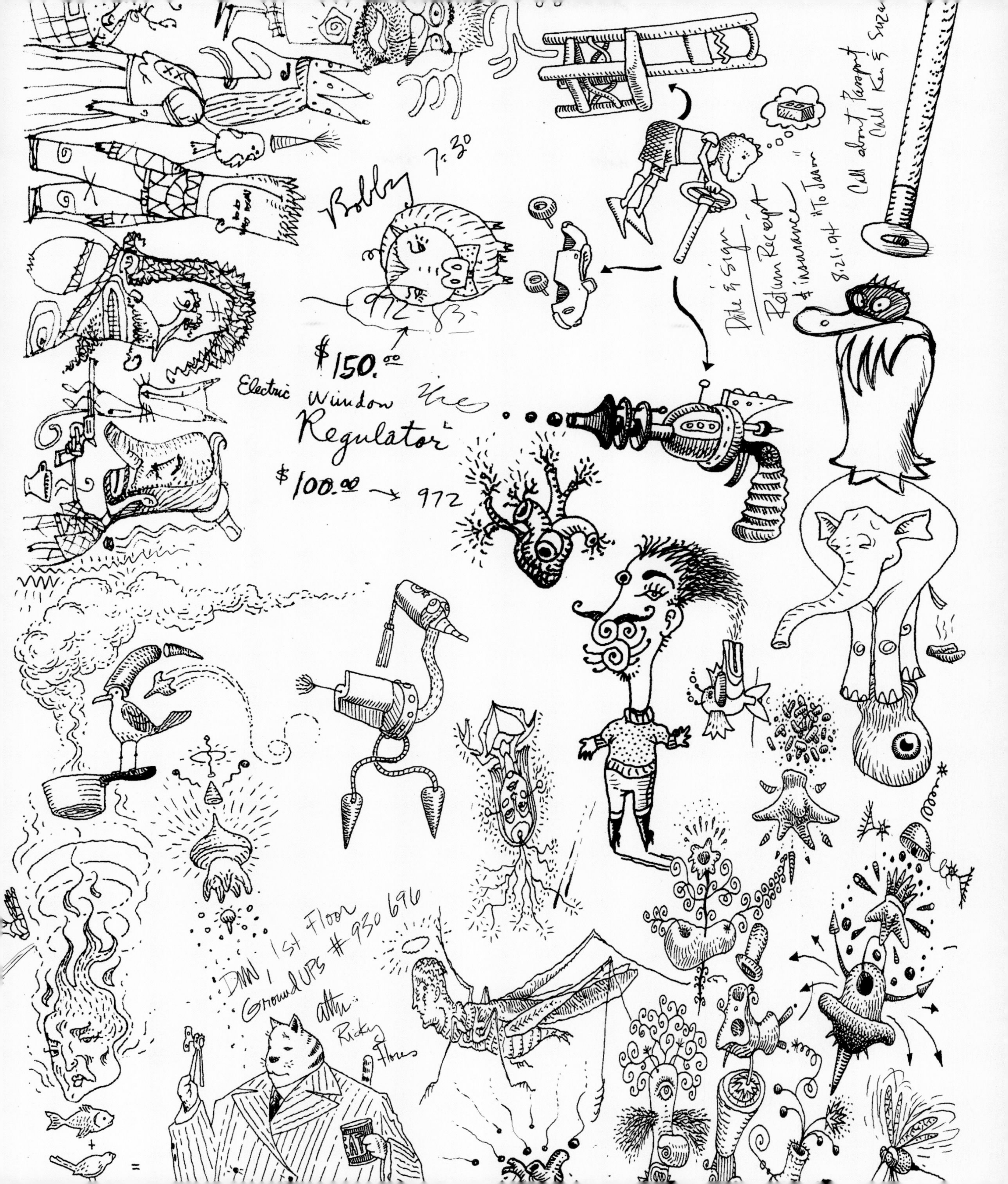

Bobby 7:30
$150.00
Electric Window Regulator
$100.00 → 972
Date & sign
Return Receipt
insurance
8.21.94
Call about Passport
1st Floor
Ground UPS # 930696
attn:
Ricky Flores

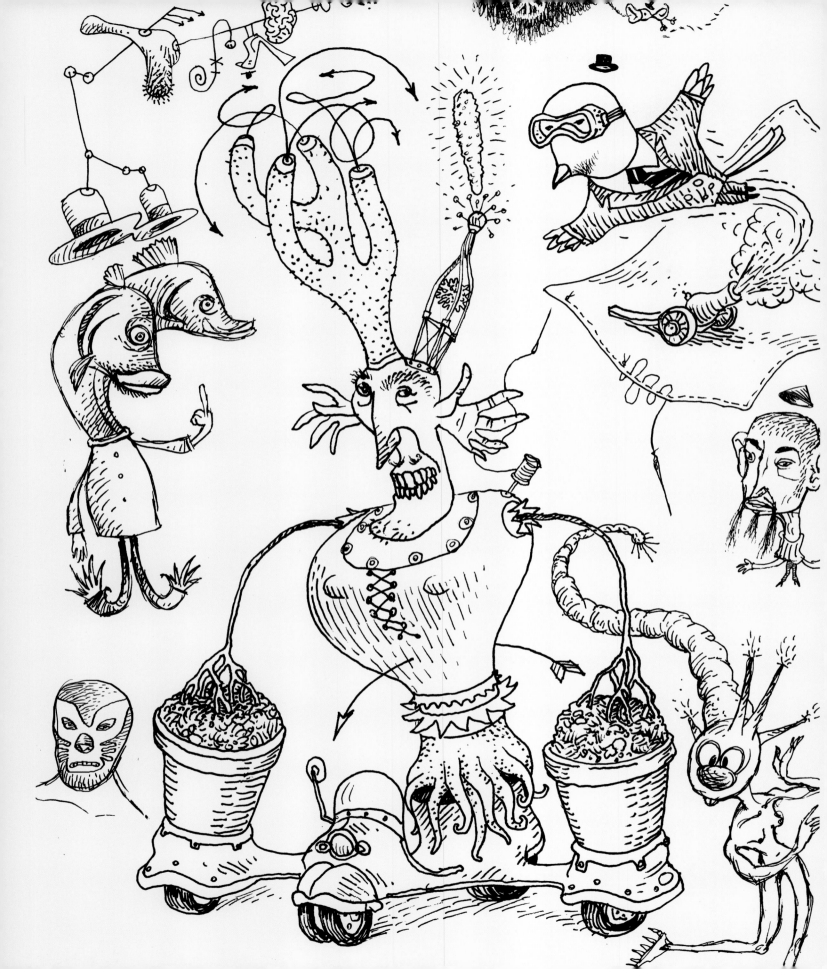

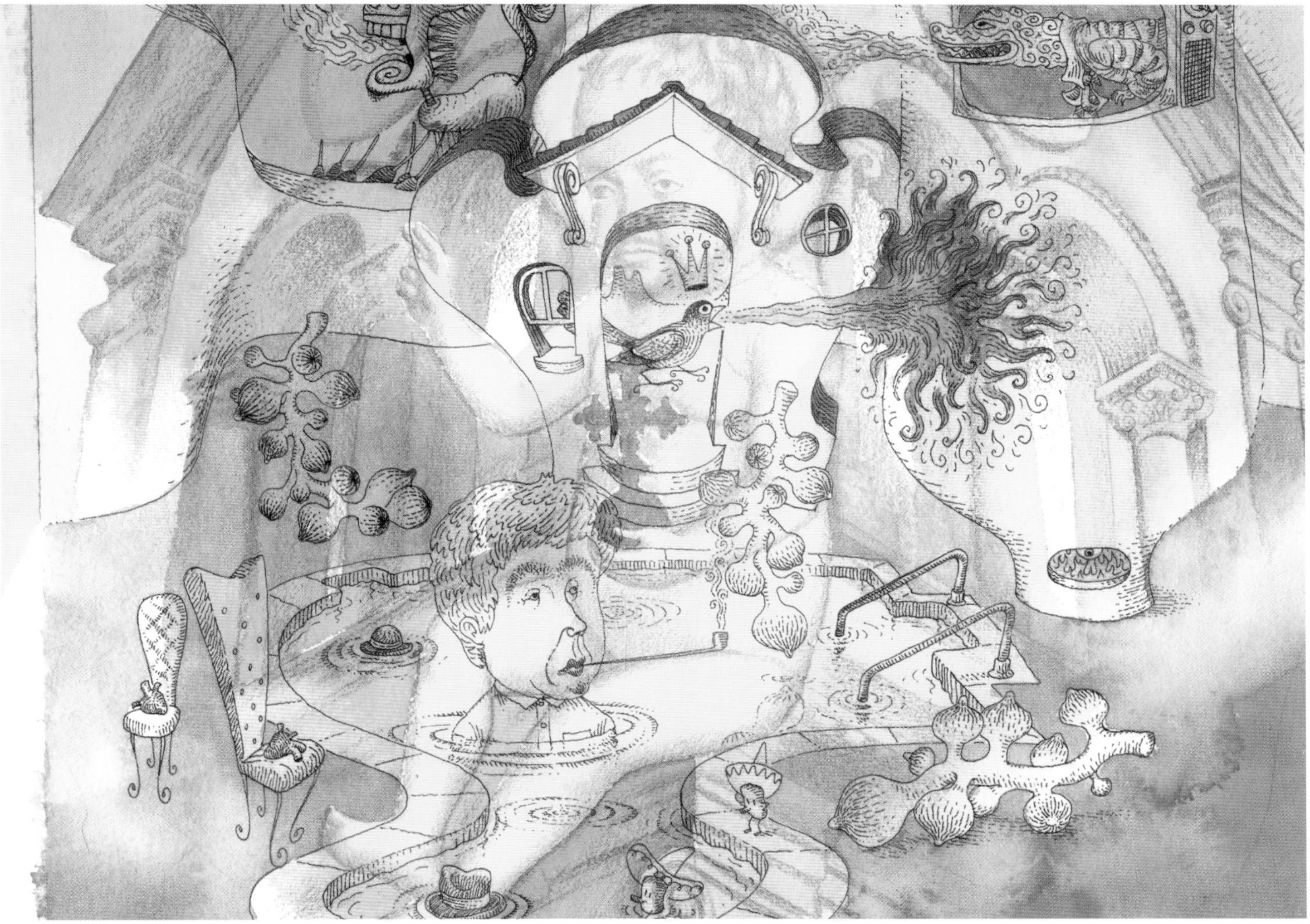

Unfinished, untitled (2001, watercolor, colored pencil, india ink, 12" x 17"). This experiment was not particularly successful, but it was interesting. I find that I can't see both the color image and the black-and-white one simultaneously. I have to concentrate on one and ignore the other. I enjoy this sort of visual/mental exercise.

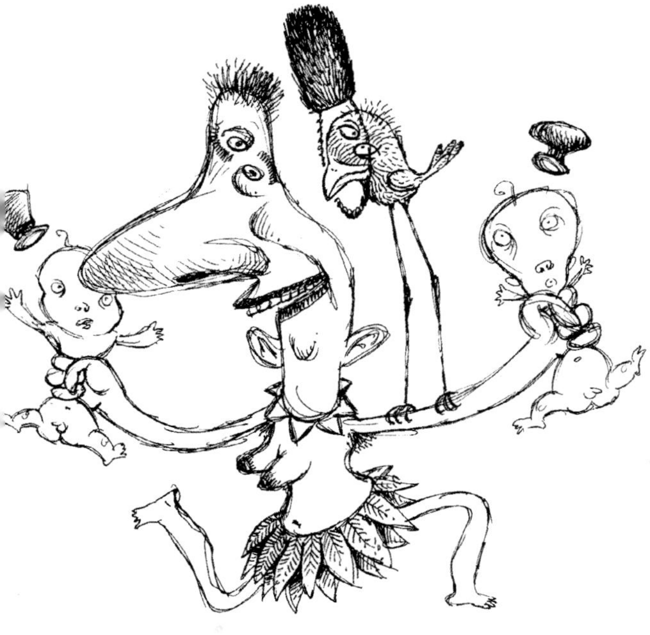

This image was part of the inspiration for the painting on pages 160–61.

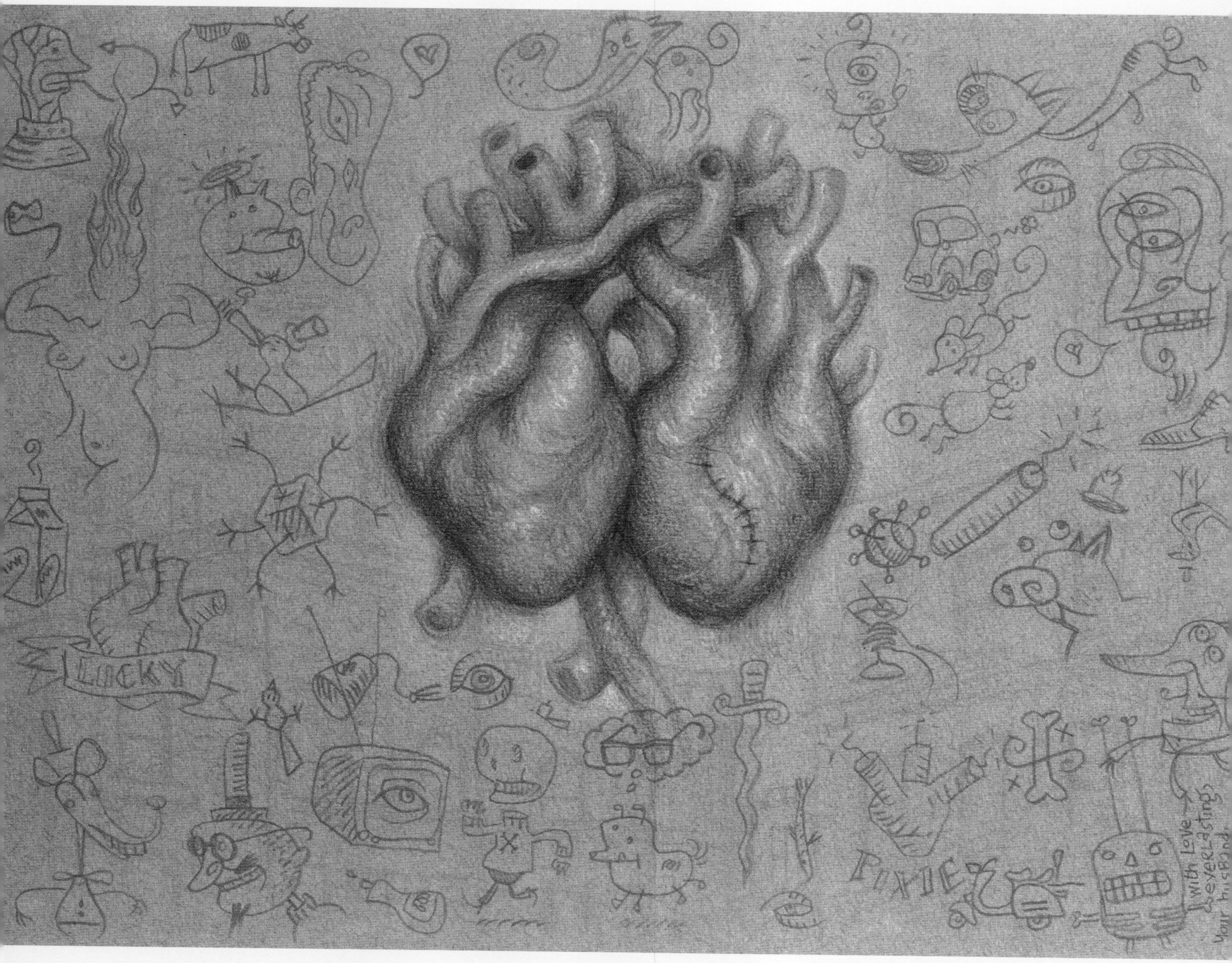
LUCKY
PIXIE
with Love
everLasting
your husBand.

OPPOSITE: An untitled colored-pencil drawing I did for my wife as a birthday gift in 2002. The stitched heart refers to her having undergone open-heart surgery when she was twenty. As a result of a routine dental procedure, she had contracted an infection that made its way to her heart. She was ill for months and doctors failed to make a correct diagnosis, even insinuating that her symptoms were psychosomatic. A valve in her heart was destroyed, and the infection caused a blood clot that made its way to her brain and caused an aneurysm. She was saved by emergency brain surgery and had an artificial valve put in her heart two months later. She's fine now, thanks.

RIGHT: Untitled sculpture (2004, wood and copper, 9½" x 6½" x 6"). Another birthday present for my wife.

181

And what exactly is that message? More often than not, it's that life is never as normal and controlled as it seems.

Behind every Norman Rockwell image of everyday American life, something bizarre is at work. At a happy Rockwellian Thanksgiving dinner table, the boy is wondering what his teenage cousin looks like naked. The teenage cousin hopes no one notices her eyes are glazed and bloodshot. The jolly, white-haired grandmother prays nobody finds out her middle-aged son is living in and selling drugs out of her basement and refuses to leave. The affable father of four is wondering how long he can hide the fact that he is gay. His wife is hoping no one confronts her with any fact that might burst her everything-is-just-fine-and-everyone-is-perfectly-happy bubble. Something like, "Honey, I'm gay."

And closer to my own interests, nobody at the table wants to know that the turkey they are about to eat was every bit as personable, affectionate, and sentient as the cherished family dog. Yet it spent every day of its life crammed into a filthy, crowded, disease-ridden pen, was pumped full of antibiotics and hormones, and likely never saw sunlight until the day it was grabbed by the neck and thrown into a truck and driven to a slaughterhouse. There it was hung by the feet on a metal conveyor chain, dragged past a metal blade that slit its throat, and cut it open while it was still conscious, terrified, and struggling. All for a few seconds of sensory pleasure in the smiling Norman Rockwell mouths.

I suspect the truth is that the "happy, normal American family" doesn't look anything like a Rockwell painting. All families, even happy, normal ones, have their share of skeletons and secrets and pain, because tragedy is as much a part of life as happiness. Maybe we developed humor as a means to cope with disaster, past, present, and future. It is no coincidence that many comedians come from particularly dark childhoods. They learned early how to use humor to deal with the painful absurdities of life.

My own childhood wasn't particularly awful. In fact, it was fairly calm by American standards. Once Dad was acquitted of the bestiality charges and Mom got out of prison, life around our house was pretty unexceptional. If it had been more tragic, I'd probably be a lot funnier. I'll never forgive my parents for providing such a stable family life, and I tried desperately not to repeat that mistake with my own children.

Someone said that tragedy plus time equals comedy. (I think it was either Steve Allen or Barney Rubble.) Finding ways to get people to laugh at themselves and the contradictions and tragedies of life is what I do for a living. In some way, it's what all cartoonists do.

Except for Jim Davis. I'm not sure what he's doing.

Syndicated cartoonists live a strange existence of contradiction: drawing one little picture every day is easy, but writing an original joke at that rate is nearly impossible. I used to worry that my muse would leave me if some horrible tragedy should befall me or my family. Would I be able to continue being funny on a daily basis in the face of real tragedy? But I don't worry anymore. If I can make it through divorce, animal abuse, and the Bush administration, I can make it through anything.

A repeating theme in my sketchbooks are characters emerging from each other's mouths, or eating each other. Since I quit smoking in 1987, I've had a serious oral fixation and am always chewing on something, edible or not. Maybe the two are connected. (I am not, however, a pencil chewer. I hate picking up a writing utensil with teeth marks in it.)

OPPOSITE: *Family Food Chain, 1958* (2004, watercolor, colored pencil, ballpoint pen, 16" x 12"). My version of what mainstream American family life must have been like for many Americans around the time I was born.

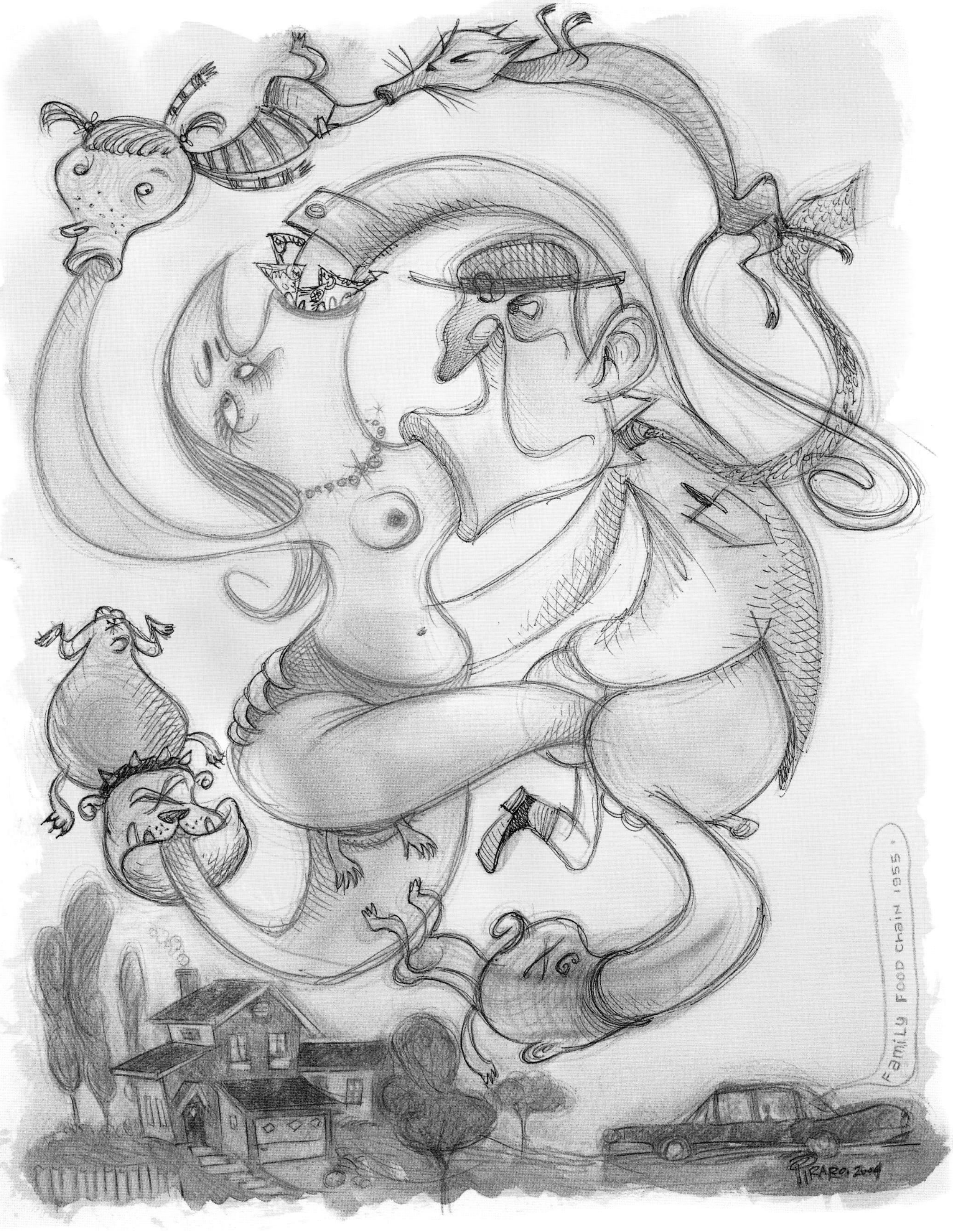

FAMILY FOOD CHAIN 1955
PIRARO, 2004

My favorite cartoons

Some of the cartoons in this section are what I think of as my best, and others are ones that readers have mentioned to me numerous times. These two lists rarely coincide, so I never know who is a better judge of my work, you or me. When choosing cartoons for a book, I try to gather a bit from both.

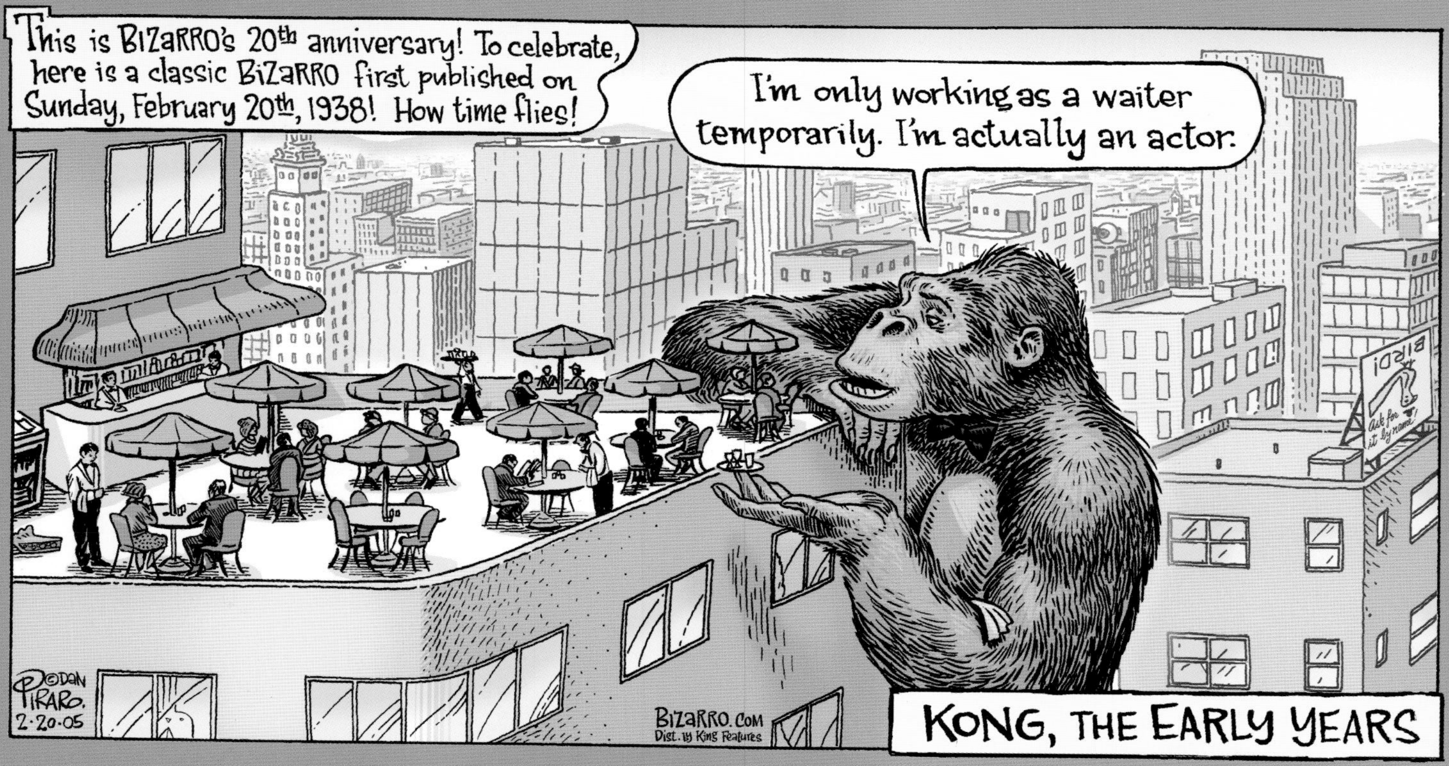
This is BIZARRO's 20th anniversary! To celebrate, here is a classic BIZARRO first published on Sunday, February 20th, 1938! How time flies!
I'm only working as a waiter temporarily. I'm actually an actor.
KONG, THE EARLY YEARS
©DAN PIRARO 2-20-05
BIZARRO.COM
Dist. by King Features

On the twentieth anniversary of *Bizarro*, I used an old Sunday comic in a new way. The line art is the same, but I've changed the captions, added a few elements here and there, and completely recolored it. The old one (see page 45) was colored by numbers in the way comics were since the beginning. It is a complex system that requires the use of a lot of imagination to conjure up an image of what the final will look like with all the colors in place. It also made it very difficult to get interesting effects. I colored the new one in Photoshop on my computer, which is how I have done all my coloring work since the mid-nineties. My favorite nuance is the way that I moved the tray from his palm to his fingertips. This tiny change is the result of twenty years of cartooning experience.

I understand the financial motivation for franchising, but I hate how it's homogenizing America. With small pockets of exceptions, the whole country is becoming remarkably uniform. I think national chains like Pottery Barn and The Gap are one reason why. (2004)

BELOW: Will Franken is a cross between a stand-up comic and a performance artist who performs regularly in San Francisco. The guy is brilliant. I included his name here as an homage to his answering-machine routine in which furniture talks about a "special offer from Personifications Enterprises." (2004)

BELOW, RIGHT: I got a complaint from a reader on this one, thinking I was making fun of the way Asian immigrants speak. The mind reels. (1995)

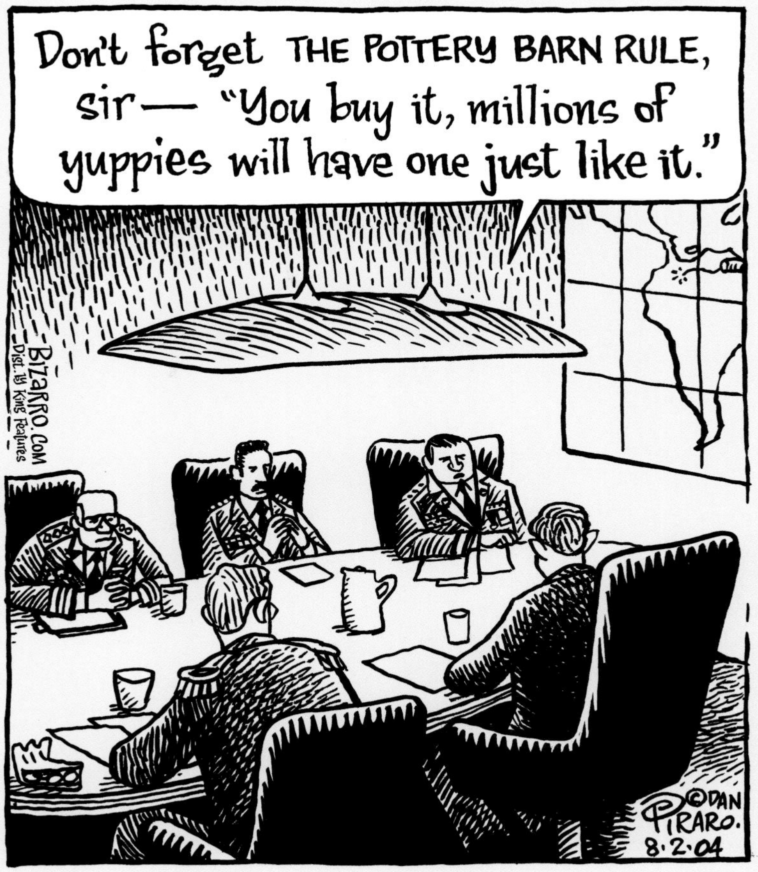
Don't forget THE POTTERY BARN RULE, sir— "You buy it, millions of yuppies will have one just like it."
BIZARRO.COM
Dist. by King Features
©DAN PIRARO. 8.2.04

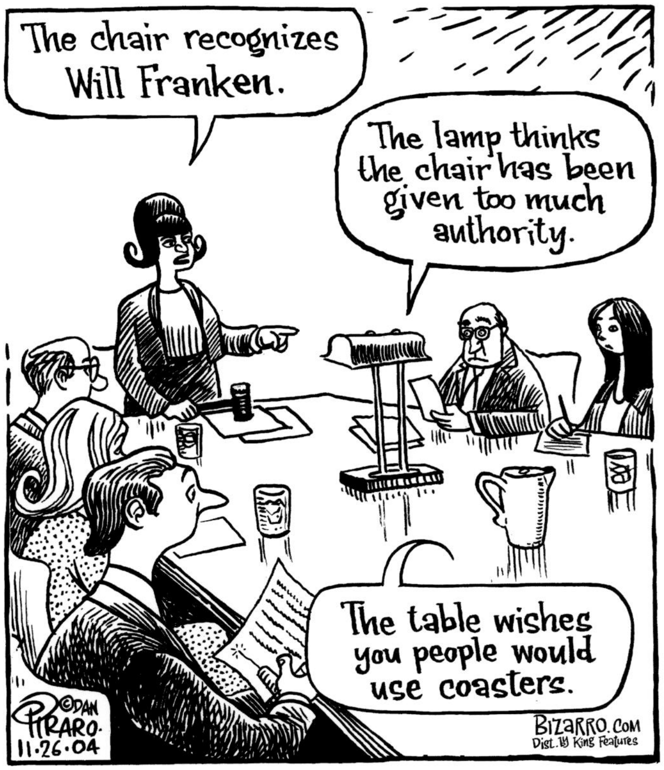
The chair recognizes Will Franken.
The lamp thinks the chair has been given too much authority.
The table wishes you people would use coasters.
©DAN PIRARO. 11.26.04
BIZARRO.COM
Dist. by King Features

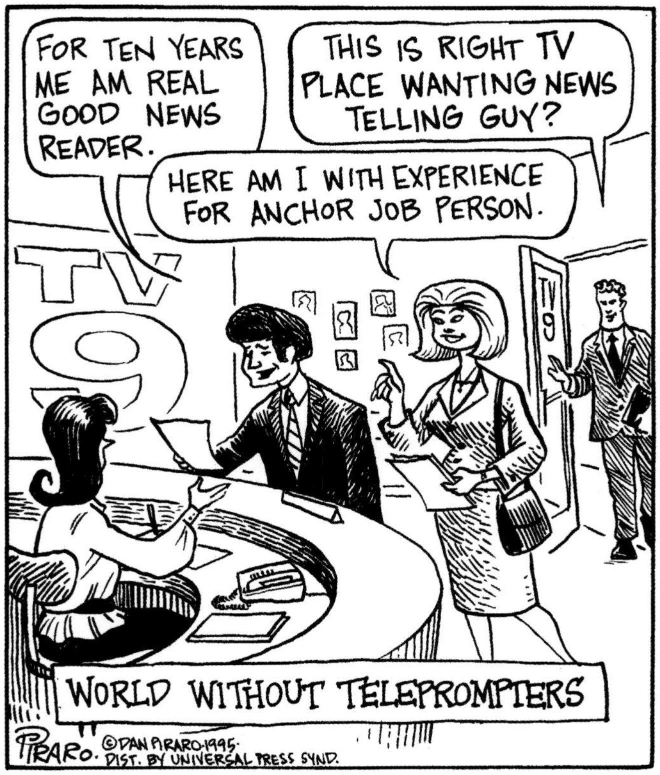
FOR TEN YEARS ME AM REAL GOOD NEWS READER.
THIS IS RIGHT TV PLACE WANTING NEWS TELLING GUY?
HERE AM I WITH EXPERIENCE FOR ANCHOR JOB PERSON.
TV 9
WORLD WITHOUT TELEPROMPTERS
PIRARO. ©DAN PIRARO 1995. DIST. BY UNIVERSAL PRESS SYND.

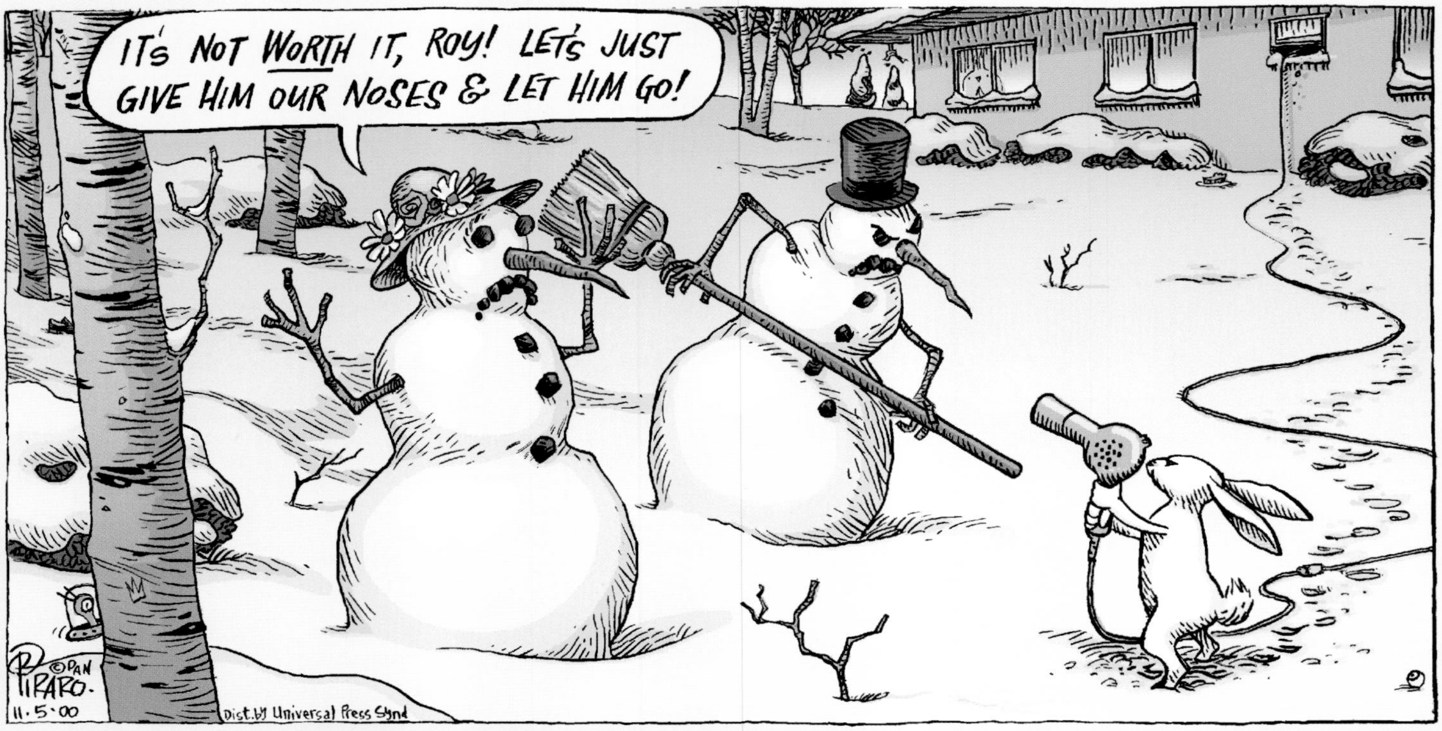
IT'S NOT WORTH IT, ROY! LET'S JUST GIVE HIM OUR NOSES & LET HIM GO!
©DAN PIRARO. 11·5·00
Dist. by Universal Press Synd

I'm not particularly proud of this cartoon, but dozens of people over the years have told me it is their favorite. It also holds the distinction of having the longest electrical cord ever drawn in a syndicated cartoon. (2000)

RIGHT: Newspapers are very Victorian about comic content. This one verged on crossing the line, but somehow snuck by. (2000)

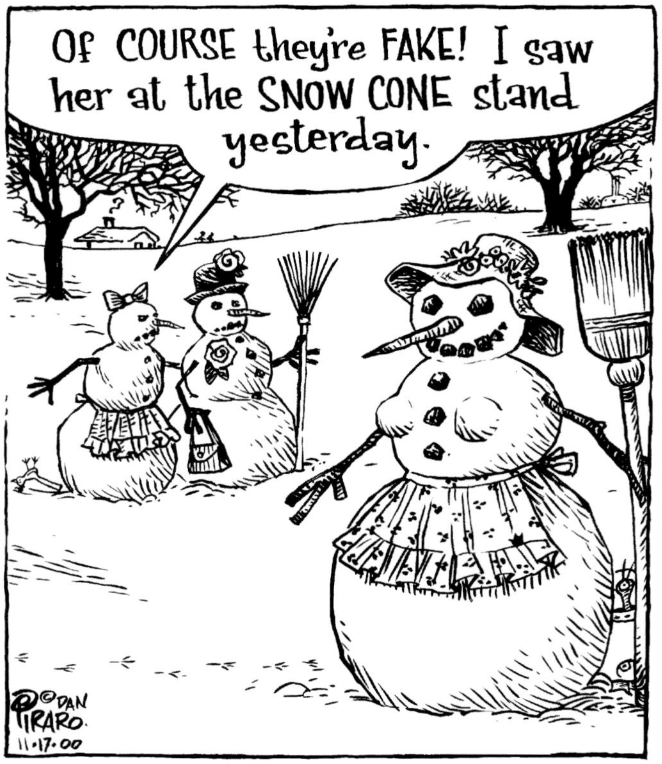
Of COURSE they're FAKE! I saw her at the SNOW CONE stand yesterday.
©DAN PIRARO. 11·17·00

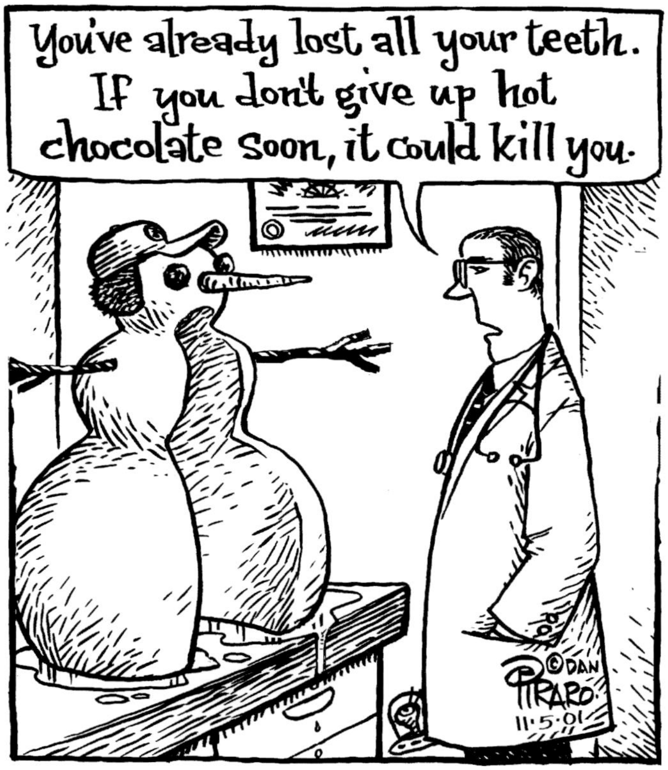
You've already lost all your teeth. If you don't give up hot chocolate soon, it could kill you.
©DAN PIRARO. 11·5·01

But will he listen? (2001)

I've done quite a few cartoons over the years about snowmen in various stages of melting. Perhaps it's my way of dealing with my own mortality. (2004)

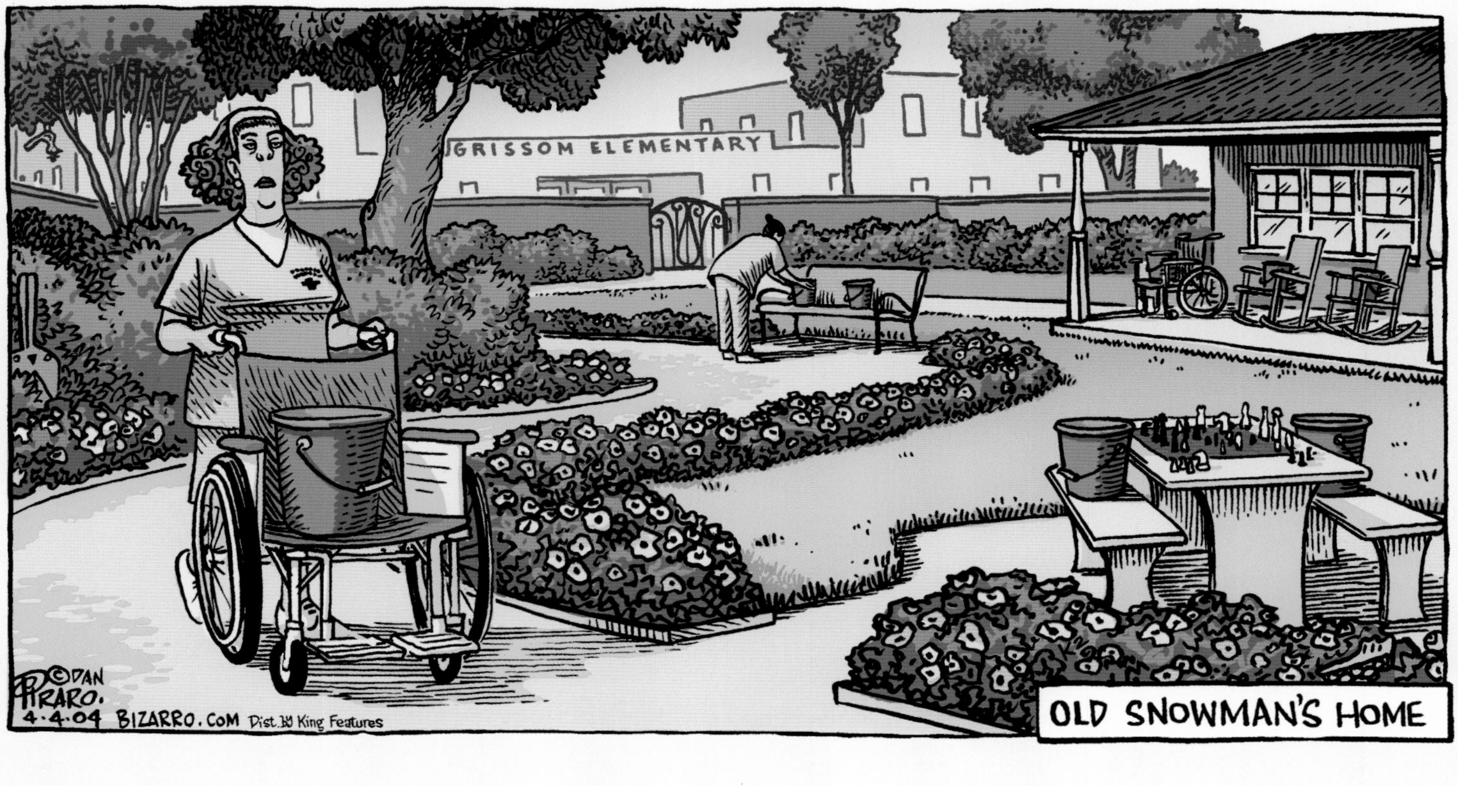
GRISSOM ELEMENTARY
©DAN PIRARO. 4·4·04 BIZARRO.COM Dist. by King Features
OLD SNOWMAN'S HOME

Another incredibly fertile area for gags is the therapist's couch. I'm not addicted to counseling like a Woody Allen character, but I've made very good use of it during rough times in my life.

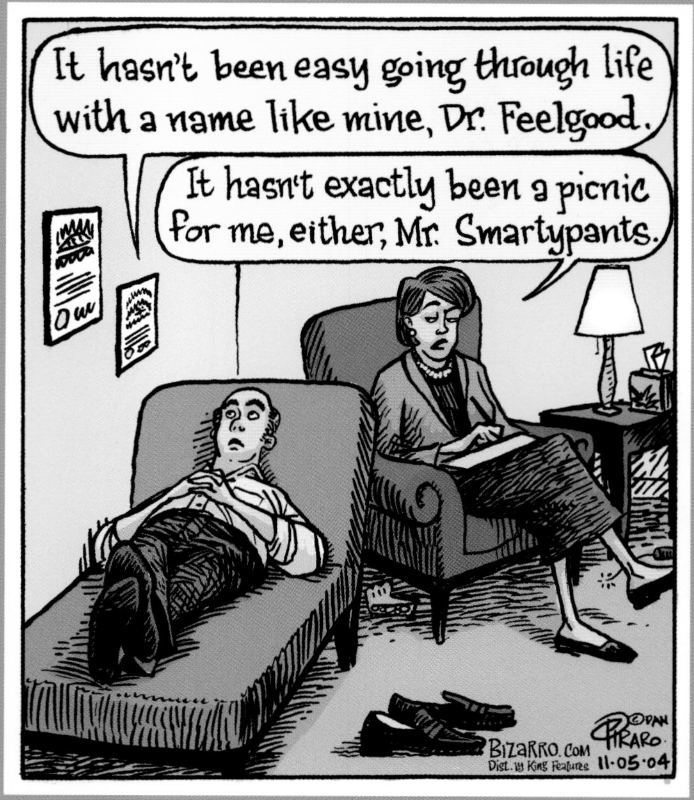
It hasn't been easy going through life with a name like mine, Dr. Feelgood.
It hasn't exactly been a picnic for me, either, Mr. Smartypants.
©DAN PIRARO.
BIZARRO.COM
Dist. by King Features
11-05-04

BELOW: Two similar jokes about parents as therapists. I think both work well. (2001, 2004)

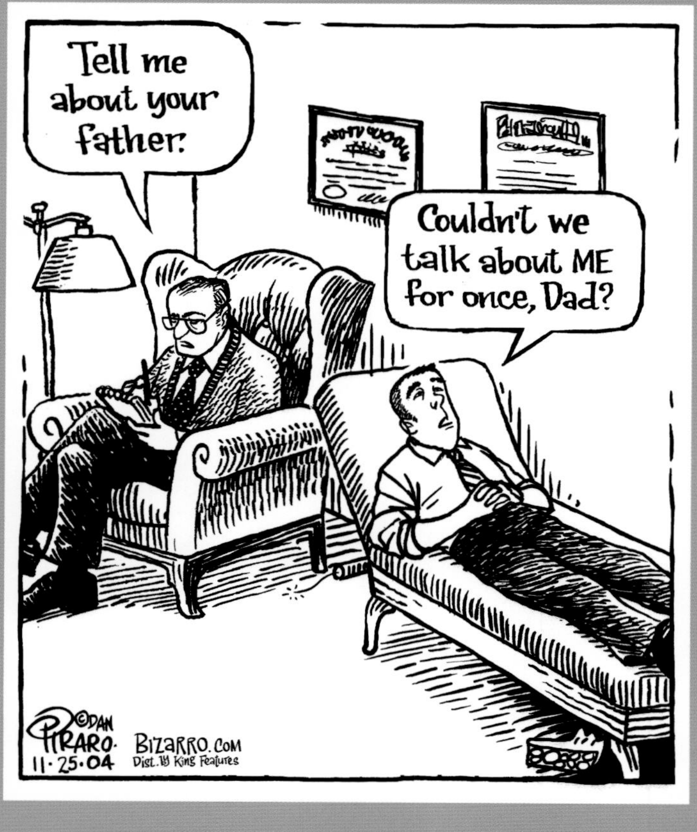
Tell me about your father.
Couldn't we talk about ME for once, Dad?
©DAN PIRARO.
11-25-04
BIZARRO.COM
Dist. by King Features

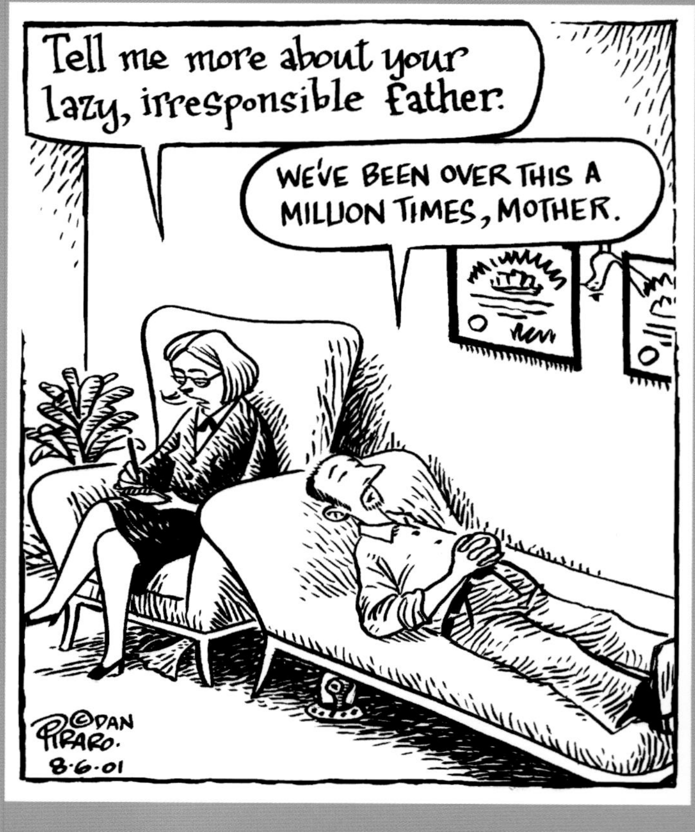
Tell me more about your lazy, irresponsible father.
WE'VE BEEN OVER THIS A MILLION TIMES, MOTHER.
©DAN PIRARO.
8-6-01

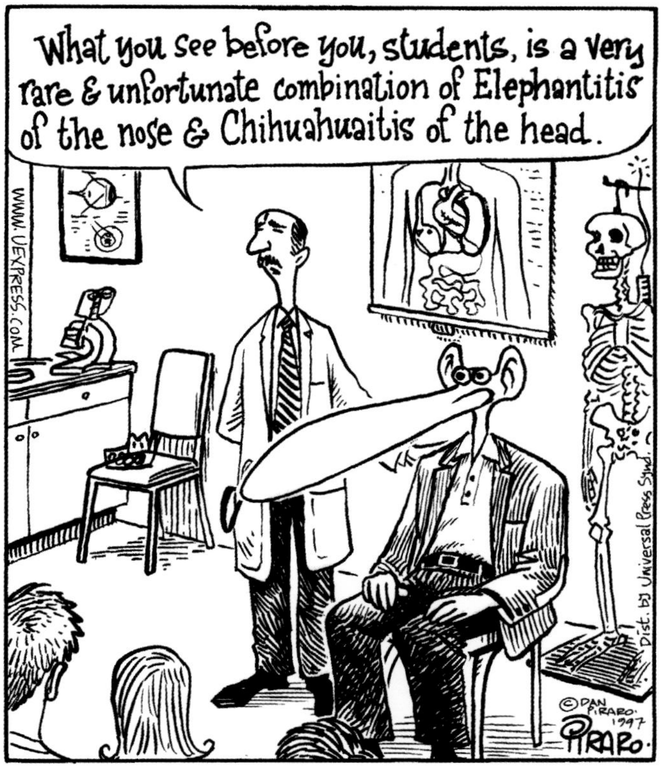
What you see before you, students, is a very rare & unfortunate combination of Elephantitis of the nose & Chihuahuaitis of the head.
WWW.UEXPRESS.COM
Dist. by Universal Press Synd.
©DAN PIRARO 1997
PIRARO

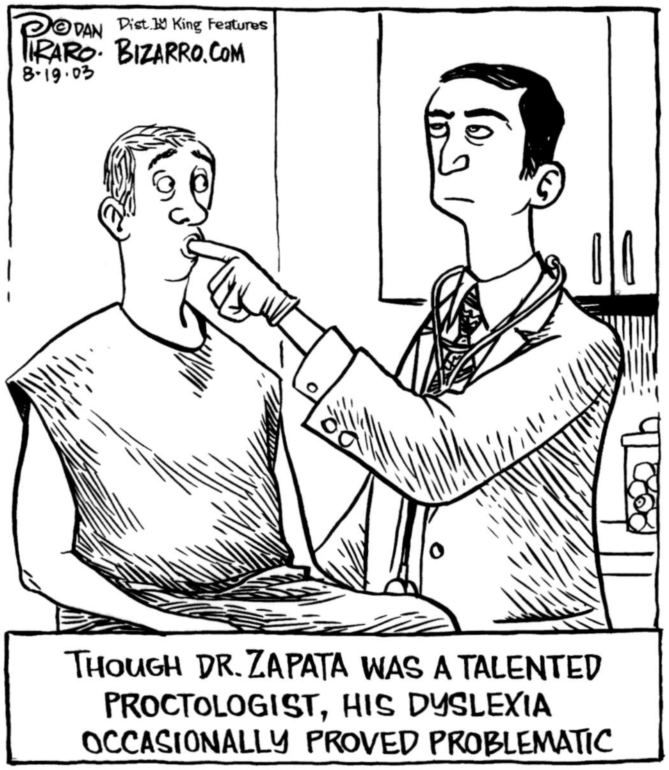
©DAN PIRARO 8·19·03
Dist. by King Features
BIZARRO.COM
THOUGH DR. ZAPATA WAS A TALENTED PROCTOLOGIST, HIS DYSLEXIA OCCASIONALLY PROVED PROBLEMATIC

The first time I heard of elephantitis was when I visited a sideshow attraction at the Oklahoma State Fair as a young teen. I've always thought the name seemed indelicate and very unscientific. It does offer plenty of humor opportunities, however. (1997)

ABOVE, RIGHT: I got a couple of complaints about the "indecency" of this cartoon. How do people who are this easily offended get through a day? Do they cry themselves to sleep every night? (2003)

RIGHT: This cartoon never fails to get a big, extended laugh when I use it in my stage show. I find it particularly amusing to listen to the delayed waves of laughter. Some people get it instantly, another group gets it a few seconds later, and then you can hear murmuring as people explain it to others before there's a last wave of laughter. (1996)

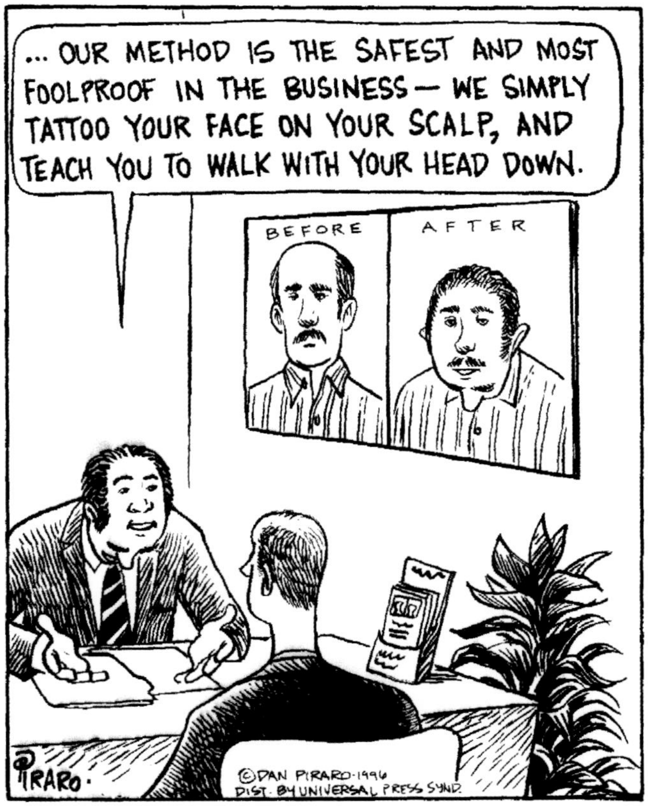
... OUR METHOD IS THE SAFEST AND MOST FOOLPROOF IN THE BUSINESS — WE SIMPLY TATTOO YOUR FACE ON YOUR SCALP, AND TEACH YOU TO WALK WITH YOUR HEAD DOWN.
BEFORE
AFTER
PIRARO
©DAN PIRARO·1996
DIST. BY UNIVERSAL PRESS SYND.

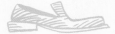

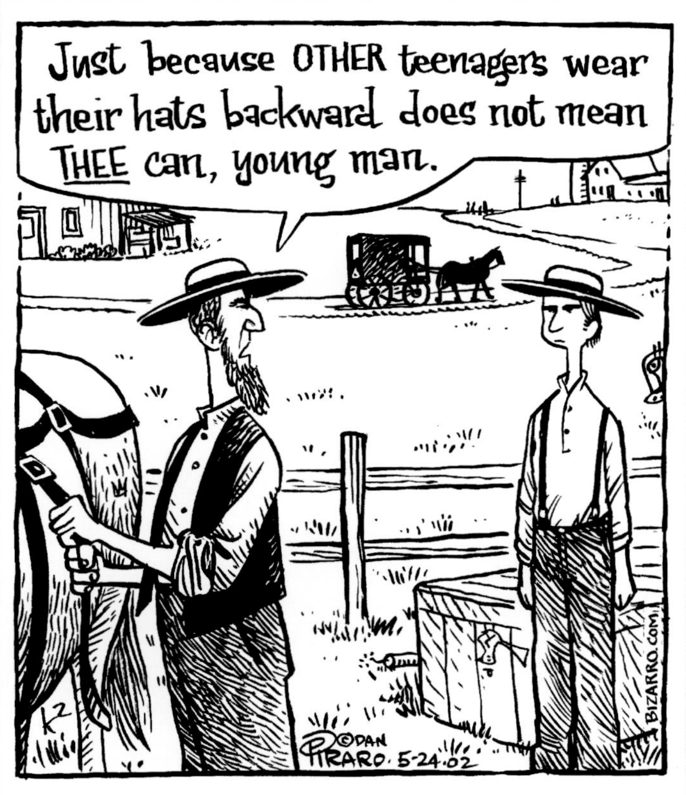
Just because OTHER teenagers wear their hats backward does not mean THEE can, young man.
©DAN PIRARO 5-24-02
BIZARRO.COM

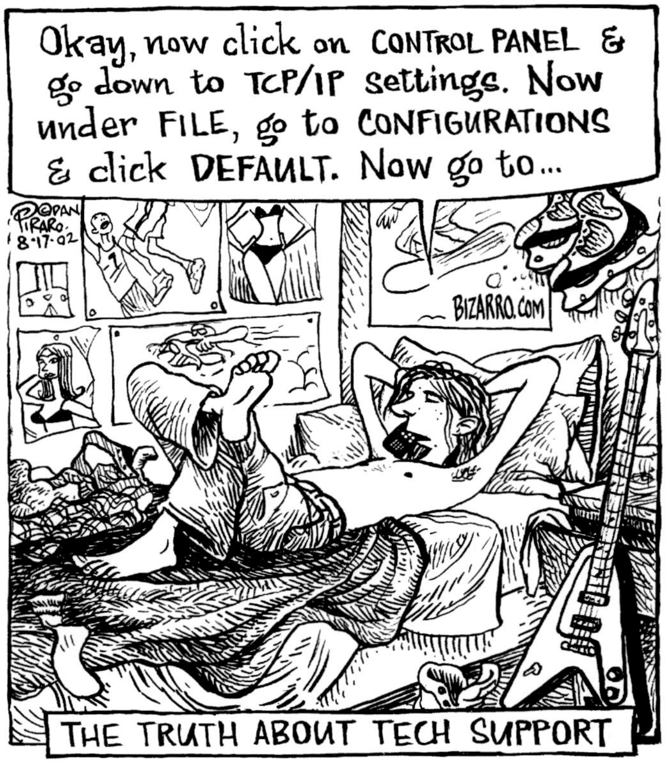
Okay, now click on CONTROL PANEL & go down to TCP/IP settings. Now under FILE, go to CONFIGURATIONS & click DEFAULT. Now go to...
©DAN PIRARO 8-17-02
BIZARRO.COM
THE TRUTH ABOUT TECH SUPPORT

Here I get the rare chance to make fun both of people who wear baseball caps backward and of the Amish. How often does that happen? I am fascinated by the fact that the only reason the baseball cap was invented was to keep the sun out of your eyes with the bill, but the fashion is to wear it backward. This is how easily amused I am. (2002)

ABOVE, RIGHT: This is who I envision when I'm talking to tech support. Except nowadays the bedroom is in India. (2002)

RIGHT: I am proud of this one because it's tough to come up with a new take on an old subject. (2001)

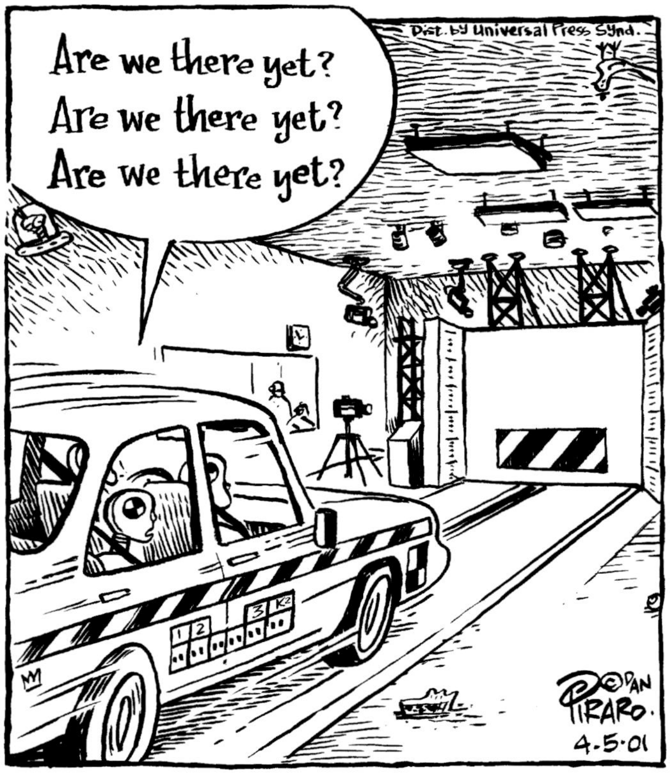
Are we there yet?
Are we there yet?
Are we there yet?
Dist. by Universal Press Synd.
©DAN PIRARO. 4-5-01

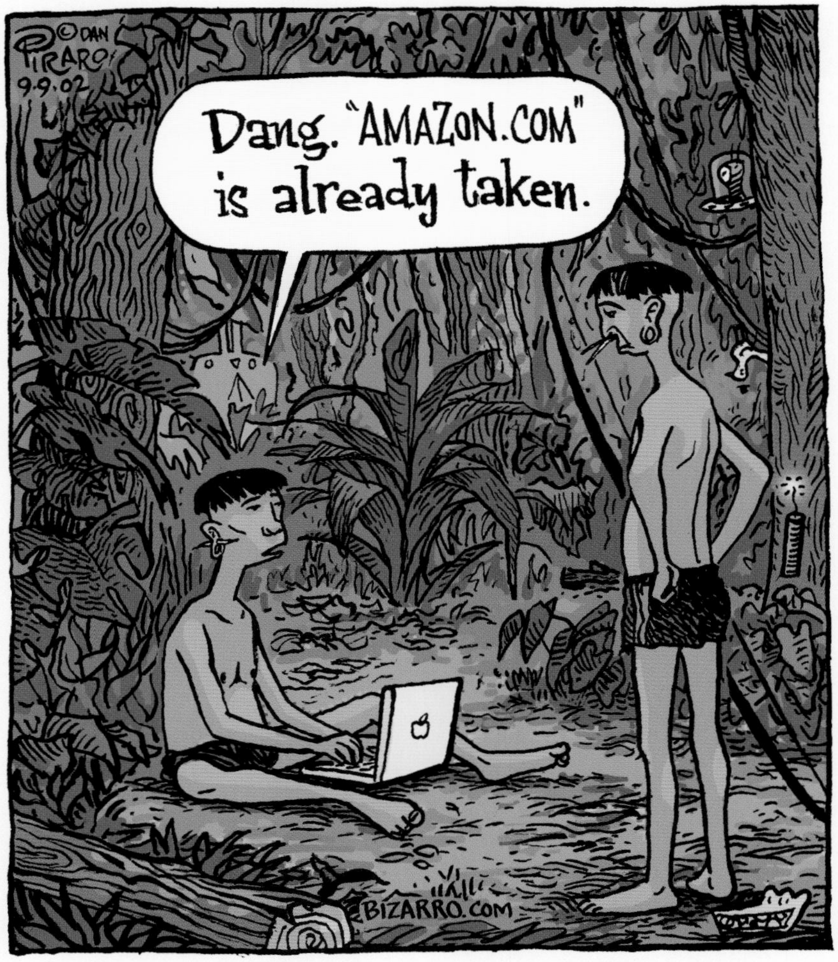
©DAN PIRARO 9.9.02
Dang. "AMAZON.COM" is already taken.
BIZARRO.COM

I consider this to be one of my best efforts. (2002)

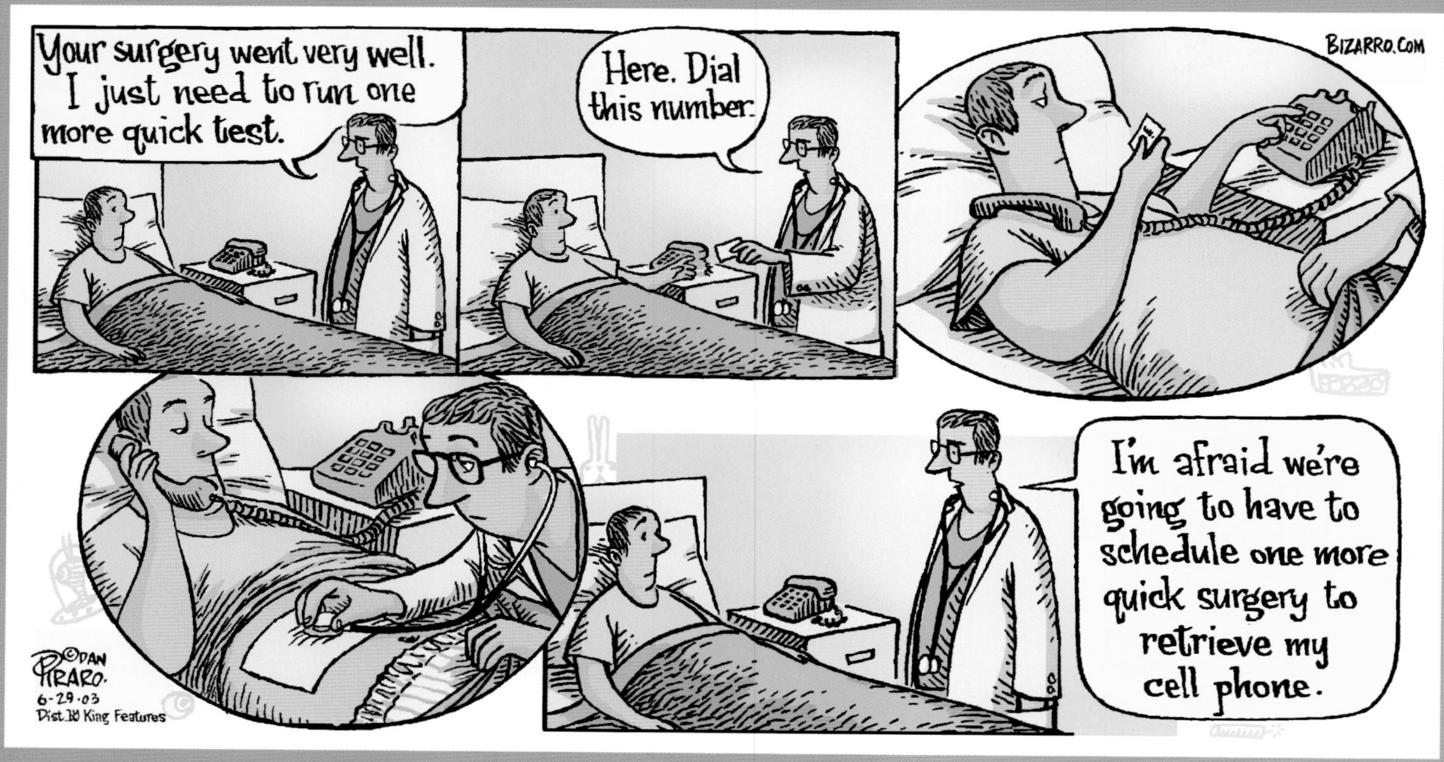
BIZARRO.COM
Your surgery went very well. I just need to run one more quick test.
Here. Dial this number.
I'm afraid we're going to have to schedule one more quick surgery to retrieve my cell phone.
©DAN PIRARO. 6-29-03 Dist. by King Features

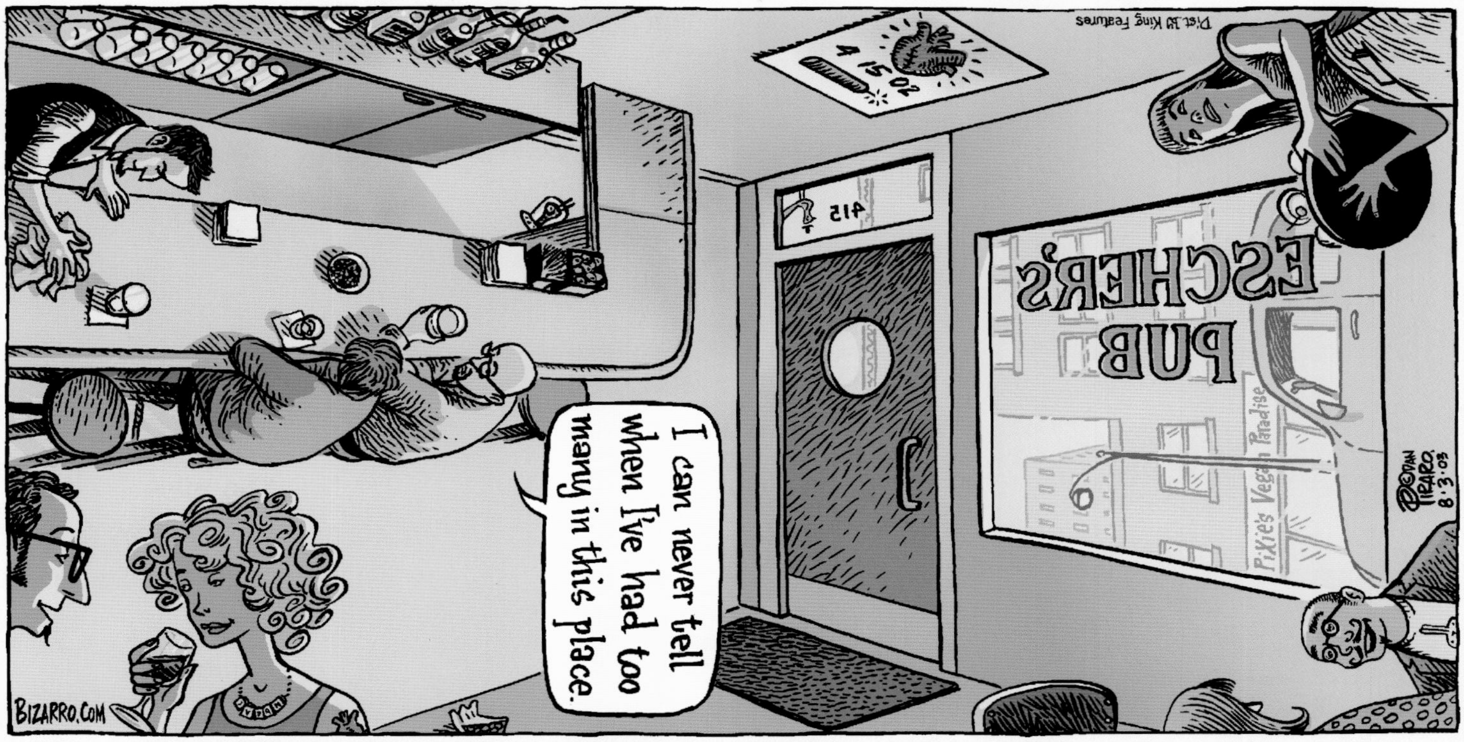
I can never tell when I've had too many in this place.
ESCHER'S PUB
Pixie's Vegan Paradise
Dist. by King Features
DAN PIRARO 8·3·03
BIZARRO.COM

I've admired M. C. Escher since I was a teenager and have done a number of cartoons based on his work. This one features a bartender who looks like Escher himself, Ashley and me in the lower left corner, and a vegan café across the street. One of my nicknames for Ashley is Pixie. On the wall is a poster featuring our wedding date and a heart with stitches through it to represent the open-heart surgery Ashley had at age twenty. (2003)

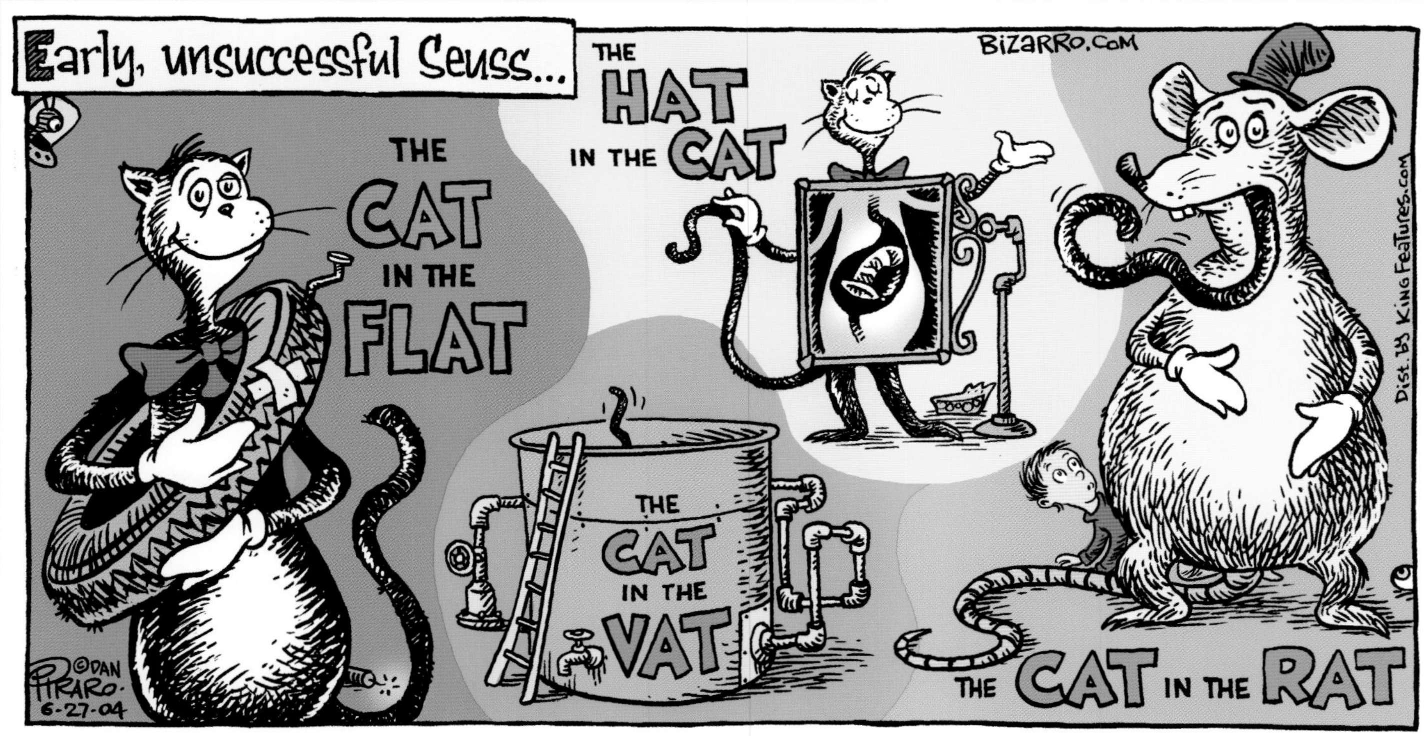
Early, unsuccessful Seuss...
BIZARRO.COM
THE CAT IN THE FLAT
THE HAT IN THE CAT
THE CAT IN THE VAT
THE CAT IN THE RAT
Dist. by King Features.com
©DAN PIRARO 6-27-04

I don't trust anyone who doesn't love Dr. Seuss. (2004)

BELOW: A unique tribute to *Peanuts*. Notice the guy in the right foreground is reading my travelogue book, *Bizarro among the Savages*. (1998)

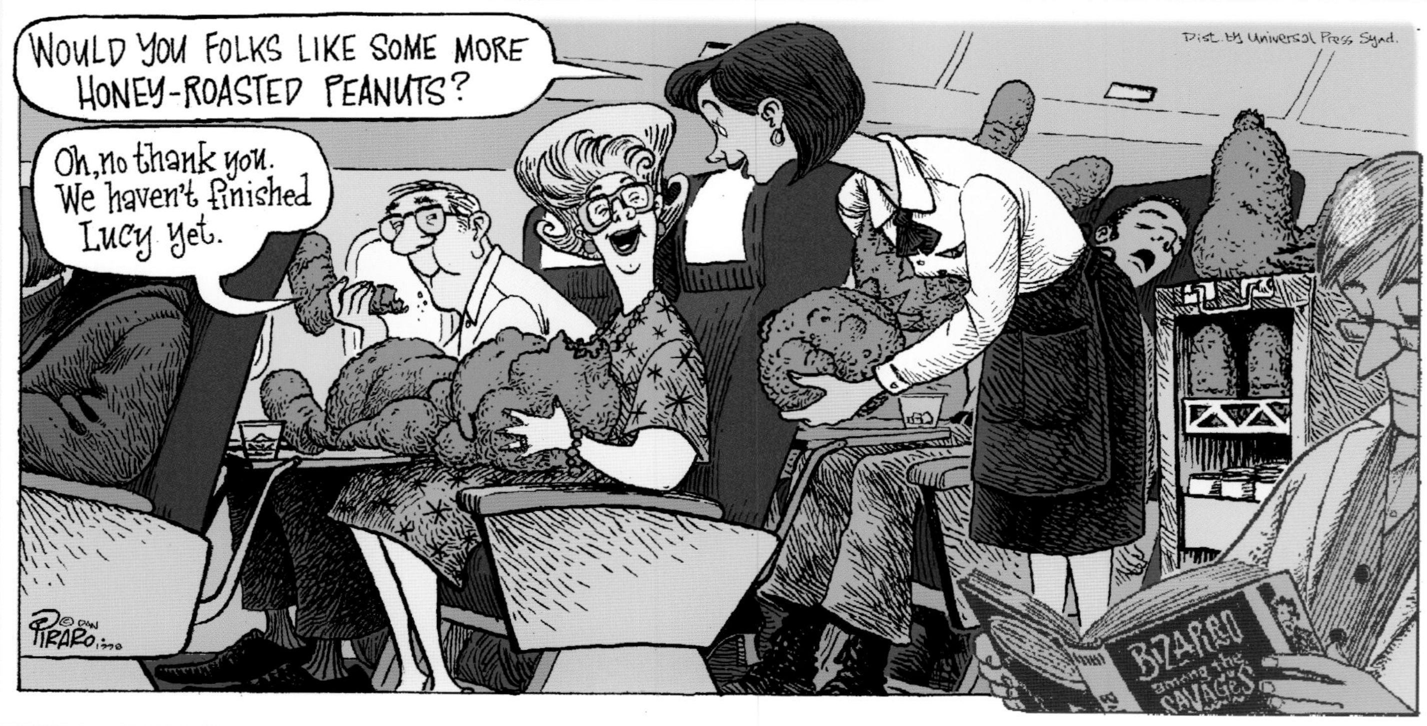
WOULD YOU FOLKS LIKE SOME MORE HONEY-ROASTED PEANUTS?
Oh, no thank you. We haven't finished Lucy yet.
Dist. by Universal Press Synd.
BIZARRO among the SAVAGES

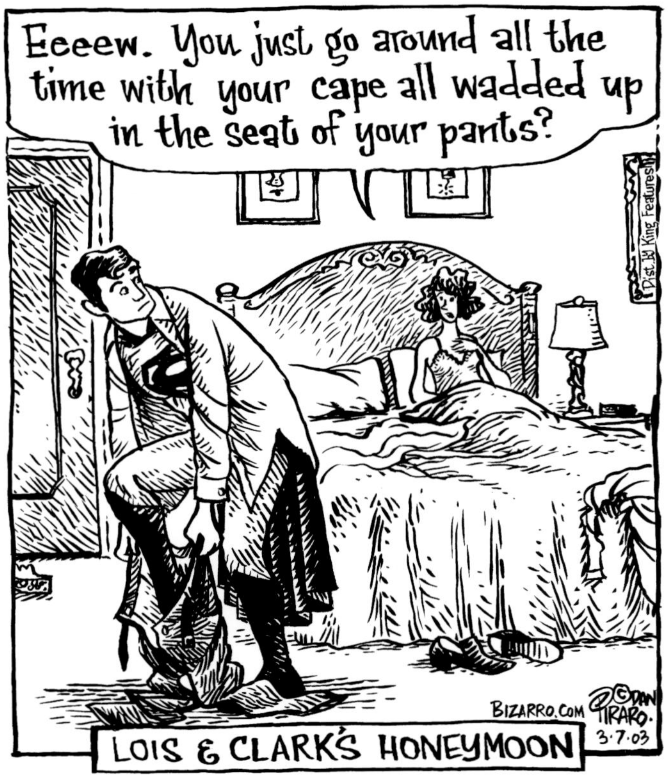
Eeeew. You just go around all the time with your cape all wadded up in the seat of your pants?
Dist. by King Features
BIZARRO.COM
©DAN PIRARO
3·7·03
LOIS & CLARK'S HONEYMOON

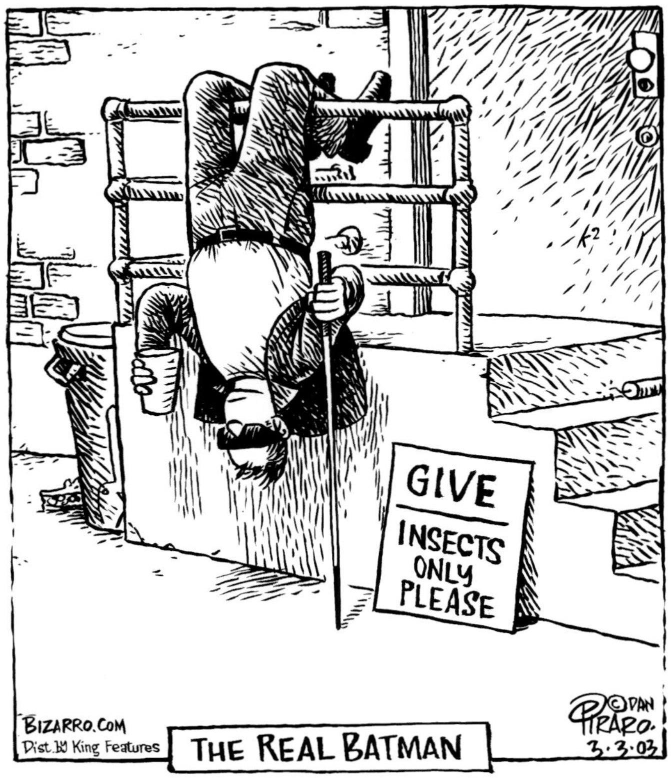
GIVE
INSECTS ONLY PLEASE
BIZARRO.COM
Dist. by King Features
THE REAL BATMAN
©DAN PIRARO
3·3·03

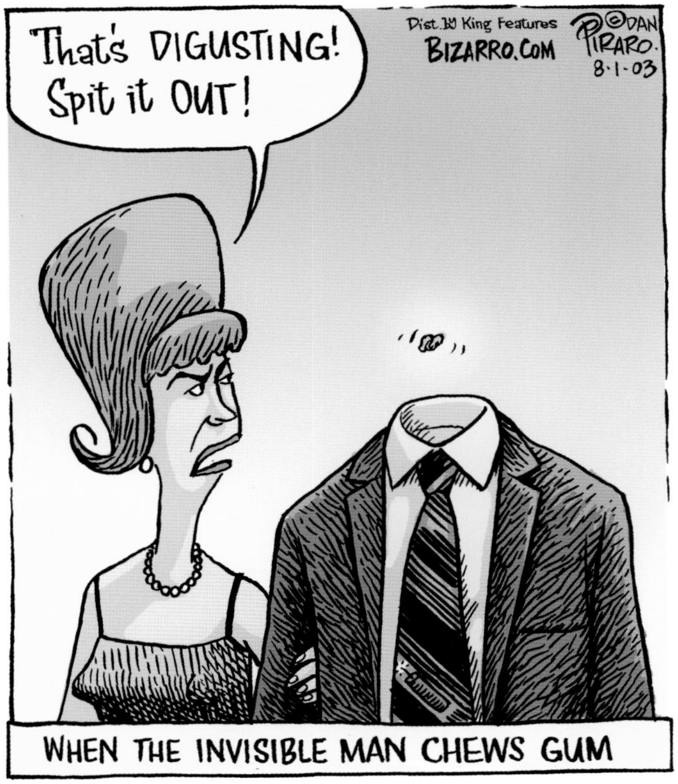
That's DIGUSTING! Spit it OUT!
Dist. by King Features
BIZARRO.COM
©DAN PIRARO
8·1·03
WHEN THE INVISIBLE MAN CHEWS GUM

Literal interpretations of fictional heroes, like literal interpretations of the Book of Genesis, are always fun for the entire family.

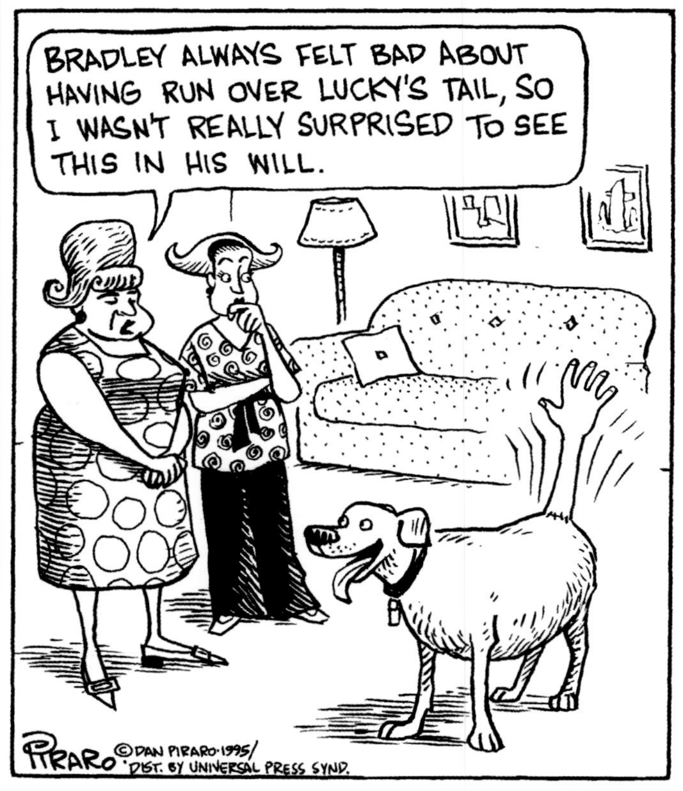
BRADLEY ALWAYS FELT BAD ABOUT HAVING RUN OVER LUCKY'S TAIL, SO I WASN'T REALLY SURPRISED TO SEE THIS IN HIS WILL.
PIRARO ©DAN PIRARO·1995/ DIST. BY UNIVERSAL PRESS SYND.

Lucky was my dad's childhood dog. Lucky's tail was run over by a car once, and because they could not afford proper veterinary care, my grandfather took him down to the basement, removed the crushed appendage with a hacksaw, sterilized it with whiskey, and bandaged it up. Lucky lived many more years but would never again go near the basement when my grandfather was around. (1995)

BELOW: An easy shot at an anti-drug TV campaign in the early nineties. (2001)

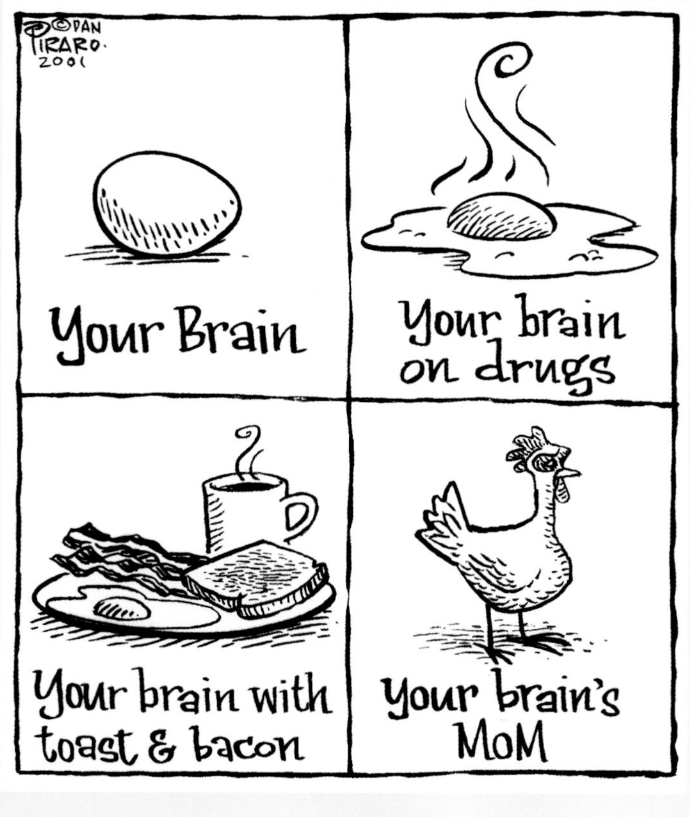
©DAN PIRARO· 2001
Your Brain
Your brain on drugs
Your brain with toast & bacon
Your brain's MoM

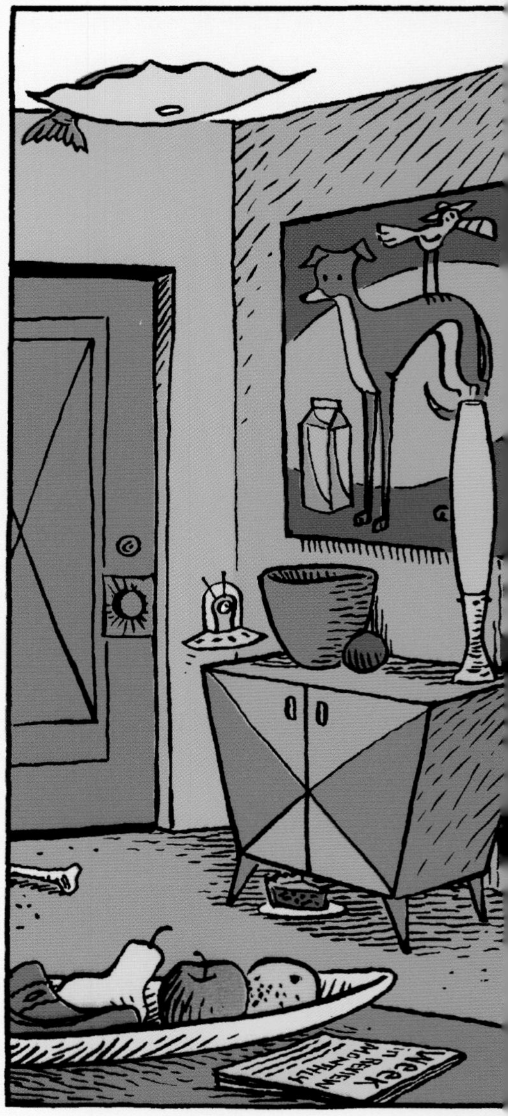
Week

I'm a big fan of modern furniture, both contemporary and from the fifties and sixties. Somewhere along the line I began including in my cartoons furniture that I either owned or would like to. This one has both. (2000)

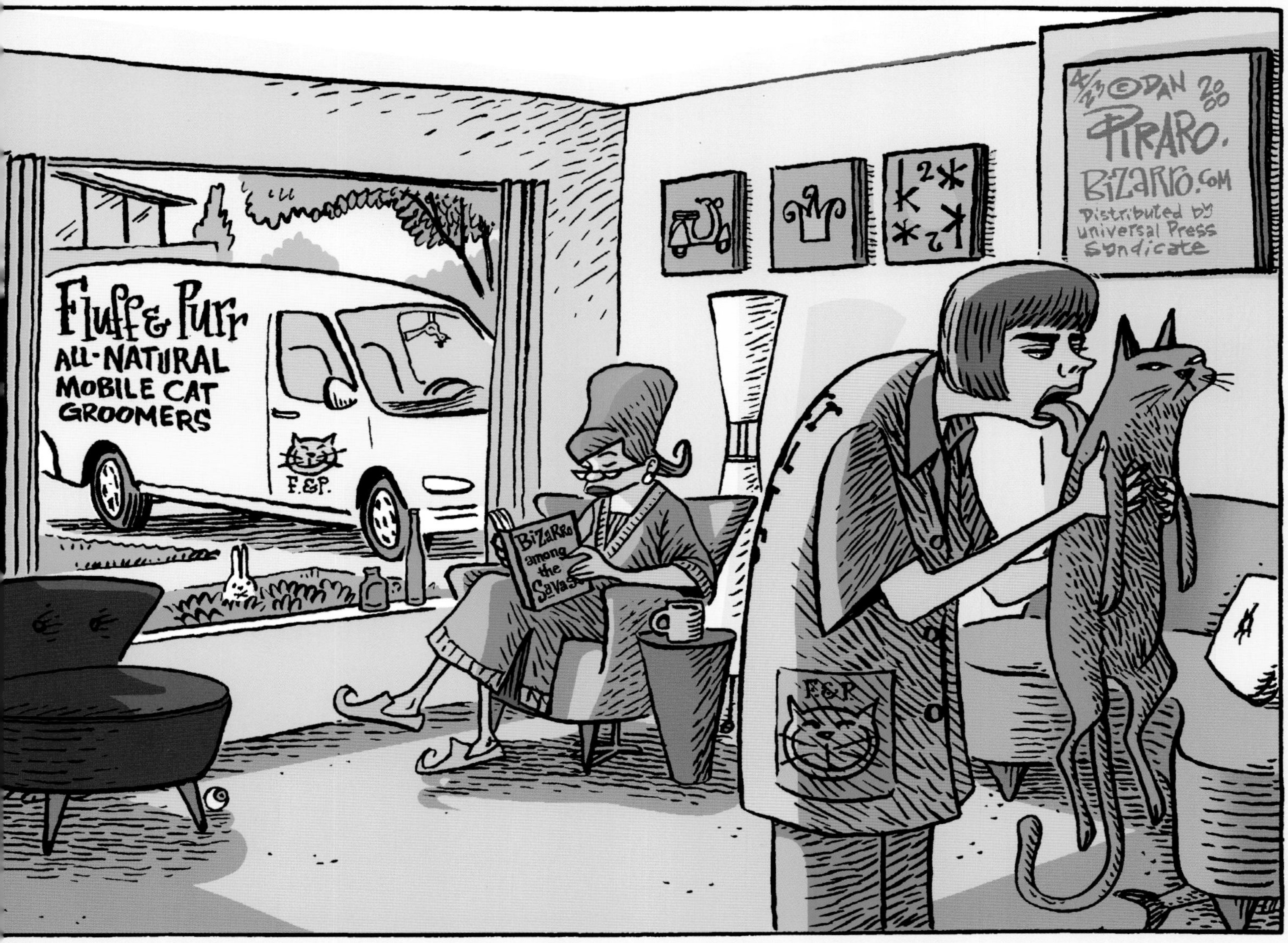

Fluff & Purr
ALL-NATURAL
MOBILE CAT
GROOMERS
F.&P.
BiZaRRo among the Savages
F&P
4/23 © DAN 2000
PiRARO.
BiZARRO.com
Distributed by
universal Press
Syndicate

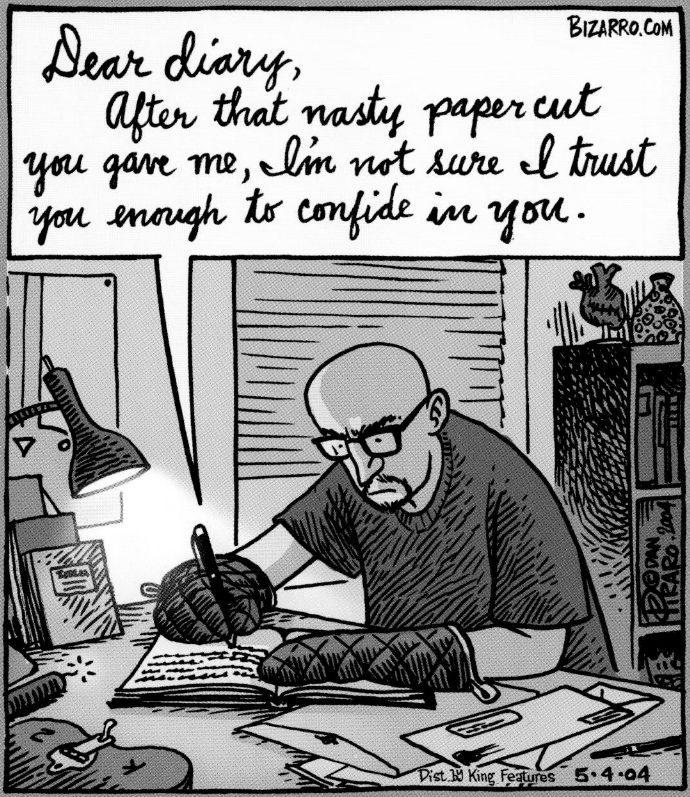
BIZARRO.COM
Dear diary,
After that nasty paper cut you gave me, I'm not sure I trust you enough to confide in you.
Dist. by King Features 5·4·04

A person's relationship with a diary is an interesting thing. Some write to themselves, and others as if they were talking to another person. Does anyone actually write "Dear Diary"? Who the hell are they talking to? (2004)

BELOW, LEFT: A different take on the age-old question "Does size matter?" (2000)

BELOW: Like most of my cartoons, this one was meticulously researched. That really is what it says. (2004)

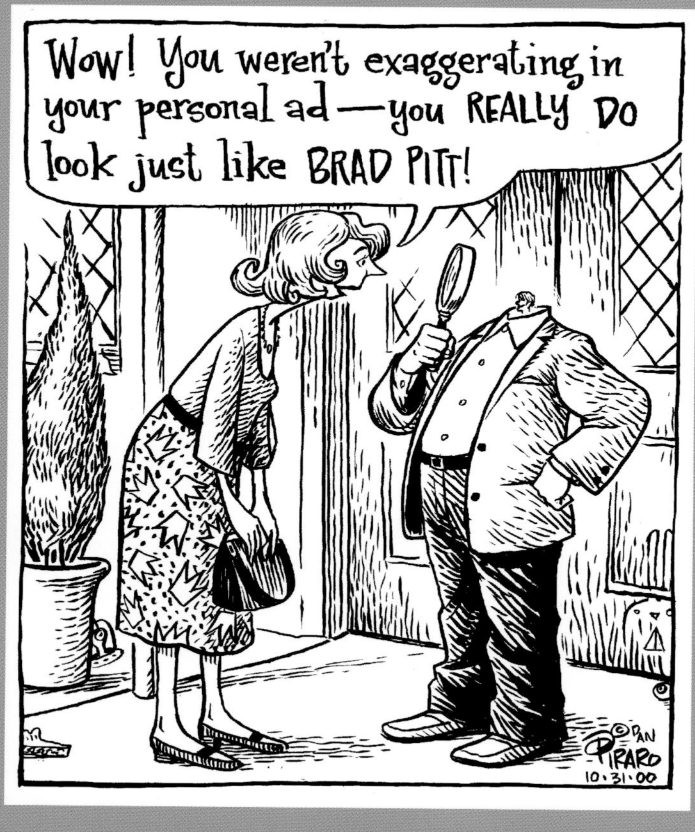
Wow! You weren't exaggerating in your personal ad—you REALLY DO look just like BRAD PITT!
©DAN PIRARO 10·31·00

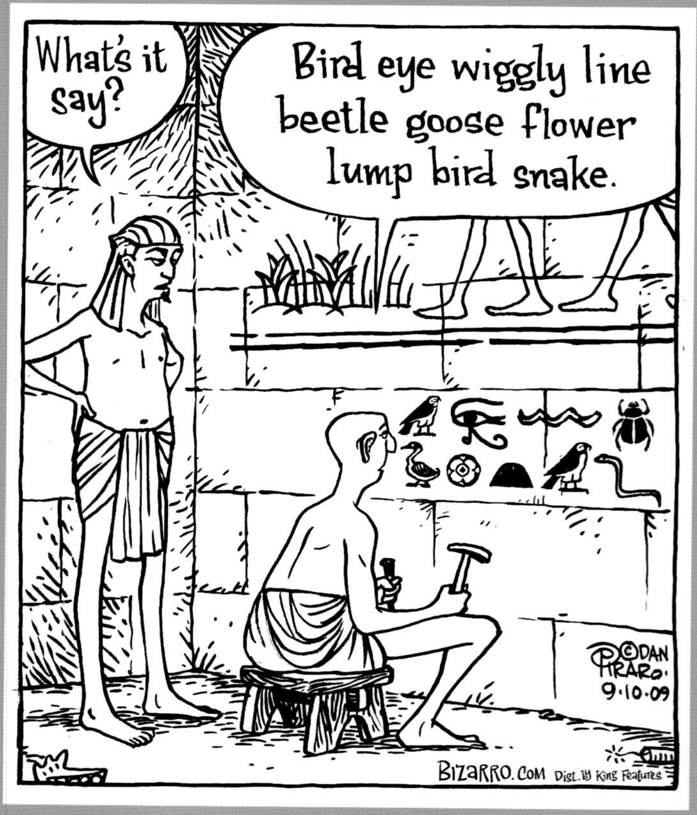
What's it say?
Bird eye wiggly line beetle goose flower lump bird snake.
©DAN PIRARO 9·10·09
BIZARRO.COM Dist. by King Features

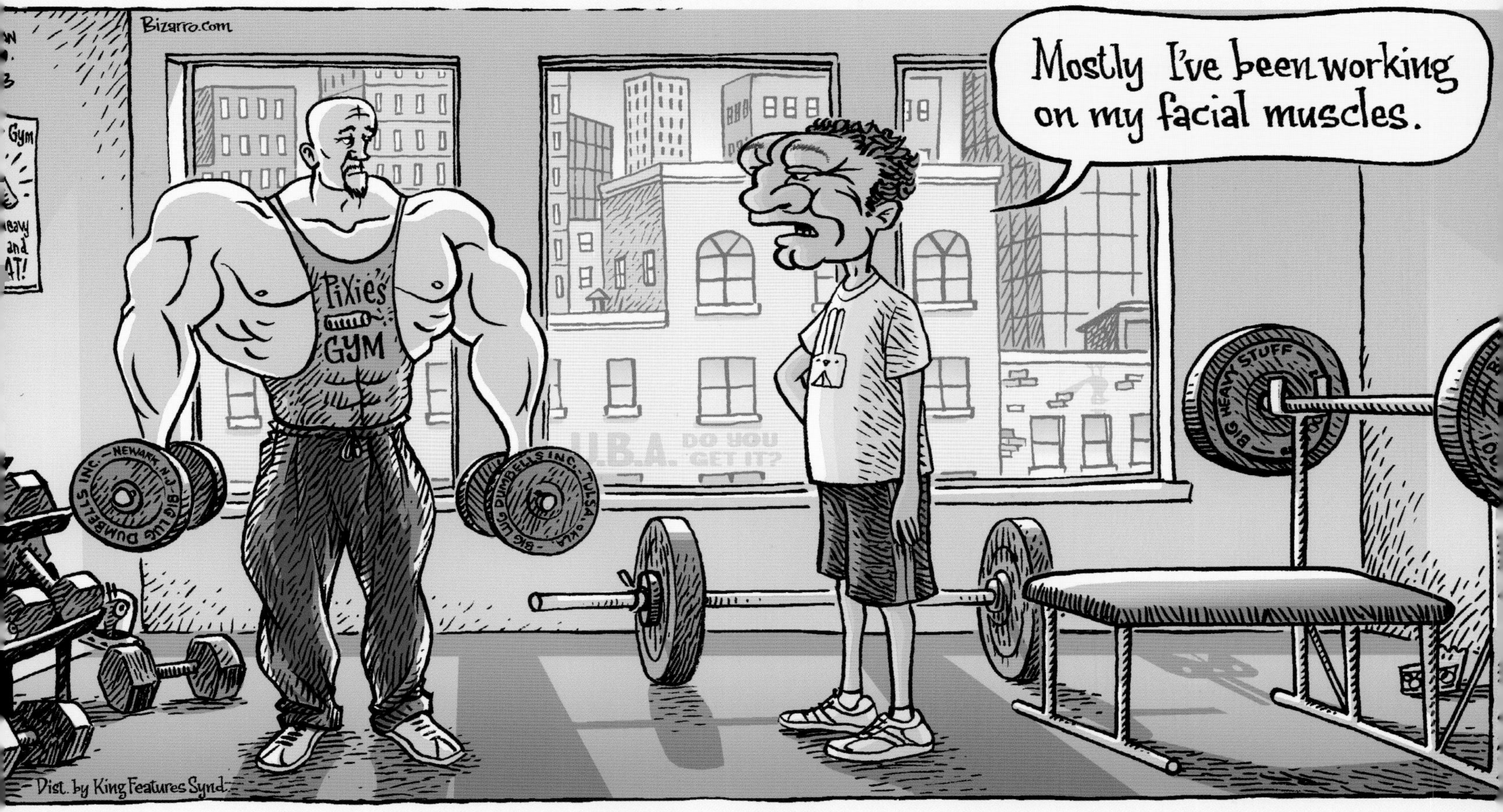
Bizarro.com
Mostly I've been working on my facial muscles.
Pixies GYM
Dist. by King Features Synd.

As a teen and young adult, I used to think it would be cool to be a big muscle man. Now I see it as a ludicrous deformity that tells the world that you've got three or four hours a day with nothing better to do than lift heavy stuff. I still like to exercise and stay in shape, but I no longer fantasize about looking like an inflatable toy. (2003)

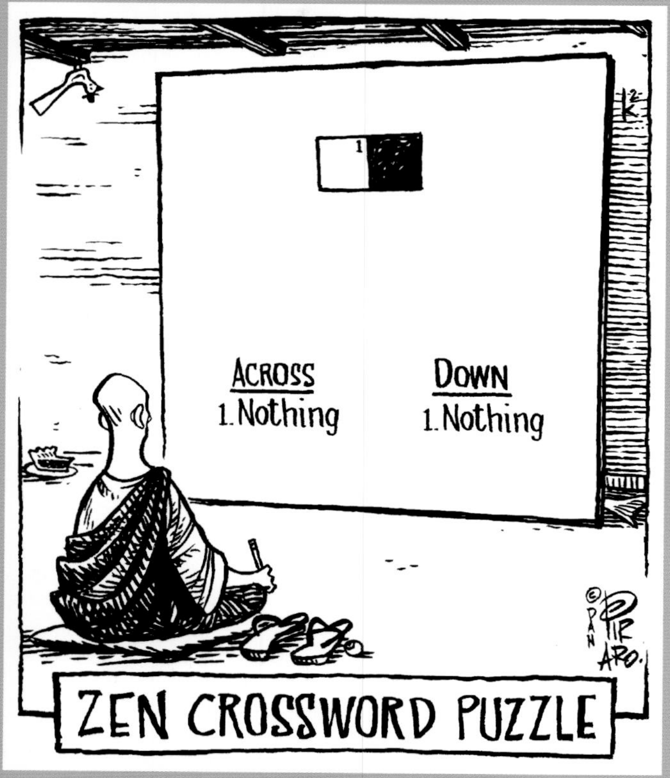
1
ACROSS
1. Nothing
DOWN
1. Nothing
ZEN CROSSWORD PUZZLE